Fieldwork and Lawnwork

Fieldwork and Lawnwork

MEMORIES AND REFLECTIONS OF AN ANTHROPOLOGIST

Anna Kushkova and James L. Peacock

LUCKY PRESS   CHAPEL HILL, NC

Copyright © 2023 by Anna Kushkova and James L. Peacock
All rights reserved

Published by Lucky Press
Chapel Hill, North Carolina
Designed and produced by Julie Allred,
BW&A Books, Inc.

Front cover: This painting is by a farmer/artist of Bali, Indonesia, whose land is near Klung Kung, a major kingdom. James Peacock saw it and bought it in 1962 when traveling in Bali with friends Joko Sanyoto and Ohio State political scientist William Liddle. At that time, Bali retained many of its traditions; for example, when swimming we saw young men joyfully washing a body in the surf, preparing for cremation. This meditative painting depicts the landscape of rice fields, hills, and trees, as well as a child and its father or grandfather, perhaps alluding to fieldwork and kinship in this patrilineal society.

Library of Congress Control Number: 2023915724
ISBN: 979-8-218-26313-3 (paperback)

To the city of Chapel Hill, a memorable and gratifying station in my anthropological journey.
—*Anna Kushkova*

With gratitude to Florence for our shared life, we dedicate these memories to our children and grandchildren as well as others who make the future.
—*James Peacock*

Contents

List of Interviewees ix

Preface *by James Peacock* xi

Introduction *by James Peacock* xv

PART I Interviews 1
by Anna Kushkova

1. Family and Early Life 3

2. Becoming an Anthropologist 25

3. University Career 35

4. UNC Department of Anthropology 43

5. Fieldwork 73

6. Consciousness and Symbols, the Nike Course, and Other Courses 141

7. Service 197

8. Scholarly Impact 261

PART II Reflections 269
by James Peacock

Afterword 313

APPENDIX 1 Belief Beheld—Inside and Outside, Insider and Outsider in the Anthropology of Religion   317
by James Peacock

APPENDIX 2 The Narrated Self: Explorations in the Psychology of Religion   333
by James Peacock

APPENDIX 3 Public or Perish   351
by James Peacock

References   355

Acknowledgments   361

About the Authors   362

List of Interviewees

Anna Kushkova (AK)

Cameron Nimes (CN)

Cecilia (Cece) Conway (CC): folklorist specializing in African American music

Dan Patterson (DP) and Beverly Patterson (BP): folklorists and musicologists

Diane Robertson (DR): community activist

Florence Peacock (FP)

Herman Greene (HG) and Sandy Greene (SG): leaders of the Center for Ecozoic Studies

Jim Peacock (JP)

Katherine Leith (KL): friend of Florence

Leedom Lefferts (LL): anthropologist focusing on Southeast Asia

Nerys Levy (NL): artist and friend of Florence

Pete (Richard) Andrews (PA): scholar of climate change and past president of the Retired Faculty Association at the University of North Carolina at Chapel Hill (UNC-CH)

Robert Daniels (RD): specialist in Africa and anthopology at UNC-CH

Ruel Tyson (RT): professor emeritus of religious studies at UNC-CH; founder and former director of the Institute of Arts and Humanities

Steven Rich (StR) and Sandra Rich (SaR): neighbors

Susan Reintjes (SR)

Bill Peck (BiP): scholar of religious studies

Preface

James Peacock

A few months ago, I discovered a manuscript by Anna Kushkova, "Fieldwork, Lawnwork, Gardenwork: Memoirs of an 'Aged Anthropologist,'" in a box of books and papers relocated to an office in Alumni Hall at the University of North Carolina at Chapel Hill that had been recently assigned to two of us retired faculty in anthropology. The manuscript focuses on the discipline and the Department of Anthropology at UNC-CH and extends to many aspects of the university, the state, the nation, and even the world as a mirror and sometimes an agent of such forces.

Anna's interviews draw out such aspects of anthropology. Her project is quietly revealing. Academics and anthropology, which are the twin interests of Anna's project, are likewise that way, as is her work.

I knew that Anna had interviewed colleagues and researched my work, but this was my first look at the manuscript. I contacted her to suggest that I add my comments to her work, and the interviews collected here are the result of that collaboration. My aim has been to add context and to do so anecdotally, tracing experiences that range from early childhood to recent projects and events through October 2022.

A word about Anna: she is an accomplished scholar. A native of St. Petersburg, Russia, she defended an equivalent of a Russian PhD in her native city and then came to UNC on a very prominent fellowship, the Royster, and completed a monumental study of Jewish ethnic entrepreneurship in the former Soviet Union. We met when she became my teaching assistant in Anth 135/435, Consciousness and Symbols, and we worked together for many years. She is currently living in Jerusalem working on a seminal project concerning Russian history, which she drafted while at UNC while a Royster Fellow. Before she departed, she undertook these interviews with a range of people on her own initiative, and I thank her for doing so. The result will grow in value as a history of certain efforts.

Fortunately, I have had the time to work with Anna's materials as I approach eighty-five. From Malinowski's diary of his time in the Trobriand Islands to Clifford Geertz's account of Cohen and the Berbers in Morocco, many precedents exist of anthropologists and others recording their experiences.

I began my account with *A True Lucky Jim* and much is added here, thanks to Anna's perceptive interviews. I am deeply grateful to Anna Kuskova for her brilliant and compelling research and insight, which is the basis for this joint publication.

The phrase "fieldwork and lawnwork," which Anna uses to title her interview project, was suggested by Dr. Carol Crumley, an archaeologist and anthropologist formerly at UNC-Chapel Hill and currently at the University of Stockholm. Fieldwork refers to the research that anthropologists, including archaeologists, undertake in places away from home. Lawnwork, by contrast, refers to work undertaken close to home. The "field" is foreign, while the "lawn" is domestic. Much of Anna's fieldwork, for example, has taken place in Ukraine, Moldova, the USA and Israel, while her home is Russia. Much of my fieldwork occurred in Indonesia, while my home is the United States. Further, much of my professional work has related to my university, also in the United States. This distinction between home and not home is not rigid, but it captures an important aspect of much anthropological research—that is, being abroad, in the field, as compared to other work, such as teaching or administration, which tends to be carried out at home or closer to home, on the "lawn." The accounts Anna and I provide include both sites. The same is true for most anthropologists; they are fieldworkers but also administrators, teachers, or performers of other types of work. This was even true of the great German poet Johann Wolfgang von Goethe. His day job was as an administrator for a German count in a relatively rural area, compared to his birthplace, Frankfurt.

It was in 1966 at Princeton University during the spring semester of the first year of my appointment as an assistant professor that I created a version of the course I would eventually teach with Anna. I introduced a version of this course at UNC-Chapel Hill in 1967, when I moved there, and the course was taught annually until I retired. I also taught a version of it as part of visiting professor stints at the University of California in San Diego and Yale University. I published a book, *Consciousness and Change: Symbolic*

Anthropology in Evolutionary Perspective, based on the course in 1975. I also taught courses on other subjects, including Southeast Asia, general anthropology, and the required graduate seminar in sociocultural anthropology, but Consciousness and Symbols was distinctive in that I taught it for many years and used it to introduce a subdiscipline sometimes termed "symbolic anthropology," namely, the study of symbols. Students were required to complete a research project and take both a midterm exam and a final exam, as well as having an option to present a "sensuous presentation," that is, a study of selected symbolic forms, to the class. I read all of the students' papers, graded them, and usually discussed them in person during meetings scheduled during the semester. Thus, I became somewhat acquainted, sometimes well acquainted, with each of my students, even though, in time, the classes became fairly large, with fifty to seventy students, after having begun quite small, with perhaps twenty students. The students ranged from sophomores to graduate students and sometimes were auditors. After the classes grew in size, I usually had a teaching assistant to help with grading, but I always also read and graded papers and exams. Many of my students became friends and colleagues and remain so; some are among Anna's interviewees.

The main advantage of Anna's method, which consists of interviewing, is spontaneity, and the main advantage of spontaneity is that it prompts ideas and memories that other methods, such as writing, might miss. The reader will hopefully accept the result.

Introduction
James Peacock

1960 to Present

The 1960s were notable for several reasons. Among them was the election of John F. Kennedy as president of the United States; I watched him proceed down Commonwealth Avenue. Notable too was the expansion of universities and colleges, which resulted in an increase in academic jobs that by 1970 had leveled off. I benefited from this boom in hiring and took my first academic position, at Princeton University, in 1965. In 1967, I moved to the University of North Carolina at Chapel Hill, where, with the exception of some visiting professorships, I stayed until the present.

During the 1960s and 1970s, in the North Carolina Research Triangle, where I largely operated, students experienced increased access to drugs and freedom, and faculty experienced increased access to research funds. The Research Triangle flourished then, as it still does, and similar developments occurred elsewhere, as they still do, but neither the funds nor the jobs are as plentiful in many academic situations as they were then.

The Research Triangle was initiated by a student of Howard Odum's, according to William Friday, late president of UNC, and was supported by the then president of Wachovia Bank, who wrote a master's thesis in history while also serving as president, and by others who represented both academic and business foci. Essential also were expanding funds available through both private and governmental grants, such as from the National Institutes of Health, the National Science Foundation, and the Ford Foundations. The Research Triangle also included numerous large companies such as IBM and academic institutions such as the National Humanities Center. At UNC, for example, as at Duke, North Carolina State University, and throughout the nation, research and service as well as academic and teaching elements expanded to meet new demands and to exploit the ready supply of funds. Administrative elements also expanded, often outrunning academic ones. Examples at UNC include the medical school, the school of public health, the business school, and so on.

Even in a little-known field such as anthropology, expansions were apparent, facilitated by huge differences between wealthy and poor nations. For example, in 1962, when I undertook fieldwork in Indonesia, I depended on a grant from the National Institutes of Health, which paid me several hundred dollars per month. This money was sufficient to support my wife, my child, and myself at Harvard in graduate school, and in Indonesia, where costs were very low for my lifestyle—that is, living in a slum in a nation with a per capita income of a hundred dollars or so—this was more than sufficient for our needs. We were living with a family, owned no car, ate what others ate (i.e., rice, bean curd, and tea), and had ample funds to provide a gift to the family with whom we lived. We benefitted from the remarkable kindness of the two families who hosted us and with whom we remain friends. This description is not meant as an ideal, for the discrepancy between "first world" and other nations remains huge and unfair as well as ecologically dangerous. Tourist industries serve many needs, to be sure, but they often convey stereotypes, for example, that Bali is typical of Indonesia. This is akin to thinking that Disneyland is typical of the United States, though this comparison too is misleading, for Bali is not Disneyland but a remarkable and genuine culture that has cultivated its achievements to meet the desires of tourists as well as to maintain itself.

Anthropology underwent a spurt of collaborative work intended to direct the discipline toward improving society. Roy "Skip" Rappaport from the University of Michigan and president of the American Anthropological Association (AAA) in the 1970s helped stimulate this effort through a grant from the Wenner-Gren Foundation, which brought a group of us together in Arizona to brainstorm ways to do this applied work. We met several times at a ranch in southern Arizona, and then I was assigned the task of driving a bus to northern Arizona to continue the effort, resulting in an edited volume. Later, several of us held meetings of the AAA and joined other colleagues in publishing a book with the association. A spinoff is a trio of lectures that I delivered at Princeton, which was reprinted by University of Michigan Press in memory of Rappaport. A lecture of mine on applied anthropology also appears in a volume edited by Richard Fox, who was then president of the Wenner-Gren Foundation in New York. These discussions stimulated many of us to do projects in applied anthropology, which for me included the creation of the University Center for International Studies (UCIS) and the FedEx Global Education Center at UNC.

Now, back to the Research Triangle. During its development and related efforts nationally and globally, there were many advances. These include: SAS Institute, led by Jim Goodnight, which became a leading software company and also created a superior environment for work and education; the School of Public Health at UNC-CH, now endowed by Gillings, a school that leads in combatting the pandemic; Carolina for Kibera, created by Rye Barcott, a former student of mine, which is a community effort in Kenya to improve outcomes in one of the largest slums in Africa; the Rotary Peace Fellows program, which has branches at Duke and UNC and funds and oversees a thousand "fellows," including doctors and teachers who earn a master's degree at these schools and then carry out work with the World Bank and many other organizations and nations; and partial support of a tenor from Swaziland and a Black cellist from Charleston, both among the most talented musicians today. Hillary Clinton is credited with the phrase "It takes a village . . . ," which is true, of course, from bankers to teachers, governments to musicians, and artists to the leaders of many faiths and commitments.

We former presidents of the AAA continue to collaborate, in some cases overseeing association issues or acting as advisors and assessing various departments of anthropology nationally, as I did for Harvard, Brown, LSU, California, and others. Our "village" was national, others were international, and still others were both while they focused on disciplines other than or in addition to anthropology, for example, the American Society for the Study of Religion. This society meets annually and includes approximately a hundred people focused on the study of religion, including scholars, administrators, and others of varied faiths and disciplines. Members often travel far and inconveniently (as I did recently) at their own expense, but the result is considerable loyalty and collaboration.

Our "village" created and was involved with many organizations and projects both nearby and writ large. Obvious ones include local church, school, family, political, and community efforts, some of them culturally or ethnically diverse. These efforts introduced me to Talie, the young tenor from Swaziland, near Kenya in Africa. In Swaziland, now Eswatini, a tribe is headed by a king with many wives. Talie is now studying in Miami, Florida, and recently won a major operatic competition in New York; Florence, my wife, helps support his study. Also remarkable is Sudibyo Markus. Sudibyo is from Pare, a small town in Java, Indonesia. We met in 1970 when I studied Muhammadiyah, a Muslim organization with some thirty million members in Indonesia. I congratulate him on his recent book, *Islam and the West: Light on the Horizon* (the English translation of his 2019 book *Dunia Barat dan Islam*). A Muhammadiyahan since his student days, Sudibyo sets forth a vision for such convergence and unity. His work as well as his friendship are an essential basis for my work.

More local is Pete Andrews's Nike project at UNC-CH. Nike, the sportswear company, bestowed a large grant on the UNC basketball team, and students protested, staging a sit-in at the chancellor's office. The chancellor wisely approached the students diplomatically, and his lawyer, Susan Ehringhaus, even more diplomatically served them food. Pete Andrews, then chair of the faculty, organized a course to explore the issues the students raised, followed by a committee to address them. Nick Dido, in the business school, and I joined in. Several students, including activists, took the course, and we also established a committee comprising students, faculty, and administrators to deal with the issues. The chancellor appointed this committee. On the last day of the course, I was waiting in the yard of the international center when a man appeared wearing a suit and dark glasses. He was Phil Knight, the president of Nike. He attended the class, which focused on recommendations by the students. Several days later, he invited the students to attend a press conference he was giving in Washington, DC. The Nike president stated that Nike would accept many of the students' recommendations about labor situations. This led to a working collaboration between our committee and Nike to deal with labor issues and carry out reforms. We worked with numerous companies around the world and locally. Later, Rut Tufts organized a national coalition of universities to work on this issue.

Several kinds of collaboration, both international and local, occurred during this period. For example, we were approached by several countries about setting up branches of UNC-CH overseas. One country was Qatar. After some discussions with representatives of that nation, the Queen of Qatar sent her private plane and flew a planeload of faculty and administrators from UNC to Qatar to view facilities there. We met at the queen's palace for a banquet and viewed facilities where several universities had already established branches. Later, several of us also went to Jakarta, Indonesia, at the invitation of a major bank. Our group included the provost. Neither of these projects eventuated, in part because of lack of support from the board of trustees at UNC-CH. However, numerous collaborative projects between various faculty at UNC-CH and institutions abroad flourish today, including one with Gadjah Mada University in Indonesia, where Dr. Carla Jones, now an associate professor at the University of Colorado, worked with Dr. Ida Adi, whose dissertations I supervised. Prior to my becoming director of

UCIS, Craig Calhoun launched a large project in Eritrea, a nation in Africa that gained its independence from colonial and then Ethiopian rule in 1993. Assisted by funding from USAID, UCIS collaborated with faculty and others in Eritrea, building a new university, including a law school. Several of us from UCIS, including Niklaus Stein and myself, were present at the celebration of the new nation. We joined in dancing in the street that evening and departed the next day, as Ethiopia bombed the airport.

The alumni association draws on many faculty to serve as lecturers for alumni tours, such as those I accompanied to Singapore, Indonesia, Bangkok, and Tahiti. When I served as chair of the faculty, I invited faculty and alumni to donate their books to the library in the Alumni Association, which resulted in a fine collection that is now ready to update and is available to alumni and others. Alumni, faculty, and friends organize numerous and varied groups dedicated to discussing politics, Jungian psychology, religion, and education or finance; many are led by us faculty retirees.

The pandemic, of course, curtailed many activities and projects.

Florence Peacock's autobiography is, in part, the highlight of my book *A Truly Lucky Jim*, and she is interviewed by Anna Kushkova in this volume. A few highlights from Florence's life are as follows: Florence was born and raised in Covington, Georgia, southeast of Atlanta. She excelled in singing from early childhood through college and graduate school at the Yale School of Music. Her sense of pitch was so accurate that composer Paul Hindemith relied on her to sing his complicated scales. Later, she was able to sing the Javanese music that is based on pelog and slendro scales rather than on Western ones. Recently, she performed a Javanese classical song on a Zoom presentation in Surabaya, Java. Each summer, she studies and is a soloist at the Oberlin Baroque Workshop, focusing on baroque music and baroque dance, which she also learned. Her many performance venues range from the Atlanta symphony to Oberlin College, and international locations include Japan, Russia, Germany, England, and Indonesia. Usually, she performs classical music, but recently she performed the role of Minnie Pearl in a concert of country and western music. As a student at Yale, she was a soloist with the Yale Repertory Company in an off-Broadway play, *John Brown's Body*, in New York. She lights up any occasion; a friend commented on her speech when she and I helped inaugurate the atrium of the FedEx building at UNC-CH; he said I was adequate but she was superb.

A remarkable aspect of Florence's singing is that she lost much of her hearing in her twenties and yet has continued singing at a very high level

Florence Peacock. Photo: Catharine Carter.

with the use of a hearing aid. She developed otosclerosis, which means that the hammer and stapes cease to properly contact. She went to a topflight ear specialist at the University of Pennsylvania who had reported nearly 100 percent success in correcting this condition. Unfortunately, in her case, the operation destroyed much of her auditory nerve, leaving her nearly deaf. She continued to sing by relying on perfect memory for pitches and text, and after some years she underwent an operation by an outstanding surgeon in Tennessee that partially corrected the condition. She also obtained an excellent hearing aid. With this aid, she continued to sing at a high level and does so still.

Florence inherited from her Aunt Florence the ear malady but also a generous heart and energetic spirit, which she expressed in both fieldwork and lawnwork, as defined above. Often she supported musicians and music students who were talented but poor. One African American bassist lived in our house for many years while he studied at Northwestern University. An anthropology graduate student, Jennie Smith, was living with us when she won an award as an outstanding teaching assistant. A young candidate for Congress stayed with us off and on while campaigning. Several boarders were fellows at the National Humanities Center. Florence also hosted many community events as well as her grandchildren. I was the lawn-worker along with Jim Flanagan, who had studied classics at UNC. Today we live in an apartment, and our guests are often grandchildren who love to visit Florence.

Looking to the future, grandchildren remain prominent in our lives. Nick is at Duke, studying a combination of medicine and engineering and will soon participate in a conference in Singapore. Yanni has entered his junior year at Harvard, majoring in mathematics and history. Flora is a sophomore at Davidson, focusing on English, Bella attends Cary Academy, the SAS school near Raleigh, and Lucia continues at the Duke school. Louly is performing and composing music and writing a book titled *Wonder Woman Bleeds*, Claire continues to publish works in photography and literature, and Natalie carries on her clinical practice while presenting and coediting in the field of clinical social work. Florence performs vocally, singing both country and western and baroque music. We all try hard to evade the pandemic.

Florence and I celebrated our sixtieth wedding anniversary on August 20, 2022.

At this moment, major issues on all our minds include climate change, the Russian invasion of Ukraine, the ongoing COVID-19 pandemic, and unrest in the United States, including the US presidency in the upcoming election.

PART I Interviews
by Anna Kushkova

CHAPTER 1

Family and Early Life

Peacock Family History

Anna Kushkova (AK): Professor Peacock, thank you for speaking with me. So, if you were to go back in your family lines, both of them, how far would you be able to go?

Jim Peacock (JP): Oh, hundreds of years.

AK: Could you tell me more about this?

JP: My grandfather's brother. The reason is, he was a coach . . . He coached the Carolina basketball team from 1915 to 1918, his name was Howell Peacock, and he is buried in the old Chapel Hill cemetery. That's the only connection I have to Carolina. It's him. So, that's my father's side of the family. OK. Now, I was not born in North Carolina. Not Tar Heel born or Tar Heel bred—though I may become Tar Heel when I'm dead. So, forebears. As far as I know, my forebears on my father's and mother's sides were from Great Britain, mainly, although there was a German connection. And on both sides, they had ancestors who had . . . they probably came to Virginia initially. Maybe in the 1600s or in the 1700s.

AK: So, some of the earliest European settlers?

JP: Yes, among the earliest. And so, on my mother's side, and her ancestors—their name is Pearson. And so, the first Pearson who, as far as I know, was in North Carolina, came to Wake County and built something called Yates Mill. It's a major gristmill, and they have reconstructed it now . . .

AK: Oh, it's still there?

JP: Oh, it still runs! It's been running for three or four hundred years! And it's there, and they built a visitors center, and it tells the history of it, and tells about him. His name was Pearson. Samuel Pearson. And what it says is, that in 1700 and something, Samuel Pearson came from New Bern to Wake County with a slave and his young wife, who was fourteen, and built this mill. And so, that's that part of the family. But then some of them moved to Alabama and Georgia; that's on my mother's side.

AK: Is it far from here, this Yates mill?

JP: No! It takes about half an hour to get there. I never knew about it until fairly recently.

AK: Have you been there?

JP: I have been there, several times. They have a Yates Mill Association. The reason it's called Yates is, he sold it to Mr. Yates.

AK: OK, that's your mother's side.

JP: Yes. Pearson. Now, the other side . . .

AK: Let's stay with your mother's side. So, some of them . . . most of them moved to Alabama . . .

JP: Some of them did.

AK: And what were they doing there?

JP: Many things! (laughs)

AK: Were there any prominent people whom you know about? Who you were told about when you were young?

JP: Yeah. One of them is my mother's father. So, my mother's father, whose name was Rogers . . . my mother's mother's name was Pearson. Laura Pearson. And my mother's father was named Alpha Clayton. Alpha, you know, like the first letter in the Greek alphabet: Alpha. Alpha Clayton Rogers. So, Alpha Clayton Rogers was a businessperson and a farmer in Elmore County. Elmore County is near where the capital of Alabama is located, Montgomery. And my mother was born in Montgomery, and then much later I was born in Montgomery as well but did not stay there. Because my father was drafted into the army, and we moved around a lot. So, Alpha Clayton was a farmer and a businessman. He was very successful, apparently. And he was elected to the legislature. The state legislature for that state.

AK: Which must have been . . . when?

JP: Let me think . . . when was he born . . . He was born in the late 1800s, probably. And somewhere . . . I have some of that history that I can produce. He died about 1939. He had cancer, and he died in New York City, because he had gone there to try a new experimental cure for his kind of cancer. But he died. So, that's my grandfather.

AK: Did you meet him? Oh . . .

JP: I did meet him, but I was about two years old, so I don't really remember him. OK—so, that's on my mother's side.

AK: Clayton—how many children did he have?

JP: Four—Laurie, Claire, Louie, and Clayton. A. C. Rogers had four children. One was my mother, whose name is Claire. And one was . . . and the only boy was named . . . Clayton. And Clayton married twice. His first wife . . . He was in World War II—almost everybody was in World War II, in his generation, my relatives. And he married a woman whose name was Margaret Dickenson. And they had a son whose name is Steve, and he is my first cousin. And he lives there now, in Elmore County. He lives on a lake there. OK, so, his first wife died, and he married again, to another person who is still alive, whose name is Emily, Searcy, maiden name, but her married name is Rogers. And Emily is still alive, she's about ninety-five maybe. And she lives in Birmingham; it's a major medical center for Alabama. And Emily and Bub had two daughters. One of them is Mary Emily. (laughs) She went to Harvard to college, and then went to medical school, and is now a physician. She is my first cousin, and she is probably fifty years old or something like that.

AK: Fifty?

JP: Fifty something—like that. Maybe older, but . . . I think about fifty. And she now lives in Ohio, and she is a physician. She was an all-American soccer player. And then she has a sister, whose name is Cynthia. Cynthia has two daughters, and both of them came up and graduated from NC State.

AK: What are their names?

JP: I have to check and find. See, I don't know them very well because they are much younger than I. But I can ask Cynthia. And Emily. And they'll probably be happy for you to interview them.

AK: Yes, that would be nice! Not just colleagues and friends, but also family members.

JP: Well, you can just call them up—they live in Birmingham. But they may even come up to . . . they come to visit sometimes. But not usually and not us—they come to see their daughter, daughters—that's why they were here. So, that is my family on the mother's side, and I already told you about my family on the father's side.

AK: Tell me a little bit more about your mother.

JP: My mother lived . . . she died when she was 101.

AK: Tell this wonderful story about this last evening when she danced . . .

JP: Oh, well, I wasn't there but . . . She moved into a retirement home and she used to say: "One morning I'll wake up dead." And so, that's basically what happened. But that night . . . she never lost her mind or her mobility, but she had pretty much become blind and deaf when she was that old. So, apparently, there was some kind of attendant at this place, and he invited her to get up and dance with him. And so they did a little bit, apparently. And then that night, or maybe, next morning, she died in bed. That's basically that story.

AK: You also said, one of the last days she went to a place . . . something like Dunkin' Donuts to drink coffee with her . . .

JP: Oh, that . . . let me show you—look right behind you: see that picture on the wall?

AK: Yes.

JP: The artist is from South Africa, and she . . .

AK: The green one?

JP: The green one, yes. And she lived . . . she and her husband, Peter . . . Peter and Faith—Faith is the name of that artist . . . lived next door to my mother and father when they were very old. And they were really . . . they were friends. And so . . . so, Faith would call my mother and invite her to have coffee at Starbucks. There were not many places . . . this is a small town in Georgia. But there was this Starbucks, where they would go and have coffee and talk. And she did that almost until she died. With Faith. And that's Faith's painting. And she did many paintings.

AK: So, your mother lived in this seniors' place in Alabama . . .

JP: In Georgia. I should have explained: so, my mother was born in Alabama, Montgomery, Alabama, and my father was born in Columbus, Georgia. They are both fairly large cities. But they are not so much apart, they're maybe forty miles from each other. Maybe more than forty, maybe a hundred or something. But they met. And so, my father was in the D-Day, as I mentioned, and when he came home—he was an electrical engineer—and when he came home, he and a friend of his set up an electrical contracting business in a small town in Georgia, which is called Tifton. It's in Tift County. Have you ever heard this singer, who sings around here, her name is Tift Merritt? Anyway. She is not from Tifton, but her family is the Tifts. The Tifts were a prominent family who founded Tifton. So, that's where my mother and father lived after World War II, when they came back after World War II.

AK: Both in Tifton?

JP: In Tift County, Tifton. They lived there from 19 . . . let me think . . . I was eight years old when they moved, so, let me see . . .

AK: Let's now speak a little bit more on your mother's ancestry—chronologically. So, when did they come to the United States?

JP: I think . . . I'll have to check on it, but . . . in the 1700s.

AK: So, a little bit later than . . .

JP: No, I think they both . . .

AK: You said 16 . . . [for Jim's father's ancestors]

JP: I think for both of them . . . they both came in the 1700s, and they both ended up in North Carolina about 1720 or so. And I'll have to . . . I'm not sure how far I can get into the prior . . . but they came from England, they both did, and by about the 1700s their forebears were in the United States.

AK: Interestingly enough, North Carolina sort of drew both of the family lines . . .

JP: It did. I think they probably entered the United States in Virginia. You know, most people at that time, they either came through New England . . .

AK: Boston?

JP: Yeah. Or Virginia. Florence's family, on her father's side, came through Connecticut. On her mother's side they came through South . . . probably, South Carolina. But mine, they came through Virginia. And by the 1700s, they were in North Carolina.

Family and Early Life

AK: Were they middle-class or . . . ?

JP: I think . . . yeah . . . well, so, Pearson built a gristmill, and at that time a gristmill was a key institution, because it took the farmers' grist and milled it. And so, yeah, I'd say, middle-class. And then I think the same was true about my father's ancestor, although I don't really know too much about what he did—he was a farmer, I think.

AK: What was their last name?

JP: Well, his was Peacock, and my mother's ancestry was Pearson.

AK: Any special people in that line? Again, maybe you heard stories about them?

JP: (laughs) I have to think about that. Well, my grandfather's brother, who was the coach of the UNC basketball team and who married the daughter of Froggy Wilson . . . Have you ever seen Wilson Hall at UNC?

AK: Well, there is Wilson Library.

JP: Yeah—that's a different Wilson. Wilson Hall is the Zoology and Biology Department, and it was named for him. That was my father's father's brother's wife. He married the daughter of the person named . . . his name was Wilson, he was apparently a very prominent biologist, I think he was in the National Academy for Science. Anyway, they know everything about him over in the Zoology [Department]. But his name was Wilson. He is buried in the Chapel Hill Cemetery. If you go there . . . one day we'll go, and I'll show you . . .

AK: The one that's on campus?

JP: Yeah. And my grandfather's brother is in there, too. And my grandfather's brother's wife. We'll do that one day. We'll take a picture of them. So, that's them. No, I don't think there were any famous . . . no presidents. (laughs) No . . . I think there might have been a . . . anyway, that's enough. They . . .

AK: And they stayed in North Carolina all the time?

JP: Well, just . . . no, they were all living in Georgia, none of them moved to North . . . I mean, there are Peacocks all around North Carolina, but in my immediate family they stayed in Georgia. Some moved to other places like Texas, or somewhere. But my immediate forebears were in Georgia on my father's side and in Alabama on my mother's side. And most of them did very well, but I don't think anybody was famous. There was one possible relative who is a renowned writer. What's her name? She wrote a novel called *The Heart Is a Lonely Hunter* . . . Carson McCullers.

AK: That's your relative on your father's side?

JP: She is reputed to be a relative. And my mother used to date her husband before he was her husband. Anyway—Carson McCullers. I have to think about it, but I don't think there was any George Washington or anybody like that. But they were, as you say, middle-class. Maybe a little better than middle-class in some cases like my grandfather, who was in the legislature, Alpha Clayton.

AK: Were there any academics?

JP: A few. Well, my grandmother is worthy of mention. On my father's side. Her name was Minerva and she was a first cousin to Miss Lillian, the mother of President Jimmy Carter. That's not a big deal, but that's her. Her maiden name was Gordy. Minerva, and her sister Mary and her brother Schley, it's a German name, they were all living in Stuart County, in Georgia, in the country. And their mother and father reputedly died young because of a flu epidemic. They died in their thirties, I think.

AK: It's something like 1912, 1913 . . . ?

JP: It was before that.

AK: But it was an influenza epidemic?

JP: Precisely. So, they died, and that left my grandmother and her siblings orphans. So, they moved . . . they were adopted by a relative in Columbus, Georgia, which was the largest city in that area. And this was in the 1800s. Women did not normally go to college then. Her sister Mary did—and Minerva did not. She went to normal school, that was teachers' college, and became a teacher of math, mathematics. And Mary did not marry and went to the University of Chicago. And that was when you could go there I think even without a high school degree—but it was one of the top universities then, as it is now.

AK: Very few women there at a time?

JP: I think so. So, she went there, and Minerva married my grandfather, whose name was the same as mine—James Lowe Peacock.

AK: You are the third one with the same name.

JP: Yes, I'm the third one. She married him, and they settled in Columbus, and she taught school. When she was sixty, she decided: "I am going to college!" And this was back in the 1940s, 1946 maybe. So, she went to Auburn, which is the engineering school. And she went there because it was nearby, it was about thirty-five miles away. And she majored in mathematics, and she apparently had the highest mark of any student, even though she was sixty years old. This was Minerva. And meanwhile Aunt Mary, her sister, slightly older sister, went to the University of Chicago, and she got a degree, and then she became a teacher, and she taught at a teachers' college, which was called Johnson City, in Tennessee. And while she was there . . . she was unmarried, and in the teachers' college they had a nursery, where children who were abandoned were taken care of. So, she saw this little girl in the nursery, and she said to the president: "I am going to adopt that child." And her name was Emily, and she is my first cousin today. And the president said: "You do, and I'll fire you." Because, see—she was unmarried. And she said: "Fire me, I'm adopting her."

AK: But why wouldn't he allow her?

JP: Because she was unmarried . . . I mean, at that time perhaps he thought that an unmarried woman should not adopt a child. I don't think it was in the law, it might have just been his . . . opinion.

AK: Did he fire her?

JP: Yes. She said: "Fire me, I'm adopting her."

AK: Perhaps he thought that with the child she won't be able to dedicate as much time to her [work at the college]?

JP: Perhaps so. Or whatever. For whatever reason. Oh, and by the way, you can interview Emily! So, she adopted Emily—we call her Emie—she is not as old as I am, but she might be in her seventies. So, this was Aunt Mary. And she went on, and she found another job at another place, and then eventually retired and moved back to Columbus. And she was famously tactless, abrupt, and lived to be ninety. She died when she was ninety.

AK: So, how did your parents meet?

JP: Oh (laughs) . . . OK. My mother went to a women's college, which was called Huntington, and my father went to an engineering school, which is Auburn.

AK: So, he already has this company in Tifton and goes to school, parallel?

JP: No, he went to school . . . prior to that.

AK: When were they born, your parents?

JP: He was born in 1912, my mother—in 1913. And so, she went to a women's college called Huntington in Montgomery, and he went to engineering school called Auburn—it's still called Auburn. And she went to summer school at Auburn, when she was in college, and that's where they met.

AK: In 193 . . . something, right?

JP: Yes. He graduated from Auburn in 1934. So, they met around that time, and they got married. . . I was born in 1937, I think they married in 1936. Something like that.

AK: Was it this "love from the first sight"?

JP: No. My mother had a rival suitor, who was head of a football team, his name was Jack. And so, my father was competing with Jack, and my mother was trying to decide between Jack and Jim—that was my father's name, Jim. And finally she decided on Jim, and she wrote a telegram to him, and we have a copy of it, her telegram to him, says: "You win. Meet me at 8." And that was her answer to his proposal. And so, they got married, and they moved to Tifton, and he initially worked for Georgia Power, that's a

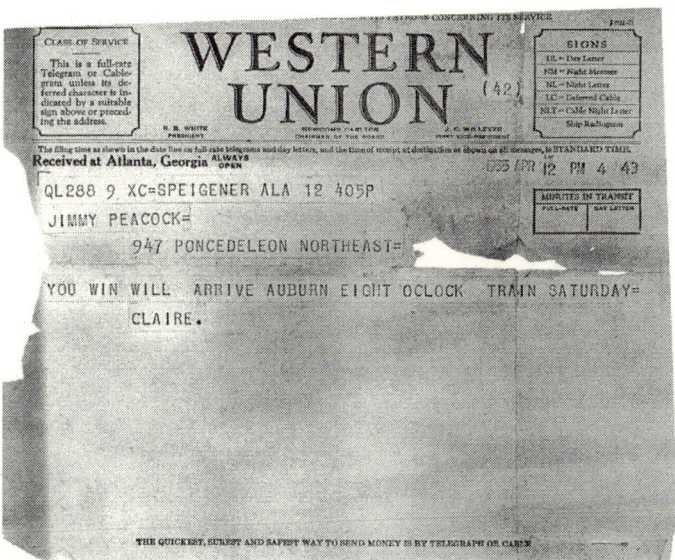

Telegram sent to James Peacock Jr. by his future wife.

Family and Early Life   11

James Peacock Jr. in the US Army, 1945 (?).

big power company, like Duke Power or something like that. And then he went to war, and then he came back, and they settled again in Tifton, and he started this business. So, that's how it happened.

AK: Perfect! This telegram . . . !

JP: Yes, it's a wonderful . . . I mean, it's so . . .

AK: It should be in the book!

JP: We will put a copy . . . my sister discovered it: after my mother died . . . my father had a footlocker, you know, a trunk, and it was sent from Europe, after the war ended . . . He had been in D-Day and all that. And in that trunk . . . and I have the trunk, and in the trunk he had many things he wanted to keep. One of them was a letter from me that has some funny little drawings about . . . what he was doing. It had pictures of bombs and things. And then one was that telegram. My sister discovered this telegram, and I have a copy of it.

AK: We absolutely need both of them for the book.

JP: So, let me make a note, and I will find . . .

AK: So, the telegram and your letter to your father during the war.

JP: I have them . . . I just have to . . . you know, when we moved, there were so many . . . but I have them . . . Those are absolutely available. And my sister, by the way, if you want to talk to her . . . .

AK: This was my next question. But let's stay with . . . So, then you lived in Tifton, and then . . . how did you move later on?

Dad in D-Day

JP: So, we moved to Tifton, I started the third grade there. I had already been to several schools because he had been moving around . . . they had been moving around, we all had been moving around. Getting . . . moving . . . training for D-Day. So, he came home, he was shot . . . wounded, but he did survive, did not die. He recovered, came home, and then decided to do this business in Tifton, and then we moved to Tifton.

Here is an account by James Peacock Jr. He notes "not a diary—written from memory about Dec 20, 1944," he also notes "Jan 12, 1944, left family at Columbia, S.C. moved by train to Camp Kilmer N.J. then went to England and eventually embarked to invade beach at D Day."

> I get off the boat, wade in, but notice Tourvielle can't get radio on his back. I wade out and help him. I get in about 20 yards when I get hit near top of my boot by a shell fragment. I see it coming like a fast baseball. We hit the dirt then run like heck for the sea wall. I stumble and fall in the road, a medic shows up. I give Sgt. Critchfield my map and 536 Radio and tell him I'll come up as soon as my leg is bandaged. My leg bleeds but doesn't hurt, I hobble to aid station, they dress it (I don't want any morphine). There was plenty of shell fire on the beach I had a ring side seat from the aid station but was too scared to look up much. Ammunition trucks are being hit quite frequently and there is a heck of a racket all the time, but it was miraculous how few men were hit and killed. The medics were doing a good job, especially the doctor of beach

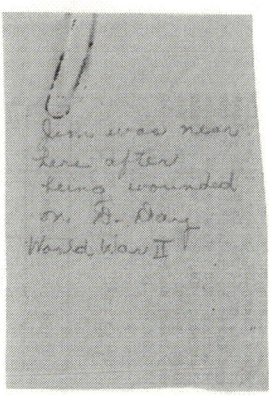

A note on James Peacock Jr. being wounded while at the front line.

Family and Early Life 13

"bri." An ammo truck burns and blows up about 15 feet away. Why none of us were hit I don't know. I see about 100 prisoners being herded down the beach—blond and dressed blouses, not the defeated soldiers that you see later. Trucks and jeeps hit an occasional string of mines and are demolished. We hear small arms fire up the beach and know that the 22nd is catching it. I see two planes fall in flames. I couldn't tell but they must have been our planes: P-38s and P-47s were up high most of the time. Germans start dropping some big stuff on the beach probably 150 mm. but we were behind the sea wall and didn't get hit—I dig a hole with my hands. Finally they (the command) decide that the tide is right and we are to be evacuated, I hobble over to a medic jeep and crawl in . . .

Going back further, here is a bit of background. I was born in Montgomery, Alabama, near where my mother's family lived out in the country and also in cities. However, soon after I was born, my father was inducted into the army, as were most of the adult men in our family. My father was an electrical engineer and became an officer in the Corps of Engineers but later was in the artillery and then the infantry, finally joining D-Day, where he was shot but survived. On the way to D-Day, he underwent training at many camps in the United States, from New England to Oklahoma to South Carolina, and where he went so did the rest of us, my mother, driving with my sister and me, starting when I was three years old and she was one year old. Since the army did not provide housing for families, we would live wherever was available, usually in a room with a family near the army base. Thus, we lived in a room with different families in New Jersey but later in an apartment in Columbia, South Carolina, where I attended two of the four elementary schools of my first year of schooling.

After my father went overseas, we moved in with my mother's mother in rural Alabama, and I went to the fourth first grade school, out in the country. My mother had met a Black mother in New Jersey whose son and I became friends; he impressed me with his model airplanes. Back in Alabama, the main African Americans I knew were servants and workers. In any event, I did not grow up, as some Southerners did, with a Black nurse, so I missed, as far as I know, this aspect of the experience of many Southerners and others as well. However, I was exposed to history of the Confederacy because both sides of our family, father and mother, had ancestors who were in the Confederacy. One was killed at Petersburg. My father and I discovered his uniform at the County Clerk's office in Stewart County. So, later, did Jimmy Carter, who was also a relative of that person. Carter's mother was first cousin to my grandmother on my father's side, but I did not meet Carter except briefly because my grandmother and her siblings were orphaned, then adopted to a relative in Columbus, Georgia, to which they moved, while Carter remained near Plains, Georgia.

AK: One thing I wanted to ask about is your parents' wedding ceremony . . . Recently I came across this journal that was called *Southern Weddings*. Is there anything special about a "Southern wedding" and did your parents follow this "Southern pattern"?

JP: I don't know that there is, and I don't know that they did—they did do one thing, unusual: they got married on a leap year. They did it as a bit of a joke because they said, well, if we get married on a leap year, we'll only have an anniversary every four years.

AK: They married on February 29?

JP: Uh-huh.

AK: Good sense of humor.

JP: Yeah.

AK: And where did they get married?

JP: They got married in Speigner, Alabama.

AK: And were there many people present?

JP: Oh, I don't know. I wasn't there. I doubt that it was many because it was in a small country church.

AK: Were they both of the same denomination?

JP: I think so. I know my mother was Methodist, and I think my father was, too.

AK: Was your family religious in any sense?

JP: In some ways, yeah. My grandfather on my mother's side was a leader in a denomination that was called "Methodist Protestant." What it stood for was "lay leadership." In other words, instead of having bishops to be the leaders, the laypeople were.

AK: So, Methodist Protestants are not the same as simply Methodist?

JP: No. So, here is a brief history of Methodism. And I'm not an expert, but

Family and Early Life 15

this is briefly. So, John Wesley created Methodism, and he was an Anglican, in England, at that time. And, so, it's an offshoot of Anglicanism. And then in America there were several kinds of Methodists. There was Methodist Episcopal, Methodist Protestant, and others. Methodist Episcopal was still related to Anglican. Methodist Protestant did not want bishops to be in control; they wanted laypeople to be in control. In 1939 several of these groups banded together and formed the United Methodist Church. If you go to downtown Chapel Hill, one of the tallest steeples—that is called the University United Methodist Church. There was Methodist Protestant, and Methodist Episcopal, and then there was a group that was a Midwestern German evangelical group. And they all bound together, and that created United Methodist Church. These United Methodists were white on the whole, although they had Black members. But also there are churches that are primarily Black. The AME Zion is one of those.

AK: And your grandfather was . . .

JP: Methodist Protestant. He was one of the leaders. Alpha Clayton Rogers.

AK: He was everywhere! He was in business, he was in the legislature . . .

JP: Yes, he was a real leader. But I didn't know him because he died almost at the time I was born.

AK: And he was elected an elder in this church?

JP: I believe so. My mother's father.

AK: So, your mother was obviously brought up Methodist.

JP: Yes.

AK: Did she pass it on to the children? How did you feel about this Methodist background?

JP: The first experience that I can remember, almost first . . . so, when my father went off to war . . . WWII, my mother and my sister and I went to live with my grandmother. And my grandmother lived on a piece of land, and there was a small church on that land, which is where my father and mother got married. So, we would go to that church on Sundays.

AK: And that was where?

JP: It was on my grandmother's property. It was in Speigner, Alabama. It was very informal. I used to go there barefoot. And I had a dog, and the dog would go with me. And we would usually just sing songs, sing hymns. Rarely did we have a minister at that time.

AK: Did you go there willingly—or were you made to go there?

JP: No, I went willingly, it was fine, I just went . . .

AK: Did they try to educate you in any specific way, like, here is a boy who can grow up and become somebody important in the church?

JP: No, I don't think so. I remember that they would read some passages from the Bible, because for much of the time there was no minister. And then we would sing some songs—that was about it.

AK: And there was no communion of any kind?

JP: Communion? I don't remember any. Not then, not there . . .

AK: Pieces of bread or something . . .

JP: I know . . . later, when we were in our bigger church, they would have communion. They would have grape juice and bread.

AK: No wine?

JP: No.

AK: Did your sister go with you to the church?

JP: Yes.

AK: Tell me more about your sister, how her life course was developing . . .

JP: Yes. So, she was three years younger than I was . . .

AK: And her name was . . .

JP: Claire.

AK: Claire? Like your mother's name?

JP: Yes, she was named for my mother. And she is very intelligent, my sister. She is very good pianist, and she wrote a master's thesis in literature, about a writer whose name is Flannery O'Connor. And I think my sister met Flannery O'Connor—she said, she met her one time.

AK: And so, she was teaching literature?

JP: She was teaching English in high school in Alabama. And she had met this man who went to the same college that she went to, and they got married. He was a Methodist minister, and then he became a social worker at the VA hospital, Veterans' Administration hospital.

AK: Does she have children, grandchildren . . . your sister?

JP: She does. She has a boy and a girl, and they have several children, each of them. My sister's son lives in Iowa. And my sister lives in Dothan, Alabama—it's a biblical name, I think. "Let us go down to Dothan."

AK: Tell me about how some of your early interests, how they began.

JP: My father was an engineer, he had been at Georgia Tech, and then later at Auburn, which is the equivalent . . . engineering school. And my mother was interested in psychology. She used to subscribe to *Parents' Magazine*. And it was for parents—about parenting. And my sister and I used to read it, even though we were the children, (laughs) and I remember one time I said to my mother, or maybe my father and my mother, and I said: "*Parents' Magazine* says, we ought to have family council, where we discuss problems together." Well, they didn't . . . (laughs), but . . . maybe you get a picture. I had an interest.

Sigmund Freud or some spinoff was important in teenagers, mainly by the idea of the unconscious. My mother had some psychological notion in mind when I threw a rock at our windshield. I said, at age four, I heard a voice, and she said, it is your conscience.

Theology came into play in my teenage years also but not very seriously. My grandmother, with whom we lived, had a small chapel on her land, where services were held on Sundays, usually (unless she called them off by party line), and consisted mainly of singing songs from the hymnal. I attended, barefoot, with my dog, Rusty. When he died, I asked my grandmother if he would go to heaven.

When I was a teenager doing construction work I painted a picture. It shows an old man pleading with a foreman, perhaps for work or to keep his job. In the background is a worker carrying a two-by-six on his shoulder. He is probably a friend from school who was working on the job. I mentioned him to my father and he replied, "He is the scum of the earth." I do not know what he meant, possibly that his father was an alcoholic. Similarly, on a job I observed the son of a company owner working on the roof with the workers. I spoke admiringly about him to my father, and he replied, "He must not be a very good manager if he has to work with the workers." These comments were not typical of my father, who was extremely democratic; perhaps they came from his military experiences where he was an officer.

Growing up, my main interests were visual and manual. I drew a lot, and a teacher at the country school in Alabama expressed appreciation. I was also a good reader but did not write anything except a few letters, such as one to my father in England before he went to D-Day. He saved it, and it included drawings of bombers and bombs. This was when I was six or so. During wartime, toys were constructed out of cardboard, so I saved Kix box tops and did that: slot a to tab b. Every morning I would run out to the "sandpile" at dawn and make elaborate tunnels for my plastic soldiers. I lost one and dreamt that I found it, perhaps a symbol of my father, facing D-Day.

Result? Like the construction work: good job but not monuments for the ages. I might have learned better from my father. When I was eleven or so we painted a bookcase. I asked him why we had to paint the back of it, as it would be against the wall. He replied, "The gods see everywhere." He was trained as an electrical engineer, but when he was seventy-five, he started making furniture, initially seeking advice from Mr. Bargerin, who made fine furniture, for example, for the Jimmy Carter library, and my father then made beds, tables, and chests of drawers for his children and grandchildren until he was ninety.

AK: Did you ever serve in the military?

JP: So, a little bit about my family background. My father, as I've said, was in D-Day, and my uncle, who was one of the founders of the Green Berets, was in Merrill's Marauders in Burma . . . In World War II, men in my extended family were drafted, volunteered—not all, but most served. And I came along . . . I expected I'd do the same, but the Korean War had already finished, and Vietnam had not yet started. When I went to college, I did the Reserve Officers' Training Corps (ROTC), but I started college at a state university, Florida State, and I did ROTC for that year. Then I transferred to Duke. Duke did not have Army ROTC. So, I could not continue it.

AK: But it's not mandatory, I mean . . . ?

JP: No, it's not mandatory, but I was already doing this. And in fact, a friend and I almost volunteered to be in the US Army. When I was a freshman in college, we went to the recruiting office to sign up. But my father said, "Don't sign up to do that for them, because you're going there as a private."

He had been a captain, and then a major, and I think he was right—He knew . . .

AK: What it was about!

JP: If you went in as a private, you're treated as dirt, basically, was his point. And so, my friend did not sign up for this program, and I did not sign for this program, so I did not go in the army. And then I went to graduate school, and at that time we were not at war; this was before Vietnam. And I got a fellowship at the graduate school, from the US government—National Institutes of Health, NIH. Many of us did at that time. So, it's a federal fellowship. The head of NIH wrote a letter to my draft board and said, "Please, exempt Peacock because he has an assistantship from NIH." So even though I was eligible, I was exempt, at least for a moment, and then later Vietnam began, but by that time I was already married, I had children. If you were married and had children . . . I was exempted. It was not a physical thing, nothing like . . . trauma or anything. I didn't attempt to be exempted.

AK: You mentioned how your father saved one of his great-grandchildren when he was ninety years old?

JP: Oh, yes. He was ninety-two, I believe, and one of the . . . small grandchildren, I have to think, who it was . . . was probably about two, dashed out in the street. And he dashed out and grabbed her.

AK: From under the car?

JP: From . . . before she got under the car!

AK: Was it here in Chapel Hill?

JP: No, in Alabama.

AK: What a great thing to do when you are ninety-two.

JP: Yup. Well, the reason I thought of it was because the child's mother, who is Louly . . . so, Louly is the one who told that story. She really . . . was grateful to my father.

AK: And so, how did you meet Professor Peacock, who was not a professor yet . . . ?

Florence Peacock (FP): He came there . . . I was there for three years . . .

AK: In Yale?

FP: At Yale. And he came there the third year. And he was studying the Indonesian language . . .

AK: How much older is he?

FP: He is not older—we are the same age, except I'm three months older than he. And I had a girl friend who lived near me—this was in a dormitory, because we had a girls' dormitory. And I was president of the dormitory. See, for some reason people thought that I could do stuff like that. And because they thought it, I did it. But I'm not sure I was that qualified. Anyway, my friend, Edith Jacobson, again, Jewish, said: "Now, there is someone in my class . . . she was studying the Indonesian language, too—who talks exactly like you. And his name is James Peacock." She said, "I want to introduce you." So, I said: "OK, but I won't go to dinner with him unless you go with me."

AK: What did she mean by "talks the way you do"?

FP: Same . . . Georgia . . . Jim was from Georgia . . .

AK: Southern, Southern . . . OK.

FP: So, somehow he called me, and we had a date, but I said, Edith is coming with us—and he said, fine. But he paid for food, which is a miracle.

AK: For all three of you?

FP: Uh-huh. And so, we went to a nice restaurant, and he seemed to find me interesting. He was very refined. But: it was dark as we were leaving, this was . . . (laughs) something (?) I liked, even though it might have been a little . . . quick. Edith was walking ahead of us, so he grabbed me by arm, and pulled me behind a tree, and gave me a marvelous kiss. Well, from then on . . . oh, my goodness! I really like this guy. But that was it, see? He was never too pushy. But then he called me and said: "Will you come over to . . . ?" He had a one-bedroom in this huge building, three stories. Unheated. And with a tiny kitchen, which everybody in the hall used to do cooking. So, he said: "Will you come over, and let's have a date, and listen to . . . " He loved Wagner. And he had these recordings, and he played Wagner. And I said: "Oh, I'd love to do that." So, I went there, we went up to the third floor, and he made hamburgers, they were terrible, but I didn't even care! And we took our plates into his bedroom—he had a twin bed—and we sat on the bed, and we covered up (laughs) with this thing that his grandmother had sent him, which was a heated sheet, not a heated blanket. So, we sat there and we listened to Wagner. And we ate our supper, and we talked, and we had a good time. Then I went home—maybe he took me home, I'm not sure, but I went back to the girls' dormitory. And this was so funny. So, after that we didn't date.

AK: Does he remember this first date?

FP: I think so. After that we didn't date, because I started working and doing concerts and studying so hard! And so, one day he saw me walking down the street, beside where everybody buys books and stuff. And he (laughs)—he is always kinda funny! He grabbed me by the arm again, and he said: "I need to see you!" (laughs) I thought it was so funny! So, I think we dated again, then I said: "Sorry, I've got so much to do, because I'm in this concert." So, he said: "OK, when is the concert?"—I told him, and I was doing the whole recital: lots of work! One was a piece for eight cellos, Bachianas Brasileiras, which was written by a Brazilian composer . . . I can't quite remember his name. Gorgeous piece! And I sang the solo, and they played. And I thought—fine, I knew it. I would get excited but not afraid. So, I sang the whole concert, everybody seemed to love it, and . . . I had three boyfriends there. One was from Alabama, one was Jim Peacock, and one was . . . I think, a musician, but . . . And my mother and daddy decided to have a party, a kind of dance party for me after this performance. Because they were there. And they arranged this—it was at the country club, so I went there, and I danced with this guy from Russia—fabulous dancer, somewhat older than I. And we just swirled around, and I just loved it . . . we did just wonderful dancing. Jim never got a chance to dance with me, but he danced with my very good friend at the dormitory.

AK: Is he a good dancer? Was he a good dancer?

FP: He danced! But, anyway, I didn't get a chance to dance with him. I think he danced with my mother, and he danced with my very good friend. And he told my very good friend that he wanted to date me, and she told me. But . . . and I had a great time, but see, what this one guy, who turned to be a very religious guy, from Alabama, told Jim at the door—he said: "I'm in charge of Florence." Telling Jim not to pay attention to me—but anyway. So . . . I didn't know that, and kept dating all these three . . .

AK: But he didn't listen obviously . . . ?

FP: Well, he didn't get a chance to dance with me, which I missed. But then mother and father stayed two days after that, and they said, "We want to take you and a friend out to dinner." And mother said: "You just choose somebody and invite him." So, I chose Jim. And I remember the sound of his voice when I called him: it was the most beautiful voice. And he seemed very pleased, but not out of control. And I think he rode with us to their house, or to the restaurant, and from then on we kind of liked each other. But again, I kept dating other people. And I had made another friendship—it was more than a friendship—with a guy whom I had met, from Chicago, at a music camp. Whom I liked so much! And he wanted to come visit me, and . . . this is kind of tragic, and that was one year before my current boyfriend, a Yale lawyer, had left, and he told me that he'd met him and said: "Do not date Florence—she is my girlfriend." I did not know all this stuff—he told me later. And I liked him a lot, too, and he kissed me also, and I liked that. But it's better that I decided on Jim. Anyway . . . boy, that was a complicated time for me. So, I graduated from Yale, I did not stay for graduation, which I have always regretted. Because I knew I was getting ready to get married. And I wanted to get home and plan the wedding. But the wedding wasn't till August 4, so I should have stayed, but I didn't. Got home, started planning the wedding . . . you know, I didn't actually like the way they did weddings, but I did it anyway . . . making a big deal out of it. But my mother . . . oh, she had the most beautiful party at our house upon the hill, the one that my daddy had built. My mother and my father, they adored Jim Peacock—oh, what a relief!

AK: How about his parents—did they like you?

FP: Oh, we visited them. We got on the train to south Georgia from Covington, Georgia, to visit his parents in the spring before I graduated, and they totally loved me! (laughs) I thought, anyway. I thought they did. And his mother—oh, she and I just got along completely well to the last breath. And his father had a lot of respect for me. His father was in the Second World War, and this had a huge effect on him. And his sister, who we're going to see this weekend, his sister Claire is just about one year younger than I . . . so, she was dressing when I arrived, and I . . . Jim had come to pick me up at the train station, and I had on a suit, I remember, it was not sexy, but . . . chic. And so, when I got there, his mother was very very friendly, and his father was respectful. And his sister was still dressing. And then finally she came around, and met me, and I was really glad to meet her.

AK: So, did you know anything about what your husband, or future husband, was doing, what was anthropology?

FP: He never asked me to marry him. All he said was: "Will you go to Indonesia with me?" And I laughed, and I said: "I'll think about it." Well, my mother wouldn't have let me go unless we were married . . . but I wasn't going to go unless we were married, either.

AK: This was almost like a marriage proposal . . .

FP: Yeah, but he never said: "Would you marry me?" So, a few days later I was with him, this was at Yale, and we were in a practice room, listening to music. Which is a closed-door situation, but that's where he asked me. And I think we must have been there again, and I said: "I would like to go to Indonesia with you. But I can't go unless we're married." So, I think finally he admitted that he wanted to marry me. And that was almost at the end of the time when we were both at Yale.

AK: And you were both twenty-two or something at the time?

FP: No. See, I graduated when I was twenty-three.

AK: So, did you know anything about what anthropology is . . .

FP: Oh, yes. By then I did because I wanted to do what he wanted to do. See, for me it was fun. So, I listened to all of those tapes and recordings of people speaking Indonesian and telling you how to speak Indonesian. And I also looked into the dance, the beautiful Indonesian dance, and the *nembang*, which means singing. And they have a different tone system: five-tone system, seven-tone system, not on our pitches, different vibrational frequency. I loved that!

AK: Wouldn't your family and friends here in the United States say something like: "Oh, you would be really crazy to go that far and live in a slum, why would you do that? Can't you stay home?" . . . Were there any comments like that?

FP: Nobody ever said that to me. And yet I know now that my mother and father were very concerned, and that Jim's mother and father were very concerned. When we departed . . . the day after we married, I handed my mother this beautiful white night gown that I had worn for, like, 5 minutes, and I just handed it to her, like, mother, you take that, it takes up too much space. I never wore it again! I don't know where it is!

AK: So, they didn't tell you anything, but they probably thought . . . and were anxious about you . . .

FP: Yeah, but my mama and daddy always were positive. They knew that that's the way to go through it: just stay positive and enjoy . . .

(5_Peacock_Florence_04_12_2018)

CHAPTER 2

Becoming an Anthropologist

Milledgeville, Snake Handlers, and "Everything Margaret Mead Ever Wrote"

Anna Kushkova (AK): Tell me more about how you got interested in anthropology.

Jim Peacock (JP): I started working on the construction jobs when I was thirteen, and I guess I got up and went up there in the morning, and came back at night. And when I was probably eighteen, I was working in south Georgia selling pots and pans at night, mainly at night, because customers were single working women, they worked during the day. And so, during the day sometimes I had an opportunity to read that book *The Human Animal*, by Weston La Barre.

That is when I heard about Weston La Barre, who was a psychoanalytically focused anthropologist. So I was majoring in psychology, but it was . . . an experimental kind. Psychoanalysis came into play, and with Freud, of course, the symbol is absolutely crucial for dream interpretation and other things. So . . . and I had already got interested in psychoanalysis as a teenager. In fact, I had never met a psychologist or analyst . . . we lived in a very small town in south Georgia, there was no psychologist there. And I never met one, and I was curious. So, in order to meet a psychologist, I rode the bus to Milledgeville. The state of Georgia had one of the two largest mental hospitals in the country. The other one was in Long Island—they both had something like twelve thousand patients. And it was in Milledgeville, Georgia. People used to say: "You're gonna go to Milledgeville," meaning—"You are crazy." So, I got on the bus, and I got to Milledgeville. And I met this psychologist and talked to him and found out a little bit about what psychologists did.

In 1959, I began studying social anthropology at Harvard. Before that, I studied psychology at Duke, and in fact I was president of Psychi, which was the psychology majors club at Duke, and I had worked with a clinical psychologist whose name was Charles Spielberger—who later, I believe, became president of the American Psychological Society. I was his research assistant, as an undergraduate, a senior. And I had a friend whose name was Chris Crocker. There was no anthropology major at Duke then, but there was a sociology major, and there was one anthropologist whose name was Weston La Barre. And Chris was majoring in sociology, but really specializing in anthropology, and Weston La Barre was his mentor and teacher. I frankly hardly knew what anthropology was, except Chris had told me about this field . . . this field called anthropology. And I had a job selling pots and pans in south Georgia, which in a way was doing anthropology—fieldwork of a sort . . .

Weston La Barre, whom I had not yet met, published a book called *The Human Animal* with the University of Chicago Press*—and I read it during the summer.

I didn't focus on any particular aspect in psychoanalysis then, but I just read things I could find. For example, I read . . . There was a library in our town, but it was very small, and one book that I found about psychology was by William James. And I read what he said about psychoanalysis, and he had this description of the censor. You know, Freud had the idea that the super-ego was a guard and would prevent unwelcome thoughts from coming through—like a prison guard. So, I read this metaphor, and frankly I didn't quite understand it: good lord, have I got a prison in my head?! But I read a few things, not much. And then I took this trip to Milledgeville. What I am getting around to saying is, I had an early interest in psychology and psychoanalysis. So, then, later, when I went to Duke, I decided to major in that, but most of psychology in the major was experimental. And so, I did experiments teaching pigeons to pick keys and things like that. There was little opportunity except when I met Weston La Barre, who was an anthropologist, but who was very infatuated with psychoanalysis, from the anthropological perspective. In *The Human Animal*, he interpreted a lot about humanity from a psychoanalytical point of view.

The first job that I was offered was, when I had almost finished my dis-

---

* Weston La Barre, *The Human Animal* (Chicago: University of Chicago Press, 1954).

sertation in 1964 . . . I was invited to come to Cornell and make a presentation. I spent a whole day or two meeting everybody. And basically, they made me an offer, which I turned down. I'll tell you why I turned it down. And by the way, there is a book by Benedict Anderson . . . in his memoir he mentions me . . . although he gets the dates wrong, and I think he gets some of the facts wrong, but he calls me "that Parsonsian." And I was! I mean, I was maybe not so much a Parsonsian but an anthropologist, and maybe a synthesizer of various points of view. I did not see myself as a specialist in Indonesia. And that's what this position was, or at least that's the way I saw it, and I just turned it down because I just didn't think I was qualified in that way.

I wish to clarify a bit. First, I admire Benedict Anderson's own work and brilliance, which is why I invited him to give a keynote address at perhaps the most important conference I have helped lead, namely the Rockefeller Foundation-sponsored event on the US South, which I organized with Ruel Tyson, mentioned above. Anderson in his speech made a suggestive comparison with Indonesia, that the US South continues to glorify the Civil War, whereas Indonesia suppresses memory of its experience with Gestapu, the year of living dangerously when a million people were killed. Whatever opinion I may have of Anderson's comment about me in his memoir is a minor detail from long ago that does not detract from my admiration for his huge contribution ranging from Indonesian studies to global understanding of history and culture.

So, anyway, this was my last year in graduate school, 1964. I was invited to come to Cornell and give a talk and meet all the people. And it was in winter, like, in December, and Cornell is . . . there is a lot of snow in Cornell. So, all the flights were canceled to Cornell, and I drove instead. And I remember, when I was driving, the snow was high in . . . places. But I got there, and I gave at least one talk . . . This was in December of 1964. And Benedict Anderson was a student there, he was probably my age, maybe a year older . . . but at the time he was there . . . he and I were both graduate students. He was a PhD candidate in political science at Cornell, and I was a PhD candidate in anthropology at Harvard. Benedict Anderson was . . . already regarded as a leading . . . scholar of Indonesia. And Cornell had a particular slant on things, which was area studies. So, instead of theory, it was learning about a place. Whereas Harvard was more of a theoretical place. And so, nobody taught about Indonesia in Harvard, and there were specialists at Cornell in Indonesia studies. So, I gave a talk, on an Indonesian working-class theater called ludruk, and it had these two types of dramas, type T and type M. Type T was traditional drama, type M was modern. And I had worked out these paradigms for each type in relation to the social vision that they demonstrated. I remember a question Benedict Anderson asked me—he asked about a particular older form of ludruk, which was there during the Dutch time. So, you can get a sense already of the view he had, which was different from mine: mine was more theory, here was a picture of a paradigm, illustrated by these two types of theater. His was more the history of it. So, he was more historical in approach, I was more theoretical.

Senior year [at Duke], I took some courses in anthropology. There were two, I believe, and one I audited. The two that I took . . . they were general courses . . . These were the only . . . anyway, they were general courses, for undergraduates or anybody. And I took those, and also I audited a seminar, and it was for graduate students, and it was psychoanalytically focused. So, then, as I mentioned, I was president of the psychology club, and I had an idea, and that was, well, let's have a lecture. Well, I had seen a book—and read a book—by Weston La Barre, which was called *They Shall Take Up Serpents*. And it was a study of snake-handlers, especially in Durham. So, I invited him to lecture on snake-handlers. I thought we might as well spread the word that he is going to give this lecture. And somehow I did, in a newspaper or something, so some snake-handlers came to the lecture. (laughs) And this slightly embarrassed La Barre because it turned out that he had never been to a snake-handler . . . service, apparently. But he had graduate students who did this fieldwork. Anyway . . . he . . . this was 1958–1959, my senior year at college. But the good thing that happened—this is how I got into anthropology—was La Barre invited Chris Crocker to go with him to the meeting of the American Anthropological Association, in Washington, DC, in the fall of 1958. Chris Crocker, who was my friend, invited me to go with him. So, the two of us went, we slept on the floor in La Barre's room, and he had a roommate who was a Mexican anthropologist. And it was like going to the circus—I mean, it was so fascinating to me because there were people from all over the world, people like Alan Lomax, who recorded things everywhere, Alfred Kroeber gave a kind of keynote, and the subject was, basically, the meaning of anthropology. And one of the things he said, was: anthropology is sensory. It deals with things you can touch and feel, for example, archaeology deals with artifacts, and cultural anthropology . . . record and see and photograph . . . all of this was very appealing to me because I was . . . mostly what I had done as I was growing up was make things and draw things. So, that sounded . . . I thought of becoming an architect. Probably, would not have been good at it. But anthropology was very compelling by comparison to psychology and other social sciences that were much more abstract in the sense that they did not, on the whole, focus on seeing and hearing and smelling . . . All of that led me, almost immediately, to apply to graduate school in anthropology. I switched to anthropology on the spur of the moment. I was attracted by the fact that anthropology involves *holistic research* . . . things you can see, hear, touch . . .

I was not really switching from one field to another, I was thinking of combining them . . . And so, I applied to four programs, and I was accepted to each of them. Chicago, Stanford, Yale, and Harvard. And the reason I chose Harvard was they had a program called "Social Relations," which combined sociology, psychology—clinical psychology and social psychology—and anthropology.

There were two sociologists there—Talcott Parsons and Robert Bellah. And in the spring of 1960—this was my first year at Harvard—those two, Bellah and Parsons, gave a seminar, which was called . . . "The Sociology of Religion." There were . . . maybe thirty people in the seminar, including me and another person in social anthropology, Terry Turner. And the third person whom I did not know at the time—who is . . . who lives here, his name is Bill Peck. And most of the other thirty seemed to be older and more advanced than I. And as the semester went on, the others would say things, talk sometimes—and I never said a word! At the same time that I was taking this seminar, I started reading Talcott Parsons, and that was due to the influence of another fellow student—Tom Kirsh.

The sociology of religion course was optional. There was a required seminar, which those of us who were entering the program in social anthropology took. And at the first class, they gave a list of anthropologists, and said, choose one and then you write a paper about that person. Well, the one I'd heard of was Margaret Mead. And, for example Terry Turner chose Lévi-Strauss. Well, I'd never heard of him at the time—this was 1958. I think he published *The Structural Study of Myth* around that year. But Terry Turner already knew about that because he had majored in history at Harvard, and he somehow knew about it. I didn't. I didn't know about any of them—except Margaret Mead, so I wrote about her. I read everything . . . every book that Margaret Mead ever wrote, and I also read a number of papers that she had written because at the Tozzer Library at Harvard they had many of her unpublished papers. So, I wrote this paper, which was fairly short, but it was a kind of synthesis of her. But I had never met her, I just . . . she was one of the few I had heard of. So, that was in the fall of 1959.

Tom Kirsh, who was older than I and had been a sociology major at Syracuse University, I believe, told me about this sociologist called Talcott

Parsons. Talcott Parsons synthesized many things—psychological, sociological, cultural—in something he called "the theory of action." And that was very inspiring to me.

At the time I was fascinated by Parsons's theory of action, Robert Bellah, another sociologist at Harvard, wrote a paper called "Notes Toward a Systematic Study of Religion." The focal idea of this paper was action is guided by meaning.

For this Harvard seminar I chose—and I have no idea why—I chose German mystics of the fourteenth century and wrote a paper about them. They were called "God's Friends," Gottesfreunde. Terry Turner wrote this magnum opus about symbols. Terry was a strong, vigorous person, and about three in the morning he knocked on my door, and he said: "I've done my paper!" And he gave me a copy, and it was this big, thick paper about symbols, from many points of view. Cassirer, people like that. And then also in the seminar was Bill Peck, and on the last day of the seminar, he and I were scheduled to present our papers, and his was a synthesis of religion, and I'm sure symbols were involved, and it was kind of a scheme for understanding and studying religion. So, I think that was in a way a birth of *symbolic anthropology*, because each of us in a different way was focusing on the role of symbols.

And in the writing of Talcott Parsons, symbols became much more central. In 1961, he published a book called *Theories of Society*, where he importantly introduces the level of culture. He was a sociologist, and a lot of his work had been focused on what you call "social systems." But now he added the dimension of culture. And symbol was key, different kinds of symbols—the *expressive symbol* is one. That would be like art—and then other things.

AK to Bill Peck: But how did you first meet with Jim?

Bill Peck (BiP): Well, we first met because we were in the same program at Harvard, in a class by Robert Bellah and Talcott Parsons. There were about sixty students in the class, and one of our jobs was to present results of our work to the whole class of sixty. They picked Jim and me to do our report on the same day. And when we met seven years later, we came to Carolina at the same time, we started teaching elsewhere . . . I went to Williams College, Massachusetts, and he went to Princeton University. . . Anyway, we hadn't seen each other . . . we didn't know each other, we just remembered everything the other had said in their presentation. (laughs) So, when we met, we started talking about the same issues, and we said: "By the way, what is your name?" (laughs) Jim Peacock—and I'm Bill Peck.

AK: But you were not majoring in anthropology, right?

BiP: No, I took religious studies.

AK: Like Ruel Tyson?

BiP: Yes, yes, I was a colleague of Ruel Tyson . . . I only met Jim in that Talcott Parsons [class] . . . which was essentially a form of anthropology. It was called Social Psychology. So, that's how we met. And we came here, we looked across the room and said: "Don't I know you from somewhere?"—and we said: "Oh, yes!" And then we both recited each other's speech. (laughs) And then—what is your name? (laughs) That's how we got to . . . that was already in Chapel Hill.

AK: When you were reporting at Harvard, this was a common project of yours, or . . . ?

BiP: This was just a course requirement of Talcott Parsons, there were about sixty graduate students in this class.

AK: Do you remember what you were speaking about?

BiP: I did a presentation on Black civilizations. Lloyd Warner, I think, an anthropologist who worked on the Aboriginal Australians. And he did his on medieval monks.

AK: It's almost like you exchanged your future topics at this point . . .

(19_Peck_Aug_26_2019)

Robert Daniels (RD): As undergraduates at Harvard, we were told . . . because there was a departmental library we used to go to—we were told: "Don't talk to graduate students, they are under too much stress."

(1_Daniels_22_09_2018)

Florence Peacock (FP): Cora Du Bois was Jim's professor in graduate school. And she had visited Indonesia, she lived in Bali, which is much easier than living in Java, but she knew about Java, I think, maybe I'm wrong about that . . . I'm pretty sure that's what she did. But she was one of the first

... now: maybe she also did her research in Java . . . But anyway, Cora Du Bois set Jim on going to Indonesia and being an anthropologist.

AK: So, she was of strong influence upon Dr. Peacock?

FP: Oh, huge!

(5_Peacock_Florence_04_12_2018)

Princeton and the Beginnings of the Anthropology Department

AK: What about David Crabb?

JP: David Crabb and I . . . so, my first job was at Princeton University. Princeton at that time . . . this was 1965, did not have an anthropology department. It had a sociology and an anthropology department. And what they had been doing was they used to hire one anthropologist, and then they'd hire a much larger group of sociologists; it was mainly a sociology department. And in each case an anthropologist would teach there for several years, and then go on to somewhere else. And I could tell you who these were . . . Paul Bohannan, Africa, for example . . . They were temporary and they didn't stay because there was no department properly—that was the main reason. So, then they hired me. And David Crabb was already at Princeton, appointed in the Linguistics Department. He was a linguist—but an anthropologist, too . . . And I taught two courses, one was a graduate seminar that had mainly sociology students—there were no anthropologists at the graduate level, but there were sociologists. And then I also taught an introduction to anthropology . . . cultural anthropology I think it was. That course had a hundred students—introductory . . . cultural anthropology. And then I had a graduate seminar. I gave lectures, and also they had something called . . . they were really discussion sections. But remember, there were no teaching assistants. So, I taught twelve discussion sections.

AK: Preceptorials?

JP: Preceptorials they were called. Then David Crabb and I had this idea: why don't we start an anthropology department? All the other Ivy League schools had them, and had had them for a long time. Princeton didn't . . . David Crabb and I started the department, and then I was going to mention another person . . .

AK: Tom Kirsh?

JP: No. The person who was most crucial in helping us to start the department was Professor Black. Cyril Black was an eminent professor of history at Princeton. He specialized in eastern Europe. Aside from scholarship he was a leader in administration and he supported an effort to create a department of anthropology. David Crabb and I joined him around his kitchen table and within a few minutes planned how to accomplish that task. Step one was to contact leading chairs of departments at Princeton and propose anthropology as a minor for those departments. Following his suggestion, I telephoned relevant chairs and made that proposal. Doubtless owing to his backing, each agreed to these proposals. Very shrewd of him to suggest that we offer a modest proposal to each (i.e., a minor rather than a major), and as I recall, each accepted. Thus, following Black's suggestion, we were able to bring forward a proposal for a new department, which already enjoyed considerable support. Further, we then got approval to hire two new faculty members. Then we published a series with a prestigious press, started several new courses, and were "off to the races." Several years later, after moving from Princeton to UNC, I realized how lucky we were to launch our project in a wealthy private university with supportive leaders at a time when universities and disciplines were expanding.

CHAPTER 3

University Career

"He must have been one of the anointed ones in the graduate school at Harvard. He must have been."
—Robert Daniels, September 22, 2018

"Gee, what an anthropological life he has lived!!!"
—Leedom Lefferts, September 23, 2018

"What does an academic life entail?"
—James Peacock

Stereotypes of "Academic Life"

Jim Peacock (JP): Most people don't have a clue about academic life. I mean, the students think . . . if they think about it at all . . . that what you do is you teach them and grade their papers. And that's about as far as they go. Most laypeople may not even think that far. Even very wealthy and sophisticated people . . . My relatives used to ask: "What do you do during the summer?" There you are, you got a four-month vacation or something like that. Anyway, they don't understand. Now—what's the relevance of helping them understand? Well, one relevance is—unless the wider public understands, we are just not going to get support for this profession. And for a long time maybe that didn't matter so much. Like, I was very lucky when I came along. But it matters a huge amount for your future and for our daughters' futures. And for all the students' futures now.

Anna Kushkova (AK): . . . but then we have to start with a general description of the academy and social sciences, and in particular anthropology.

JP: Right, and I thought of a way to introduce that, and that is partly by ... so, major figures in the history of ... So, these will be people like Max Weber or Woodrow Wilson, who was one of the few ... probably the only American president with a PhD. And who was a college professor before he became a governor ...

AK: But also practical things, like division of the four-field anthropology, or liberal arts: most people in the world have no idea what liberal arts are, so ... And that in its own turn has to do with whom we're writing for, who is the audience. So, on the one hand, we already more or less agreed that it's for people, for nonacademic people who have no idea about what's going on in the academy. But also, and following what you say in *Grounded Globalism*, there are so many people coming to this country right now ...

JP: Good point!

AK: ... some of whose children would go to universities, colleges ... who have no idea, no source, nobody who can tell them anything ...

JP: Good point!

AK: So, it might be some kind of disambiguation of what the academy is—not only for Americans, who don't have much knowledge of this, but also for the increasing number of immigrants ...

Fieldwork, Lawnwork, and Housework: A Tripartite Structure of Academic Life

JP: Fieldwork, lawnwork, and housework: you want me to tell you about those?

AK: Yes, absolutely. "Lawnwork" is something I came across in your course synthesis ...

JP: So, fieldwork is for work undertaken in some place far away, lawnwork is conducted in places nearby, and that would be the work with primitive Baptists and Pentecostals in Durham, and then the housework is work with the legislature and that sort of thing, that's not field ... I mean, that's not anthropology, it's ... it's ... you can call it what you like.

AK: But it's work with the legislature related to your profession, or in general about ... ?

JP: Related to the university mainly.

AK: Like, public service?

JP: Precisely. One overall perspective that I have thought of, and we've already discussed briefly, is sort of a question, and that is: what is an academic life? And so, I start with the simple trichotomy for that, which universities' decree have given out, and that is: teaching, research, and service. And the course is an example of the teaching part; the research, which we discussed, is mainly fieldwork for me; and the service part is something we have not discussed very much, but I can go into that a little bit.

With me, teaching and research intersect somewhat, which we've already discussed, and that is how fieldwork sometimes entered into the teaching. The service part . . . the relation to service part is less obvious, but it is there, and I can go into that. So, today, then, we will talk about the intersection of teaching, research, and service. By the way, I thought of a quotation from Goethe, and it was something like "Die Tat ist Wahrheit." *The Deed is Truth.* I think it comes out of Faust. It reminds us about the connection between thinking and doing.

"I Am a Student"

JP: They used "armchair anthropologists" for old-fashioned anthropology, the ones before Bronisław Kasper Malinowski. Well, Malinowski introduced the idea that fieldwork was the great thing, but before that . . . they were all "armchair anthropologists," I think he used that phrase himself. But anyway—they referred to people like Sir James George Frazer, who once said about . . . somebody asked him, had he ever met a savage?

AK: God forbid! (laughs)

JP: But she [Cora DuBois] did not mean that about me, I don't think, because at the time I had not really begun any fieldwork, I just was a student.

AK: I see that this expression is about the relation of your research and your field, or the absence thereof, but we should probably come up with a term for scholars, anthropologists who are writing for purely academic purposes, without any intention to put their ideas into practice.

JP: Right. Well, the way that I saw myself at that time was: *I am a student*. I have an opportunity now to be a student. Someday, I thought, I'll be a teacher. That was as far as my ambition went—to someday teach, but not now. I must study. And so, I was offered a teaching assistantship by one of the professors, his name was Douglas Oliver, but I turned it down.

AK: Here at UNC?

JP: At Harvard, when I was a student. And I turned it down for two reasons: first, I had a fellowship, so I did not need that money, and second, I thought: now it's the time to focus on studying. So, I tried to read everything in the world!!! And, by the way, I was the first person . . . I was the youngest person in my class, with the least background in anthropology. But I was the first one to finish my dissertation. And that was simply because . . . that was my . . . I thought that this was something I should do—finish that.

AK: So, you said, although you focused on reading and writing, you hoped that someday you would be teaching . . .

JP: I did. That was my goal—to be a teacher.

AK: Is it—or was it—possible in America to get your PhD and then do research only, without teaching?

JP: It was . . . in fact I won a postdoctoral fellowship, but I turned it down to take a teaching position. The reason I did, was—I thought: what I want to do, all I wanted to do, is teach, and so, even though I had this opportunity for postdoctoral research, I thought, I will not do that, I also have an opportunity to teach. And so, I'm going to teach! And so, I stopped being a student, and I started being a teacher. The other part, though, that I did not anticipate, was that I would also become an administrator. And as I've already described to you, that happened because the teaching position that I got was at a school that did not have an anthropology department, and so I and this other person, David Crabb, started one. And so, both of us became, to a certain degree, administrators who organized the department and hired people. I did not anticipate doing that. But I did.

Arriving at Princeton: "Good Samaritans"

JP: Do you want to know the story of our arrival? It might be interesting for you with your Jewish connections. So, I finished my PhD at Harvard in 1965 and graduated in the spring. And I had had a fellowship during that time, but the fellowship ended, in May, I think, or in June. And so, I did not have . . . that was my income basically. And then the job at Princeton started in September. So, between June and September I basically had no income. So, Florence and I . . . and we already had our new child, Louly, who was probably a year old then. So, I had this old car, which I mentioned before, probably . . .

AK: The one you used to go to AAA meetings in Chicago?

JP: Yes. It was . . . Association for Asian Studies . . . I also used it selling pots and pans, and it had been all over! It's a good car. Chevrolet, 1953. And so, we got in the car and drove to Princeton. I had no money—almost no money at all. So, we had a banana, which we gave to Louly, and the money—I used to buy the tickets on the expressway. And so, we arrived in Princeton, late at night, and I wondered, how are we going to eat? We had already rented an apartment, so we had a place . . . We went to the apartment, it was called Magie, they were apartments for faculty. I had a key to the apartment somehow, and we opened the door, and there was a basket of food. And the food came from a Jewish couple, whom we had known in Cambridge, Massachusetts. His name was Bill Michaelson. And I think his wife's name was Ellen. And he was a sociologist, and he had just taken a job at Princeton, at the sociology department.

AK: People of your age, not, like, much older?

JP: Oh, yeah . . . they were our age. And so, they followed . . . a custom of greeting the new arrivals with food. It was a basket of fruit, and bread, and cheese. And it was the way we managed to survive over the weekend—it was a Friday. And then, Monday, we went to the bank, and opened an account, but we didn't have any money to put in it. But they said, you can . . . in essence, you borrow a little bit of money until you get a paycheck. Because they didn't start paying until, you know, a week or two later. Anyway—that was one of the most gracious things, and when I think of Judaism, I think of that! It was like a "good Samaritan" . . . Christian. So, we arrived in Princeton, and I began to teach soon after that.

"What Do the Faculty Do? They Teach."

AK: Three things: teaching, research, and service.

JP: Correct. I kept teaching the whole time, I never stopped teaching. And by the way, I never missed a class that I know of without planning for a substitute, except when I was run over by the taxi, and that was when Florence replaced me for one day, and students said, it was the best class . . .

AK: (laughs)

JP: But otherwise, I just kept teaching the whole time . . . If I think of my fellow graduate students—almost all of them became . . . they went into teaching. A few might continue to do research only, but very few, very few. I think this is related to a history of American universities, which is the following . . . if I may quickly summarize a little bit. If you think just about any American university, including, say, Harvard, which is the oldest—it was a college, that's what it was called. And a college meant, a place where students go to learn. And the faculty teach them—that's what they do. The idea of a research university mainly came into being in the late nineteenth century, after the model of Germany and perhaps other places as well, like Russia, maybe France. But in the United States, up until the late nineteenth century, what you had were colleges, that's what UNC was, that's what Harvard was, that's what William and Mary, the second oldest, had. And so, the faculty—their main job was to teach. And then, with the advent of the research universities, then research became an increasingly important part. At UNC, the state appropriation to the university is almost entirely to pay faculty to teach. And it's called the "instructional budget." The research part comes from independent grants, which come often from the federal government, not the state.

AK: Is it because UNC was established so early, 1793, and that sort of laid the tradition of . . . ?

JP: Partly—but it's also true pretty much throughout the . . . [nation]. Anyway, I was just following the standard practice, which is: you get a doctorate, and then you become a teacher. And the idea of research being an essential part was increasingly important. And the paradox then was . . . still is, perhaps, that although you're hired to be a teacher, your status . . . your tenure, for example, depended on your research. So, you're hired to be a teacher, but the most important criterion for tenure was research and publications. So, therefore, I did both. I already mentioned—my first year of teaching at Princeton, I had a pretty heavy load, I had twelve preceptorials (discussion groups), and two courses, and no TA to help.

JP: If you ask a layperson, or an alumnus, most of whom were undergraduates, not more, or maybe they went to law school—but mostly their experience with faculty was as . . . a teacher. And so, if you ask them what the faculty do, they would probably say, "they teach." And if somebody asked me, "What do you do?" I would probably say, "I teach." In fact, I continued to teach, I never stopped teaching, and I had large enrollment . . . but I also did not stop research, and I did not stop service. I mean, all three of those things, but . . . so, there is a *difference between reality and perception*. The perception by most laypeople is—"he teaches" or "she teaches." That's what

Epitome. James Peacock's study at The Cedars, ca. 2018. Photo: Anna Kushkova.

faculty do. The reality is, they do a lot of other things. Now, the third thing that we were to talk about, was the service part.

AK: This "trichotomy" as you called it—when did it emerge as a trichotomy? In the history of American education.

JP: I think it emerged at the turn of the twentieth century. When colleges became universities.

AK: What do you mean "became"? It was a shift . . .

JP: A shift! Because so-called colleges, like Harvard college, is still the main unit for Harvard University.

AK: But this was not just the renaming of colleges into universities?

JP: No, it was adding a whole dimension of activity, which was research. And then with that became more and more administrative responsibilities, and that was partly because . . . as you increase complexity, you need . . . anyway, you get more and more deans and presidents . . .

AK: We mentioned at some other point this theoretical turn that started happening in the American academy somewhere in the 1970s . . . So, I was wondering if you can think about this right now and then later on: did it have any impact on your work?

JP: A lot! So, when I was an undergraduate, I was in psychology. And also biology to some degree. And so, I thought about things as based on individuals, whether it be an organism or a person. And then, when I got into anthropology, it was sort of a wake-up call: it's not just individuals, there is culture, and there is society. That made a big impact on me! Lab work became fieldwork.

CHAPTER 4

UNC Department of Anthropology

Creation of Anthropology Department at UNC

Jim Peacock (JP): Guy Johnson . . . he started social anthropology at UNC. It was at the fiftieth anniversary of the teaching of social anthropology at UNC. I asked Guy Johnson, who was in his nineties, to tell the history. Well, he told two parts.

Anna Kushkova (AK): Oh, that's the Malinowski history?

JP: Yeah, that's one part. The other part was Joffre Coe, and that was the creation of the archaeology program at UNC.* The other part was about himself and Howard Odum and the creation of social anthropology at UNC. But the first part was about Coe.

So, the archaeology part was this: there was a high school student, his name was Joffre Coe . . . [To Cece Conway:] Do you remember Joffre Coe? Big old guy . . .

Cece Conway (CC): When did he leave? I don't remember that I knew him.

JP: He was around when you were here.

CC: But the archaeologists were in the basement!

JP: They were separate. They were in the basement, that is exactly right. There was a big break, a separation, between the archaeologists in the basement and the social anthropologists, who were upstairs.

---

*Joffre Coe, Father of North Carolina Archaeology, https://www.ncdcr.gov/blog/2015/07/05/joffre-coe-father-of-north-carolina-archaeology.

AK: Well, the break is still there!

JP: You are right. OK—here is what happened, according to Guy Johnson. Joffre Coe was a high school student in Greensboro, and he started doing archaeology as a high school student. And I think he even helped start an archaeology club . . . he even lived with Guy Johnson one time. I mean, he lived with the family of Guy Johnson when he was a student at Chapel Hill, I believe. But before that, he was at high school, and he was already doing archaeology. And then he came to Carolina as an undergraduate, and he applied to WPA—that was a Depression-based funding for lots of things, including building highways, for example, the Blue Ridge Parkway and all of that stuff. And Joffre Coe somehow managed to get a grant, which, according to Guy Johnson, was eight hundred thousand dollars. A tremendous amount for the Depression time!!! So, he got this huge grant, and he started an archaeology . . . club maybe. So, the federal government granted this huge amount to this college sophomore—they didn't realize he was a college sophomore. And when they did, they said, OK . . . he earned the money, but they said to Frank Porter Graham, who was president of the university at that time: "But you have to hire a full-fledged faculty member to administer the money."

AK: So, it was a mistake on their part? They didn't realize he was a sophomore student?

JP: They didn't realize his status, but it was a good proposal! So, they just . . . on the merit of . . . So, anyway, according to Guy Johnson, Frank Porter Graham, who himself was legendary, was on a train to New York, and on the train met a young archaeologist, who was . . . I can't remember his name . . . and hired him on the spot to be the faculty person in charge of this giant project. And so, that guy stayed just long enough to collect the money and start the program, and then he took a job at Tulane and left. So, it was in the hands of a sophomore, Joffre Coe.

CC: Now—how long did he . . . just enough for the money to arrive?

JP: The guy who was hired stayed only a short time. But Joffre Coe . . .

CC: . . . he stayed forever.

JP: He was a student, but then he went to the University of Michigan and got his PhD eventually. And James . . . Jimmy Griffin, who was chair at the University of Michigan, and they were good friends . . . He was kind of legendary, Joffre Coe. He was really the creator of archaeology in the

Southeast. I don't know about the money part, but he managed to . . . now, this is Guy Johnson's account, I never checked it out. But that is the account that he gave to everybody who was present [at the conference]. So, that was the first . . . one part, which was the creation of archaeology. Then came the Malinowski thing. How they were sitting at the Meeting of the Streams—what is now Kenan Memorial Stadium. Malinowski, so charismatic, inspired Johnson to go study with Sapir at Yale and Radcliffe-Brown at Chicago, then introduced social anthropology at Carolina.

(12_Peacock_Conway_July_30_2019)

AK: What about John Gulick?

JP: John Gulick was . . . and by the way, his son . . . Florence knows his son very well, his name is Jim Gulick, and he is a lawyer in Raleigh. John Gulick was from Massachusetts. And he was in the war—I think he was an ambulance driver in Europe. So, John Gulick actually hired me to come here. Gulick was the chair of anthropology when Daniels was hired, and when I was hired, and when a lot of others were hired. Because it was about 1966.

AK: You were hired probably a couple of years prior to Bob Daniels.

JP: Correct. I was already on the faculty when he was interviewed, and that's why I went to the airport to pick him up. I may already have been associate chair then, I'm not sure about that. Anyway . . . He is a couple years younger than I am. And by the way, Bob Daniels's interview with you was very gracious. He gives me a lot of . . . pluses . . .

AK: That will be my next question, but let's go back to John Gulick. So, he is from Massachusetts . . . What kind of a person was he, how he treated other people, how people related to him at the department . . . ? What was his style?

JP: He was matter-of-fact, but not quite like Honigmann. So, here is how I met John Gulick and how I came to be hired: he and I were sitting next to each other on a flight from one of the AAA meetings. We were flying to Boston, because I was a graduate student at Harvard, and he was doing a postdoc at Harvard. He had also done a PhD at Harvard. So, we talked and we had a really good conversation. And (laughs) it was the best conversation I ever had with him. We talked . . . So, later I was hired, and really, he was the craftsperson of the department. He designed the graduate program, for example.

AK: However, at some point the department switched from four fields to three concentrations—was it under Gulick?

JP: That was later. Carol Crumbley, who was an archaeologist, she was involved in that. It was an attempt to bridge, instead of split up the discipline into four fields, you know, archaeology, linguistics, ethnology, and . . . physical anthropology.

AK: And also, as far as I understood, this was when more and more anthropologists who would come to teach at the department would lack the four-field education.

JP: There was a correlation, and that is true. What tended to happen later was people like, say, Margaret Wiener, who was at Chicago, I think did not have background in physical anthropology. And others. Because at that point around the country the four-field thing was diminishing, and specialties started meeting separately. So, that is correct, and that was . . . but that was tending to happen later than Gulick.

AK: But about Gulick . . . Bob Daniels said, "Linguistics has been . . . I would say an 'orphan child' or a 'dead child' of the department—from the beginning."

JP: That's probably not true from the beginning, but it became that . . . When I came, there was one introductory course, it was called Anthropology 41. And it was a four-field course. And everybody was supposed to teach it.

AK: Did you teach it?

JP: I did. The first year I taught it twice. I taught Anthro 41 in the fall, and I taught Anthro 41 again in the spring. So, eventually, this was part of the shift from the four fields to the three [concentrations]. We quit doing Anthropology 41 and started doing these specialized things. Like, Glenn Hinson taught whatever he teaches . . . the US South, and somebody else would teach something else. And it would be kind of divided according to your interest.

AK: So, one could become an anthropologist not having taken a class in physical anthropology or sociocultural anthropology . . . ?

JP: That's right. For graduate students . . . although for undergraduates, I think they are still supposed to take all four fields.

AK: So, there existed a course where you could take all four of them at once?

JP: Well, in a way. But you are right, and Bob is right: things started splitting up maybe in the 1970s.

AK: And Gulick was still chair at the time?

JP: Let me think . . . no, I think the chronology went like this: I believe that Gulick was chair in the late 1960s and into the early 1970s. And then Honigmann was chair in the early 1970s, and then I became chair in 1975, I believe. And did so for five years, till 1980. And then other people later . . . Dotty Holland, and Bruce Winterhalder, whom you don't know because he left, and so on. And Bob described this reading course that Terry Evans, and Bob, and I taught. It was . . . there was no credit, and we would meet . . . we would take turns meeting at each other's house. The three of us.

AK: And whose idea it was?

JP: Just the three of us . . . Terry and I, we used to play tennis together. And Bob and I would play volleyball together, and we were just buddies at that time. And frankly, I don't remember how we came up with that idea, the reading seminar . . .

AK: But what kind of purpose did it have?

JP: The purpose was to just explore . . . and it was focused on social anthropology, cultural . . . just to explore issues in that area. So, we read a lot of things . . . Terry Evans had studied with Max Gluckman at the University of Manchester, and I had studied with Talcott Parsons at Harvard, and Bob Daniels had studied with other people at Chicago. But it was just reading stuff that was current. So, we would read things by Gluckman, or Radcliffe-Brown and Kluckhohn . . . Geertz maybe, he would come in later . . . And we would just meet every couple of weeks, maybe even once a week . . .

AK: And you invited students, right?

JP: Oh, yeah, they were the reason . . . yeah, it was kind of an ongoing reading group, I think it was for no credit, and we would do it as an extra and would read all these things, and nobody wrote anything, but we would read them, and discuss them . . . And there are students today, around, who participated in that. One of them would be Jeff Boyer—he just retired from Appalachian State. He is a friend of Dotty's. He was in that group, and he remembers.

AK: What about Terry Evans? Do you know where he lives now?

JP: I think he still lives in the same house. It's right off of Estes Drive. I have not seen him lately. I hope he is OK. I heard that he may have some problems, but I don't know for sure.

AK: And you had a common grant, I believe ...

JP: Oh, yeah—the "Transcendence"! Terry and I had a grant mainly in the summer of 1979. The idea was this: social movements—the idea was that they were utopian and wanted to transcend the current situation. So, we got a grant from the National Institutes of Health (NIH) and the grant was pretty large, and it was enough to finance maybe half a dozen students. One of whom was Jeff Boyer, who did a study in Honduras.

AK: So, for this grant you were not working in the United States?

JP: We worked in different countries. I did a little bit in Indonesia for my portion.

AK: So, you were studying very different social movements.

JP: Correct. Different social movements, and they had in common the idea that they would transcend current society toward some kind of utopia. It was a very broad scope.

AK: And it's interesting that you got a grant from a health ... organization.

JP: In that day, the NIH funded a lot of social science research.

AK: Not anymore?

JP: Not as much. And that's a change in society ... My graduate study, and that of hundreds of others, was partly funded by the National Institutes of Health. So, ours was a group grant, funded by them, and it was enough to have several students to do a full year of fieldwork. For my part, I did just one summer in Indonesia, but I worked with another student, whose name was David Howe, and he did a study of Sumarah, a mysticism movement in Java. So, David lived in Surakarta and studied Sumarah, and did a dissertation about that, and so on, totaling eight studies, I believe, each for a dissertation. And Jeff Boyer went to Honduras and did a dissertation on that, etcetera.

Beverly Patterson (BP): [Have you heard about] Jim's contacts with Guy Johnson?

AK: Oh, yes—this was in 1930s, when Malinowski came here, and this Guy

Johnson was a sociologist, and they had a chat, and Johnson was so . . . conquered by Malinowski's charisma that he became an anthropologist himself and went to Chicago, right?

Dan Patterson (DP): He came here with Howard Odum, who came here to establish the Department of Sociology and Anthropology—that's what it was called. And Guy Johnson was its first graduate student and wrote a book on John Henry and another book on blues and spirituals.

AK: That's Odum institute in Davis Library, right?

DP: Odum was the major figure on the campus at the point when he was setting graduate programs in the university. Edwin Greenlaw was the one who was probably the dean of the graduate studies. He was an English professor, but he became dean of the Graduate School, and he established the Graduate School, and he brought Odum here to establish the Sociology and Anthropology Department, and he had been a major politician in the South to do that.

(7_The_Pattersons_Feb_9_2019)

Creating an Anthropology Syllabus

Robert Daniels (RD): It was four fields, and everybody was supposed to teach undergraduates, there was always a great concern about the "body count" . . . John Gulick forever tried to get general agreement on what was going to be in the introductory course. He could never get people to agree on the same book, could never get them to agree on the same syllabus . . . at one point they had a theme where everybody was going to write down the three things that every graduate student absolutely must read their first year. And, you know, there were about fifteen of us at that point, maybe . . . maybe twenty . . . there was about 3 percent overlap. It was unbelievable. So, that was always a problem . . . always a problem. There was a point when somebody wrote down, you know . . . of course, for Jim it was going to be Max Weber, etcetera . . . one person said: "Everything by . . . " and [another would say] "Nothing by . . . "

AK: So, it would skew to this particular person's interests . . .

RD: Right, absolutely. And then there is a whole question: as we get more and more people in the department . . . it was decided that we could do . . . it would still be called Anthro 41 . . . we could do an introductory-level course, but its content could be . . . specifically that way, or that way, or that way.

And so, the argument became . . . the anthropological . . . you know, what makes anthropology is not the content, it's the approach. And therefore I don't have to teach . . . whatever, you know . . . Van Gennep, you know. I'll introduce students to what anthropology is all about and teach it this way, not the other. So, that worked for a while because we got to the point when not everyone had four-field backgrounds. And we finally got [to the point] when you don't have to take Anthro 101 to be an anthropology major. (laughs) It's a long story, and I'm involved in that.

OK, here is the weird thing about being at the department: you almost never hear your colleagues give a presentation, except for a job talk if you got there first. And then . . . unless you team teach with them . . . but even that's so difficult.

AK: Is it customary to read your colleagues' articles or books?

RD: Well, it's supposed to be . . . There's complete contradictions between . . . what you are supposed to do, what you have to do, and what you thought your job was all about . . . what your intellectual career is.

AK: . . . and what you actually do—or don't do.

RD: Right. And you can't get your work done because of your job!

(1_Daniels_22_09_2018)

Departmental Crisis and the "Meaning" Seminar

RD: Late seventies or early eighties . . . the department got into a kind of . . . Well, my own doctoral work was about initiation and age sense. So, that's the way I see the world. We got into the age of crisis. The department started with John Honigmann, he was a big name, John Gulick, Joffre Coe, who started the North Carolina Archaeological Society when he was in high school. And George Holcomb, who was a dean of research and also a physical anthropologist. And Joffre was . . . he was described as a "mandarin"; he was this enigmatic old round fellow who sat there and terrorized students by not saying anything. And he founded research laboratories, which were originally research laboratories for anthropology, but were renamed correctly in archaeology. And then they hired people like . . . Julie Crane was one of the first . . . women, god bless her.

AK: But how many women were there originally, when you came? 10 percent? 20 percent?

RD: There were two . . . one was Mary Sanchez.

AK: Two out of how many people?

RD: At that point maybe ten. . . So, we got to this point . . . and I'm trying to think in the early seventies, something like that, when the four-field approach was just breaking down, because there were a bunch of people who were not really trained in the four-field approach, and there were too many undergraduates, and there was no way to get eight sections of Anthro 41, etcetera. Terry once . . . taught . . . 450 students in one lecture.

AK: 450?

RD: Something like that.

AK: Where can you put all these . . . ?

RD: Hamilton Hall. You have to interview him! It was like in megachurches. And he had six TAs and all the rest of it. So, the Meaning seminar . . . So, what happened, was: we decided we had to redo the graduate program. And that took at least a year and a half of head-banging and faculty meetings. Faculty meetings used to be awful! They used to be like people with invisible blowguns and invisible poisoned darts . . . *pshut*! at the other guy . . . and you suddenly realized—*poiiing*! You know, what I mean? It used to be awful. And Dotty Holland was the one who kind of . . . I wouldn't say it was all her idea, but she was the one who kind of crystallized it into . . . transitioned into . . . instead of four fields into these different foci. And so, what happened now is they decided to rename all of them that didn't make any sense anymore. Carole Crumley was key on this because she did both ethnography and archaeology, and she didn't have any problem combining those things. And working in France on pre-Roman to Roman . . . and then up to today, and look at the gardening practices here, and look at . . . you know.

AK: But not everybody was like this.

RD: Not everybody was like this—absolutely not! And she kind of . . . Joffre was this kind of old male bull in control of archaeology, trained at Michigan, and . . . she didn't fit in that pattern very well. Thank god, things have changed. But there has been a rocky road.

AK: And Dr. Peacock—did he take sides, or . . . ?

RD: No, I'm not aware he had done that. But for a long time we had this upstairs-downstairs problem with socioculturals and archaeologists being two different worlds . . .

AK: Who is the "big brother"?

RD: You know . . . not even speaking the same language. I was one of these weird guys who would agree to be the fourth or the fifth member on an archaeological doctoral committee. Because there was not enough personnel. And I didn't mind! Reading archaeology dissertations and offering what little I could. Anyway. So, we came up with four concentrations. And they were: evolution and ecology, sociocultur- . . . social systems and meaning, anyway. And I was the one who said, we should treat them as water holes in the Kalahari. With somebody in charge of who is coming and going, but everyone is welcome to come and go. So, you could have a sociocultural meeting, and Carole Crumley shows up, and nobody says: "Excuse me, you are not one of us," right? Because we were trying to un-boundarize the four fields. And that really worked pretty well for a while—the problem was, we never had any of grad students to any of these alleged . . . (?) So, what happened with all of these, was Terry, and Jim, and I . . . I'm not sure who else . . . decided that what we needed to do was to have an off-the-record fund . . . evening meetings, maybe once a month, in one person's house or another, and we all pick something to read. An article. And then we would have a discussion—this was the Meaning seminar . . . The Meaning seminar was started by Jim, and me, and Terry, and I supposed Dotty was on this for a while, and Winterhalder. He went on to California. There would be fifteen of us, or so. Three or four faculty, and the rest—grad students.

AK: Oh, grad students were there, too?

RD: It was intentionally for the grad students listed in the "meaning" concentration. And it was . . . everybody should take badges off, and you could say, which one. It's an open discussion. And some were really good.

AK: And this seminar was not in the syllabus?

RD: No, and it wasn't graded, and it wasn't on anybody's record . . .

AK: A reading club basically?

RD: Yeah. And that ran off and on for . . . I want to say for three, five years at least. We finally burnt down. Well . . . people changed . . . You can ask Jim about the "Meaning" seminar.

(1_Daniels_22_09_2018)

RD: I owe my tenure at UNC to Jim Peacock.

AK: Yes, this is something I wanted to start with . . . he said, you are one of these people who've known him for decades.

RD: He and John Honigmann were standing at the fence when I got off the airplane in January 1969 for my job interview trip. Well, it's a long story. Of course I was nervous to begin with, and we took off in Chicago out of this winter muck . . . I was very nervous. It was my first job. And so, as we get descending into Raleigh-Durham, we start getting a lot of turbulence, and I felt very uneasy. We get off the plane, you have to walk down the stairs, and there is a crowd of people, you know, forty, fifty, I don't know—there are two guys in tweed jackets, with mustaches—instant tribal recognition! And there is John Honigmann, whom I only knew by name, it was a big name in the department, and Jim Peacock, who is 2.5 years older than me.

AK: Was it customary for professors to meet potential . . . candidates?

RD: Yes.

AK: Really?

RD: Not as a senior professor—but, yes. And give them a [fill-in?] on the way to the town. These were two nights and three days of an interview—a job talk, you know . . . I had to talk to archaeologists, I had to talk to the dean . . .

AK: It was already this four-field discipline?

RD: Yes. But I . . . get off the plane, and John Honigmann is going to get on the same airplane in twenty minutes. And he takes me into the lounge, gives me a black coffee. And all I wanted was to go the men's room . . . I thought I was going to be sick. And he interviewed me, and I have no idea what he asked me, what I said.

AK: Right in the airport?

RD: Yeah, over black coffee. And then Jim Peacock drove me into Chapel Hill. And that's back when there was no interstate. And Highway 54 was two lanes and seriously crowded any time you rode, and there were two places where there was a one-lane bridge, and you had to wait for people coming the other way. And I kept thinking: "What kind of a school is going to be at the end of this road??" Anyway—so, that was Jim Peacock, and he was absolutely . . . one of the most gracious people I've ever met. I mean, he is a prince. I don't know anyone who has anything bad to say about Jim Peacock.

AK: Did he look . . . princely?

RD: No!!! He looks like Abraham Lincoln, you know.

AK: OK . . . in terms of mustache . . .

RD: Well, he is tall, and slightly stooped over . . . Only in the sense that he had to stoop over to talk to people. No, he used to run for miles, and . . . we would be at a meeting and lunch, and he would pull out his lunch, and it would consist of three pieces of apple, a piece of cheese and a stick of celery or something. And he'd say: "Gee, I want a burger!" (laughs) Anyway . . .

AK: So, on the way to the university—did he, like, comfort you in some sense . . . ? Your nervousness . . . ?

RD: I just remember it was a pleasant drive.

AK: And so, you went through the interview . . .

RD: Gave my job talk . . . And they offered me a job and I didn't think twice about accepting.
    . . . So, I was hired . . . John Gulick was the chair, he was the first chair. I think it was in 1965 that the department separated out from sociology . . . When I was hired, the ethos was still that everybody taught undergraduates and that everybody took a turn in teaching what was then Anthro 41, Anthro 101. On a four-field basis. We were all trained on a four-field basis.
(1_Daniels_22_09_2018)

RD: He . . . let me think about all of the people I met over at his house! I mean—Louis Dumont, Edmund Leach, Eliade . . . and, gosh, you name them! Rodney Needham . . .

AK: So, Dr. Peacock initiated bringing of all these people, like Dumont, Leach, and Eliade to campus . . .

RD: Many more! I can't think of all of them right now . . . Vic Turner, certainly . . . oh god . . . Mary Douglas? Who wrote about purity and danger?

AK: Margaret Mead.

RD: No, no . . . it's British . . . I don't know how he knew these British anthropologists, but he knew all them.

AK: And he was doing this in the capacity of the head of the department, or it was his private initiative . . . ?

RD: I think he did this even before he became head of the department. Of course he taught over in Oxford for one or two rounds . . .

(1_Daniels_22_09_2018)

AK: You mentioned those people who were either coming from abroad or publishing their books . . . and in relation to this, Bob Daniel says: "Let me think about all of the people I met over at his house! I mean—Louis Dumont, Edmund Leach, Eliade . . . and, gosh, you name them! Rodney Needham, Mary Douglas . . . " Tell me about this fascinating . . .

JP: How did they come? (laughs)

AK: Right.

JP: OK, so, I became chair in 1975, and this would have been during the five years that I was chair. He is right. Sometimes (laughs) it was by a simple . . . this was kind of Jewish entrepreneurial Soviet Union. So, I'll give you an example . . . So, Rodney Needham . . .

AK: . . . whom Bob Daniels describes as being "crazy as a loon."

JP: Yeah, I think that is absolutely wrong. He is not crazy as a loon, he is a fabulous person, but eccentric in some ways. So, here is how I got Rodney Needham . . . paid for him to come. Duke, which always had more money, contracted for him to come and speak, at Duke. And paid his way, honorarium—all that. And so, I said—look, how about if you also come to Chapel Hill? So, the cost for me was three dollars—to drive him [from Duke and back].

AK: So, you stole him in a way, like . . . (laughs)

JP: With Duke I did this various times. Because they had a lot of money, and we didn't have any, I mean, really, zero: the department had essentially zero for speakers. But I also knew these people. Partly because in 1980–1981 I had a Guggenheim, and I went to England, and so I got to know a lot of these people there, and they invited me to give papers, so I gave talks at Cambridge, and Oxford, and London, and then I invited them to come [here]. And many times I would do it when they were already invited by somebody else. So, they were already in the country. So, that's how I get all these people. They are all British. I just took advantage of their being invited by somebody else, to come from England, and then I would just get them to come to Durham. I remember Edmund Leach, for example. I think he came to Johns Hopkins . . .

AK: But that's pretty far . . .

JP: But not as far as his coming from England. So, usually . . . I don't think I ever paid for anybody to come from England, but then the British would come to other places that had more money, and I would just invite them to Chapel Hill.

AK: And that was your idea to invite them in such a way?

JP: Well, I had a particular anniversary in mind: about 1935 or something like this, the first course in social anthropology was taught at Chapel Hill. And that happened because Bronisław Malinowski visited Chapel Hill. He was a friend of Howard Odum, who, by the way, was the reason that Franklin Roosevelt brought the New Deal to the South . . . I mean, Odum was a big deal in that time. And so, he invited Malinowski, and he came, and a student of Odum, Guy Johnson, met Malinowski. They sat at the Meeting of the Waters, which is now Kenan Memorial Stadium, and Malinowki was very charismatic, and he inspired Guy Johnson, who was a sociologist . . . student, to also do social anthropology. So, he went up to Chicago and Yale, studied with Radcliffe-Brown at Chicago, and Edward Sapir at Yale, came back and taught a course in social anthropology. He was still alive at that time when I was chair, and so I said: "Look, let's celebrate the coming of social anthropology to Chapel Hill by having one or more seminar or colloquia with social anthropologists!"

AK: When was this?

JP: This would have been around 1979 or so—it was when I was chair. It was . . . maybe fifty years later. It was roughly half a century after his . . . the first course. That was the rationale. So, we had these social anthropologists come, and we had colloquia, I remember one of them was in Gerrard Hall.

AK: So, it was in relation to this anniversary that all these people came . . . ?

JP: Right. I invited these social anthropologists to come from England. Except that usually I tried to arrange it when they were here for some other reason.

AK: And then you invited them over to your house?

JP: Yes. They were all sitting . . . this was not in the house that we lived in on North Boundary, this was before that. We lived in a small house on Willow Drive. 1305 Willow Drive—you can still see the house. And I remember they were all sitting on our sofa—Victor Turner, Mary Douglas . . .

AK: Did I ever sit on that sofa?

JP: Nope . . . this was at Willow Drive . . .

AK: And you didn't take it to North Boundary?

JP: I think not. You should ask Florence what happened to that sofa. But I remember very well—we're all sitting there . . . Victor Turner was sitting right beside me, Tom Beidelman was sitting next to him, Beidelman who had studied with Rodney Needham. Mary Douglas and her husband, they were both there. Stephen Douglas, I think, his name was. So, Beidelman was a (laughs) a "disturber," you know—so, he started talking about how Victor Turner "sold out." He was sitting right next to him, and in a very loud voice he went on and on about . . . "Victor Turner—sold out!" Meaning that he abandoned his fine-grain ethnographies that he did with Ndembu (a tribe in Kenya), and then he started writing about history and drama and all that . . .

AK: But "sold out" to . . . whom? Or what?

JP: Sold out to publicity—something like that. He gave up the craft in order to address wider audiences.

AK: And so, what was Turner's reaction?

JP: Turner listened, and then he stood up, and I remember he stood up right in front of Tom: he was a sturdy guy who had been a rugby player. Stood up in front of Tom and said: "Tom . . . —and he was Scottish—Tom, we, Scots, believe that if you are going to criticize a man, you do it to his face, and not to his side"—something like that. (laughs) And so, we had . . . confrontations . . . but not vicious ones, they all knew each other . . .

AK: So, the department would not allocate any money for these parties?

JP: They did not have any money essentially. They didn't have any money for speakers. When we would . . . later, and maybe then, also, if we had a visiting speaker, and took him or her out, we would have to pay, we would divide it up. And Dotty has this memory of . . . one time the question was: "Do I owe you five dollars, or do you owe me five dollars?" (laughs) And we

Professor Peacock at his office in Alumni Hall, with a student.

still kick each other about that. I mean, that's the way we would do it—you know, if you have six people and one guest, the six would cover the one. That's the way the department would pay for a guest—it just didn't have any money for that kind of thing.

Important Conferences

JP: Ruel Tyson and I organized a conference at the Friday Center. We had more than four hundred people who attended. It was about the US South but including more than just "Black" and "white," and the Civil War and everything—it was about . . . oh, we had a title for it . . . it was more about diversity in the South. And we had thirty workshops as part of this conference, and as I said, four hundred people, and then we invited four guest speakers: Benedict Anderson, Katherine Bateson, the daughter of Margaret Mead and Gregory, Allan Gurganus, who is a wonderful writer who lives in Hillsborough, and Bland Simpson, the superb writer and pianist for the Red Clay Ramblers.

AK: Which year was this?

JP: In the 1990s. I have to look, which year it was. 1996, probably 1998 or 1999. It was when I was also starting . . . or helping start the Center for the Study of the American South. So, it was about the South, but with a more global angle. So, we invited Benedict Anderson, and here is what he said . . . He was a very good speaker. By the way, he is British . . . Irish . . . And he said . . . he sort of compared the Indonesia of the Suharto period and the US South and the view of revolution by each. So, the view of revolution by the Suharto people referred to the revolution of 1945, when Indonesia fought for its independence, and the revolution that he referred to for the US South, the Civil War, which in another way was its fight for its independence, and he said something like this . . . That during the Suharto period, which is after the war of independence, and after something called Gestapu, that Indonesians were repressed from discussing that period. By comparison, in the US South people glorified that period, and it was a major topic of celebration. An interesting point, I thought.

Blockade Runner Conference

CC: One of the things I want you to record me and Jim talking about is that Jim organized a conference at the Blockade Runner, at the beach. We were there at the ocean, and it was wonderful. I went down there with

Dotty and Bill, and that's when I became real close to them. And Rodney Needham was one of the keynote speakers at the conference, and we got a better chance to . . . and we gave some talks . . . and he would say thing like (laughs) "That's on page 32 in my book."

(11_Conway_July_29_2019)

AK: Now that you mentioned Rodney Needham, one thing we didn't discuss yesterday was the conference at the Blockade Runner. Can you tell me more about it? Blockade Runner . . . what is it exactly?

JP: It's a motel. In Wilmington. On Wrightsville Beach. That's where we had the Southern Anthropological Society meeting. Rodney Needham was a distinctive person in many ways. One was that he had been in the Second World War on the Burma frontier and had been shot by the Japanese, and a gurkha pulled him to safety. Gurkhas are short but ferocious people who live in the highlands of Burma.

AK: Yesterday, Cece mentioned Edmund Leach . . .

JP: I met him, and I brought him to Chapel Hill to speak. It was part of the same effort to commemorate the creation of social anthropology at UNC, the fifty years . . . And so, I invited . . . this conference, not everything happened the same day. Let me tell you whom I invited and who came. They were: Victor Turner and Edith Turner, Edmund Leach, Rodney Needham, Mary Douglas, Tom Beidelman. They were all very distinguished social anthropologists. They were all British except Beidelman.

AK: How about Ben Anderson?

JP: That was another affair . . . he was not involved in this one. I did invite him, and he did speak, but it was at a conference on the US South.

AK: And what was the exact name of this conference?

JP: I think it was just "Commemorating Fifty Years of Social Anthropology at UNC."

AK: And it was in 1980-something?

JP: Probably earlier than that. [To CC:] When did you go to Wrightsville?

CC: I'm not . . . I think it was pretty early . . . well . . . it could have been around 1980. Dotty came . . . you brought her to see a film with you, the draft cut.

JP: Here is the way to figure it out: Guy Johnson began teaching . . . taught what his claim was, the first course in sociocultural anthropology in 1926. Fifty years from then makes it 1976.

CC: That makes more sense to me.

JP: And these were really the top social anthropologists of that time.

AK: And you got a grant to bring them to UNC?

JP: I had no grant. It was by hook and by crook!!! (laughs) For example, I got Needham . . . Duke paid for Needham to come from England, and I paid for him to come from Durham to Chapel Hill!!! (all laugh).

CC: Very clever!!!

JP: And I think Needham came . . . when he spoke at Wrightsville Beach . . . he didn't charge . . . he just came, so it was a favor. And I remember (laughs) with Leach it was a little bit of a mix-up. So, I remember, what his honorarium was—it was five hundred dollars. Here was the deal—here is how I got him to come. He had already come to Baltimore, to Johns Hopkins. He had a visiting appointment there. And so, I paid for him to come from Johns Hopkins. I really had to be chintzy about it, because we had almost no money at the department. Chintzy—meaning, do things on the cheap.

CC: Were there two separate conferences?

JP: The Wrightsville was separate . . . absolutely! The Wrightsville one was a meeting of the Southern Anthropological Society, and I think I was its president at that time. And the name of the motel was the Blockade Runner. And this was a much more vigorous organization. And . . . maybe I'm confusing . . . these people, they all came together for a panel, and I don't remember if Needham came to that panel, but then he came to Wrightsville Beach. And Leach did not come for that panel, he came himself, and he gave a talk called . . . something like "Bible as Myth." (laughs) And I suggested that that was not a good title for this . . . Southern town . . . Back to Wrightsville, Guy Johnson and his wife, Jillian, they were both there. And there was music . . . it may be an opera . . . there was a musical . . .

JP: Well, we did a square dance—it's, like, with mountain music and . . . barn dance is another name . . .

CC: It's called square dance in the South. But what I'm getting at is that he might have given a different talk then, or he and Jillian maybe gave a talk together rather . . . that had some music . . .

JP: Of the two of them, he was the main . . . he wrote spirituals based on negro spirituals. And Florence sang some of them once, in church. And she said, they weren't very good . . . they were kind of based on spirituals like "Swing Low, Sweet Chariot" and things like that. And the place where he did that research was in South Carolina . . . It's on the coast. He was sort of a folklorist type of a sociologist, he did the study of the John Henry myth . . .

CC: And song. Odum collection . . . a lot of blues songs. And he had a long bibliography. That's a conference I was at. Johnson's wife was the first woman who wrote a study of Southern traditions, and it's a fine book that's out of print. She was fabulous!

JP: They were both from Texas, but he was tall and laid-back, and she was a dynamo!

CC: Her first name was not Jillian, but Gian!

JP: I was going to ask Cece what she remembers about the square dance.

CC: Of course, I remember!

JP: Here is what I remember . . . and I want to make sure I'm not talking about another SAS meeting . . . There was a guy, and I can't remember his name . . . from the University of Colorado, who was a gynecologist, and he did abortions, and so, they were doing the square dance. And the way you do the square dance, men go left and women go right . . .

CC: Do-si-do . . .

JP: Do-si-do . . . and you meet . . . But some of the women objected to his health policies, and so they would not accept his hand, when he would offer it to . . . and as a result, the whole dance got really screwed up. (laughs) He'd be sticking out his hand, and nobody would receive it.

CC: You see, that may or may not be at Wilmington, at Wrightsville . . .

JP: It certainly was at an ASA meeting.

CC: However, at that square dance . . . Rodney, it turned out, did not dance. Presumably, from an old British war injury, which he wouldn't talk about. Since he was not going to dance, I sat with him throughout the dance, and he also would not tell me the war stories. Because . . . it's something we just don't talk about.

JP: He was also older than a lot of people there. So, the square dance, it was either on the way there, or on the way back . . . and Rodney asked if could get a cup of tea. And so, we stopped at the Hardy's, and he saw a sign that said "Mello Yello," and he said: "What is Mello Yello?"—to which the waitress said [speaks with a Southern accent]: "Here, get some, so you won't ask about it"—and stuck a can of Mellow Yello in his hand . . . (laughs) What happened to Frank Manning was Frank had done his . . . he was my first PhD student, and he was from Boston. And he was red-haired and red-faced, and he did his fieldwork in the Caribbean, and he got melanoma and died of that. Very sad . . .

AK: Because he got too much exposed to the sun?

JP: Yes, exactly. Especially if you are fair. He was a red-haired Irishman. Great guy, great person . . . I picked Rodney up Needham at the airport, and he walked out, and he had no luggage. And I remarked about that, and he said: "Well, I have this suit, which I'm wearing. And if you show me the cleaners, I will stop and let them clean it," which he did.

CC: What did he wear when they were cleaning it?

JP: I'm trying to remember—maybe he just stood in the corner while they cleaned it. But I know that when he walked out of the plane, he was empty-handed. He was a very fastidious person, and he was in the military, and he was neat, and his handwriting was very tiny. He would write on the spine of the book.

CC: And he gave a talk before we went to Wrightsville.

JP: Yup.

CC: In a room with probably mostly anthropologists, but we were kind of . . . it was a more informal room, and people would ask him questions, and he would say: "That is on page 44 of my book." (JP laughs) He didn't have to recite it for anybody.

CC: One of Dotty's students, Carole . . .

JP: Oh, the one who gave a paper on Alcoholics Anonymous?

CC: Yes. So, first of all, we had been partying late and everything, and Bill Lachicotte kindly called my room to be sure I'm awake before our session, and then . . . I was giving my paper on this fellow, Tommy Jarell, we've seen the movie about him. When Carole gave her paper, she said: "OK, the first paper I heard today was about firemen. And the next paper I heard was about bluesmen, and that was by someone who looked like a bluesman, in a shirt . . . And I'm giving a paper"—and she said—"I hope" (laughs) "on Alcoholics Anonymous, but I hope nobody will think I'm an alcoholic."

JP: She was one of humorous . . .

CC: That was funny to say—I never heard her say that!

AK: Anything else about this conference?

JP: I remember the way it began. Johnson said something about the sea. No . . . maybe that was the person who introduced him, who made that comment, not him. He said, if you look behind us, you'll see the Atlantic Ocean. And on the other side is England, and on this side we are. And then maybe he said, next to England is Africa, or something like that. He wanted to say that the ocean connects the various cultures, including Black, white . . . and all of us who are here.

(12_Peacock_Conway_July_30_2019)

The Carolina Seminars

Sandy Greene (SG): I was hired by Ruel Tyson in 1981 for . . . it was a pilot program that was funded by the Massey and Weatherspoon families, the Carolina Seminars. And Professor Tyson hired me to be his administrative assistant, or program assistant, modeled on the university seminars at Columbia. And after . . . I guess it was two or two and a half years, they did a review of the program and decided that it was a good program, and worth continuing, so it became a permanent program in 1984. It was a wonderful opportunity to just take something from the ground up . . . and Jim was named the second director in 1997. So, that was when I met him—when he became the new director of the Carolina seminars. And all of that time it was just the two of us, I was the only employee. We had grad students who would work as repertoires for each seminar, but . . . It was great! Jim . . . during the year we would oversee the conveners, in a sense that we really wanted to give them freedom to do what they wanted within the guidelines of our program. But what we would do, would . . . try to identify new topics, people that might be interested in presenting new topics, helping them form a proposal, and then accepting or . . . I don't know . . . we didn't reject anyone. (laughs) And finding potential Douglas Hunt lectures. The Douglas Hunt lecture is funded by the families, the Massey-Weatherspoon families, and it's administered through the Carolina seminars to honor Douglas Hunt, who was, for many years, a special assistant to the chancellor. He was a wealth of knowledge and was a connection to Columbia University. And he sort of shepherded the idea of starting the Carolina seminars. So, that's the connection between the Douglas Hunt lecture and the Carolina seminars. So, Jim . . . because he was so out there, with . . . the population, you know, different universities in the area, different academic fields, he networked and connected so well, he would just find topics, or find people, and he was always full of ideas . . .

AK: He described to me how he "stole" people from Duke, especially the Brits, who would come there, and Duke would pay for their stay, and he would just come there in his car . . . people like Mary Douglas and many other British anthropologists, and then bring them over to UNC, because the department never had money for that, but Duke had.

SG: Well, they were already here, right?

AK: Right! But the connections! He already knew all those people!

Herman Greene (HG): He has been a member of our board, the Center for Ecozoic Studies, which is the center that . . . We say, our mission is to advance ecology in culture as the organizing principles of societies. And he has been very helpful to us, providing funding to our work, helping with some funding through the Carolina seminars we had. We had a conference on the works of Thomas Berry, we had . . . we brought five people that wrote about his work, and had twenty-eight papers presented about him. That was in 2014. And Jim has one of the papers in that issue. He has been a friend to us, he is friend to both of us, and I'm sure I'm not alone in feeling that he is really getting me all the support he can, and has made me feel that my work is important. Really, one of our most important board members . . .

SG: Well, there is always something . . . funny happening. You know, a problem needing to be solved, and Jim finding a way to do it, and it not being a crisis . . . And it mainly . . . you know, thinking about Carolina seminars—we would have these big events that we would plan, the Douglas Hunt lectures, you know, we would send out invitations, and the year that we had the musicians from Russia, the Moscow conservatory, we were catering dinners for the donor families, and all of this planned, and really, we didn't know, until just a few days, that they were actually coming. Because of visa issues. (laughs) And we were just planning away this event, and I had a serious knot in my stomach because (?) they were on the airplane, we were just not sure, because there was a person we were dealing with, who was coming with the group, and she was sort of . . . well, she spoke English, so she was who we dealt with, and she managed the visa application process at her end, and one of the musicians was legally a minor, she was seventeen, I think, at the time, and so there were all of those little things that hadn't fallen into place, and we were getting down to the wire, and we had not yet started to think, OK, what do we . . . what's the plan if we have to cancel? But they got to the plane, and they got here, and it was a wonderful event, but it was kind of nip and tuck, and getting the reimbursement process through the university, because normally they want to mail checks. That wasn't going to work because they really needed to be given money here, so they could cash it . . . And all of those little twists and turns . . . Jim just deals with it, you know? Just . . . there is always something that seemed to happen, but they were all things that were completely out of our control. And Jim's ability to just . . . deal with that and turn it into something that you just laugh about. And we had Thomas Berry who collapsed after his Douglas Hunt lecture, and I think Jim ended up going with him to a hospital, and then taking him back to the Carolina Inn, because they discharged him . . .

HG: . . . he wouldn't agree to stay.

SG: He didn't agree to stay for treatment, and I think he just told Jim he wanted to go back to the Carolina Inn and have a scotch at the bar.

AK: That's treatment! (laughs)

SG: So, that's what they ended up doing! (laughs) But then I remember we had the dinner for the donors, and I think Florence came in at one point, because everybody was wondering: where is Jim? Where is Thomas Berry? And Florence came in and said: "They won't be able to attend the dinner because he is in a hospital," Thomas Berry was, so . . . There was always a lovely dinner that we hosted. And, anyway, it was really a lot of fun.

(8_The_Greenes_March_28_2019)

Personal Style

Dan Patterson (DP): I think, Jim . . . any sphere of life he is going to operate in, he'd be gracious, and attentive, and unpretentious . . . sympathetic—whether it's a professional meeting, or it's something informal in his house, or it's just friends at a meal, or students—it's just his nature.

Celebration of Professor Peacock's eightieth birthday at his house at North Boundary street, with Anthropology Department faculty, 2017. Photo: A. Kushkova.

Celebratory portrait presented by members of the Anthropology Department to Professor Peacock on his eightieth birthday, 2017. Photo: A. Kushkova.

AK: He never had conflicts with anybody?

DP: He probably . . . you can hardly be a department chair without having some very difficult people that you happen to work with, but I never imagine he lost his temper—at least, in public. He would always be attentive, and patient, and helpful, and supportive. I must have gone to him sometimes, or . . . for example, when we had the Southern Folklife started, and he was always on . . . moving from one place to another . . . (?) library system. Then we got an offer from somebody: we could buy the John Edward M(?) collection that was housed at UCLA, but UCLA was not doing well with it, and it was a huge collection of country music. This would put us on the map. They had a publication, and put us on the map, and so—if you had twenty to twenty-five thousand dollars, you could have it at UNC library.

AK: But at that time it was huge money!

DP: That would be 1980 . . . 1985. I went to the department chairmen, and I think Jim . . . if he was chairman that year, he gave money for it, I know that anthropology did, I can't remember . . . walking in and seeing his face . . .

(7_The_Pattersons_Feb_9_2019)

SG: I just worked with him daily on a personal level from an administrative standpoint. So, I don't have experience with his writing or, really, his academics. I saw him more in an inter-collegial relationship, from an administrative standpoint. How effective he was in motivating people and developing ideas for discussion. Asking questions. So, that's how my relationship with Jim looked . . . and I have a thought, and if I don't say it, I'll probably forget it, and I don't want to do that—he is so well respected, I think, because of his ability to communicate and work together with people. He . . . you mentioned, Herman, he has a generous spirit and is such a trustworthy individual, so honest and . . . And a lot of this, I think, was reflected in how he worked on campus with other faculty. And I remember when he was asked to head . . . it wasn't a committee, it was during the time when there were quite a few students filing complaints against faculty. Well, I remember this in particular, and I can't remember the instance that triggered it. But this was—and you probably have this in your notes—the chancellor put together a . . . I'm guessing, it was the chancellor—put together . . . oh, gosh, it has been so long! They wanted to put . . . some kind of . . . resource available for students, who wanted to confidentially discuss problems they were having with teaching faculty.

AK: Anonymously?

SG: Anonymously. Whether it was . . . sense of harassment, or . . . whenever there were sensitive issues, at the time there was no really well-established resource for students. And as I recall, Jim was asked to head that up. I don't remember how long it lasted, I don't remember what it was called. But that was reflective of how people felt about him.

AK: He was perfect for this particular position.

SG: Because students loved him, and the faculty . . . well, he was chair of the faculty, he was very highly respected. And that's really a position of extreme trust. And I'm not sure what his charge was from that, you now, whether it was counseling, or . . . Ask him more about that! But he was a big part of that. You know, his interpersonal skills, the way he was able to connect, to motivate people . . . I'm not that good at really describing things . . . I mean an "anecdote" is the way he dresses. (laughs) I'm not good at describing it, but, you know, sometimes with baggy shorts and his running shoes and some shirt that is not tucked in, and . . . they don't match . . . (all laugh) He is a distinguished professor—maybe that's part of it: he is esteemed, but totally . . . not self-absorbed, I guess, I'd say. He is not trying to present himself in any special way to other people. He is just genuine.

(8_The_Greenes_March_28_2019)

Sandra Rich (SaR): When we were with them, they were telling these wonderful stories of things he was finding and that he would wear his father's clothing. Which was, I thought, wonderful, because, again, Jim being who he is, he didn't care if he was wearing something that was fifty years old—or something brand-new.

Steven Rich (StR): (laughs) Especially as an anthropologist, it was just perfect!

SaR: He was excited and amazed at some of the things he found, and I can't really be specific, but it was just . . . to watch him talk about it, to see the look on his face, and the way he would describe things that he found . . . and books, too.

(9_The_Riches_July_24_2019)

Susan Reintjes (SR): Ichabod Crane is a fictional character and a protagonist in Washington Irving's short story "The Legend of Sleepy Hollow." [Looks up the image in the Internet] "A tall, lanky individual . . . he is a local school master and has a strong belief in all things supernatural . . ." I mean—that is Jim, right? (laughs) "All things supernatural including the galloping Hessian of the hollow, or headless horseman . . ." OK, here is my impression of Jim Peacock: so, he is perennially curious, he is just a perennial student. He is so knowledgeable and so perceptive, and extremely sensitive. So, there is this balance in him that men often don't have: between intellectual capacity and emotional capacity. Many men have the intellectual capacity but are shut emotionally, and many men are emotionally open but don't have intellect. So, left and right brain. I would say, his left and right brain are very balanced. I always picture him . . . I was on a Jungian board for a while, so I can picture him coming to the Jungian lectures, and he has to lean down a lot, because he is so tall, he is six foot seven, isn't he? And he is also so lanky, he probably looks taller. But he is also always leaning down—he is perceiving. He is a constant perceiver. He is so incredibly perceptive, he is constantly listening . . . Very sensitive being who is always perceiving. And he is looking for a deeper level. So, I think he is constantly looking to go deeper. That's why I think came to the Jungian program.

(14_Reintjes_Aug_9_2019)

CC: And here is another . . . here is a fun little example. There are several . . . the potentially humorous. So, Jim was finally gonna come to the folklore conference. And something came up, and he couldn't go to the session. He was to chair the session. He rode his bicycle over to my house and gave me his paper, and then I chaired the session. (laughs)

AK: Was this an AAA meeting, when he bicycled . . . with the paper?

CC: No, AAA is his typical meeting, American Folklore Society was not his typical meeting, but he was going to come this year, but then he couldn't and . . . this was twenty years ago. But the point is, how conscientious he was. And he used to bicycle to class from Willow Drive, and people die on those bicycle trips, so it was a relief to all of us, when he wasn't bicycling.

(11_Conway_July_29_2019)

UNC Department of Anthropology at Leisure

JP: The best thing the Anthropology Department ever did: we played volleyball every Friday afternoon! (laughs) Right next to Bynum Hall. And one afternoon, I think, in December, it was actually snowing, and we were playing volleyball, and then this jerk came around, from the administration, and he was measuring the site, and it turned out later that they built a fountain there that destroyed the court. And I remember pointing out to him, when he was measuring, I said: "Look, how important this is, that we are playing volleyball in the snow!" But that didn't . . . [change anything]. I know him pretty well, he is still around, and he was not a horrible person, but he was very . . . ethical. If he had a task to do . . .

CC: That's not called "ethical," that's called . . . "fundamentalist." (laughs) That was . . . that meant a lot!!!

JP: Anyway—he destroyed our . . . culture.

AK: That was only men who were playing?

JP: Noooo!!! Everybody!!! And people who were just walking by would join in the game!

AK: And for how many years was this going on?

JP: Years! Many years! Twenty years!

CC: And the English Department had the volleyball game.

JP: But theirs was somewhere else . . .

CC: It was out in the country. I went to both of them.

JP: I wish I went to the other.

CC: Well, the other one didn't have the team spirit, you know, so I preferred the anthropology.

(13_Peacock_Conway_McCanless_July_31_2019)

Professor Peacock at the department graduation, 2011.

CHAPTER 5

Fieldwork

"His pencil was moving rapidly across the blank sheet as he listened and watched."
—Gerakan Muhammadiyah in *Purifying the Faith*, 1978

"Sometimes people would say: 'Well, what is your religion?'—and I would say: 'My religion is anthropology.' I tried to stop, look, listen and observe . . . I just never pretended . . . but on the other hand I've tried not to remain aloof."
—Cecilia Conway, July 29, 2019

"And here is another important thing, and maybe it came up with the Muhammadiyah step: when he'd be asked: 'Well, what's your religion?'—he would respond: 'I'm an anthropologist.' And I think that shows why he would wanna go back home to the South."
—Cecilia Conway, July 29, 2019

Choosing the First Field of Study

"'Watch out for the dogs, they bite.'"
—Cora Du Bois, with reference to her own advisor, Robert Löwe, about fieldwork

Jim Peacock (JP): We had no training whatsoever in fieldwork at Harvard at that time . . . No course in method or anything like that . . . since we had no course in fieldwork, we asked each of our teachers if we could spend an evening with them and get their accounts of their fieldwork. To guide us.

And we did that with several of them. So, that was it. Now—Cora Du Bois, when I was getting ready to do fieldwork, I asked her if she had any advice, and she replied . . . she said: "This is what my advisor, Robert Löwe, said: 'Watch out for the dogs, they bite.'" . . . I understand the metaphor, basically, watch out for any threat, or trap.

JP: Back in 1960 you needed to choose a country for your fieldwork during your first year. You had to choose a place where you're going to go to do your fieldwork. I had no clue where I was going to go to do fieldwork. Tom Kirsh had chosen Thailand, and he lent me a book, it was by Ralph Linton, and it was called something like "Most of the World." And it just had little sketches of different places. And I looked through it, and I saw Indonesia. I knew nothing about Indonesia, but . . . it said, it's a Dutch colony—or was, and I thought—well, I've studied German, maybe it would help me to learn Dutch, and any way, Indonesia sounded like it was diverse, it had so many different . . . And so, I just thought—well, I'll choose Indonesia. You could go anywhere, but of course you had to work out an appropriate project, and get the funding, and all that. At that time, it was rare to do field research at home. That was before people started doing fieldwork much in the United States.

JP: I did not join several group projects—that I could have. One of them was led by Cora Du Bois, who was my advisor, and it was in India, Bhubaneswar. Another one was led by David Maybury-Lewis, and it was in Brazil, and he was one of my favorite teachers. There was a third one, which was in Chiapas, Mexico, led by E. Z. Vogt, who was also one of my teachers.

Anna Kushkova (AK): Why did you say "no" to all of these?

JP: I didn't really say "no," I just didn't say "yes," I didn't pursue any of those.

AK: Were they taking their students for field trips?

JP: Yeah. They all went to each of those places, and they worked together.

AK: For a long time, or for a short . . . ?

JP: Well, a fairly long time—for a year or two. And so, it made it really easier, I think, for their students. So, it tended to be kind of a company, so if you went as an assistant to one of these projects, then when you took your oral exams, your advisor would tend to be kind of . . . at least be in your camp, would support you, because you were working for him—and it was usually a "him." Except for Cora Du Bois.

AK: And you don't have to look for field research money, it's already provided, everything is paid . . .

JP: Right. Basics and all that kind of stuff.

AK: Ideal!

JP: So, look: why didn't I join one of those? Well, number one: I don't think anybody asked me to, although I had a very good record. And number two, I had already kind of decided on going to Indonesia, with no good reason, but that's what I decided to do, and nobody was going to go work there. And third, I was just kind of independent. And fourth, sort of stupid . . . I mean, I should have realized the advantage of doing these things that way, but I didn't really think about that. So, I had to do it pretty much on my own . . .

Anecdotes about Cora Du Bois

JP: Once . . . I was at a meeting, there were four or five of us who went to the meeting of the Association of Asian Studies in Chicago. So, there was a panel, Cora Du Bois was on a panel, along with several other scholars, who I think were not anthropologists. And two of them were a husband and wife. And so, they talked about how useful it was for the two of them to be doing fieldwork together. Well, Cora Du Bois was a lesbian, and she was in the field alone in Alor, and so, she sat there listening to them about how useful it was to have a spouse. And then they finished and she said: "Well, there is always the typewriter." Which I thought was an excellent corrective.

I remember something else, another kind of comment: when I was a graduate student, my advisor was Cora Du Bois, and she once said to me . . . I think she had just given me a drink . . . Scotch . . . because she drank Scotch, and she smoked a lot, and she said: "James, you would measure your drink instead of drinking it." And she said that to say, you know, "you are being so analytical about everything." And I remember the first paper that I wrote in her . . . in the only real course that I took, which was a seminar . . . I wrote this paper, and at the end she said: "This reads like an aged humanist." When I was twenty-one or twenty-two, and she might have been sixty or something . . . she was kind of taunting me, or teasing me for being so analytical. Well, I was a student, and in a way I thought what I should do then was to study, not do other things.

I finished two years of graduate school and had decided to go to Indonesia. And I went to Yale to study the Indonesian language. They did not teach it at Harvard, so I went to Yale.

I received funds to research a very general topic in Indonesia, called "Nation to village communication," to focus on the way the nation communicates with the village. But after I passed my oral exams, I came up with a more specific field proposal, the study of ludruk. And they didn't reject it, but they said, it needed more work. So, this was in the summer, of 1962, that I really dug into writings by people like Kenneth Burke and others about drama, literature, and theater—I didn't know anything about that stuff. And then I submitted a new proposal, and they accepted that.

But at the time, unless you had some real connection, it was very difficult to get a visa to go to Indonesia. Very, very. And the only people who were getting visas were people who were sponsored by the Ford Foundation, or Fulbright—because they had offices in Jakarta to help you. But if you were just a lone individual like me, the chances of getting . . . What you needed was a semi-resident visa, where you can stay for a year or more. But this is where I had amazing luck. I went to the embassy in DC, the Indonesia embassy, and I just walked in and met this cultural attaché. And he knew a former cultural attaché, whose name was Joko Sanyoto, and he wrote Joko, and so when I went, with no hopes for any result, to the Department of Foreign Affairs in Jakarta, and amazingly, this guy Joko Sanyoto—he was there! And within half an hour we had the so-called Dinas visa, which allows you to stay for a year, and fortunately, you could come and go without getting an exit permit, which was a big deal, because things were up and down for a while, it was near a year of living dangerously, and if you need to leave quickly . . . Connections worked! It was just like magic.

Ludruk and Geertz in Indonesia

JP: Now, in 1960 Clifford Geertz published *The Religion of Java*, which is in many ways based on Max Weber's *The Religion of India* and *The Religion of China*. And in *The Religion of Java*, Geertz described a theater form called ludruk. I read the book, and I wrote to Clifford Geertz. And amazingly, he replied with a thoughtful letter. I mean, I was just a student, and he was at the University of Chicago. Along with the letter, I sent him two papers— well, one paper and one proposal. The paper was a study of Sukarno, who was then the president of Indonesia. And the proposal was for the study of ludruk. And so, he wrote back and he said: "Your paper on Sukarno is interesting, but your proposal is . . . " I don't remember, what he said . . . "Useful," or something like that. But then he said, the problem of studying ludruk is that they . . . he said, it would be like studying . . . participating in . . . at the time the French and the Algerians were at war, he said, it would be like studying the Algerians at the moment—or something like that. He said, ludruk is so full of controversy . . . he said, they are homosexual, they are communist, you know—they are really . . . they are wicked from the point of view of the Indonesian elite, or government—it's really an illicit form. Meaning—they can be imprisoned and things like that. So, he said, I'm not saying "don't do it," I'm just warning you . . . So, that's what he said.

AK: What would draw young people like these two (Sudibyo and Amien Rais) to Muhammadiyah?

JP: Well, let me tell you about Sudibyo. Now, first of all I want to insert a surprising connection. When he was about twelve years old, Clifford Geertz and Hildred Geertz, and about seven or eight other anthropologists came to his hometown, which Geertz in his book *The Religion of Java* calls Mojokuto. But the real name of that town was Paré.

AK: In which books does Geertz . . . ?

JP: In his books he refers to it by the pseudonym Mojokuto, but the actual name was Paré. It was a town, not a village—maybe, eight or nine thousand people. You know, Indonesian towns, they don't look as big as our towns because people live cramped all together. So, Sudibyo mentioned that in passing, and he said to me: "Hildred Geertz gave us these tests, they were called thematic apperception tests." And they are: you look at a picture and you tell a story. And he said: "I told her all these various stories." Believe it or not, if you go to Davis Library at UNC, all of his stories that he told are there. His stories. The reason they are there is . . . there was an anthropologist, or probably a psychologist named Burton Caplan. Not the same Burt Caplan who was on the faculty at UNC. And he reprinted all of these stories and put them on microfilm, and they are in libraries all over the country. And so, they are Sudibyo Markus's stories. But they don't give his name.

AK: Was it a program of some sort . . . ? Interviewing indigenous children . . . ?

JP: Something like that. She was doing it, Burton Caplan oversaw it, and it was done in various parts of the world, and it so happened that . . . the Geertzes were involved in a project, which was a group . . .

AK: Do you know the name of this project?

JP: Yes. It was at MIT, and the director of it was named Rufus Hindon. And then another leader of it was Douglas Oliver, who was a professor at Harvard at that time. They were not present, but they gave the money and

Fieldwork 77

they oversaw the project. There were not many, maybe six or seven people who went to that little town . . . But he [Sudibyo] told me about being interviewed by her . . .

AK: Did he remember her name, Geertz?

JP: Oh, yeah. And he still would—if I emailed him right now, he would tell you!

AK: Now—sure, but he was a twelve-year-old boy at the time.

JP: But he remembers all of that. I'm sure he would tell you all about it. I never have asked him very much about it.

AK: Can you send him a small letter asking to describe that encounter with Geertz?

JP: I'll be glad to do that! Ludruk had this horrible reputation. Ludruk was allied with the communist party somewhat, and remember, not long after we were there, a million people were killed by the military, including ludruk people—some of them. So, it was a major bad thing.

Ludruk performances were held in many places. Sometimes in a village or in a neighborhood—but in this case it was called the People's Amusement Park. With clear communist allusions. Anybody could go there if you just paid the ticket, which was virtually nothing. And all the people there were really *rakyat*, the low-class people. And sure enough, like Geertz said, ludruk was full of . . . it was all men, and many of them were homosexual, and male prostitutes, and then they had clowns, and the clowns were hilarious, they were brilliant! And they were mocking everything, but especially the elite, sometimes the government . . . sometimes they were arrested and things like that.

I went to eighty-three ludruk performances. But in addition, I just did everything and went everywhere. Sometimes with that family.

Part of ludruk's perspective was, in a way, a Marxist one. The point of view of *rakyat*, the working class. I don't think I disagreed with them, I just was . . . disturbed by their situation, and in fact the whole situation in Indonesia, because it was terrible. Seventy-five thousand beggars in Surabaya, for example, where we were living. The family we were living with were literally hand-to-mouth, and on, and on, and on like that . . . I didn't have any moral dilemma I can think of, it was more just fear, fear for them and fear for us sometimes. Fear and quandary, what to do, and then, of course, as many as a million people were slaughtered, and that was a real tragedy. But one time I was in a kampong, that's the slum, and this man, who seemed to be drunk, attacked me, shouting slogans of *merdeka*, that means "freedom." And that was related to the independence movement, throwing off the colonialists and so forth. My response was simply—when he sort of attacked me—I simply grabbled him and stopped him from doing it, I didn't hit him or anything, but I just stopped him. But that was very rare.

In the Field with the Ludruk Study

JP: At ludruk performances, if anybody asked me, like, who are you, what do you do, stuff like that . . . I would say . . . there is an Indonesian word for the anthropologist, or anthropology—*kebudayaan*, "culture." "*Ilmu-kebudayaan*," the science of culture. They actually have . . . well, most people in that place would not understand that word. It'd be like saying that to somebody in . . . So, what did I say? Well, you know, actually, I heard speculation by various people, why has this guy come to these things? And one of the speculations was, he really likes to watch these guys act as girls. Something like that. Or—he enjoys . . . Anyway—people wondered and would ask, why are you coming, but mostly they didn't—they just, you know, there you are, here is this weird guy . . .

Basically, I positioned myself as just a spectator. And I never . . . not then, anyway, attempted to join in the performance, you know. To do a dance or something like that.

My basic posture was—I'm just a spectator. We would sit on the front row. I used to be dressed in normal dress, just a shirt and some trousers . . . I would be taking notes, recording, probably—sometimes, not very much. And would go backstage and take photos.

One time this ludruk was going to go out in the country, and the way they traveled was an old truck, and all the troupe would stand in the back of the truck. There wasn't room to sit. So, I went with them; Florence did not go. And we went to some village they were making their performance in, so they had a kind of makeshift stage, where they would change clothes, and some actors would put on women's makeup and stuff. And I sat back there with them, and we were all sitting on the ground, or they actually used to have a little mat. So, two or three of them said: "You know, if you are doing stuff with us, why don't you become more like us?" And so, they gave me a sarong (which is just a cloth worn by both men and women), and they said: "Just put on the sarong"—and I did. And that kind of broke the ice a little bit, because usually I just acted as a spectator. But I was in the middle of every kind of situation where I was just a spectator.

They thought often that we were Dutch. I mean, they didn't distinguish. The word is *blanda*, or *londo*—it just means "European," or "white person."

AK: As various political events/developments were happening in the American society and globally over your anthropological career, which of those were most significant for your professional approach to teaching anthropology? For instance, the Cold War was going on—did it produce any influence upon . . .

JP: Oh, yeah. Because Indonesia had the largest non-ruling communist party, and therefore Russia and China to a degree were both involved in Indonesia. And so, when Florence and I went there, well, I already mentioned, twenty-six out of twenty-seven districts, including the one where we lived, were under the communist party. So, the Cold War . . . we were involved in the Cold War by extension, or by . . .

AK: By default!

JP: Yes, by . . . we were living at that time. Much more involved in it there than we were in the United States . . . While we were there, the communist party was very strong and very . . . present. So, I learned about them directly through my friend who was part of it, and did ludruk, and all that kind of stuff. It was just all over the society,

AK: They are usually all over. (laughs)

JP: Two years after we came back, they had the Gestapu, and that was when the communists got slaughtered, a million of them. There are many books about it. But we were involved because people we knew were killed or imprisoned . . .

AK: But you were safe, even though you were Americans? Did you feel any pressure . . . ?

JP: Well, we were safe, but we could have been . . . it was risky, somewhat risky, and supposedly people were paid to keep track of us, but nobody ever arrested us, anything like that, and I think mainly . . . we had friends.

AK: You were surveilled probably.

JP: I think we were surveilled. I am told that we were.

Anecdote from the Field: Ludruk

JP: Here is a quick comical example. We get to Surabaya . . . Joko Sanyoto, who got us a visa, and then he said: "Well, you need a place to live. My mother-in-law lives in Surabaya, so you can live with her!" Or, with them, actually—they were a family. And we did. And I'll tell you more about it—it was, you know, it was in a slum, really, called *Jalan gundi*. So, we got there, we settled in, and then I wanted to go to ludruk. So, we went to ludruk.

AK: Together with Florence?

JP: Yeah. So, we marched in (laughs), and remember—I only had a little bit of Indonesian then. And I said to this guy: "*Saya mau ke belakang!*" It means, literally, "I want to go to the back," you know, like backstage, but colloquially it means "I need to go to the bathroom." They didn't have any bathrooms, but if you needed to go to the bathroom, you'd just go back behind. Anyway—that was an example of the naiveté. I guess I probably knew the difference. They didn't react in any particular way . . . you know, Indonesians and the Javanese especially are just so polite. Usually. And I think he probably just asked something like "Do you mean . . . going to the bathroom?" And I said, no, I don't.

Anecdote from the Field: Florence on the Indonesian Language

Florence Peacock (FP): Yeah! I wanted to [learn Indonesian]. . . Jim was studying Indonesian, I didn't study in that class, I studied on my own. And they spoke . . . almost nobody spoke English except for the wealthy. And we were not hanging out with the wealthy. So, we were living in a slum, so to speak. But I loved it because of the people. The Ibu, our mother, was very kind to us. We came to Jakarta, in Jakarta we met Joko Sanyoto, who had been living in the United States. And Joko put us in touch with someone in Surabaya, who put us in touch with someone who was good to live with in a slum. So to speak, slum. So, we went to live with this family, and . . . Ibu Marsosudiro: Ibu means "mother," Marsosudiro is their last name, but they put it first instead of last, and I don't know what her first name was, but I just called her "Ibu," mother. And Bapak Marsosudiro met us at the train station—we were taking a train all the way there from Jakarta. And he had a white suit, standing at the train station, not a station, it was just a stop. He was standing on the tracks—very refined gentleman. And so helped us to take our luggage—he was an older man—take our luggage to their house. It was modest, some of it had dirt floors, but see—I didn't care. I was twenty-three, I guess—at the most I was twenty-three. No . . . I was twenty-five! By the time we married I was twenty-five. So, it didn't bother me a bit! They put us in their only bed, and it was a bed with a mattress. The matress had *tingis* in it, bugs, they couldn't help it. So, every day I would put the matress outside in the sun, the *tingis* would come out, I would kill them, then I would put the mattress back. So, for two nights the *tingis* wouldn't bite. They did not like Jim, they did not like his taste, they bit me every night.

AK: Not everybody would like it and would stay any longer in these conditions, because the difference must have been huge!

FP: It was huge!

AK: But you didn't mind . . .

FP: Let me just say: I was absolutely determined, as I am now, and my father put that into me. I was determined to do it. And I thought: I love Jim Peacock, I can hug him in bed, and I can do anything. So, I had no fear! And even more so: it was wonderful. She would put us around her table—they'd have rice, delicious rice, we picked it with our fingers, which we always washed—that was the rule in Islam. She was not Islamic, she said: "I am what everybody is around me, no matter, what they are." (laughs) So, she changed any time . . . So, we had these round-the-table meals, and we would eat the rice, and would put a tiny bit . . . if they had meat, they would shred it, and sprinkle it on top of the rice. It was delicious! And vegetables sprinkled on top of rice. And we would eat this and would always be so hungry, but there was this family, who embraced us.

(4_Peacock_Florence_05_11_2018)

Florence's Impressions from First Trip to Indonesia

AK: What were your impressions about this "proletarian drama"?

FP: It was fascinating. I've been, you know, to the musical theater, and it was their form of musical theater, but it was more refined.

AK: Really?

FP: But not real refined. It was not like *wayang orang*, which is extremely refined . . . dance. And *wayang kulit*, which is with the puppets, we have those puppets. So, this was for the lower class, but I never mind being with any class. In fact, I found it extremely interesting.

AK: And it's only men playing, right? Transvestite . . .

FP: Yes, in Islam they didn't allow women on the stage. So, men played women's parts, and they would be probably gay, I'm not sure. They would be wearing sarong and kabaya, which is a jacket, and they'd put in pads for breasts, and they'd come out and sing in the counter-tenor. Someday I can sing you those [sings a couple of lines]—beautiful songs. Boy, I loved those songs.

AK: Were there any women among the spectators?

FP: Yes, women could be spectators—most were men. Sometimes the Russians would come. Three Russian men . . . and I would give them a nod. But they spoke Russian, and if we ever spoke, we spoke bahasa Indonesian. In fact there were lots of Russians there. But this would be part of a . . . like, a fair. So, you could go to ludruk, but you could also go to other things. But I liked it.

AK: Did you feel like an anthropologist yourself in some ways?

FP: No, no, I just felt like myself. I tried to analyze the music, and I did. And Jim used that, and I liked to be with the . . . cast, especially with the people who were playing the females, and they would say: "Oh, look at my skin—it's lighter than yours." They were very sweet people. And one day I saw one at work, very slim, handsome, in men's clothing . . . had to be very careful, because Islam did not believe that men could be gay. But it was not strict Islam; they would let the women wear these jackets that really made their breasts show a little bit . . .

(4_Peacock_Florence_05_11_2018)

Florence Bitten by a Rabid Dog

AK: Do you remember any funny episodes, anecdotes from any of the field trips you made together with Dr. Peacock? Anything funny, or anything that's worth mentioning that stayed in your memory? Some encounter, some episode . . . ? Maybe pleasant, maybe unpleasant.

FP: I don't remember anything unpleasant.

AK: But you were bitten by a dog!

FP: Yes, correct. OK, the unpleasant was . . . again, I didn't think of that . . . I did know it was a rabid dog that bit me. And I was near a warong . . . a place where you can buy a cup of tea on the street and little snacks. And so, they were across the street from where we were living at the time, which was what they called the balakang of a nice house. And the man who owned it was a psychiatrist, who had studied in the United States. Very nice to Jim and me. He had a wife who was strict Muslim, and . . . she was still kind. So, I was crossing the street to the house where we lived, and out of a ditch came this dog—*puf*! Foam. Bit my leg, just like *shumpf*! I had no time . . . I mean, there was no way . . .

AK: Foam around her mouth—that must have been a rabid . . .

FP: See—a rabid animal, no matter even it's a human, all they want to do, because they cannot swallow, they try to bite you trying to get some fluid into their bodies. So, they will bite you—even if it's human. So, don't get around them, unless they are chained. In Indonesia they would chain those people to their beds. So, anyway, I knew I was bitten by a rabid dog. And the warong just closed their doors, everybody on the street closed up. And I don't know what happened to the dog, because I saw . . . all I saw was that he bit me, and I had to run into that place and close the door. So, I rushed to the pot of the boiling water, or water that had been boiled, and I rinsed the place off, but I could see that it had broken the skin, and the teeth marks were there. So, I ran . . . I think I ran to the Ibu, to the mother. And I said: "Ibu, I was bitten by the rabid dog." And, boy, she was really upset. She was so good, she said: "We will go to the doctors, and they will give you the serum." Now—they were very tight on serum. . . because Indonesia was just poor. And so, first of all . . . and this was, like, either . . . the next day, because you have three days. Next day we went to . . . very properly done . . . she and I went to a doctor, at a hospital . . . no, we first went to . . . no doctors, doctors at the hospital, period. They said: "We do not have the serum." We would have a cup of tea for half an hour before she would bring the subject up. Then we go to the next. On the third doctor we were at a hospital, and he said: "Yes, I can give you some serum." It was the horse embryo serum. Which was the way . . . not in the United States—we have the duck serum here. The horse serum was from an embryo. So, we got the serum, her son, who was studying to be a doctor at a very highly regarded school, and I think it was an American-built school, but it was for the Indonesians—he said: "I can do the injections." So, we went . . . he got the injections, he brought them home, and he started injecting them into the stomach. I didn't care—he was a completely devoted young man. To medicine. Almost a doctor, but not quite—just studying. So, he would give me those, in my stomach, on a daily basis. After about the first eight injections I woke up one morning, and I couldn't walk. I was paralyzed from the hips down. So, it was . . . I was allergic to those injections, to the horse embryo. So, Ariawan, that was his name, said: "We will half the dosage." And so, instead of having twenty injections in all, I had to have thirty. Then he started doing half doses. And even though it would . . . I still had some immobility, I could shuffle along. So, we finally had all the injections, and I didn't get lethal disease, but, I mean, this disease is a kiss of death if you don't take injections.

AK: So, these people helped you to find this serum to begin with, and then do the injections, so it's not just about the dog, it's about the relations with people with whom you . . .

FP: It would have been terrible . . . because, see, just to get from Surabaya to Jakarta, you couldn't fly, you took a train that was fourteen hours. By the time I would have come to Chicago, I would have lost a day. And you just can't wait if you wanna live. So, the serum that I was sent from the United States by Jim's cousin who was a doctor, got there way too late to help me. But it was the duck serum. And we gave it to the people at the Embassy so that they could give to anyone . . . because it was so rare . . . So, we gave it to the people at the Embassy, and they did it . . . there was a child who was bitten by a rabid dog in Java, and I think, Surabaya, and they used it on that child. A boy from America. So—that's the only bad thing that happened, except for the volcano that erupted during the week of the biting, which caused black darkness in daytime.

(4_Peacock_Florence_05_11_2018)

Florence on Women in Indonesia and in the American South

FP: And to me, people came on in a friendly, happy manner, and—sincere, especially the women. And they are the leaders of the family—I don't know if they still are now. But they were the leaders. They are the ones that . . . if the man made money, had a salary, he would bring it home to the woman, give it to her, and she would disburse it. And she would always—the ones that I knew—be very honest and very precise . . .

AK: Did it strike you, this empowered role of a woman?

FP: Yes. I liked it. And in a way, Southern women are like this. See—we pretend that we are not, that we are submissive, that we are beautiful, and really inside we are tough as nails. That's the truth!

AK: So, it's particularly so in the South, you think?

Florence Peacock with women in Indonesia, 2010.

FP: It certainly was that way when I was growing up.

AK: So, it sort of matched your type of disposition toward other people and yourself, when you saw that in Indonesia?

FP: Yeah, but I think most women are like that. African American women were particularly strong. They really led the family.

. . .

FP: The people in the kampong, which is a slum, but a nice slum . . . I realized immediately the dominance of the female. The mother. Ibu—that's what you call mother. And we call our mother in the household Ibu. Ibu Marso. Because her last name was Marsosudiro.

AK: What age do you have to be to become this "Ibu"?

FP: You have to have a baby.

AK: So, a young woman of twenty can become that already? If she has a small baby, she is automatically the head of the household?

FP: As soon as she has a baby. But if there is an older ibu in the household, she is head. That's OK, because it takes responsibility.

AK: In many cultures, like in the Gypsy culture, the older a woman becomes—and she is mother, grandmother, maybe great-grandmother by that time—the more authority she [acquires].

FP: That's correct. Same thing. I liked seeing that happen, because when I had come from the United States . . . it was different. My father was head of the household. My mother was really head of the household (laughs)—you know what I mean. She ran the show, and he made the money for the family. Very different kind of thing, I mean . . . the men, at least in the slums of Indonesia, didn't have a great position.

(5_Peacock_Florence_04_12_2018)

Muhammadiyah Study

JP: In 1969, I got a grant from the National Science Foundation to study Islam in Malaya. But unfortunately, they began having race riots in Malaya, and so I was unable to get a visa. In my fieldwork in Indonesia, I went from the low class to the middle class to the upper class—eventually. And each one had a different cultural perspective. And so, this was a kind of move to the middle class, Muslims. And I had planned to do it in Malaysia, but they had race riots there. And Florence and I, we had two small children. Instead, I went to Singapore; it was sort of a refuge, really. And I did a study of Muslims in Singapore.

But this is what happened: we arrived in July 1969, and around maybe November, something like that, our middle daughter, Claire, developed a very severe kidney problem. And there was a doctor in Singapore who really saved her life. He said, if she doesn't get an operation, she will die in two months. So, my wife traveled back to the United States with our daughter. When they went back, I decided to go back to Indonesia, which I didn't plan to do. But now—no children, and no wife. OK—so, now I will come to my fieldwork. So, on the spur of the moment I decided, I will go back to Indonesia, and I will study Muhammadiyah.

I got my visa through what is called the LIPI—Indonesian Science Foundation. I got their approval for my plan, and then I went to the office of Muhammadiyah, maybe January the second or something like that, just after New Year's Eve. And I walked in . . . I had no contact, never met any of them, it was all on the spur of the moment. So, I walked into the office of Muhammadiyah in Jakarta, and they were praying, and there was one guy at the front, who was a secretary. And I just said to him in Indonesian, "I want to study you." And I showed him a letter, I believe, from LIPI, which gave me at least . . . the government approval. So, much to his credit, he said: "We have a council of twelve people, and you must go to each one, and tell them your plan, and then they will vote, whether or not to approve of your plan." I mean, that was incredible that he was so courteous and smart, and no-nonsense. So, that's what I did. The twelve people lived all over Jakarta, which is a huge city, probably about twelve million people. These twelve people were the leaders, one of them was the minister for industry for the nation of Indonesia, one, a most famous writer, Hamka, and others. So, I went to each one, by all kinds of conveyance. I just interviewed them, I asked each one about his life. Which was one of the plans, by the way, which I had for my own project, which is to get . . . in Indonesian they call it *riwayat hidup*, which means "life history." So, my plan was to get stories of Muhammadiyahans. And so, I started with these twelve men. And I think that was, actually a useful approach. Because each one really seemed to like to talk about himself. They were men—they were all men. And I was thirty-one or thirty-two at the time, and they were probably in their sixties. And so, it was kind of student interviewing . . .

And so, then, after several weeks I had interviewed all of them, and they voted that I would be permitted to do the study. And so, then they wrote a letter, the office did, that said that I was authorized to study Muhammadiyah. I took the letter . . . I had the copy of the letter . . . and I found that there was a boat that would go to many of the different islands of Indonesia for about ten dollars. Twenty-five hundred miles for ten dollars, but you had to sleep on the deck. And I thought, well, that's a great way to do it. There were at least a thousand people who were going to get on the boat, and they were going to go deck-class, just like me.

And I was so . . . dumb, you know, I had not asked what I should bring. It turned out, I should have brought a mat and a cup: a mat to sleep on, and a cup to drink out of and a plate to eat out of. I didn't have any of those. But I had huge suitcases in which I put tape recorders and cameras . . . We would stop at each port along the way, and I would get off the boat, the boat would usually dock for about two days, and they would unload things, because it was mainly a cargo ship and did not have very many cabins. Everybody was really on the deck, and the cargo was the load. So, when they would stop, I would get off the boat, and I would somehow make contact with the local Muhammadiyah chapter. And almost always they would invite me to stay with them, in one of their houses. And I'd stay with a family, sometimes for several days.

This trip took several weeks. Eventually I returned to Jakarta, the capital. So, then I got on the train and I got to Yogyakarta, which is not the capital of Indonesia, but it's a provincial [town]. So, Yogyakarta is the headquarters of Muhammadiyah, and that's why I went there eventually, after I did my trips around the islands. Muhammadiyah has several thousand branches all over the islands of Indonesia, which extend for about twenty-five hundred miles. So, finally I went to Yogyakarta, the headquarters for Muhammadiyah. They had an office there, on 99 Ahmad Dahlan street. Ahmad Dahlan is the founder of Muhammadiyah. So, I went to that office, and I met an administrator, Jindar Tamini. I told that story about what I wanted to do, and I showed him the letter, and he said: "OK," and he procured the place where I could stay.

It was with a family, who were Muhammadiyahans. So, I moved into that place; it cost me about two-to-three dollars a month. If you were living as an ordinary person, it was very cheap. By the way, I never had money in the bank, I had just brought traveler's checks. But I didn't need to spend very much.

So I lived with a family, and one of the first activities that I observed there, was: they had a meeting of the women's group of Muhammadiyah, which is called Aisijah. It's the name of the favorite wife of Mohammad. And so, they had this meeting, which normally I would not have been able to visit, or see, but I was living in the house, and so I did—I saw a lot of it. And participated in just about all of it. They were just having a meeting, and I was . . . sitting in one of the rooms, and I just . . . I remember one time they asked everybody to sing a song, and so, they asked me to sing a song, and I sang "Ade zur guten Nacht . . . " in German.

Time went on, and I participated in many other events. I met two guys who are still good friends of mine, Amien Rais, who was the president of Muhammadiyah and Sudibyo Markus. The two guys were students, and they were in their late twenties, and I was in my early thirties. They included me as a kind of honorary member of what was called a *Pemuda*—Muhammadiyah, "The Youth of Muhammadiyah." We went on a retreat. We went up to the mountains, and we excreted in a river, and we made fun of each other's anatomies . . . I think you get the picture . . . And they told some dirty jokes, and I told one or two that I could remember. And we became kind of buddies, and that led later to several camps, one of which was with students that I went with, and the final one was with branch leaders. And the two guys, my friends, have remained my friends all these years.

Professor Peacock's Indonesian field notes mailed home.

Muhammadiyahan Spirituality

AK: Did you feel from the beginning of the first trip, when you didn't know much, didn't know anybody, how you were progressing, how you were moving in the culture, how you were learning more about it . . . Did you feel how your knowledge was changing and how you became more and more part of it? Not in the sense that you would eventually join a culture, but how you would progress in it. Did you have this feeling of movement?

JP: I did, probably—somewhat. But, number one, I did not join the culture, number two, I did not become a specialist in that culture. You know, there are people who are specialists . . . on Asia, Indonesia, or Hinduism . . .

I wanted to study Islam and just learn . . . but oh . . . I did . . . yes, I had a project in mind: it was to study life histories. Biographies. And so, I did do that. I did it partly in Singapore, partly in Indonesia, and then I did it somewhat in Malaya, but I couldn't stay there, so I did it with surveys. But mainly I did it in Indonesia and Singapore.

AK: Surveys—so, you used some of the quantitative methods . . . ?

JP: I did. And I wrote a book about those three: Singapore, Malaya, and Indonesia, and I gave the results of the surveys.

AK: Were you using questionnaires . . . ?

JP: Yes, I was.

AK: I have some suspicion about questionnaires . . .

JP: I do, too!

AK: What kinds of questions did you have in your . . . ?

JP: Well, I had a whole bunch of them. And I spent a huge amount of time analyzing them, and they have not played a very strong part in anything I've done . . . but while I did surveys, I also did fieldwork. I lived with Muhammadiyahans, I took part in their training camp, I interviewed them at length, and that's what I ended up basing my work on.

AK: And you didn't choose this topic of Islam and Muhammadiyah in particular because of some "fashion" in the academy? I don't think this "fashion" was there yet at the time . . .

JP: You mean . . .

AK: I mean, now everything related to Islam . . . you're doing Islam, you're doing terrorism . . . and there so many jobs for that . . .

Fieldwork 91

Excerpts from Professor Peacock's Indonesian questionnaire.

JP: That's right. No, I did not follow that then. My theory was based on Max Weber. The *Protestant Ethic and the Spirit of Capitalism*. So, my theory was ... or my question was: how did the Islamic ethic differ from the Protestant ethic in terms of life histories? And so, I did all of these life histories with Muhammadiyahans and others. And then I in some degree compared it to protestant ethics.

AK: That's a very interesting twist. Did it include business ethics?

JP: Oh, yes. Because most Muhammadiyahans were businesspeople.

AK: Was this book published—where you compare the two ethics? What's the title of the book?

JP: *Muslim Puritans*. So, that was based on surveys but also on the interviews and other stuff. But then I also did a short book, which was called *Purifying the Faith*. And it's kind of ironic, but that book had a lot more . . . it became well-known among Muhammadiyahans. It was short, and kind of simple, and it told about different personalities, individuals . . . So, now it's . . . it's translated into Indonesian and published by Muhammadiyah. So, it had more impact, I think—at least among Muhammadiyahans.

Five Trips to Indonesia

AK: How many did you have altogether, and for how long?

JP: OK. The last one was in 2010, and that one was for the hundredth anniversary of Muhammadiyah. So, the trips were these: 1962–1963, that was the study of ludruk, for one year. The second one was the study of Muhammadiyah, and that was 1970. And I was actually . . . we were in Singapore for three to four months, and then I was in Indonesia eight months. The third one was in 1979, and that was when I did the study with my student David Howe, of Sumarah. The fourth one was in 1996, several months.

AK: So, seventeen years later, between 1979 and 1996?

JP: Correct. In 1996, what we did was . . . we lived with this woman, Tati, whom I mentioned, and her sister . . . and we lived with them . . . I have to think for how many months . . .

AK: Approximately . . . ?

JP: Maybe five or something like that—in Yogyakarta. In a way, I did not do field research, but I did some field research. Kind of mixed in with . . . just being with them, living with them.

AK: And these are your major field trips.

JP: Yes, and then in 2010 we went there again, for a shorter period, but it was for this congress. And again, we connected with Tati and her sister. But not for that long a period, maybe for two weeks or something. We worked with a Korean political scientist, much younger than I, but she had studied Muhammadiyah. And she and I later attempted to . . . we wrote some things together . . . mostly unpublished. So, that was 2010.

Indonesia, 2010.

Indonesia, 2010.

Indonesia, 2010.

Indonesia, 2010, with Sudibyo Markus.

AK: Why are those things unpublished? Would you consider reworking them now and submit for publication?

JP: I don't know if it's worth it. What she and I tried to do was basically to combine a young person and an old person, a person who had more recently studied Muhammadiyah and a person who previously studied Muhammadiyah . . .

AK: That's an interesting perspective.

JP: Well, we could probably do something of interest there, but I did not do new fieldwork.

Three Classes of Indonesian People: Proletarians, Middle-Class, Wealthy

AK: Did you feel like your informants from Muhammadiyah or other people, since they knew, or they thought how wealthy you are, did you feel any . . . did they give you their consent faster knowing that you are so rich, or . . . The feeling that you're so wealthy, whether true or not, but for them it was real—did this fact change your communicative format with your informants?

JP: Well, OK—it was different with Muhammadiyahans than previously. The first fieldwork . . . my so-called informants were poor, I mean, they were proletarians, but then some people we knew were wealthy. Relatively wealthy.

AK: And those proletarians, they were also Marxists . . .

JP: Well, some of them were.

AK: . . . so, against the very principle of riches . . .

JP: That's right—at least some of them were . . . to some degree would profess—right, the Marxist point of view. And there were a lot of class . . . divisions and stuff, so—yeah. But with Muhammadiyah it was different. Muhammadiyahans were middle class, most of them originally were small businesspeople, merchants, and they did things like they wove batik, and they had a batik . . . cotton industry. How . . . so, it wasn't the same . . . it was not me and the proletariat, but it was me, an American, you know, sort of middle-class person with other middle-class people, who certainly were not wealthy but had viable means of livelihood. They were not beggars or destitute. And some of them were pretty well-off. But they were not rich. Most Muhammadiyahans in my experience . . . they were middle class. So, we had in a way... a simpler relationship, and more equal relationship, than with the first group... And then later, my third trip, the group that I got to know were mainly aristocratic. That doesn't mean they were wealthy, but they were relatively well-off. And they had... by the way, a lot of people had servants. Even though by our standards their income was very low, relatively low, they would have two or three servants, who would survive by being their servants.

AK: So, you covered three different classes...

JP: In my three trips—all three.

"Wow" Experiences in Indonesia

JP: It was my third trip to Indonesia. It was 1979. Before going to Indonesia this time, I stopped in Cairo, and... I'll go into the "wow" experience... A former student from here, her name is Hind Khattab, she is Egyptian, and lives in Cairo. So, I looked her up, and she introduced me to one of her students. And her student was from a wealthy Arab family, but she was studying in Cairo—I think, maybe at the American University. And according to Hind, she, well, a few months ago she had been riding around in... not shorts, but... social clothes. But now she converted to a kind of fundamentalist Islam. And so, she's wearing a burka. So, I met this student, and then she invited me to meet with her guru, who was a police captain in Cairo.

AK: Hmm... interesting... Muslim guru who is a police captain?

JP: Yup. And so she and a friend of hers, who also is a student, they are counselees, he counseled these young women, maybe others, too. She had a dream, this student. And she went to the guru's place, and she told him the dream, and I'm sure I wrote it down somewhere, but... But there was something in her dream and her conversion experience that really touched a chord in me. And not that I converted, but I just was... at the time I was really alone and isolated...

AK: You were there alone, your third trip?

JP: I was there alone, yeah. And I think maybe this... so, this experience... and it was probably not a "wow" experience, but it sort of struck a chord because it put me in touch with something or somebody who represented a broader, a bigger force. Well, then I went on in Indonesia...

AK: But what was the dream about?

JP: I don't remember. As I said, I probably wrote it down, but I don't remember. But I went on to Indonesia in order to connect with a former student of mine, his name is David Howe, who—and I already told you about him—he was the one who had started studying this mystical group called Sumarah. And he was . . . he and his wife, new wife from Brazil, were living in Solo (Surakarta). And he had become connected to this group, Sumarah. So, again it was kind of the same "wow" experience. Again, I was sort of alone, and I appreciated his and hers, his wife's, friendship, but also the guru, Father (Pak) Wondo, whom I got to know, by going to their sessions—Sumarah.

. . .

JP: At a Sumarah meeting Pak Wondo the guru asked if anyone had had a dream. And I said: "I had one last night." I dreamt that a friend who in reality is dead was alive in my dream. And the guru replied: "That's OK, if, when you dreamt, you realized it's a dream." Well, that was a kind of a small "wow" . . . wake-up . . . call . . . wake-up dream, because in a way, it's kind of Buddhist that you . . . you think about your thinking as you're thinking it, as opposed to just I'm thinking, I have a dream . . .

AK: Did you ever collaborate with, like, indigenous scholars, in Indonesia?

JP: Yeah, in a certain way. Well, Muhammadiyah translated the book that I wrote about the movement. Within Muhammadiyah there are several anthropologists, indigenous anthropologists. Oh, and there is another person I worked with, studying Muhammadiyah, and he is Dutch: Niels Mulder. So, I had already begun my work on Muhammadiyah, and I moved to Yogyakarta, which is where the headquarters of Muhammadiyah is. And I was living with a Muhammadiyahan family, and this Dutchman rode up on a motorcycle and said: "Hey, I'm Niels Mulder, and I'm doing fieldwork in Yog-Ja." That's how they say it, Yogyakarta become Yog-Ja, and Surakarta becomes Solo: these are nicknames. Anyway—he had rented a big house in Yog-Ja, and he invited me to move in, and I did. And so, then we did fieldwork together.

AK: For his or for your project?

JP: Well, it was for his project. But . . . these two are complementary. The Sumarah are mystics, and Muhammadiyah deplores mysticism because . . . they are very much like the Calvinists and Pentecostals in a way: they deplored mysticism because it unites god and men. Whereas Islam puts god way up there. It's very much like Calvinism. So, anyway, I worked with him on the Sumarah, and he actually didn't work with me very much on Muhammadiyahans because he didn't like them very much. Or at least he just focused on his own thing.

AK: So, you were just helping him a little bit . . .

JP: Yes and later I became the chair of his committee at the University of Amsterdam. That's where he did his PhD.

AK: Did you use any of these materials in your own works?

JP: Only indirectly: I put them together just in little essays. So, one of those essays was in a book, edited by Edward Brunner. I wrote an essay contrasting three philosophies. One was Muhammadiyah, and let me see, how I divided up . . . Sumarah, Muhammadiyah, Pentecostals, and Primitive Baptists—all four of them.

AK: What was the title of the article?

JP: I think it was called . . . religion and life stories, something like that.

AK: And which year was it?

JP: I'll find it for you. It was probably about . . . 2000 . . . And the point of it was . . . it kind of took . . . it tried to show how each of the theologies was expressed in the shape of the life story. It might have been called something like "Life Story and Religion."

The Anthropologist and the Locals

AK: Last time you said that you pretty much worked alone except for the project with Ruel Tyson and the Pattersons . . .

JP: However, when I said "alone," I meant "not with other anthropologists," but I was often collaborating with Indonesians of one kind or another—not anthropologists. For example, the guy who just sent me this email in the morning: he is a really interesting person. His name is Sudibyo Markus. He changed his spelling somewhat. He was . . . when I first met him, there were two guys in Muhammadiyah, Sudibyo and Amien Rais. They were both in their late twenties, and they were graduate students. Sudibyo was a medical student, and Amien Rais was a student of political science. They were both at an Indonesian University called Gadjah Mada. Sometimes the spelling has changed: originally it was Dutch spelling, and then it became a more British spelling. Gadjah Mada is a university in Indonesia, which is about the size of UNC. It's one of the two main universities in the country, and it's in the city of Yogyakarta. And that is also headquarters of Muhammadiyah. Which is why I went there. So, I met these two guys. I was thirty-one or thirty-two . . .

AK: Pretty much the same age.

JP: Yes, but they were students, and I was a professor. But we really hit it off, and they included me in something called Pemuda Muhammadiyah, "Youth of Muhammadiyah." And by "youth" they were fairly elastic in their category . . . if you are below forty or something like that. And so, I got involved with various activities with them. And then Sudibyo, who was just about my height, very unusual for an Indonesian, he and I were almost the same. And they sometimes called us "twins": we looked kind of alike. And we acted kind of alike. Well, Muhammadiyah had training camps, and I went to several camps in stages. And the last one was with branch leaders. And these two guys who were kind of young neophytes were involved in that camp for branch leaders, who were older than we were. So, it lasted about two and a half weeks, and we went out in a village, and used the village school as the headquarters for the training camp; we slept and ate there.

AK: Did they provide any introduction to Muhammadiyah for you?

JP: They did. Well, I already knew a lot about Muhammadiyah, but it went through a sequence. We had physical training in the morning, we ate breakfast, which consisted of bean curd, tea, and rice, and then we had lunch, and then we had supper. Always the same thing . . . So, I participated in a lot of their activities; we did a retreat in the mountains, and we did this and that. And we had lots of arguments with each other! He, as you can tell from his name, Markus, which is Mark, he had gone to a Catholic missionary school when he was a little boy. Probably, before Hildred Geertz interviewed him. And then, as a youth, he converted to Islam and then joined Muhammadiyah. And so, I asked him about this experience. I asked him about it, after he invited me to visit his family. So, we were on a train, and I asked him about this experience, and he told me.

AK: And his family was still Christian?

JP: Well, that was an interesting thing. So, I met his family—his mother, his father, and some of his siblings. It was a fairly large family, maybe eight or nine children. And they were everything: one was a communist, one was a Buddhist, his mother was a Muslim . . . And this was right after the time of Gestapu, which is when communists were exterminated. So, one reason we

Fieldwork

Indonesia, 2010.

had all these arguments, was that he had become an anti-Christian zealot for Muhammadiyah. And he was going around the country haranguing the Christians. Some Muhammadiyahans chastised him for being too vehement.

AK: How about the family? Were there any quarrels about religion . . . ?

JP: No—not when I was visiting. And they seem . . . Javanese are very courteous. Today he might be able to comment on some of that. So, he wrote me

Indonesia, 2010.

an email about two years ago, and he said: "You would not believe me today, compared to the way I was then, because now I'm collaborating with Christians on various projects and things." So, that's him in a nutshell.

AK: But why did he convert from Christianity to Islam to begin with?

JP: He told me: "I did not have any conversion experience." He said: "Christianity was like a black cat in a dark room, it was mysterious and incomprehensible. Islam was like coming into the daylight. It was so clear." And the second thing he said, was—he quoted Malcolm X. And he said: "When Malcolm X did his pilgrimage to Mecca, said that it was like he met his brothers," something like that. And he said: "That's how it was for me . . . combination of clarity and companionship."

AK: So, did you have those conversations at the time when you were visiting these camps? Did you talk about Muhammadiyah with these two guys a lot? Like, what kind of introduction did they provide? Was it mostly, like, connecting with other people, or some substantial thoughts that you shared?

JP: (laughs) Sudibyo liked to tell dirty jokes, and that was part of our camp friendship. And so, the last day of the camp we all got into . . . they had a few cars, and the cars were touring various projects that Muhammadiyah was doing in that province. And so, Sudibyo and Amien said: "OK, we want to get into this car and tell some dirty jokes together!" And they invited me to join them. And so, we got to sit in the back seat and I could tell you a lot of these jokes if you wanted me to. And I told them one that I remembered from my fraternity. And you know, it's just kind of a typical teenage guys getting together. So, and that was the last time I saw Sudibyo for many, many years. But I had seen Amien Rais several times because he became the head of Muhammadiyah, and then he became a candidate for president of Indonesia, he got thirty million votes, but was not elected. But he had a lot to do with their electing the first and only woman president. But Sudibyo was doing other things, and so I never saw him again until 2010. And they had their one hundredth year [of Muhammadiyah]. So, I had not seen him since 1970, and it was 2010. Forty years. And I thought, I bet he is really mad at me—you know, we had not had any contact . . . and we saw each other, we embraced. I mean . . . that has rarely happened to me, maybe rarely happened to him. We were just so glad . . . at least, speaking for myself, I was so glad to see him! He looked exactly the same! So, since then we've been in contact by email, but he has not been here since, and I have not been there since.

AK: Has he traveled to the United States?

JP: I think he did once or twice maybe, during that time that I did not have any contact with him. So, he is still one of the leaders.

Anecdote from the Field: "Four Cars Crash at an Intersection..."

JP: Muhammadiyah had a very viable organization—at that time, six million members. They were clearly and rather fundamentalistically Islamic. And sometimes, I got in arguments with them about doctrine or something like that. At the end of my fieldwork... toward the end... so, the last ... one of the last things I did, was—I participated in a training camp for branch leaders that Muhammadiyah held. And when the camp ended, some of the participants asked me if I would... first of all, they asked me: "Will you critique Muhammadiyah?" And then some of them asked me if I would come to their branch and speak, just give my opinion or whatever about Muhammadiyah. So, I did, and I sort of created a joke. And it was based on an Indonesian joke that a friend of mine told me... told us. And it actually happened to be the same guy whom I mentioned, Joko Sanyoto, who helped us get a visa. So, he told a joke: four cars crash at an intersection, and they ask, who is at fault? And the answer is: the Dutch! So, that was his joke, an Indonesian joke, that said: look, we're scapegoating, we are blaming somebody else. So, I adapted it a bit, and I had it: four cars crash, who is at fault? Answer: the Christians! That was probably a pretty brave joke, but they were polite, they didn't shoot me.

"American Muhammadiyahans," or, Southern Fundamentalists

JP: When I say that Muhammadiyah was "fundamentalistically Islamic," I mean that they were people who treat the sacred scripture as literally true. There are many groups in Indonesia, and Muhammadiyah is only a minority, even though they are many. Another group are more the aristocrats, intellectuals, and syncretists. So, one of them, whose nickname is Tati, came here to graduate school, in the English Department. And for various reasons I gave her a ride to Atlanta. And on the way there is a university called Bob Jones University, which is a fundamentalist college in South Carolina. And I said to Tati, who was more aristocratic and also... she is not a fundamentalist Muslim... is not and was not... she died recently. So, I said, how would you like to see a fundamentalist Christian college? And we just pulled off the road, it was off of 85, and drove through the campus of Bob

Jones, and she saw a young man and a young woman standing there. They were very neatly dressed, and the young man and the young woman had short hair . . . So, she looked at them and she said: "Muhammadiyahans!"—this was her little joke to say, they are like Muhammadiyahans, they are fundamentalists!

Sudibyo Markus . . . and the other person is Tati. Her full name is Jukortati Imamurni. Tati came to Chapel Hill as a graduate student in English literature, in the English department. Here is something about her: she is a member of the nobility in Yogyakarta. Now, Yogyakarta is one of the two court cities in Java, and she was a member of a large royal family. And she lived in a house, which was owned . . . it was in a palace complex, she lived in an old house, probably a hundred years old, with her sister whose name was Retno, who was a bit older, and had gotten a doctorate in the Netherlands in philosophy. And Tati came here . . . they were spinsters, both unmarried. They lived together in this old house, and they had servants, and they had several students who lived there. I met her here, in Chapel Hill. She got various fellowships, she got a Fulbright. She could have gone to any university she wanted to, but she chose to come to Chapel Hill because it had strength in Southern literature. And when Tati was a young woman, she read William Faulkner. And she also had had a fellowship in Australia and had studied Victorian literature. The reason she chose UNC was to study Southern literature.

AK: As a PhD student?

JP: Uh-huh. And she was assigned one of the leaders in Southern literature, his name was Louis Rubin—he is dead, but he was well-known in that field. But—two things: first, I don't think Rubin paid too much attention to her, and second, they said to her: "You cannot study Southern literature, you have to study British and American literature," and that meant Hawthorn and people like that . . . Shakespeare . . . And she said: "Well, I've already done that, in Australia. I don't want to do that again." Dan Patterson, who was then director of the folklore program and professor of literature, welcomed her and included her in his group of folklore students, and that became her main home. Then I discovered that she was living in an unheated basement somewhere, and she was from Indonesia, so she was not very happy there. I think maybe Florence gave her a coat, or somebody did.

AK: But she was from a royal family! She didn't have means to . . .

JP: Well, she . . . I'm not sure, what the reason was . . . it's an old story, and that is: foreign students were not very welcome and not taken care of.

AK: Which year was this?

JP: This was about 1994, something like that.

AK: And so, she was in her thirties or something?

JP: Probably. So, Dan and Beverly sort of tried to help her and included her in the group, and they introduced her to me and Florence. And so, we became friends, and then she decided to go to another school. Because with her fellowship she could go just about anywhere. So, she was thinking about Emory University. So, I said, I'm going to Georgia, I can give you a ride to Emory University, which I did . . . It turned out that she did not go to Emory—but she did decide to transfer, so she transferred to the University of Maryland. And she specialized in American studies, and she wrote a dissertation on bingo. She did fieldwork, I think, a Catholic church, where the older people played bingo, and so, she wrote a dissertation about that.

AK: From Southern literature to bingo!

JP: Right. I think she chose that partly under the influence of having been with folklore people. So, then she returned to Yogyakarta, the court city—it's an old city with royalty . . . the sultan of Yogyakarta gave much of his palace and so forth to create a new university, which is called Gadjah Mada, that's a name of a renowned general in Javanese history. So, she started a new program there, which was called American studies. And her sister meanwhile had also become a faculty member, so the two of them were . . . And her program attracted various people, four of whom later came to Chapel Hill. And one other who came and actually lived in our house for a few weeks. I just wanted to bring her in because she is a person of importance.

AK: Why do say she is a person of importance? In which way?

JP: In various ways. One of the ways is that she and her sister kind of *bridged* Florence and me and our earlier time, which was in Surabaya, and the way that it bridged, was that . . . one of the two . . . we lived in two families, one of them was the slum family, one of whom now lives here. The other was family that had a connection to the royal family of Yogyakarta. And so, later, Tati and her connection to the royal family, and that earlier family and its connection came together . . . with us. And then we connected them to a professor and his wife at Harvard, Byron Good, who is still a medical anthropologist, and he is still doing research there, in Gadjah Mada. So, that's part of that. And the other connection is through Sudibyo Markus, the one from Muhammadiyah.

Fieldwork 107

AK: And how are these two connected, Tati and Sudibyo?

JP: Yogyakarta is a court city, and there are two major institutions there, one is Muhammadiyah, whose headquarters are in Yogyakarta, and whose founder is Kyai Haji Ahmad Dahlan, who created it in 1912. He was a cleric at the royal mosque in Yogyakarta. And the sultan of Yogyakarta is kind of mixed of Hindu and aristocracy, and the more Muslim part is more . . . merchants, and not really . . . I mean, they are and they aren't, the two entities, the kind of a . . . two extremes of Indonesian society, and that is to say, pious Muslims who tend to be merchants, on the one hand, and sort of the royal family, which is somewhat Islamic but also mixed with Hinduism and all that . . . and aristocracy, on the other. So, Sudibyo Markus is more of the Muhammadiyah element, but also somewhat part of the . . . tradition, and his family . . .

AK: The family that was all diverse in its religious . . . ?

JP: Correct. Including Buddhism and all that—I told you all that. So, in a way, these two individuals, Tati and Sudibyo, illustrate, in many ways, the core features of the Indonesian nation and its cultural aspects . . .

AK: And it also reflects the three stages of your work: you first worked with the proletarians, with the ludruk, and then you moved to the middle class, the Muhammadiyah . . .

JP: . . . and then finally this aristocracy!

AK: So, they represent the second and the third stages . . .

JP: Lower, middle, and upper . . . !

AK: Sudibyo in the middle and Tati in the upper.

JP: Right, but in the beginning, there was proletariat, which was ludruk. Very simple. And there were other connections that put all that together as well, but personally Sudibyo and Tati were, I guess, in some ways, my closest friends, but not the only ones.

Anecdote from the Field: "On a Boat with a Chinese Man and His Mistress"

AK: Oh, the cabin—you said, there was a cabin on that deck, and you said, you'll tell me later, what it was about.

JP: OK, one cabin. There might have been more, but I knew of one. So, everybody on the boat, just about, was Indonesian, and we were all sleeping on the deck. There was one cabin that was occupied by a Chinese man, and his mistress, and her daughter. And after a few days on the boat I think he perceived that I might appreciate a little bit of privacy. Because I was on the deck, and there were thousands of people, and they would keep asking questions . . .

AK: And you were the only two different people, right? Him being Chinese, and you being American?

JP: Yes indeed. I was certainly the only . . . *londo*, the only white person. And he may have been the only Chinese. Probably was. He and his mistress. So, yeah, we were kind of alike. So, he invited me to just come and . . . visit in their cabin for a little bit—I did. And then later, as the boat . . . went to many different islands, and when it came to one, he had an idea, and he said: "You know, we could catch a flight from here to Jakarta. Would you like to come with me?" I think he had decided he had enough of the boat. And so, I did. And so, I went with them to Jakarta, and I spent a night or two in his house, and we went around the city, and he introduced me to a lot of things that the Chinese did, like gambling and stuff, and we went on a bamboo roller coaster—he, and I, and his mistress, and her daughter.

AK: Did the Chinese have a higher status . . . ?

JP: They were much wealthier. Ninety-five percent of the wealth in Indonesia is owned by Chinese people, by some measures. Even though they are, like, 5 percent of the population.

AK: Oh, that's something you mentioned during my defense, comparing the Chinese in Indonesia to Jews in Europe.

JP: Right. Many make this comparison. And so, they are often persecuted, and so forth.

AK: And of course, he and others regarded you as another wealthy person because you are American, and all Americans are millionaires as we all know, which is something that brought you together . . .

JP: Right. Everybody on that boat asked me: "How much do you make per year?"

AK: Did you answer in truth?

JP: Oh, sure, yeah, I told them. I mean, as far as I remember, I just told them what I made. Which was enormous by comparison, partly because of the exchange rate.

AK: If you need two or three dollars per month to live there . . .

JP: Exactly.

Fieldwork as a Quest

JP: Here is another aspect, maybe—PTSD, Post Traumatic Stress Disorder. And how fieldwork engenders that, and I think that actually I'm having a bit of PTSD. Not now, but I'm remembering those things. Not that they were horrible, but this or that . . . I mean, the whole thing is very demanding—fieldwork . . . I wasn't doing traumatically dangerous fieldwork, but when I think about what I did, and how I did it, I just think: "Good God! How did I do that???" And it's kind of a . . . it's Southeast Asia traumatic in the sense that I think: "Good Gosh! That was a close call!" I could have . . . you know—this could have happened, that could have happened . . . There were so many things that could have gone wrong . . . Just that I did it, I survived it . . . and I'm sure with you it's . . . and many fieldworkers . . . you know, we talk about PTSD for combat veterans . . .

AK: Do you think it's a common feeling among the anthropologists, have you ever spoken to your colleagues about that? PTSD as applied to the Southeast Asia field experience?

JP: Not literally, but it's so obvious when you just think about it, I mean, when anthropologists get together, they just talk about their experiences . . .

AK: PFSD—Southeast Asia Field Stress Disorder! (laughs)

JP: And I'm sure that many combat veterans or people who think they were that would turn up their noses at the idea that this would be [seen as traumatic] . . . One of the distinctions I thought of for myself at least, between, let's say . . . like, my father was in D-Day. That's obviously a dangerous situation. And I think he actually had some PTSD later, maybe his whole life.

AK: When was he born, which year?

JP: 1912. But I think with us, you and me, and our fieldwork, one of the differences with the military is: if you are in the military, many times you are a part of the group. And the group is part of the command hierarchy, that tells you what to do. When you are an anthropologist, it's just you. And I think it's a difference with archaeology as well. The archaeologists often do a dig, and they are together. With much fieldwork you are alone—an outsider to the natives.

AK: Would you say that you had the same degree of this PTSD when you think about your fieldwork in Indonesia, on the one hand, and in America, on the other?

JP: What I did in America . . . I did a lot! But no PTSD.

AK: OK, so, maybe it has to do with . . .

JP: Being in a different state . . .

AK: Then that supports my original assumption that it's a semiotic shift that [happens] when you do research in a culture that's different from yours . . .

JP: Sure!

AK: Symbolically, semiotically, including the language, including significations . . .

JP: All that! All of that, absolutely! And . . . but I think being . . . if you would have gone as part of a platoon, say, a military platoon, it—sure, it might be a different language group, or different terrain, but you are part of the group. Also, a lot of times you have mediators, you have interpreters . . . The best thing that I can say about various fieldworks I've done . . . well, and broader, here—is friends. And some of those friendships and not just friendships, but . . . helpers, are really amazing, you know. That they would help you for no good reason. I mean, without any benefit for themselves, actually.

AK: That reminded me of two things. In a formal analysis of a classical fairy tale . . . like the one that was developed by Vladimir Propp . . .

JP: Oh, I know—I read his work carefully . . .

AK: Some of his characters . . . position of the characters as "helpers." They help you. Not necessarily for no reason, maybe there is some kind of mutuality, reciprocity . . .

JP: Right, but many times they just appear, out of the blue.

AK: And then I thought of one of the topics of our course, which is the initiation story, which we discussed all three semesters that I was TA-ing for the course, and how this usually young person proceeds with the quest . . .

JP: Right.

Indonesia, 2010.

AK: That's basically the same: a fairytale is also a quest. And that's interesting about the helpers . . . and of course, field research is a quest.

JP: Yup! . . . When we went to Indonesia in 1962–1963, we were thrown into a social upheaval, but I did not . . . I was still an observer. That was my position, an observer. But as always happens, we became connected to certain friends and families . . .

AK: "Complicit" like Geertz . . .

JP: Something like that. I'm not . . . yeah, Geertz, that's another question, how he is like that and different from . . . And then later, in my second fieldwork, with Muhammadiyah, in some ways I was even more involved, but I still was basically an observer. So, while all that was going on, I was still essentially a teacher, researcher.

From Muhammadiyah to Pentecostals/Primitive Baptists

JP: In 1970, I did eight months of study of Muhammadiyah. And they are fundamentalist Muslim. So, I came back from that and I met Ruel Tyson—he now lives in The Cedars. So, he and I had a conversation about Muhammadiyah, and that led us to discussing fundamentalism in Christianity. So, we decided that we would start doing fieldwork together, and we did it for years and years. And our first fieldwork was with the Pentecostals.

AK: . . . and the snakes, right? The snakes are the Pentecostals?

JP: Correct. And then later we decided to go to the mountains and work with Primitive Baptists.

AK: It was a continuation of Muhammadiyah, but not a direct one?

JP: That's right. They were . . . sort of on the same line. So, that's how that happened. And so, we did that . . .

AK: For how many months or years . . . ?

JP: We're still doing it (laughs) . . . in a way. But mainly it was in the 1980s.

AK: And did it change . . . in which ways was the Primitive Baptist project different from the previous ones?

JP: I really liked the Primitive Baptists. They are poor, on the whole, but they are very sturdy and committed, and sometimes they are surprising. I'll give you an example. So, one time Ruel Tyson and I . . . drove all over the mountains to go to all of these churches, and I interviewed people. So, one time we went to interview a Primitive Baptist man named Calvin Yates. So, Calvin . . . we interviewed him, he had about an eighth grade education . . .

AK: That's not too much . . .

JP: It was in a time when the schools didn't go any higher than that . . . in the mountains. So, after the interview I've noticed a photograph in the living room, and I asked, who are they? And he said: "They are my daughters."—"But who are your daughters? What do they do?" And he or his wife said, well, "This daughter is a professor of Old English in Ohio, and this daughter sings with the Waverly Consort." They are one of the best baroque music groups in the world. So, here was this young woman, coming out of the mountains, way in the backwoods, and is one of the best singers . . .

AK: And the other one is a professor.

JP: So that was . . . sometimes with Primitive Baptists you find surprises like that.

AK: So, although they are "fundamentalists," as you said, this fundamentalism doesn't really constrain one's free choice, so to speak . . .

JP: Not necessarily. I mean, they were actually very tolerant and liberal in some ways, for example, one of their beliefs is that . . . well, it's in predestination. Predestination of the world. Before the creation of the world, God has decided who is saved and who is damned, but it doesn't matter where you are from, or which, if any, religion . . . I mean, you can be a Russian orthodox or something . . . And on the other hand, if you happen to be a faithful member of a church where you go every Sunday, it doesn't mean you are going to be saved. So, it's all preordained. So, in that sense it's liberal . . . because it doesn't imprison you in your . . . You cannot dictate . . . nor do you know if you're saved or damned. And you can't choose to be saved or damned—so, that's Primitive Baptists.

AK: Also related to this: we all know that academic life is very precarious, it depends on so many factors, from financial factors, to family factors, to anything in the world.

JP: You bet.

AK: Were there any cases in your academic career when you would have done something—a project or a trip or whatever—but external circumstances prevented you from doing so?

JP: Yes. So, one example was—1969, I got a grant from the National Science Foundation to go to Malaya and study Islam, and just before I left, they started having riots in Malaya, and I was unable to get a visa. And so, we went . . . Florence and I and our two oldest daughters went to Malaya, but could not get a visa . . . so, instead we stayed in Singapore for a few months . . . and then I went to Indonesia and . . .

AK: And "lived a year dangerously." (laughs)

JP: Sort of. Well . . . that would have been earlier . . . I joined with . . . Muhammadiyah in 1970.

AK: I watched this film, *The Year of Living Dangerously*,* particularly that year when you were there . . .

JP: We were, but it was earlier. *The Year of Living Dangerously* was 1965, and the study of Muhammadiyah was 1970, so it's five years different. In 1970,

---

* *The Year of Living Dangerously* is a 1982 Australian romantic drama film directed by Peter Weir and cowritten by Weir and David Williamson adapted from Christopher Koch's 1978 novel *The Year of Living Dangerously*.

I met Ruel Tyson . . . he was in the Religious Studies Department. So, we thought, what if we do fieldwork together on fundamentalists?

AK: So, it was his suggestion?

JP: I think, jointly. Because I had just been doing that in Indonesia, with Muhammadiyah. So, we said, what about if we do it here? So, we started doing that. And I had just . . . the thing that I presented at AAA was about Mary Steadly's involvement with that, with Ruel. She was in the folklore program at that time—she was a student of Dan Patterson. So, we started going around, first in Durham, going to many services, and we met all kinds of . . . at that time we were focusing on Pentecostals, in Durham mainly. So, the three of us then were in different ways . . . I was working with each of them separately, but then . . . let me think, when was it? Probably, 1980 or so, we got a grant from the National Endowment for the Humanities, NEH, for about thirty thousand dollars—at that time I think it was the largest grant from NEH that anyone had at Carolina, and it was the three of us. And it was to study two streams of Protestantism: one was called the Arminian stream, these are the ones who believe . . . Arminius was a Dutch theologian . . . it's not the country [Armenia], it is a brand of theology . . . So, these are the two main . . . one is "I chose to be saved," that's the Armenian way, the other is a Calvinist: "God chose whether I'll be saved." Before the creation of the earth.

AK: Predestination?

JP: Predestination—you've got it. So, these are the two mainstreams of Protestantism. And so, we decided to do an ethnographic study of these two streams, and how they work out.

AK: The three of you are: you, Ruel Tyson and . . .

JP: Dan Patterson. So, then we chose Pentecostals to illustrate the Arminian approach, and Primitive Baptists to illustrate the Calvinist. And then we set about doing fieldwork. Both of us. And later all three of us. Beverly as well, who married Dan. She and Dan met—he was a bachelor—they met while we were doing fieldwork together, and then they got married. For the Primitive Baptists, we did the work mainly in the mountains of North Carolina and Virginia. For the Pentecostals, we did it among Black people, Native Americans, and white people. So, we did this work over some years, in the 1980s.

AK: I see a book here, written by her in 1995, *The Sound of the Dove: Singing in Appalachian Primitive Baptist Churches*.

JP: These were the women in the Primitive Baptist church. And then Ruel and I published a book called *Pilgrims of Paradox*. And that was just Primitive Baptists.

AK: So, she is more in the music part . . .

JP: She is an ethnomusicologist. And then we also published some other things, but we have BUSHELS of field notes!!!

AK: Do I understand this correctly that this tripartite project, you, Dan, and Ruel . . .

JP: . . . and Beverly!

AK: OK, this quadruple project—was it the first group project you've ever been involved in?

JP: That's essentially correct. Most my fieldwork has been alone, although sometimes I also worked with some students—like David Howe in Indonesia. In 1979. David Howe got his PhD here, in anthropology, and he studied the Sumarah, which is a mystical . . .

AK: Oh, I remember!

JP: And so, I went there in 1979, and worked with him, and also another person, whose name is Joseph Errington, who is now a professor at Yale. So, we worked together on that, but it was mainly for his dissertation. Joe and I kind of pitched in, and then I had other students involved . . . But you are essentially correct: the only group project that I participated in was this one.

Research on Primitive Baptists

Leedom Lefferts (LL): I discovered that he had actually done a study, here in Western Carolina or Virginia, on Primitive Baptists. And it just so happened that my heritage is Primitive Baptists. [LL's grandfather was a very well-respected minister in Virginia. Leedom is his second name, given after one of his grandmother's last names—this is a family tradition. So, the Leedoms and the Lefferts are the two lines that got married in Pennsylvania. His first name, Harris, is the same as his father's, so he was called Leedom at home from the start.]

But anyway—I found out about his work with Primitive Baptists, and I read his book. I read it—I said: "Yeees! Yeesss! Right on!"

AK: So, you recognized . . . ?

LL: Oh, yes, I'm recognizing it! Even though this is Western North Carolina, and he [his grandfather] was just north of Washington, DC. So, he was more Middle Atlantic as opposed to South . . .

AK: So, you are saying that what you read in this book, *The Pilgrims of Paradox* . . .

LL: Resonated with me! There is something that's different, but something is the same. It's been a while since I read it, because I read it four years ago . . . Tyson is a sociologist, and he sort of bowed out of it, I have a feeling, whereas Peacock carried it to its conclusion.

(2_Lefferts_23_09_2018)

AK: So, Dr. Peacock said at one point, explaining your joint projects, first with Presbyterians and then with Primitive Baptists . . . I asked, how did you switch to this topic after you did Indonesian proletarian theater, and then Muhammadiyah, and he literally said: "I did eight months of study of Muhammadiyah. And they are fundamentalist Muslim. So, I came back from that and I met Ruel Tyson . . . So, he and I had a conversation about Muhammadiyah, and that led us to discussing fundamentalism in Christianity. So, we decided that we would start doing fieldwork together." Do you see this development the same way or? How did you start this project?

Ruel Tyson (RT): That's blurry to me, but here is what happened: when he left for Indonesia, I was . . . I'd say "charged," but I don't know who was charging me, but anyway, here is what happened: with the help of a wonderful person, who was in her MA course at UNC . . . I'm tempted to put a long parenthesis here about her, but I'm going forward. She was assigned to be my helper. And since I don't drive, and I never have, she was the driver.

AK: Her name was Beverly, right?

RT: Beverly, right.

AK: Who later married Dan Patterson?

RT: That's right . . . No, I'm sorry . . . her name was . . . unfortunately, she is deceased. She was at Harvard . . . the first female . . .

AK: Oh, right—Dr. Peacock mentioned her . . . Mary, I think . . .

Fieldwork   117

RT: That's her. Anyway, she was a driver, and I was . . . a notetaker, I guess. So, we left Chapel Hill . . . it's about a two-hour drive down the country, it's south of here. And I'm going to be difficult on names, because I'm losing it. We would go down on a weekend, and I was being very local in my suggestions, so I said: "We cannot be observed in the same locale for . . . over night." So, we found a tourist home for her that took her in and offered breakfast, and for me, I went to a very cheap . . . six rooms, all in a row, and they were probably ten miles apart, but a very clean . . . So, what we did, we started introducing ourselves to what we called "preachers." And by showing up and asking permission to visit.

AK: Showing up for services?

RT: Yeah. So it happened . . . this was in the summertime, and we were able to identify two churches who held services at different times, so we started attending each, and we thought we were being very smart by not mentioning that we were seeing that before. After three weeks, we came to a church one day, and the minister intercepted us and said: "I heard that you were visiting so-and-so one's church." I said: "How did you know that?" He said: "Oh, they told us over the radio this morning." (laughs)

AK: So, they were very different churches?

RT: Yes.

AK: And how did you present yourselves?

RT: Just . . . right out, "We are from university, we want to learn about your religion." And they were very hospitable. So, you'd go there, and it so happened that we began going to each of the churches during . . . I'm trying to think what they called it . . . but anyway, in that community there is a week when everybody goes to the beach, and everything closes down. But these two churches thought that was sinful, so they never closed down, and we were going there, and it wasn't unusual to have only six worshippers there. Because they put on a series of services every weekday, and afternoon, and every weekend, and every night!

AK: So, they were very strict in their . . . beliefs and practices?

RT: The attendance was slightly better at night, but not close to the weekend.

AK: And these are Presbyterians?

RT: No, these are . . . (laughs) . . . each church is . . . they are more connected to the tribal . . . each minister, not only cares for a local group of people, but they are notorious for exchanging pulpits, as they would put it, as far away as up in the north coast up in the eastern edge here. They drive all over the world up there. So, they exchange all the time . . .

AK: But these are not Primitive Baptists?

RT: No, no. They share some few features, but . . . So, we would go there, in the afternoon, about two o'clock, and sometimes there would be only one other person there, the minister and his wife, and so, slowly, people began to come. And there would be singing, there would be . . . If the wife was there, she might give a testimony and would invite everyone present to do so as well. And one of the . . . so happens . . . that I have . . . let's see . . .

AK: If you are looking for the book *Diversities of Gifts*, I have it.

RT: In there . . . actually, I haven't read that in a long time. That would be good to connect right here . . . because I had two wonderful helpers . . . my assistant. As we translated this . . . we recorded it . . . but boy, I would think . . . I don't know, how many hours we put . . . it turned up . . . we'd put around maybe . . . eight pages, but those eight pages took us . . . I don't even know, a long time.

AK: And you were already doing some formal project, or you were doing the "reconnaissance" of the field, so to speak?

RT: Well, I . . . maybe Jim already told you that—let's go back for a moment. Early one summer we decided to canvass every church in Durham, North Carolina, and so, he would be driving, and I get terrible . . . on mapping and so forth. (laughs) And so, we would spend . . . he always reminds us . . . we had very little money, so he would drive us over to the Durham County line, and we would try to make appointments, to reach the minister . . . We used the Yellow Pages, that's what we were using. And so, during the course of that summer, when we were both working together, I don't know, what the count was, but we saw the churches, we tried to have conversations with the minister, and we were really looking for a place to do fieldwork. And we found one. Again, the identity of the group . . . it was a large denomination, there were several . . . I used to know all the words they were using . . .

AK: To describe themselves?

RT: Or . . . we were in the same circle . . . that would not be the word they used, but . . . So, we started to go to church there and made good friends

Fieldwork

with the preacher and his wife. She had her own job, so she was not part of the . . . but she was always present. They had a congregation of forty to fifty people, that's in Durham, so we already had our . . .

AK: So, you were trying to find your field basically? That's why you went from church to church . . .

RT: That's right.

AK: It cannot be then connected to the fundamentalism in Indonesia that Dr. Peacock had studied prior to that?

RT: Well, you know, I have no recollection of any explicit conversations about any comparisons. He was probably . . . I would have reminded . . . it would become a motif . . . but as far as I remember, any comparisons at that stage of exploration were not paramount in our concerns.

AK: They probably emerged later.

RT: That's right! I think . . . I'm guessing . . . I'm sure we got close to fifty churches. Many of them were obviously not what we were looking for, they were mainline churches, Baptist and Methodist . . . We were looking for more exciting churches.

AK: That's my next question: now you can find lots of books on any denomination, church . . . so, that was not the case at the time? You were looking for a church that had not been studied before, right?

RT: Honestly, I don't think we were wise enough to look at that . . . no, we just dropped in. And spent that whole summer going back and forth.

AK: Without any grant money, just on your own?

RT: On our own. So, it was probably next summer that we split, and he went away, and I went down to . . . where I was talking about first.

AK: Aha, with this woman?

RT: Aha. Right. So, *Diversities of Gifts*—if you read it, you'll know more than I remember.

AK: And so, then he gets back from Indonesia, and you decide to do a big joint project together . . .

RT: But we didn't have any leave from this place, so we were working on the weekends. And we got one of the largest grants ever made when we began doing the Primitive Baptists in the mountains. I think we got some local support from the university.

AK: So, this was something you were doing parallel to teaching, service . . .

RT: That's right.

AK: And then there was this National Endowment for Humanities . . .

RT: That was the big one. It gave us two years of support, and every summer we studied that particular group of churches . . . It has two churches in Virginia and two churches in North Carolina, and it's a perfect line-up . . . you should go and have a look.

[RT doesn't know Leedom Lefferts; AK tells about his Primitive Baptist background.]

RT: One of their [Primitive Baptists'] commonplace claims is "We are a dying denomination." And they seem to enjoy this melancholy report, and truth is, I don't know how many of them we got to know, are still living.

AK: Which of the groups you studied are most . . . interesting for you—and why?

RT: It would be the Baptists . . . Old Baptists. There, in the mountains. I think we got closer to more people in that group than we did in any other. With a couple of exceptions—like, once . . . Jim will be able to remember her—once we were in Durham, doing the survey, and someone told us about this lady who was . . . I don't know the word . . . ecstatic . . . a special kind of preacher. And we finally got an appointment with her. And she was upstairs, in a rental building, a very small building, in Durham, and she invited us to meet her there. And we got started interviewing her in a usual way, and then she turned the interview to us, and before it ended, she had us standing up with her hands on both of our heads. Each by head . . . prayer song, and telling us something . . . we had the spirit (laughs), and we were both tongue-tied . . . And that fit well with her need to preach . . . We finally dissolved our connection literally, and then a funny thing happened: we got into Jim's car, and drove maybe two to three miles, and I said: "Jim, you reckon that she was going to turn that little fan off?" That was the only thing in that upper room that was electrical . . . And we both: "Let's go back! Let's go back and see." But it was locked, and . . . sloppy us, we didn't even bother to get the address, we gathered that she would give it anyway. So, that was a little . . . nervy.

Fieldwork   121

AK: Maybe she was taken to the heavens for her preaching? (laughs)

RT: Yes, that's right, that's right . . .

AK: Did you feel any change, after you've worked with these different people, including this woman—did it produce any personal impact upon you?

RT: Yes . . .

AK: Did you feel the spirit? (laughs)

RT: Oh, no . . . but it did educate me to a degree of respect for the Primitive Baptists of the Mountain district. And their hospitality was extraordinary. And their view of the world was systematically hard, and here is how it goes: they did not believe in election. At least they would not know about it—if they were. They hoped they were elect. And so they would confess—that would be their word to use—that on some occasion, while plowing on the upper fields, they found themselves singing . . . and they again hoped that the Holy Spirit was touching them. But they never claimed that it was. And that was the attractive feature I felt for that particular group of people. They were hard—that's one of the words they use—"We are hard people. We are hard-shell." And they mean by that—as against the Evangelicals. They looked down on them: "Those are Evangelicals, it's so easy for them," they say. And I think connected with their severe view of election . . . they were very, very charitable. And would . . . well, Jim and I were invited to spend a night with an elderly couple. And by the time to go to bed, we found that we had to walk through their bedroom to get upstairs to ours. The same was true when we needed to go to the bathroom. That was part of the deal, that was not unusual for them. And the truth is, many of these people were . . . owned lots of land, and they were very frugal, boy, they were not hungry!

AK: So, it's not a poor community? They were pretty well-off?

RT: Yeah, yeah, but they would never brag about that. They would say: "We were blessed." But they would never brag about that.

AK: So, it was like this Weberian work ethic . . .

RT: That's right.

AK: Do they proselytize?

RT: Never! And that includes their own children. One (?) we encountered about this: "Well, I reckon my daughter, she is going to school down in Chapel Hill, she will become a Methodist . . . that's a little sad . . . " But then again, there is a cycle, I think . . . if they . . . most (?) of them come back to . . . some did . . . the longer they were there, the likelier they would begin to move in with the older people who had been there a long time. And there is very little mobility. And that's why they say: "Oh, they'll go down to Chapel Hill and become (?), and then they'll come back." But . . . they wanted them to come back—that's how they managed . . . at that point they were agricultural. Previously there were a lot among them who worked in mills—cotton mills and so forth. But that was beginning to die off already back then.

AK: So, you liked this hard-shell type of philosophy?

RT: Hard-shell, definitely, yes. But one of the things I found . . . so, their very severity was . . . I would say "balanced," but that's not a good word here. Their very severity seemed to evoke much charity and help-giving.

AK: Even though they were not trying to bring people in, they were . . . ?

RT: Exactly!

AK: A weird type of exchange . . .

RT: Yes. I'm sure we must have recorded some of the better sermons that we found . . . I couldn't tell you where they are.

AK: I found your papers, 1970s–1991, at the Southern Historical Collection: is that where they are?

RT: Yes, and I was up to . . .

AK: How many? Are they in boxes, or . . . ? How much material is there?

RT: I've lost that number, but . . . there must have been at least six to seven churches . . . they go to each other's church. And there is a service on Saturday afternoon, Saturday evening, Sunday morning, and sometimes Sunday afternoon. And there is a lot preaching . . . and I think Jim told you about that . . . because one of the unique features of that particular religion is the following: if they go to the pulpit, with the Bible in hand, they have read the text that they want to preach on, and . . . By the way, most of them didn't read it, but they were preaching from it. So, if they would preach for a few minutes, and they felt that the Holy Spirit was not with them— "Well, brothers, I'm getting out of the way, and let's brother so-and-so try the speech . . ." But of course they only did when there was another brother to call in . . .

AK: And it's only men who can do that?

RT: That's right, only men, yeah. And then the apex of their . . . we would say "liturgy" is that once a year they hold this . . . what would it be called? . . .

AK: Like, convention?

RT: It was a certain service, in which washing of feet occurred. And that was fascinating, because you had older women having their feet washed by a younger woman . . . there was always sexual . . .

AK: Ah! Women—to women, men to men . . . ?

RT: Yes, that's right. And older men being washed by . . . they did each others! Reciprocity! And my wife, and Jim's wife were there on a Sunday when this happened. And they were invited to take over a hose and . . . they can tell you about all that. And then everybody who came to that service would have brought a huge amount of food and spread it . . . on the grounds with tables, outside. It's usually held in August.

AK: Not around Easter time? Washing of the feet . . .

RT: No, that's not in there . . . So, they celebrate, there is a lot of food, lots of joking and laughing, and they love to invite people for that.

AK: Do they have any dietary restrictions? Do they eat everything?

RT: No, [they don't have restrictions].

AK: Do they fast?

RT: No.

AK: Do they drink alcohol?

RT: Certainly not in the service or in the supper afterward . . . That's a good question—I don't think they do alcohol, but I'm a little wobbly on that.

AK: Is their communion under both kinds? Both bread and wine?

RT: Bread and wine. Their wine is real wine.

AK: Oh, so, the communion wine is real wine?

RT: Yes. And what was so different about them is that the deacons, after they served, everyone who was . . . they wouldn't say, who should come up, but those who felt they would come up . . . When all that was over . . . we're talking about anti . . . they would throw all the wine out of the window! (laughs) Because they are . . . "we don't want to sacralize anything." That wouldn't be their word, but that's what they meant.

AK: So, this was the most . . . unique and exotic . . . and the most attractive . . . ? But did you, Dr. Peacock, or your wives have a desire to join Primitive Baptists?

RT: No . . .

AK: Would you be able to do so?

RT: I think that would be suspect until you had been at the services for a long time. I don't think . . . that would require the local church to be agreeable, but they are . . . in their religious . . .

AK: . . . the territorial body?

RT: Right. That's pretty random . . . all kinds of fights among the different . . . so . . . and we never got to talk about their politics or . . . They were very . . . you go into their homes, and the church is bare (?), and the homes are full with things these people made or bought, and that's a dramatic difference.

AK: Would you say Dr. Peacock was easy to work with, or did he have any specific features . . .

RT: I would say, quite easy to work with. And I only remember one . . . I guess I would call it "spat," and I can picture it right now: I was running about (?), about some implication or something, and I don't know if he was feeling badly or something, and I guess he just got tired and said: "Tyson! Can't you talk about anything else, not this stuff?!" (laughs)

AK: So, that's the only . . .

RT: I said: "No!" (laughs) Anyway . . . you know, you build up certain tensions. But . . . no, it's amazingly harmonious and long-lasting . . .

AK: So, you were compatible as . . .

RT: Yes, I would say we were super-compatible.

(6_Tyson_21_01_2019)

Beverly Patterson (BP): There were several grants, not just one. At least... One of the earlier things we did before we settled in for Primitive Baptists was to look across the spectrum of religious...

Dan Patterson (DP): Maybe it was "White, Lumbee and Black" forms of Pentecostals...

BP: Pentecostal, yes.

AK: What's the second word?

DP: Lumbee—Native Americans, in Robeson County.

BP: Black and white Pentecostals, and the Lumbee—Robeson County.

AK: What's your version—why Pentecostals? Because according to Dr. Peacock's... by that time he had done Muhammadiyah, which is fundamental Muslims. And then, according to what he said, he comes back and with Ruel Tyson they think, what can they do together. And they thought: OK, from fundamentalist Muslims to fundamentalism Christians. Now—Ruel Tyson does not make this connection. He said: we were just off to Durham, and we were stopping at every church, trying to make contacts with people and with pastors, and somehow we ended up studying Pentecostals. So, what's your version of how it came about?

DP: I think it was more designed than that... my recollection is... well [to BP] you were involved in it, I wasn't, but went there once or twice I think ... to one of Durham churches.

BP: Well, I don't know whether it was the "World and Identity" project—do they use that description?

DP: This was earlier than "World and Identity"...

BP: What I'm thinking we were doing was... extremes... religious... Wesleyan belief system—and the Calvinist. Kind of on a continuum.

DP: Well, I think you did this first, and...

BP: We did the Pentecostals first...

DP: And then I was working with... because of my own personal acquaintance with Elder Evans... I love his music. And I was their connection to that thing, and then we focused primarily on Primitive Baptists for about two years, didn't we?

BP: Yes.

DP: We went to many different churches in western North Carolina, and the mountain association there . . . a number of churches in that association we focused on, and then carried it over to Kentucky, the music that you were studying . . .

BP: Well, it brings people into your life that you wouldn't have ever known otherwise. And that you like. And you see other ways of thinking. They were doing things, and we learned a lot about . . . just, I think, a sense of community.

AK: Who was the main . . . how was your group structured, a group of four, three men and a woman—who was the leader, or was there any leader . . . what kind of a group was it?

BP: Well, I was a graduate student at that point. And since I was the only woman, I got to talk to the women. When Dan would interview men, who were song leaders, and . . . special knowledge of song and music tradition that I didn't [know]—I didn't interview men. And when I tried to talk to the women about music, they didn't want to talk about music, they wanted to tell me about their family situations.

DP: I guess in that tradition, too, they would be timid about offering opinions about things like music.

BP: The women—that was not their sphere, the men took care of all of that.

AK: In this tradition . . . but in the tradition where this woman was talking about the wind going through her . . . being called . . .

DP: They could talk about their religious experience . . .

AK: But not the music.

DP: They could talk about the structure of the church, things that were going on in the church, not necessarily if they were approving of them . . . Women, at least some of them, were really the force behind . . . this organization going.

BP: Right. Because they did . . . whenever a visiting preacher would come—that was often—and distinct members of the congregation came—many people had two . . . and especially church ladies, who were leaders of the church, would have two kitchens.

BP: The women did a lot with food—bringing the community together. They did *huge* amounts of cooking. And just expected people to come home after the service, and they might have twenty or thirty people for lunch or whatever.

DP: And it took two stoves, and two refrigerators, and some place.

BP: Once, I think, it was just you, and Jim, and Ruel, at one person's house for a meal . . . Three kinds of meat, five kinds of vegetables, breads, deserts . . .

AK: What a great field!

DP: They are wonderful cooks! And a wonderful country-style food! But then usually there would be two . . . see, likely as many as three preachers in the service. One may read a prayer, and another preach, and another maybe . . .

BP: They'd all preach! They would all be invited to preach!

DP: They would all preach. Invited to preach, that's right. And a man who would be invited, would stand up and go to the pulpit, and not feel that he had the spirit with him today, because they thought they preached by God, who preaches through them. But if their inspiration (?) didn't come, they would make no bones about it, but simply: "Lord is not with me today, he is not giving me anything to say." Let somebody else come and take my place [at the pulpit].

(7_The_Pattersons_Feb_9_2019)

AK: How about this trip to Elder Evans and the washing of the feet?

Cece Conway (CC): What I remember, I was with you and Beverly and Ruel. And I think Dan wanted me to go so that Beverly wouldn't be a lone female there. And so, we went to the foot washing, and we had dinner on the grounds, it was wonderful, and I was excited because Elder Evans played the fiddle.

JP: Which was very rare.

CC: Well . . . but they never played instruments in the church.

AK: That's Primitive Baptists?

CC: That's Primitive Baptists, and it's in our movie, at a different place, and the men sat on one side, and women on the other side, and you can see a little footage . . . another group of Primitive Baptists. And then I think they stayed . . . Where did you stay when we were doing that field?

JP: There was a school . . . it might have been in a place called Glades or something like that. They had a school, and during summer there was nobody there, and that's where Dan, and I, and Ruel, and I guess later Beverly stayed—instead of staying in a motel.

CC: And so, that first night I took Beverly with me to Tommy Jarrell's in Mount Airy, and you were in . . . the fieldwork was near Sparta.

JP: That's where we stayed.

(12_Peacock_Conway_July_30_2019)

Anecdote from the Field: Primitive Baptists

AK: Do you remember any funny anecdotes, stories from your fieldwork where Dr. Peacock would play some kind of a role? Some funny situations, something funny said . . .

DP: The thing I remember most vividly is conversations we had as we drove away from an event—all four of us in a car: you, me, Jim, and Ruel. And we'd have been talking about what we have seen, and what we undertook—that was really stimulating and interesting. Because they were saying things very different from ours. Ours were much more limited, and theirs were much more ranging . . . philosophical . . .

AK: Like a mini-seminar in a car . . . ?

DP: Yeah.

BP: Right! Well, I remember something that was not really academic at all. Our living situation, when we went to the mountains . . . it was a kind of a . . . it used to be a camp for something, I'm not sure . . . they were buildings that were not being used. And so, Jim was able, I think, to rent a couple of places. One was like a . . .

DP: A little house!

BP: Well, where I lived, was a little house, it was all by itself out in a pasture. That was just down the hill from where Jim and Ruel and Dan stayed. A dormitory . . .

DP: Not too far away.

BP: Some hundreds of feet maybe. And I'm all by myself. And I discovered that there were mice in my house. (DP laughs) And I didn't really know what to do about that. So, I thought, I would report it to Jim. Which I did, and I think we ended up . . . we got some mouse traps, and got all those mouse traps all set, and caught a mouse. Or more than one mouse. And so, I went up to report that, and so I said: "Jim, what do I . . . "—I expected, as soon as I said, you know, I got a mouse in the trap, that he would come down and take it. (laughs) And I said, oh, goodness! What he said, was: "Oh, you take care of it!" (all laugh)

(7_The_Pattersons_Feb_9_2019)

AK: They also took one of their daughters to one of the countries where Professor Peacock did his research, when they grew up a little bit.

Nerys Levy (NL): They didn't grow them there in a sense . . . they took them there, but . . . Florence is the one who was in the field. And Florence was the one who really built relationships—you know, the gamelan, the music . . . she had her own life around this. And she came from a very privileged background, but she didn't mind marrying an anthropologist. Because he is honest. Florence is very honest. And she could see his qualities—I mean, he doesn't lie, he doesn't mess around, and I think people resonated with this. When he was an anthropologist, he was out there as he was, as a person, you know, he wasn't . . .

AK: . . . pretending . . .

NL: . . . removed or worried, and I'm sure a lot of people are like that, but he was of that generation, and people who followed him were much more like that, but at that generation, still, to be an anthropologist was still to be a little removed. Which is why anthropology in a sense, I think, was put aside, because people couldn't quite get . . . it wasn't social work, it wasn't . . . you know, they couldn't quite access it. People went . . . it's courses longer than medicine, you know, because of all the things you have to do. So, you tell people, it's longer than medical school, because by the time you do your required courses, then you do your language training, then you do your field, and then you come back . . .

AK: Your field and the transcription of all . . .

NL: And you are not a missionary, you know. All those things. And then you get married, and you have kids, because so long everybody . . . That's why anthropologists are so close to their students. Because it's a very long relationship. It's not just people who come through. It's like doctors with their medical students—they have very good relationships. It's not just a graduate student who goes through a graduate school, because the nature of the study, and also . . . you know, we had everybody's motorbike in our house, things in the ceiling, you know . . . I mean . . .

AK: And then they go to the same field, and bring presents from . . .

NL: This is it—it's like a family, you know. So, I think Jim, because he was very personable . . . and Florence is very personable, so to go out there with Florence . . . he didn't go out there alone, he went with Florence, and I think that was really important.

(10_Levy_Nerys_July_27_2019)

AK: Now—you are very much involved in what your husband was doing, and Florence was, too—how typical would you say that anthropologists' families . . . ?

NL: Oh, so—it's very . . . they have to be committed. You cannot be an anthropologist and be single-minded about it as a removed subject, like, maybe, philosophy. You go in and out of the university . . . sit at the table thinking about it . . . It requires a lot of physical commitment on behalf of family.

(10_Levy_Nerys_July_27_2019)

JP: First of all, let me say about Florence: she has done a lot of types of music, it's not just classical. And this is a story that y'all may never have heard—maybe Cece had. So, Florence went to Yale School of Music. But she grew up just singing anything under the sun. While she was at Yale School of Music, the Yale Repertory Theatre, which is the drama company for Yale, did a show in New York, which was called "John Brown's Body." I never saw it—I didn't even know her then. And I don't know what it was about—we could ask her. So, she was a soprano for the show, and somebody heard her, who was from Broadway, and he offered her a job . . . well, I'd say more than job, he offered her a leading role in "Once Upon a Mattress," which was about to be developed starring Carol Burnett. And I never knew that she got that opportunity until many, many years after we got married, but she turned it down. And she said, one reason she turned it down was because I invited her to go live in a slum in Indonesia. (general laughter) For which she was rewarded by being bit by a mad dog, and all kinds of things. But that tells a little bit about her musical career.

(13_Peacock_Conway_McCanless_July_31_2019)

AK: But that was a general tendency, because some time in 1970s people started performing this "homecoming," from those remote "exotic" countries or islands—back to home.

NL: And a lot of people started not to do fieldwork, they started to look at texts, and they stopped doing fieldwork. And for him to do fieldwork in the United States, a lot of people in the 1980s and 1990s were doing texts as opposed to fieldwork. There was this thing, you know, with all this postmodernism, people were reinterpreting . . . And then the outcome of this was that people went into . . . started questioning all the fieldwork that a lot of anthropologists were doing . . .

AK: Like Malinowski . . .

NL: Yeah, like, why did you do this? Why did you want to live with these Trobriands? Why did you go over . . . you know. We worked with Kenneth Emory, and we went, with my husband, to this remote island in the Pacific, which Kenneth Emory had visited, oh, in the 1930s, and had written a book *Road My Body Goes*. So, we were going back there. So, we took the book to show the people—and these were people now who saw these photographs for the first time as children, in the study, and they remember him, but the island hadn't really changed because it was so remote. But what was interesting was sharing rather than just taking, giving back. And to give back we left the book there—not that anybody could read English, we left the book there, so they can show people the pictures.

(10_Levy_Nerys_July_27_2019)

AK: Let's talk a bit about the field. You said, you did some fieldwork together with Dr. Peacock?

CC: Yes, but I will only do a little bit of that because it's better for us to do it together. When they started the Primitive Baptist fieldwork, they took me with them on the first event. It was Jim, Ann Willow, and Dan, and then Beverly went along. And I had my car. We went to a foot washing and picnic on the grounds that Elder Evans did. Of course, for me, what was especially significant was that Elder Evans was a fiddle player. And that was at a place called No Creek Baptist Church. Because they didn't have a creek—they believed in total emersion. Just like in Weber's trip to Mount Airy, they were baptizing people in the river. No creek! Very clever. Then I somehow took Beverly with me to Mount Airy, and we spent the night there and came back the next day, and then I did some fieldwork with Black folks in Boone (?) . . . Beverly and me, we left them [Jim and Dan] in one of those big houses and went to another town, where the fiddle player was, and she and I stayed together at Tommy Jarrell's, the fiddle player's. But of course, it is the case in Primitive Baptist churches that men sat on one side, and women sat on the other side.

AK: So, Dr. Peacock was working in different fields, and he started in Indonesia, and then made this "home-coming" as many anthropologists then did, and started working in the United States . . . Why do you think he made this turn to begin with?

CC: Well, one thing, which I didn't think too much about, but the fact that he liked what the folklorists did, which was all here, almost no folklorists would go to other countries, and found them interesting, they have inspired or encouraged him . . . and he also cares about his culture, you know.

AK: And he is a Southerner!

CC: Yes, he is a Southerner, a place he often had to defend, and he never gave up his global . . . Grounded Globalism is really a symbol of both.

AK: And it's also about inclusion and multiculturalism in the South as well.

CC: Uh-huh. And he was trained in the North, at Harvard, and taught at Princeton, but he came home, to North Carolina, which at the time was at least more amenable to progressivism.

(11_Conway_July_29_2019)

Mule Auction

AK: Can I ask you a question about your common experience with the horse auction? Or mule auction?

JP: Ohhh! That was with Dan Patterson.

CC: Dan Patterson, and Jim, and me, and a woman who was doing her folklore thesis . . . Page!

JP: Page . . . Holmes! And . . . if it's not on my list, I have a cassette, it's not our fieldwork, but some of the stories she recorded with the horse trader. The mule- and horse trader. And partly . . . one of the reasons it's so interesting, it's because of the characters in Faulkner's novels.

JP: Yeah, the mule is . . .

Fieldwork

CC: In *Barn Burning*, the father is a horse trader, and he does a lot of horse trading. Anyway—we went down there, the four of us, together. And the sale was in Asheboro. And I think it started about nine or ten, and I think Dan usually went to bed pretty early, so it's remarkable that he came with us. It was fun, and the man was a cool guy, and a good trader, and a good host, but the main other thing I remember when we were actually there, that a little before midnight I got to gallop around the stock-yard, on the horse, one of the horses that he had.

AK: Anything else about that trip?

CC: I remember sitting in the auction . . .

JP: Oh, I remember sitting there, but I don't remember anything . . . really . . . sensational. I mean, I remember it as a really wonderful experience.

(12_Peacock_Conway_July_30_2019)

Bill Peck (BiP): . . . all I know is that religious studies was the field I was specializing in. And whenever I would go to Guatemala, I would meet shamans there. So, I did essentially fieldwork there. So, one time we went together to Guatemala.

AK: This must have very interesting for Dr. Peacock—the shamans. This in-between-ness, in between the worlds . . .

BiP: Yes, yes—soft lens!

AK: And sharp focus!

BiP: Yes, sharp focus.

AK: Did you do any research together, like, applying for a grant?

BiP: No, we did not. Our fields were sufficiently separate . . . So, I'm an enthusiastic defender of anthropology, mainly because of my relation to Jim; he is an excellent perceiver of realities.

(19_Peck_Aug_26_2019)

AK: We don't want to produce an ideal picture of Dr. Peacock, with wings . . .

Susan Reintjes (SR): No, no—I don't see him in that way. But Ichabod Crane to me is more like that long, tall . . . and aware of other worlds. Like, headless horseman or communication with people who have died—so, that's what I do. And he was very interested in what I did.

AK: Anthropology is about mediation. Anthropologists mediate, translate among cultures.

SR: That's what you are doing, you try to build bridges between. And I'm a bridge between the world of coma and consciousness and death. [About Professor Peacock's various field trips:] He is really going far—and near, and then bridging, and bridging, and seeing the connections . . .

(14_Reintjes_Aug_9_2019)

Grants and Other Financial Support

AK: How many major grants did you get in your career?

JP: On the whole . . . another major grant was a little bit later, and this was in the 1980s, with Ruel Tyson and Dan Patterson. And that was through the National Endowment for Humanities. So, I had a fairly large NIH grant that is the one we just discussed, and then the NEH grant. And there were a whole bunch of others, but they . . . I could quickly run through them, if you want me to.

AK: Are they on your CV?

JP: Maybe . . . maybe not. NSF was . . . all right, the first grant I had was with NIH, or NMH, and that was for my dissertation in Indonesia. The next grant was a little bit later, in 1969, and that one . . . I have three grants. I had a grant from NSF, and I had a grant from Wenner-Gren Foundation, and I had a grant from SSRC, Social Science Research Council. And that was for study of . . . reformist Islam in Southeast Asia. It involved Singapore, Malaysia, and Indonesia.

AK: Were these all individual grants?

JP: Yeah, they were all for the same project. That year, that grant . . . Then I got a grant . . . I did that work in 1969 and 1970, and then came back, and then I got a grant from NSF, the National Science Foundation, and that was to analyze a lot of the information statistically. And that gave rise to one book, which is called *Muslim Puritans*. So, here was a background factor: UNC at that time, and I think even today, did not give sabbaticals. So, if you wanted to get away and do research, you had to get a grant from somewhere. So, that's what I did.

AK: If they didn't have sabbaticals, that also means that they'd have to hire somebody while you are away, right? It's not that they didn't give the money, but they won't let you go basically?

JP: You would have to provide money to hire somebody in addition to money for you to go somewhere.

AK: Wow.

JP: Although that part was a little bit flexible. You see . . . it wasn't, either . . . if you wanted to go away, you would lose your salary. So, you would need money for you to go away, and then they could use your salary for the replacement. So, those grants I mentioned, they permitted me to go to Southeast Asia, 1969 and 1970. Then I came back, and then I was chair of the department till 1980. And then in 1980, around 1980, I got this NEH grant, and that was for the work that Tyson and I . . .

AK: It was a group grant?

JP: Group grant. Then . . . so, then the "Transcendence" grant came along, and that was 1979, that's when I went to Indonesia and worked with David Howe a little bit. Then I got the NEH and did the work in the United States on Protestantism and stuff. Then I got a Guggenheim, and we went to England for a year. Guggenheim did not pay very much, but we didn't . . . cost very much, either. (laughs) That's when I wrote this short book *Anthropological Lens*. And that was really the first time when I actually got the grant to write something, as opposed to fieldwork. That was 1980, 1981, I think. Then at some point I got some visiting professorships at various places. So, I went back to Princeton in 1990, I was in Yale for part of 1986, I was at California, San-Diego, 1973—you know, just teaching, as a visitor.

AK: They invited you, or did you apply?

JP: No, I didn't apply, they invited . . . but I was just a visiting professor, those were not grants.

AK: Would that be typical for a professor at this stage of his or her life to be invited to other places?

JP: It was typical, but maybe I got invited more than some people. And maybe less than others. So, then there was a kind of a change in grant-getting in this way: so, let's see . . . 1996, we went to Indonesia again, and lived with Tati and her family. Her sister, those two. And I think there was a grant involved in that, too, but I can't remember exactly, what it was. We were there in 1996, for several months, and I came back, and they needed somebody to direct the new University Center for International Studies, UCIS. So, they asked me to do that. So, then I started getting a whole bunch of grants . . . well, some of them were already gotten, by Craig Calhoun, so I cannot take credit for getting those. But one of them . . . Rockefeller. So, Ruel Tyson and I got a grant from The Rockefeller Foundation. So, we got several grants through the Institute for Arts and Humanities. Ruel created it, but I was involved also. It's over at Hyde Hall. At that time, it did not have a place, but it was in a little building. So, we applied to Rockefeller Foundation, and so we got money to do various things. One of the first things we did was we held a conference, and it was on the Global South. That was at the Friday Center.

AK: That's when Ben Anderson was invited?

JP: Correct. We had four hundred who came, and thirty groups that met—it was a big conference. And the money came from Rockefeller. And then also I had a series of grants through Rockefeller that involved seminars, and so I taught seminars on the South. And the money paid for some visiting scholars. So, we had scholars from Japan, and Louisiana, (laughs) you know . . . from various places. And they all came, and they did a project, and so there are many books actually that were published through these Rockefeller grants. So, then I took over the UCIS and again applied to Rockefeller. So, we got another Rockefeller grant, and that paid for . . . oh, yeah, we had one or two others. Oh . . . who were they from? I think we had three or four from Rockefeller, and then we had one or two from other foundations, and those paid for postdocs for various people, like Emiliano. So, he came to Chapel Hill. He got a postdoc from us, his major is history. So, these were postdocs that had to do with global subjects.

AK: But what kind of money are we talking about—like, the first Rockefeller grant that supported so many publications, and it's the 1990s, so . . . approximately, just out of curiosity . . .

JP: You mean, how much? During those years . . . let me think . . . 1996 to my stepping down in 2003 . . . several million dollars in various grants. Some from Rockefeller, some from the National Science Foundation, some from this or that. There were one or two other foundations.

AK: So, basically, first you were getting grants for your own research, and then . . . [distributing grants among others].

JP: Precisely! That's it! These were not grants for my research; they were grants for others. They were grants for postdocs from other schools, they were grants for foreign scholars to come . . .

AK: So, once you occupied this position at UCIS, you started attracting grants for the organization to distribute them . . .

JP: Precisely—not for me. Virtually zero for me. I think that is correct. None of that went for me.

AK: What was your last personal grant so far? That you got for your own research?

JP: Very little. I mean, starting in 1996 most of my grant-getting activity was for the organization and for these other people. And as I say, it was several million dollars, but I have to kind of break it down. The only personal grant that I can think of along that time was a very small one, and it was from the Wenner-Gren Foundation . . . And what it went for was to . . . they had small grants for archiving. And so, this one went to copy twenty thousand slides that are now in the Smithsonian and the Southern Historical Collection . . . That's what that one was for. And it wasn't all that much, but it was enough to do that.

AK: Dr. Peacock started working in Indonesia, but then he moved back and did a lot of research here . . .

NL: He worked with religions here, and with Ruel, but he was also interested in . . . native people, and that included white people. He didn't draw the line at . . . Cherokees or anything, but he looked at the Appalachian religion, or Pentecostal religion, you know. Because they were getting a lot of students here, and I think he was also interested in broadening the base of UNC, getting people to come to the university. He saw the public university as a place for everybody.

AK: He gave me an explanation of how he switched from Muhammadiyah to Pentecostals: he said, in his view now, this was a transition from fundamentalist Muslims to fundamentalist Christians. But Ruel Tyson disagreed with that, he said, it was more or less accidental that they started doing this . . .

NL: Well, I think it was probably a bit of both, but I think he probably understood . . . he was probably more sensitized to different groups in your country. Because once you've been through an anthropological experience, as you know, you are more in tune with the diversity in your own situation, and you know it's not all overseas . . . You can apply everything both ways.

(10_Levy_Nerys_July_27_2019)

BiP: Jim saw all that and he remembered things about Indonesia that were parallel to things in Guatemala. Every time we ran around a corner, he would say: "This is just like Indonesia!"

(19_Peck_Aug_26_2019)

CHAPTER 6

Consciousness and Symbols, the Nike Course, and Other Courses

"A veteran course"

AK: Maybe, then, our course would be one big extended example of how academics live in this world, what they do . . .

JP: Exactly.

"I Don't Want Any Wholeness," Or, How It All Started

Jim Peacock (JP): Jung . . . I'm trying to remember, how that came in, and it maybe that . . . maybe thirty years ago I was one of the founding members of the new society in the Triangle, which was called the C. G. Jung Society. But that went back to an experience, when I had just graduated from college . . . I will try to make it shorter, but . . . I worked at a psychiatric hospital in the summer in Delaware. And one of my fellow workers was a woman named Ann Willey. And so, when I finished college, I'd just finished, and I went to Germany. And on the way to Germany I went . . . to New York, and I saw Ann Willey, and she asked me . . . or said something about, well, "Have you read Carl Jung?" And I said: "Yes, I've read. But I don't want any wholeness!"

Anna Kushkova (AK): Do you remember why you said it so explicitly, "I don't want any wholeness?"

JP: I think I was rebellious. Right. OK. So, I first taught the course . . . let me think . . . in 1966. Spring of 1966, Princeton University. It was my first year of teaching. During the fall I had taught a large course in general anthropology, I had a hundred students, and among those hundred students was one, whose name was James Boon. And also another one, whose name was Bruce Richmond. And then another one, who was Funk. Those were in the course, and one reason I remember . . . knew them . . . there were a hundred students, but we had 12 discussion sections, and they were called preceptorials. And see, I was the only anthropology faculty member at Princeton, and there were no graduate students in anthropology, and so we did not have TAs at that time. And so I was the one who did all of the discussion sections, I did all the lectures. I also did another graduate seminar, which people took who were in sociology and so forth. Carlos was another student in that beginning. At the same time that I was starting to teach at Princeton, a colleague whose name was David Crabb, was a linguist, and he also was at Princeton, in the Linguistics Department, but he was an anthropological linguist. And so, he and I had an idea of starting an Anth- . . . because Princeton did not have an Anthropology Department. In the past they occasionally hired an anthropologist . . . and some of them . . . became well known. Lloyd Fallows was one of them—he later taught at the University of Chicago, and another was Paul Bohannan . . .

AK: That's Africa.

JP: Correct. And social anthropology. But each of them were there for several years, and then they moved. So, here came . . . me. Here I came. David Crabb and I had an idea . . . we had two ideas. One was—and I'll come to that in a moment—symbolic anthropology. It was my idea, really, but it was related to the idea of starting a new department . . . starting a department in anthropology.

AK: Not just, like, introducing a course or two . . .

JP: Starting a new department. So, this was my idea—that there are many anthropology departments, but this one is a new one, and it would have to start small, and so, let's not do general anthropology, which means four-field and all that . . . archaeology . . . because there were many . . . if you look at Ivy League schools . . . you think of Harvard, Yale . . .

AK: Princeton?

JP: Well, not yet Princeton.

AK: Oh, Princeton was not yet an Ivy League . . . ?

JP: Oh, yes, it was Ivy League, but they didn't have an anthropology department. Harvard had a very old anthropology department. Yale had an old anthropology department . . .

AK: How come Princeton didn't?

JP: Who knows? . . . So, Crabb and I had an idea: let's start one! And then I had this idea, which was: OK, we have all these big old departments that have four fields, but we're starting small, so let's don't do four fields, let's focus on something! So, my idea was, let's focus on symbolic anthropology, which did not yet exist. It was not yet a discipline.

AK: Why did you call it this if it didn't exist?

JP: We had yet another idea at the same time: OK, start a department and have a focus. So, my proposal was: let's focus on symbols. And David was a linguist, and so he agreed with that idea; he liked that idea, too.

AK: Cultural symbols? Because language is a symbolic system as well, so it will be close . . .

JP: Right—semiotics, signs . . . he was a linguist. But I was a social anthropologist with an interest in . . .

AK: So, you were thinking of the symbolism in a broader sense . . . cultural symbols . . . material symbols and linguistic symbols?

JP: Correct—all of those. And so, here is what happened: I think it was that year. So, David and I made contact with a man whose name was Morris Philipson, who was the editor of the University of Chicago Press and who was a philosopher. And so, David and I proposed to him, whom I had never met, that we do a series in symbolic anthropology. Which we did.

AK: The books, you mean . . . a series?

JP: As a series. And he accepted that idea, and the first book in the series was to be my study of the ludruk. Which at that time I was writing, based on my dissertation, but I was rewriting it to make it into a book. So, I was doing that. At the same time, I was teaching in my first year, so I was creating a course in general anthropology, and I can tell you about that course later, but that's what it was. And I was teaching twelve discussion sections and was also teaching a seminar, and I was rewriting my book. Doing all those things at the same time during my first year, which was 1965 and 1966. And so, David and I went to the American Anthropological Association meeting, at least, I did—I don't remember, whether he did, or not, because remember, he was a linguist. And there I met Morris Philipson, the editor, and proposed this idea of a series on symbolic anthropology . . . And we were creating a department. And I proposed, and David agreed, that we should focus . . . on something like the study of symbols. But that was too narrow, so I think we called it PhD in Cultural Anthropology. So, we had a powerful ally, whose name was Cyrus Black. His nephew lives in Chapel Hill, his name is Stanley. He was half from Eastern Europe . . . one of his parents was from North Carolina, and one was from somewhere . . . oh, shoot, what's wrong with that brain? . . . not Russia, but one of the Eastern European countries, I'll think of it in a minute. And Cyrus Black was a senior and influential person at Princeton. He was professor of history. And he and a few others, including a linguist named Mouton, supported the idea of starting this new department. So, David and I met at the house of Professor Black, and we sat at his kitchen table, and in about thirty minutes we designed the new department—that's all it took. Because it's pretty simple. And one thing we decided to do—and I'm telling you a lot more than you need to know—but one thing we decided was: all right, there is no department right now, there is not even a major in anthropology, so let's start with anthropology as a minor. And so, we thought . . . we asked, what fields will it connect to as a minor. And there was a number, like, art history, or Asian studies, and others . . . I contacted about a dozen people in different departments and asked if they would consider anthropology as a minor for their major. And so, for example, one of them was a man named Koch. It turned out that he was the son of a Koch who created Playmakers Theater in Chapel Hill.

AK: It's like Koch, German . . .

JP: Exactly, but he pronounced it k-o-ch. So, I called him, and I expected this German professor, but instead I heard a Southern accent. And he said, "Just think of it as scotch, without a 't.'" So, Professor Koch was one of the people who kind of said: "Oh, sure, art history could use cultural anthropology as a minor." And many others did, too. They were happy to do it. So, the way we got started was that we were not even a major, but a minor. So, then David Crabb had to go do fieldwork, I think maybe to Africa, and so, I was the only person present at Princeton. And we had to take this proposal before the Senate of the university. And I remember going to this place: they met in a big chapel, and there were all these senior professors, and there I was, you know, new guy, new junior prof.

AK: Under thirty.

JP: Under thirty, but also just brand-new and unknown. And they asked me one question . . . David Crabb was a linguist, and he proposed two terms: emic and etic . . . He suggested that in our description for our new department, that we say that it deals with the emic and the etic. Well, that didn't mean anything to them, and one of the senior professors said: "Well, I looked it up in OED, Oxford English Dictionary, and there is no such thing as 'etic' and 'emic' . . ." Well, I explained that it was "phonetic" and "phonemic," and the idea is simply "seeing things from the outside and inside." So, they accepted the idea of a brand-new department! So, the next thing was, we were authorized to hire two new tenure-track faculty. And we did, and those two were—my former roommate (laughs), Thomas Kirsh, and also a student . . . a former student, a Harvard undergraduate and a University of Chicago PhD Martin Silverman. So, the next year, then, we had, instead of one and a half, or, really, one, we had four faculty members. And we had anthropology . . . I think then it was just called a "program." Not yet a department, but it became a department. All right—so, that's all was happening that year, 1965–1966, and then, so, 1966 started, the spring semester, and so I had already taught a general course in anthropology, so I had an idea of teaching a new course, which I would call . . . I don't know what I called it, but symbols—that's what it was about.

AK: You don't remember the exact title?

JP: No, but I can find it—I'm sure it's in the Princeton bulletin. So, the course . . . all right, several people participated in the course. One of them was a renowned philosopher, whose name is Amélie Rorty.

AK: Like, Richard Rorty?

JP: It's his wife. Former wife. Amélie. Very interesting person, a Jew who escaped the Holocaust and lived in West Virginia for a while.

AK: How old was she when she took the course?

JP: She was probably in her thirties.

AK: So, she was not a regular student, she was taking the course . . .

JP: She was a faculty member at Rutgers.

AK: So, she took the course just for her . . . out of curiosity?

JP: I think maybe she just audited it. But she was part of it, and she and I used to take a ride on a canoe on this lake nearby, and we would talk about this field. And then another person who took this course was James Boon.

He was a French major, and I think Florence sometimes audited the course, and Amélie sometimes audited it. And then there were several others. So, that was the first course I taught in . . . whatever it was called, in anthropology of symbols, and I can tell you some of the things we read.

AK: One question: so, there were no minimum requirements as to how many regular students should sign up for the course?

JP: Probably not, but, you know, we had a reasonable number . . . It was not meant to be a large course, it was meant to be a new course, sort of like a seminar, but it was mainly for undergraduates, because we did not have any graduate students in anthropology yet. So, things that I assigned included an essay by George Devereux. He was a Hungarian who had adopted a French name, and he had written a little essay, which was called "Art." And in that essay he set forth a . . . he was a psychoanalyst as well—he set forth an idea that art was a sublimation of the id. And so, there were lots of . . . for example, obscenities, and I can see if I can find . . . but anyway, the idea was, he gave examples of various kinds of art based on obscenities, but were sublimated into art. And then I think we might have had some writings by Kenneth Burke, it may have been Edward Sapir, who wrote about linguistic symbols. I'll tell you who for sure was not there yet, Victor Turner. He and his family were later a major influence. We would meet between UVA and UNC and I wrote the introduction to his work.

AK: Was the proportion of lecturing and the time that students were supposed to spend for their own reading and writing—was it pretty much the same at Princeton as we have it here now?

JP: Yeah, pretty much the same. This was like an undergraduate seminar.

AK: Were they supposed to produce any papers?

JP: Oh, yeah, they wrote papers. If I write James Boon, he might be able to tell me about the paper that he wrote.

AK: What were your major themes, concepts that you wanted your students to walk away with?

JP: I think the main thing was the nature of the symbol. And you have mentioned semiotics . . . on the whole I did not focus very much on linguistic symbolism, or semiotics. Though I was aware of that, with people like Thomas Sebeok . . . But at this point it was a social anthropology, and the psychological anthropology of symbols. So, that was the beginning. I taught it at Princeton for two years. And then I left, foolishly, probably, to come to UNC.

AK: Oh, straight from Princeton to UNC?

JP: Yes, 1967. And so, at UNC I think there was already a course, and I just adopted it and turned it into a course on symbols. And the one that you know, which is Consciousness and Symbols, was that.

AK: So, you adopted a course that was already taught, Consciousness and Symbols?

JP: No. It was called something else, and I think I changed the title to Consciousness and Symbols.

AK: And the Department of Anthropology was already established here?

JP: Well, that more or less happened at the same time.

AK: And at Princeton, did they continue teaching this course or similar courses?

JP: I do know a certain amount on what they continued to teach, but not exactly. I continued to have connections to Princeton, and in 1990 I spent a semester there—it was some kind of a lectureship, it was in the Religious Studies Department but had connections to Anthropology still, and . . . And a funny thing happened . . . there was an anthropology major, his name was something like Hancock . . . He was a photographer, but also, I think, a rugby player. In Princeton they had eating clubs at that time, maybe they still do. And this particular eating club had initiation rituals. And apparently, they were very obscene, and so this fellow had an idea of photographing these rituals. And he asked me if I would be his advisor for his honor's thesis, and I agreed. And he took the photographs, and he submitted his honor's thesis. Some of the brothers in the eating club wanted to see his pictures. And he said, all right, I'll hold an exhibit. Now—at that time it so happened that I was not there, I had to go to California for some reason. When I got back, it turned out, there was a big scandal. . . He had exhibited these photographs, and many of them were obscene, showing people doing various kinds of ritual action. The local newspaper learned about it, and the fathers of some of the boys got angry, and some of the boys got angry about the display.

AK: Initiation is supposed to be, like, a secret . . .

JP: Yes, it's supposed to be secret.

AK: . . . even if it were not obscene, you're not supposed to . . .

JP: Exactly! So, he violated the rules . . .

AK: Several rules.

JP: Yes, several rules. Or at least the norms—I'm not sure there were rules.

AK: Remember, several times when our students were writing about those fraternities and sororities—one paper was particularly outstanding in this respect: so, she writes about this sorority, and the history of this sorority, and now she comes to the initiation ritual . . .

JP: And they are supposed to be secret.

AK: And she says: "I'm under vow of secrecy, I can't tell you . . . but, take my word for this, this was really an initiation." Period. (laughs)

JP: Yeah. I remember at least one of those papers in our course. So, this was like that, except it was an honor's thesis, and he made it public. Anyway—the event went out to the dean, and I don't know what the dean did, or said, but he worked it out with the parents.

AK: But in terms of interpretation—it was not just a photo session he was doing for his honor's thesis—it was some kind of interpretation of the initiation, I would imagine?

JP: I am sure it was, but it was mainly photographic . . . So, that was kind of a funny outcome of the symbolic things.

So, let me continue a little bit about this course . . .

AK: How did this course develop here at UNC . . .

JP: That's what I was coming to. So, July . . . or summer of 1967, we moved here, and I think maybe the first semester I taught at least two introductory courses. They were big—like, Anthropology 41 is what they were called, and they had . . . each one had at least one hundred students, maybe two hundred. And it was, you know, physical anthropology . . . four field. Because here there were . . . as we . . . and we were just creating a department here at UNC.

AK: So, the department was not really here yet . . .

JP: Well, it was just beginning . . . When I arrived in 1967, John Gulick was the chair, the first chair for the new department, and it was a four-field department. And it already had long-established archaeology—same as what we have now. So, anyway—I'll come to the course, then. So, maybe it was in the spring, I think in the fall I just taught these introductory [courses]. And so, I did a course, which was, I think, very similar to one in Princeton. And I remember the students who were in it. I'll tell you about them a little bit. Their names are: Travis Venters, Richard Gatling, Robin Moyer, Terry Rushin. And at least . . . well, I know that Travis and maybe a couple of the others, maybe, Robin, were in the fraternity, which is called St. Andrew's Hall. It's a special fraternity: it's more intellectual than the others. And so, they were all in there, at least several of them . . . Travis, I know, and I believe maybe Richard . . . maybe Robin—I think those three were. And they all were going to do creative things. Travis Venters actually went to Princeton to do a master's degree. He was an English major, but he got a master's in anthropology, and he went to Japan, and he has married a Japanese woman, he now has two children who are half-Japanese. One is a filmmaker, and then a daughter who is doing international work. And his wife, whose name is Keiko, and he lives part of the time in Japan and part of time in . . .

AK: Chapel Hill?

JP: In North Carolina, not in Chapel Hill. And he is a poet, a very good poet. And I have one of his books that I can show you, and other of his poems. Robin Moyer is a photographer, internationally known, and he may live in Hong Kong. Richard Gatling's grandfather was the creator of Gatling Gun—it's the fastest-firing machine gun . . .

AK: Is it the one they try to prohibit right now?

JP: It's the one . . . it's much faster than that one, and it's so heavy, though, that they mainly use it on helicopters. And Richard (laughs) spent part of his life . . . he makes furniture, and he has . . . had, anyway, a factory that did two kinds of furniture: bars and churches.

AK: It's a nice combination.

JP: He said, it takes the same machine to do each.

AK: That's semiotically very interesting (laughs)—that the same . . .

JP: Right. So, these guys were all in this class, and either that year, or maybe the next, Cece Conway was there.

AK: Yes, she was here yesterday.

JP: She was in the English Department; she was a graduate student in folklore. It turned out then that there was a connection to that course, because they had just created a Folklore Department chaired by Dan Patterson, who was in the English Department and was part of the English Department and still is.

JP: And so, many of the graduate students in folklore took the symbols course over the years, for obvious reasons: it fitted in their interests in performances and music, especially folk.

AK: How large was your first class? You mentioned four people, but I imagine, it was larger than that.

JP: Oh, the first . . . it probably had about thirty-five.

AK: Uh-huh, normal size.

JP: Yes, it was normal size. It was . . . at first, the course number was 135, that was before they changed the numbers—now it's 435, as you know. So, it started at about thirty, but at various times it was pretty much in demand, and so at some point it grew to maybe seventy. And I think when you and I were doing it, it was sixty, or fifty . . .

AK: Fifty-something, I think.

JP: Fifty-something, that's what I thought.

AK: I can check—I still have the rosters.

JP: No, it was roughly that size, and we taught it, at least . . . the last time, I think, it was the FedEx building.

AK: Right.

JP: And it was in that classroom, and it was pretty much filled up.

"I Didn't Restrict It to Anthropology..."

AK: So, what did you read with your UNC students . . . ?

JP: Oh, in the beginning—yeah. Good question. Oh, I think one of the things we read, right at the beginning, maybe at Princeton, too, was Durkheim. *Elementary Forms of Religious Life.*

AK: . . . but we added Turner and Lindquist.

JP: So, what happened to Durkheim . . . so, he was fundamental from the start. And the basic idea was that symbols and society are interconnected.

AK: These were symbols on the social . . . collective level.

JP: Right. The basic idea was that the collective is . . . fundamental. You know, the Durkheim thesis. So, over the years I kept assigning . . . as one student put it, "That damn Durkheim." They hated reading Durkheim, because, you know, he was . . .

AK: It's a pretty dense text!

JP: Dense, and so forth. I tried different things; one was—I assigned a version by a sociologist, almost as stuffy as the other one. And then I found an abridged Durkheim, and I tried that for a while, and finally . . . a short book, *Communitas* . . .

AK: It's not very short, and it's also dense, because it has one zillion examples . . .

JP: That's correct.

AK: But it's much easier to read. . .

JP: With the same message, which is . . . because Turner, and that's another story, by the way—the Turners and their role in all that—and actually, I just was thinking a lot about that because I was asked to do an introduction to a . . . some sort of book to honor Victor and Edith Turner. So, I was thinking about that. And Turner actually came into the course, but not as a reading . . . I used, remember, I used the example of Kamahasani, an African whom Turner knew . . . But Durkheim was fundamental, and I would start with Durkheim, and then proceed through Weber, introducing the idea of "meaning," and then . . . Freud was there from the start, but not so much as a reading, but as an example.

AK: We didn't read Freud, you mentioned him—we read Jung.

JP: Well, that was later. I was coming to that. But Freud was key as in the essay by Erik Erikson of Hitler's Youth.

AK: Uh-huh.

JP: Later there were three main changes over the years: Jung, Pollack, and

Berry. Here is how that happened. My oldest daughter looked at the syllabus, and she said: "All the authors are men, where are the women?"

AK: That's the one who wrote about Bashkirtseff?

JP: That's her, Louly. And I thought: "Yup! You idiot (me), how could you not see that?!" So, immediately I added Griselda Pollock. And that's partly the influence of Louly. Then I asked another art historian: "Can you suggest something that has the same message, but maybe simpler?" She said: "No." And she said: "Griselda Pollock is probably best . . ." And so, I assigned Griselda Pollock.

AK: But she is not an anthropologist.

JP: No, no—they didn't have to be. In fact, most of these are not . . . And I think we read that until . . . I finally substituted Edith Turner's *Communitas* . . .

AK: Yes, this was my next question, because it was not until 2014, which, I think, was the last year, that . . . three authors were gone, which are Durkheim, Pollock, and Weber—we didn't teach Weber last time . . .

JP: Precisely. I wasn't just trying to do anthropology. The way this course came to be listed at UNC was an interdisciplinary course. Remember, I made contact with people in art history and so forth. So, eventually it came to be listed as something like Philosophical Perspectives. So, I didn't restrict it to anthropology. So, Pollock came in because Louly said to me to do it (laughs), "Have some feminist perspective!" So . . . as I went along with the course, there were several major changes . . . of approach. The first was the feminist. The second was Jung and the idea of wholeness. And the third was Thomas Berry. Thomas Berry was the ecozoic approach.

AK: And you knew him personally?

JP: Well, I had met him through Herman Greene. And that was a big change for me. I'm really stupid. I hadn't thought of a feminist perspective. I had not thought of a Jungian perspective, I've been more . . . Freud, psychoanalytical. And I had not thought ecozoic. So, all those for me were a big change, and I inserted all of these into the course.

AK: When did all of these changes happen?

JP: Well, at different times. I think the first was Jung, and then was the feminist, and then there was ecozoic.

AK: And when did they approximately [happen]?

JP: Well, maybe in the 1990s.

AK: All of them in the 1990s?

JP: Maybe. Something like that.

So, these are probably the major changes. So, then I . . . and I'll tell you about another change that was happening all the way . . . and by the way, when are we going to get to your . . .

AK: Well, first we're going to speak about you, and then . . .

JP: OK, why don't I very briefly mention then another thing that began . . . was beginning . . . So, this was the course and the way it was developing . . .

AK: This was my question about the changes: does Turner substitute for "group" or "society" represented by Durkheim?

JP: Yes. More or less.

AK: But do you think that the new framing that Turner offers—she is basically offering a new perspective on how to frame everyday experience—do you think that framing is adequate to substitute for Durkheim's "society is god . . ."

JP: Probably, not. OK, what I think is—it is not theoretically as deep, but a reason that I put Turner there was that it also connected to students' activism. Explicitly. Because a lot of her book is illustrated by student activities, sometimes of UVA, which was so similar to UNC that I thought, maybe a resonance.

AK: And it actually blended very well with your book, *Grounded Globalism*, because you also quote lots of experiences . . .

JP: That's right.

AK: . . . of your own, and some of the students' experiences as well, so these together work very, very nicely.

JP: That's right, you're absolutely right, so the *Grounded Globalism* plan was sort of bringing it back home.

AK: But before *Grounded Globalism*, did you ever introduce any of your writings, articles, books in the course?

JP: I never did until that book. I've never assigned a book that I published. I listed them in the syllabus, but they were never required reading.

AK: Was it a conscious choice never to include anything of your own?

JP: It was. And the reason that I did not, was that I thought it unfair to require a student to buy something that I had written. So, I would list them—some of the things I wrote, I listed if anybody ever wanted to look at them.

AK: As optional reading?

JP: Yeah—almost nobody ever did.

AK: Well, students rarely read optional . . .

JP: No, I knew they wouldn't, but I listed them. And the first time I broke that rule was when I published *Grounded Globalism*. I thought well, this one is more relevant to their lives than Indonesia or something like that.

Grounded Globalism and the University Agenda

AK: How about Barcott's book? We always read it—Barcott, *It Happened on the Way to War*. I have literatures for all three years that I've been TA-ing, so Barcott was in 2011, in 2013, and in 2014. It was somewhere in the end, but it was connected with what we discussed in the beginning of the course—the initiation story and the quest . . .

JP: You're right! That was the case study in the "life story." Absolutely right—you're right, I assigned that, and that was partly . . . rightly or wrongly, because he was the actual student from UNC, who had gone on and lived a certain life . . .

AK: And their age . . .

JP: And their age. And also, he had organized . . . CFK, on campus . . .

AK: Carolina for Kibera . . .*

JP: Yeah, that was my justification for it: he was an actual student, who is doing something important, and he is one of you! And then, as you know, this year he delivered the commencement address.

---

* For Carolina for Kibera, see https://cfkafrica.org/.

AK: I have a question with regard to what you just said about prominent students and Rye Barcott in particular. Throughout the course, the way I know it, you were stressing the fact that knowledge should be put into action.

JP: Yeah! By the way, I didn't do that in the beginning, that kind of got in later.

AK: Although you always stressed that your scholarly approach is that symbols become symbols when they are put in the context of some kind of an action.

JP: Yes. And vice versa: action . . .

AK: . . . action might be symbolic. So, there is this connection . . .

JP: There is a connection!

AK: But at least I remember the course, you always stressed this . . . putting it into the action . . . knowledge into action . . . for instance, one of the handouts said "Results."

JP: Yes.

AK: You went through "Purposes" and "Methods," and then "Results." You say: "Create meaningful action that can sustain or change experience . . ." And then you invite your students to think about putting fieldwork, or lawnwork, into "action, engagement, service," for instance, you say, "social entrepreneurship, center for public service, etc."

JP: Uh-huh.

AK: So, my question is basically about . . . you're basically introducing the fifth field, applied anthropology . . .

JP: Applied! I did! But not very . . . aggressively, I think.

AK: As a matter of fact, my question in relation to this was: Has this connection between knowledge and practice, or action, always been a part of the course? So, exactly, I was wondering when did you formulate this?

JP: Right. Good question. And I think the answer is "yes" and "no." (laughs) Implicitly—yes . . . The connection to action, as illustrated by Rye Barcott, is implicit in . . . by learning, or by exploring your life, and who you are, and what society is, all that—you may arrive at a direction . . . I never required anybody to do work for the legislature. It so happened that in a few cases, like, I think, maybe with Calvin Cunningham and other students—they were . . . they were doing activist work. Well, I had some others, like Nicole Welsh was working with "Nourish International" at the same time . . .

AK: I think a bunch of students were doing some kind of work, but this was independent of the class.

JP: Exactly. Precisely. And the class might intersect in some . . . but not . . . yes, sometimes there would be intersection, but . . . one of the students was editor of the *Daily Tar Hill*, for example, but I did not try to teach activism or teach field method, either.

AK: Yes, you say, "Apply to your experience/interests" . . .

JP: Yes.

AK: Rather than put it into some new involvement.

JP: Yes. Students, if they were already involved in something, they could bring it into the class, it was OK, just fine. But I never tried to push them into this.

AK: Did you ever introduce students' presentations as . . . maybe optional, maybe mandatory part, when students would present their . . .

JP: Oh, sure—every year.

AK: From the get-go?

JP: I don't know about the get-go, but it became . . . I called it . . . at first, I called it "Sensuous presentation."

AK: Sensuous?

JP: Sensuous. A little bit as a joke, meaning, things that you can see, hear, and touch. So, I had students over the years who presented on pottery, or . . . Terry Rushin was . . . the one whom I mentioned in the beginning, he was one of the tragic cases. He was a filmmaker, and he showed a film in the class, which was called *Cole, the Potter*. And it was a film about mister Cole, who was a potter. And it was a very good film, so Terry got a scholarship to Stanford in filmmaking. Unfortunately, on the way he needed money, and he sold some narcotics. And he was arrested in Texas, and he was put in federal penitentiary, and was there for years, and eventually died. After going to China, he got some bad disease. I mean, that was one of the tragic instances. But others—many others—became poets, and writers, and photographers . . . things like that.

AK: But they would do presentations . . .

JP: Yes, sometimes they did.

AK: Do you know if departments keep syllabi or schedules of classes . . . ?

JP: They may, and I probably have something, too. So, I can look and check. I have a lot of materials that I already moved to the Cedars, I could check on all that.

AK: Yes, you told me from the very beginning, before we started the interviews, that you have lots of materials for the course that you never used—somewhere.

JP: They are over there. Mostly. Papers and things like that . . . Oh! And I was going to tell you! I just got some photographs and a note . . . there were three or four students I taught in 1967, first time that I was here, first semester. One of them was named Robin Moyer. And he has become a world-renowned photographer, he lives in Hong Kong. And he just wrote his uncle, whom I know, Sam McGill, who is at Carol Woods. He sent some copies of his photographs, which are of New Guinea, and he said his inspiration was the course that he took with me in 1967. So, I have a note from his uncle. I think Cece Conway might have been the first folklore student who took that course. And then various folklore students would take it, which led me to meet Dan Patterson, who had just created a folklore program at UNC. He was professor of English. And I can tell you how he started creating a program in folklore. So, I met him, Dan Patterson, and we went together to things like . . . there is mule trading, you know, where people buy cattle . . . we went . . . we had at least one student who did a thesis on mule trading.

AK: Like, local economy?

JP: Exactly. And in other ways we started doing some work together. And I was teaching some of the same students he was. So, that was when I first came in 1967.

Anna's Perspective on the Course

JP: It's your turn to say something . . . if you think about your input and your experience in the discussions that you led, what would be the main things that you . . .

AK: Well, from the very beginning I was not sure how much students would know . . .

JP: I'm going to take notes. My turn to take notes.

AK: . . . how much students would know about the basic concepts we were operating with, for instance, "symbol." I was not sure to what extent their use of the word "symbolic" in their everyday life corresponded to what it's usually referring to in humanities and social sciences, including linguistics. So, I made sure I go through the basic things like "signifier/signified" on the linguistic level and then on the general cultural level. And in order to illustrate this . . . and this was my second year here at UNC, and I'm a foreigner on top of it, I would look at things that would catch my attention, sometimes precisely because they were symbolic of something that was not familiar to me. Or something that I saw right away as a certain symbol and would bring to the class as such for illustrating purposes. So, one thing that was helpful to me, and I hope helpful to them, was going through and illustrating things for each recitation by bringing lots of visual materials.

JP: For example?

AK: At some point I was taking pictures of . . . car bumper stickers, what people would put on their cars. And some of those were obvious symbols—like, the one they have, in one row, the cross, the crescent, the six-pointed star, and other symbols of major religions—like, united or whatever. But in other cases, symbols were less clear in terms of how you read them, and I would bring those and ask students to come with suggestions, what can this refer to. Also, with "dense" readings, with Durkheim, for instance, which I myself spent a lot of time reading and figuring out, I decided that I could illustrate some of his major ideas through . . . text that would be more familiar to students, or easier to "digest." So, for instance, I showed to them . . . and this produced a lot of laughter, but a lot of understanding . . . you know, Monty Python, *The Life of Brian*, this wonderful comedy . . . And there is a scene in the beginning, it's called "the stoning," and shows a lot of what Durkheim speaks about in a condensed form. It's a sacred ritual that takes place in a sacred place, women are not allowed to . . . so, separation. Degrees of sacredness—women are allowed to watch from the distance but not to participate. And this woman, Brian's mother, puts on men's clothes, and they walk there as if they were both men. The guy who is being stoned is a local guy who told his wife at dinner that her fish was "good enough for Jehovah." So, he utters the sacred name that's not supposed to be uttered. Then he retells the story, and everybody is aghast because he did it again, and they start throwing the stones . . .

JP: Wonderful!

AK: I don't remember all the details, but this whole scene, which is four minutes long, it all aligns with what Durkheim says about the "sacred" and the "profane" . . .

JP: Sure! Wonderful!

AK: So, I thought . . . there is no guarantee that everybody will read everything from A to Z . . .

JP: In fact, they won't probably.

AK: So, I would first probably initiate some discussion based on the text only and put some key words on the blackboard . . .

JP: By the way, did you show the film?

AK: It's a clip—sure. I would certainly show it because that would stick in their memory. It would provoke emotional response—it's funny, and it does illustrate lots of things Durkheim speaks about.

JP: All right.

AK: Or else a clip about the id, ego, and super-ego: I found this video on YouTube where both the ego and the super-ego are personified as two figures, one is white, one is red, or black, and it shows how the id and the super-ego struggle when a person, who is sitting there, needs to make a decision. How these conflicting forces are sitting inside him. This was an educational video created specifically to illustrate Freudian concepts. And then for initiation I downloaded a bunch of videos with various degrees of "scare": some of them were really terrible in showing what was done to people during initiation. [Retells the video clip on initiation at a creek in the forest; piercing of the nostrils, the water is washing the blood away and taking it away, etc.] Some people couldn't watch it, but I had lighter versions of similar initiations. So, I tried to bring in something, whether video or visual stuff, for each lesson because there were a lot of difficult concepts to grasp. Or else I would draw something of my own, for instance, Pollock's "the woman as sign," and this whole concept of "gaze," "male gaze," and this woman who was not really a human being, but a signifier upon whom . . . upon which even, all kinds of significations, whether artistic or cultural, were projected. So, that's where I returned to the theory of signs, "signifier/signified," and the woman as "sign" basically meant that she is a board upon which things are projected. And whatever those projections might be, "femininity," or "fragility," "stupidity," or "beauty"—but in none of those projections is she a human being. And I said, well, I'm definitely not Dante Gabriel Rossetti, but I'm going to draw something. And I drew a picture of this woman (laughs) in the bottom part of the semiotic sign, showing that that's where she is, she is a signifier, not a human being.

And then also my master-picture showing how animals didn't have the division between "conscious" and "unconscious" in their brain: I would always draw a rat with an undivided brain, and then a human being, where the brain is clearly divided into "conscious" and "unconscious." But these things are difficult, so I made sure to illustrate them on the blackboard . . .

JP: Good for you!

AK: Many others, too—it's just something that comes to mind right now. Connections between the course materials and individual experience . . . when we studied Lindquist, where she describes Russia in the 1990s, I definitely gave lots of examples of my own, how things were then. Basically, she speaks about this semiotic chaos that ruled the country, because many old significations basically disappeared, whereas the new symbolic world was only forming, coming into being. Lots of people were disoriented, and that's where all those healers . . .

JP: Oh, yes! As in that book that Michele assigned. Which I read.

AK: We read it last year . . . So, I explained to them what I myself remembered about this well, essentially symbolic, or semiotic disorientation, and how in this situation quack healers, all kinds of quacks, could find their niche and earn a lot of money and persuade lots of people to follow them. But also, speaking about this connection between text and experience, I learned a lot from students. Because very often I would divide them into several groups, pose a question, give them several minutes, and they would be supposed to come up with an answer to whatever question, or examples illustrating it, and they would come up with stories from their experience, all of which would be new to me. I learned a lot about the American South, for instance, when we came to *Grounded Globalism*. Because lots of kids were from the South . . .

JP: Yeah. But not all.

AK: And this was good because we could compare and contrast.

JP: Terrific! Brilliant.

AK [to Beverly Patterson (BP)]: Now—about the course. I didn't realize you took the course with Dr. Peacock.

Dan Patterson (DP): Consciousness and Symbols.

AK: Do you remember anything about it? His teaching style, the course itself, the communication during the course, the assignments . . . Which year did you take it in?

DP: It would have been in the 1970s.

AK: Here, at UNC?

BP: Here at UNC.

AK: What did you read at the time?

BP: We were reading Durkheim . . . I probably have the syllabus . . . I remember sitting out . . . he would take his class outside, sit out under a tree . . . No, I mean that we did it once or twice. It was pleasant . . . It was just likely, if you asked him a question, he would just likely turn it around: "And what do you think?" (laughs)

AK: Was he heavy on theoretical stuff? About Durkheim, or Weber maybe?

BP: Weber, yeah.

AK: Was he going deep into theory of . . . ?

BP: He was always . . . making it easy to understand, I think. Very . . . the books would be sometimes a little daunting, but he would make it very approachable—the way he taught about these ideas.

AK: So, he was not hard on the students?

BP: I can't imagine . . .

DP: I can't imagine Jim being anything but supporting.

BP: I mean—look what the tradition in the old style . . . when you went to see a professor, and his response . . .

[DP: About his friend, whose nephew went to see his professor; the latter roared: "Herein!!!" then said he was busy and, "Come bother me tomorrow. What do you think I'm doing here? Catching flies???"]

BP: Jim would be just the opposite.

DP: I couldn't imagine any . . . yeah . . .

AK [to BP]: Did you read Jung and the psychoanalytic stuff? Because Dr. Peacock told me that from the beginning, he wanted to study psychology . . . the interpretation of dreams . . .

DP: He is in the Jungian [society].

AK: So, this course—was it a popular course?

BP: Very popular. Always full.

AK: How many students were there at the time?

BP: We were in that classroom—as you enter Alumni Hall, there is a classroom to the left, so, not more than what can be accommodated in that room.

AK: Like, thirty maybe?

BP: Uh-huh.

(7_The_Pattersons_Feb_9_2019)

DP: Well, I met him, probably, first through . . . when I got (?) in a curriculum in folklore, and the previous chair of it had retired, and (?) in 1940, and so it was the oldest graduate program in folklore in the country. And it had a whole set of faculty members, who taught in different areas—music, English, Spanish, social science, and each of them had a course that related somehow to folklore, some of them more directly on the subject, some more tangential, but useful. And that's why they formed a program and called it "curriculum." Curriculum at UNC had no budget, they simply had a common interdisciplinary unity. And about that time I got a degree and I began to teach English literature—the usual introductory courses and so on, and then American lit, and Southern lit. But about 1968, Arthur Palmer Hudson, who was head of the curriculum, retired, and then John Keller, who was his immediate successor, shortly after that . . . he taught Spanish and Spanish medieval folklore, and he had some sort of explosion, and he left, and went to the University of Kentucky, carrying all the graduate students and some of the faculty members from the Spanish [Department] [with him].

AK: "Explosion" like scandal?

DP: Not a scandal, probably, just jealousy and rivalry and hurt feelings . . . And so, he left, and left the curriculum suddenly without that faculty member, without Hudson, and nobody . . . and who was going to take over these things? And I was given, I think, Hudson's ballad course because I was the only person around, and interested in it. And I did it. And that was my only qualification—the only folklore course I had read was that one. (laughs) At that point I began to try to . . . and other people were retiring . . . I began to try to put together . . . go to every department—is there anybody here who has a course that seems appropriate for folklore [curriculum]? We had built enough courses . . .

AK: For a minor or for a major?

DP: It was a major. And they could get a master's in folklore [or a doctorate in English]. We had people like Cece Conway who took a doctorate in English, with a master's in folklore. Peacock was one person I found who taught the Consciousness and Symbols course; that really was very appropriate, I think. Beverly first studied music, then she studied ethnomusicology, and then anthropology . . . So, he [Professor Peacock] was one that I wanted, and then we developed a friendship, and we taught together a lot, and then he began doing fieldwork with some of the folklore students, and some of the anthropology students who were . . . also, he had people like Beverly, in music, and in religious music, and Cece was . . . teaching on the Black Pentecostal church, wasn't she? And so, he offered courses, he and Tyson, in religious studies, a joint course.

AK: Now I understand what Dr. Peacock meant when he said that he and you were teaching some students together. So, these were students who were probably majoring in different subjects but were taking folklore classes . . .

DP: That's right . . . taking his class, and we were cross-listing his class in the curriculum of folklore . . . We did one with someone in the Geography Department, John Florin, and someone in . . . Ruel and Jim and a seminar . . . I never had a seminar with Jim, but we talked a lot. And then lots of students . . . they wrote a project that you [addressing BP] were involved in, and so was Tom Rankin, chair of the Duke Center for Media Studies. . . the Black church . . . There were three different varieties of Pentecostals . . .

(7_The_Pattersons_Feb_9_2019)

Herman Greene (HG): We formed another kicker-liner seminar. It was called . . . Ecology and Culture, I think it was, and we did that for three or four years.

Sandy Greene (SG): Ecology and Social Change.

HG: Ecology and Social Change. And he and I were cofacilitators, and actually . . . you're asking how he . . . became interested in Thomas [Berry]—it was totally interrelated to the . . . I can't recall exactly how it was . . . I mean, what his knowledge was when we started this seminar, but Thomas came and spoke in it, and Thomas . . . he had one of the Douglas Hunt lectures, and then he came to me and he said that we want to have Thomas Berry come and give one of the Douglas Hunt lectures.

AK: So, he had known this name before? You didn't introduce that name to Dr. Peacock?

HG: I'm sure I gave him some papers to read about Thomas, and later he read *The Great Work*, which he taught in his class.

. . .

AK: At some point he started this course, 435, Consciousness and Symbols, and taught it for fifty-plus years, mostly here, and he said that at some point his daughter came and looked at his syllabus and said: "Oh, there is no gender perspective!"—and he said: "Oh, my god!"—and he added a book related to gender and art. And I think that's something that might have happened with the ecologic perspective as well, because it was Durkheim, Weber, Freud in the beginning, all the classic texts, and then he started expanding, adding more contemporary . . .

HG: Yeah, that's what he did. He stayed with it longer than I did, but for the Jung Society . . . he has been involved in it a long time. And I don't know—was his undergrad degree in psychology?

AK: He started . . . his first major was psychology because anthropology was not there yet, and then he met other people at Princeton . . .

HG: So, he always maintained an interest in psychology and psychoanalysis, and when he talks about things, sometimes he would get some of the psychological analysis more than anthropological or social, and he would talk about . . . Anyway, one of his emails about the South recently was strictly from a psychological point. And he is very affirming, and he says "That's terrific!" a lot.

AK: Or "Awesome!!" (laughs)

HG: Yeah . . . almost to a fault, because he really affirms everyone and makes everyone feel special . . . somewhat uncritically. Sometimes there seems to be things . . . that he could question, but his usual response is to affirm whatever people say. So, I don't know if he has an enemy, but I don't think he has many, because his overall approach is to affirm everyone. But in the anthropology area he tries to move the profession toward engaged anthropology.

(8_The_Greenes_March_28_2019)

Cece Conway (CC): I first met Jim Peacock . . . when I first came to UNC to get my PhD. I already had a master's in English, mostly American Lit, from Duke . . . my BA and MA from Duke. And I wrote my master's thesis on the Jungian analysis of T. S. Eliot's *The Cocktail Party*. It was all literature, but especially twentieth-century American literature. But when I came to UNC, I knew already that I was going into folklore. And so, I came with an MA in English, and I went to the English Department, but I was coming for folklore, and Dan Patterson was here. I came in summer, and I took one class with Dan, a course in folklore, which was housed in English. And then I studied independently to take my Latin proficiency for my PhD as my second class and passed that. And then in the fall I took more folklore and I took Jim Peacock's class, in process, Consciousness and Symbols. It was related to folklore, and it was amazing. . .

AK: And so, how did Dr. Peacock's class then contribute to what you were doing?

CC: Well, there were several things . . .

AK: Which year did you enroll to the UNC program?

CC: Summer of 1970. And that might have been only one year after Jim arrived here. He was teaching Consciousness and Symbols—there was no book, it was just lectures. But we were doing all kinds of things like Durkheim . . . I remember a lot of things about symbols and consciousness, but not about Durkheim. But the brilliance . . . one of the brilliances of Jim Peacock was that he could summarize Durkheim in a paragraph that was clear and simple. And that made it a lot easier to deal with. And likewise with Weber . . . Protestantism and Capitalism.

AK: *The Protestant Ethic and the Spirit of Capitalism.* . . .Were you free to disagree with the texts you were reading and discussing during the course?

CC: We could do that. We had to take tests of some sort, but the main thing we had to do was to write a research paper, and I was going to the potteries, and I wrote a folklore paper . . . a fieldwork paper about pottery. It was all about consciousness . . . Jim taught me how you want to see the relationship between the men and art, that's the main . . . And that's why his course was so extremely valuable.

AK: So, the artistic component was already there, it's not just Durkheim and Weber . . .

CC: That was one . . . symbol, that was obvious, and that's how it fit with my interest, and my work, and my paper. [Art was] there in the ideas that were applicable, and he was generating these ideas that were not in some . . . text.

AK: So, you didn't really read any of those thick books?

CC: I read some of them. I read enough to deal with the tests . . . but thankfully his lectures addressed the readings in a useful way. And this was so applicable.

AK: What else do you remember about his method of teaching? You already said that he was capable of summarizing the hardest texts in a paragraph. What else do you remember about his teaching?

CC: He liked his folklore students. He liked the fieldwork that we were doing, and in some ways . . . I had read something, some ludruk drama by that . . .

AK: Yes, that was his PhD dissertation; it was already out by that time.

CC: And maybe he told us about it or something . . . But that was more related to the man and the symbols. Looking for that was the main thing.

AK: Do you remember if Dr. Peacock made any substantial comments or suggestions on your paper?

CC: He usually just supported us here or there . . .

AK: Like, he wouldn't say "Wrong . . ."

CC: No, he never did that—and he never proofread, he was more interested in [ideas].

AK: Did you expect, when you enrolled to this course, Consciousness and Symbols, that it would be so helpful for you in the future?

CC: Well, pretty quickly—I mean, maybe not immediately, but . . . It seems like... I may be wrong about this... I may have even sat in on it again at some point... And I certainly, when the book came out, I bought the book and was thankful to have that. *Consciousness and Change*, Jim's book. He was still thinking it through when I took the course.

AK: How many students were in the class when you were taking it?

CC: Millions! (laughs) There must have been... I don't know, thirty-five to fifty... In that day it was quite a few.

AK: And obviously, there were not just folklore students there...

CC: Mostly anthropology, maybe it was even a requirement, I don't know. I know that the course was always taught, because when Jim was away, Bill Lachicotte would teach it. [On her field trip, CC was working with a fellow anthropologist, who earned a slightly lower grade than she did, although she was smart. This woman asked Professor Peacock why she had gotten a lower grade, and he said:] "Your paper was much like I might have written, but hers [CC's] much more dealt with meaning of the materials." And then I thought, that might be the guide of why he liked folklore papers—we're more interested in that than theory.

AK: So, he was not biased toward anthropologists over folklorists in this course?

CC: No—he was interested in interesting, important stuff.

AK: Did you know that he had been teaching this class for more than fifty years?

CC: Well, I'm not surprised... I can just say that my experience of it was enlightening to begin with, and then having access to the book that specifically addresses... [meaning, the book *Consciousness and Change*].

(11_Conway_July_29_2019)

AK: So, in the class you taught in the 1970s, Anthro 135, there were both anthropologists and folklorists...

JP: Lots of people—these are just the two types. It was anybody who wanted to take...

AK: But these were two distinct groups, anthropologists and folklorists?

JP: Well—there were some of each. And then there were other people, who were neither. Like, Travis Ventors (?) or Gatwick, or Terry Rushin—several others who were not . . .

CC: Oh, yeah, Terry Rushin was the one that made the movie . . .

JP: That's correct—it was called *[A.R. Cole,] Potter.* . .

AK: For how many years . . . as far as I understand, the Folklore Department was developing at that time . . .

JP: Correct.

CC: That's a part of folklore curriculum.

AK: . . . and Dan Patterson was its director . . .

JP: Yup.

CC: . . . the whole time I was there.

AK: And so, folklorists would take this course pretty much all the time, I guess . . .

JP: Some did, yes. It was a 135 course, it's the same level as 435, and somewhat similar.

AK: I just don't remember any folklorists when I was TA-ing for 435 . . .

JP: They might not have been by then.

CC: Because they had a more elaborate program by the end. And once Dan left, it was less embracing of the world . . .

JP: Yes, but folklorists continued to be in it.

CC: Until about how long?

JP: Well, even then, but there were certainly not as many. In the beginning it was sort of a standard practice, I think, for folklorists to take that course, as well as some others, but later on, after Dan stopped being the chair, that was probably not true.

CC: But that may not have happened instantly because he has been retired for fifteen or twenty years.

JP: Right. But the change . . . I mean, over the years folklorists continued to take it—sometimes, but not as they did then.

CC: And once the class became 435, was it a higher level?

JP: No, it was just . . . on the whole . . . it was mainly undergraduates who took it then. In the beginning it was more of a mix.

AK: When did it change the number?

JP: Oh, not so long ago, maybe ten years ago.

AK: Because now 400-level courses are both for graduates and undergraduates.

CC: That's the way it used to be.

JP: It was that way then, with 135. They just change the numbers, that's all.

AK: Were you modifying the content or any approaches as you saw different people come in, less folklorists, or more of somebody else?

JP: Well, let me think: it was not so much that, that would cause modification. Gradually . . . several things . . . it evolved, or devolved. (laughs)

CC: It evolved, and eventually you wrote the book.

JP: I wrote the book pretty early, and then . . . Here is what happened. When you [addresses CC] took it, I'm sure Durkheim was . . .

CC: Durkheim and Weber.

JP: That damned Durkheim (AK laughs)—as one student put it, was the opening book in the course, from the beginning, and only in the last two or three years did I substitute Edith Turner's short book *Communitas*. That was kind of a simple version of Durkheim. And before that, I tried a short version of Durkheim, which was pretty good. But in the beginning, and for a long time, it was the full-fledged *Elementary Forms of Religious Life*.

CC: And the only saving grace for us was that Professor James L. Peacock is the master of summarizing eight hundred pages in one pithy paragraph (JP and AK laugh).

JP: So, that was there from the beginning. And I think, Weber, also.

CC: Yes, Weber was there when I took it in 1970.

JP: And then a few years later, my daughter Louly noticed that all the main authors were men, and she said: "Dad, you need women authors." And so, she suggested one, which was Griselda Pollock, who is an art historian and a feminist. And so, then she entered the course.

AK: That was already in my memory—2013 and 2014.

CC: How old was Louly when she said that?

JP: Probably, twenty-five.

CC: So, that would be about twenty years after I took it.

AK: It was very difficult to teach this book—it was dense and . . .

JP: She was a British . . . sort of Marxist.

AK: One of the chapters was called "Woman as a Sign," and I had to explain to them the sign in linguistics, and . . . I was drawing pictures . . . oh! Dr. Peacock is famous for drawing pictures in class, on the blackboard! We are going to include some of those . . .

CC: Very good! But there are others—I have a copy of his . . . laborers, that he drew when he was thirteen.

AK: Is it this big framed picture . . . ?

JP: No, it's not a big one, it's a small one, and it has an old man, confronting a nasty, mean foreman, and has his head in his hand, and it looks as though he is pleading, he wants not to be fired or something like that.

AK: That's social justice right there, at thirteen!

JP: That's right. At thirteen.

AK: I don't remember this one; I remember your big one, the pier.

JP: That's right, and that was . . . I never painted, except those two pictures.

AK: I photographed all the pictures you drew on the blackboard . . . Which is the book that is based on the course?

JP: It's called *Consciousness and Change*. It was published in 1975, I think. And actually, I never used it in the course.

CC: You didn't? Why not?

JP: Well, I don't know . . . On the whole, I did not assign my own books.

CC: It surely would have been a lot better than Durkheim! (all laugh)

JP: So, we didn't read that book in the course.

AK: But it has a direct connection to the course?

JP: It does. It's based on what came out of the . . .

CC: It came out four years . . . or five years after I took the course.

JP: . . . after I started teaching it. That's correct—that's basically what it was.

AK: And the fact that you didn't want to assign your own books to the class—what are the reasons for that?

JP: It's a kind of an ethic that you don't want students to have to pay for your own books. It's not illegal, but . . . Anyway, I didn't normally do it, with one exception: *Grounded Globalism*. And the reason I did that was, I didn't know any other thing like it. (AK laughs)

CC: Good reason! And even . . . I mean, I used to assign my *African Banjo Echoes* book, but then finally I ended up assigning it as one of three possible choices.

JP: Actually, what I did in the syllabus, I listed some of these books as optional readings. They were not on sale in the bookstore, you could go [to the library?]—if anybody . . . and frankly, over many, many years that I taught it, I don't think anybody ever took the initiative . . . to order the book . . . or buy it. But it was . . . some of them I listed as . . . And students complain about too much reading anyway.

CC: I'm pretty sure I have the book, and it was very helpful for my dissertation. But also . . . I think . . . I mean, Rodney Needham's book—I think of it as the main book about sensuous . . . the quality of sensuousness and . . . what might he have discussed when he was here for the conference? He wrote a lot of shortish books . . .

(12_Peacock_Conway_July_30_2019)

[AK talks about Jung and Freud as part of Consciousness and Symbols course.]

Susan Reintjes (SR): Very, very interesting. It's almost like he is a psychological anthropologist. Or an anthropologist of psycho-studies. It's almost his sidecar in a way. His interest in depth psychology and going deeper in layers of psyche and consciousness.

(14_Reintjes_Aug_9_2019)

Cameron Nimes (CN): I took one class with him—that was probably in 1974. And then . . . I have a vague memory about one other contact . . . It might have been a tutorial, that sort of thing, I did with him—it's been so long, I can't remember. And then I hadn't seen him for many, many years. But maybe a year or so ago I attended a meeting of the Jung society, and he was there. And one of the things that impressed me was that even today, these days, he was busy taking notes. Constantly taking notes, and totally engaged. Kind of interesting to see.

AK: What kind of a class was it in 1974?

CN: It was an anthropology class . . .

AK: Was it Consciousness and Symbols?

CN: That might have been it, yes . . . that sounds familiar. My interest . . . what other courses did he teach?

AK: This is his major creation that he has been teaching for fifty-plus years . . .

CN: Then that would have been it. Because my major study here at UNC was comparative religion. So, he fit right into the course work I was doing. There was another professor, his name was Bill Peck.

AK: Ruel Tyson?

CN: Let me think . . . that name is familiar. I think he might have been the head of the Religious Studies Department in those days. So, the courses I took from Dr. Peck were . . . an introductory . . . comparative religion class. And part of my amazement about him was that . . . he said it to the class. This was four hundred people, a big lecture hall—he said, "When I'm explaining things, and you don't understand, please, raise your hand, and I will explain it in a different way. And I will do this six times in any given class, and if you still don't understand it, come to my office." And I watched him do that several times. He just completely reconfigured how he made the presentation, the same point . . . brilliant! And then I took a course from him called Psychology of Religion.

AK: From Bill Peck?

CN: Yes, him. My interest was in . . . I'm not a particularly religious person, my interest was in why we have religion. And that's where Dr. Peacock's theme came in, too: the symbology of religion.

AK: Did you read Durkheim?

CN: Yes, we did. It all had a huge impact on me, but I don't consciously remember any [authors?].

AK: Was it also a big class?

CN: No, with Dr. Peacock it was probably fifteen to twenty students.

AK: When I was his TA, we had forty to fifty people.

CN: I can imagine, the popularity of the course grew over time. But this was . . . I came in into the class of 1975, I showed up in 1971, so I should have graduated in 1975, but I left school for a period of time, went to live in Costa Rica, but my last semester I was in the martial arts class, and I broke my arm (?) and was in a cast and couldn't write my final papers, and I had five incompletes, so I didn't graduate because in those days they were all papers. [Had to take notes with his left hand, couldn't read what he wrote himself.]

AK: Can you say anything about the style of his teaching, I mean, Dr. Peacock's?

CN: As I remember, it was a very interactive class, it was not all the lecture. There was a lecture, for sure, but he encouraged a lot of intercommunication in the class, and a lot of questions. So, it was an open format as far as I remember.

AK: But was he considered a strict grader in terms of how he was grading . . . ?

CN: I wouldn't have said that . . . I found him to be very open-minded and innovative in the way he presented information. It was very engaging, because my mind had always been more enrolled in philosophy, and now spiritual practice, as opposed to religion.

AK: So, while with other professors it was lecturing, lecturing, lecturing . . . and taking notes, with him it was . . .

CN: I would say it was of an open format . . .

AK: Which at the time it was not yet . . .

CN: Yes, it was not so common. But then again, the courses that I took with Dr. Peck and then another one . . . I don't remember his name . . . it was a course in religion and art, which fit very well with the study of the philosophy of religion, what else is going on in consciousness as expressed through art. The reason I took the courses I did was because initially I was trying to get into a program that was an interdisciplinary studies major, but the way they structured it, I had to plan it up to two to two and a half years ahead, to get the whole course work. And there was no guarantee that in the processes . . . of being able to register for those courses . . . that I can even get them. I didn't want to be locked in in the whole course like this, so I just stayed in the Religion Department, which allowed me to take any courses anyway . . . I am trying to think what else we read in Dr. Peck's course, because for me it was all the same investigation, and whether it was an anthropology course, or religion, it didn't make any difference. We read Dostoevsky and Herman Hesse . . .

AK: Steppenwolf!

CN: Yes, Steppenwolf, exactly.

AK: So, the interdisciplinary was already "there," as a concept?

CN: As a concept, yes, and they had a structure for it, but it was, like I said, it made me feel like I'm locked in. It was like I was made down a path, and I didn't want to fit into a structure that restricted other avenues that I might have pursued. Eventually I got what I wanted, but I got it piecemeal.

AK: Academia has changed so much over the last . . . thirty to forty years.

CN: It has, I'm sure, but I would say that for the time it was very innovative, what they were doing, and it was just perfect for me . . . I suppose if a student knew that they wanted to be a mathematician, they would take math courses. But since I had no personal direction in my life in terms of a career or what I was going to do for work . . . I was investigating the nature of my own mind, let's put it this way. For me it was really a fantastic . . . platform to begin the process of my own . . . awakening.

AK: So, it helped you a lot to . . . ?

CN: Absolutely! In the same timeframe I was introduced to transcendental meditation—I don't do this practice anymore, but it was a much broader pattern that I'd discovered in myself, being interested in the nature of human consciousness.

AK: You are probably a rare person in the sense that you benefited from the undergraduate education to the extent you are describing . . .

CN: It was very formative for me, I have to say. And I was dazzled by Dr.

Peck. Also, by Dr. Peacock, but I only took one course with him, maybe two, I can't remember. As I look back to it, it was almost as if I was being led, guided by something.

AK: [about the Jungian society] What topics do they discuss?

CN: I think it's usually to do with . . . Jung's literature, and they have speakers who come and make some sort of presentation from one of his books, or some work they've done, or . . . Jungian therapists, or . . . This is where I saw Dr. Peacock: there was a book about politics, and . . . how did he frame that? Eh . . . understanding the phenomenon of politics through the lens of Jungian psychology. Like, Trump right now. What does it say about the collective consciousness, or collective unconsciousness of our culture. Topics like that.

AK: And certainly people like Susan [Reintjes] and others were already there in the 1970s, and somehow this course was already preparing grounds for . . . social interest and practices . . .

CN: Yes! As to whether those subjects were popular in the 1970s . . . there were people fashioned like this for thousands of years—the spiritual masters, you know, the shamans . . . but in the 1970s there was a shift in collective consciousness, and awakening, in a collective way . . .

AK: [Says something about Dr. Peacock's work in Indonesia, and her guess that the West is much more "shut" to communication with anybody but human beings, and that non-Western cultures are much more open to communication with spirits.]

CN: Uh-huh. It's the implicit permission to do that.

AK: That might have also influenced his interest in Jung, and symbols . . .

CN: I would say so, because if he started in a culture that's consciously operating . . . that would have to stimulate his own awareness of it all. So, that would explain . . . his background that you just showed to me, why I found his courses so interesting, because even though he didn't talk about that material, he was obviously coming from a perspective that included an awareness of that. So that would have . . . to some degree affected how he presented Durkheim and all the rest of it.

AK: In Dr. Peacock's case, it was Indonesia to America, but then he moved to the Appalachia, where he did a lot of research, with Ruel Tyson among other people, on Primitive Baptists and some other religious groups. And that's also bridging of the experiences, because you go to the mountains, to those churches . . . how much do we know about them here in Chapel Hill?

CN: Right—and what's the underlying structure of consciousness that creates that expression . . . that version of Christianity?

AK: Right.

CN: Are they operating on another . . . frequency that is not available to the rigid Western Christian model?

AK: That's a great expression, "operating on a frequency" . . . maybe anthropologists can be described as people operating on different frequencies simultaneously . . .

CN: Frequencies of other cultures.

AK: Right . . .

CN: I am delighted to have this conversation, as I was delighted to run into Dr. Peacock again, because it sort of brought back that time in my life, which was really the beginning of my own personal journey. It was my own Jungian journey, my own unconscious, and so on.

AK: So, even though he did not introduce any specific Indonesian stuff into his course, his general approach was such that you could feel it . . .

CN: Yup! It was provocative on some level that I was not even aware of; it was compelling. So, I can trace through my life a very clear path that I didn't design, but I couldn't help but follow. There is a line . . . one of my favorite songwriters is Jackson Browne, and there are lyrics from one of his songs that goes: "It's like a song I can hear, played right in my ear, I can't sing it, but I can't help listening." So, this path that I found . . . Dr. Peacock and Dr. Peck was part of that process, something was guiding me, after the college . . . one synchronicity after another . . . Dr. Peacock and Dr. Peck, they helped launch the whole process. Dr. Peck and Dr. Peacock sort of fertilized the ground, and something . . . the process began to emerge. And the beginning of my awareness of all that came from Dr. Peck and Dr. Peacock and these courses. I can trace it all back to that . . . The overriding point is: I can trace my whole path back to the course work I did in those days, and Dr. Peacock was part of it.

(15_Nimes_Aug_11_2019)

Bill Peck (BiP): Because we were both teaching, we taught a number . . . I wanted to teach about Durkheim, so, just come over and give a lecture on Durkheim. And then I would give a lecture in his place. So, we kind of, all over the years, we kind of overlapped that way.

AK: So, you were presenting on Durkheim in Dr. Peacock's Consciousness and Symbols?

BiP: Yeah, Durkheim's theory of religion—that's very much part of my field and Jim's field. *The Elementary Forms of Religious Life.*

AK: But you never cotaught a course?

BiP: No, but . . . close enough, so one would almost say (?) we did that. I don't think we planned a course . . . He did that with Ruel Tyson—they taught courses together. But in my case, it was just . . . he would invite me to do a lecture. We then walked every day . . . maybe not every day, but . . . we walked maybe a hundred miles a week—walked and talked. He talked anthropology, and I talked religious studies.

AK: Like peripatetics—walked and talked.

BiP: And we added together, over a thirty-five-year period, we thought we were pretty close to a hundred thousand miles walking together. (laughs)

AK: Wow. Whose idea it was to start walking like that?

BiP: Oh, that came out when we went with the Peacocks down to the Outer Banks, and my son was in the long-distance running program, and we were there on the beach, and my son said: "Hey, let's go for a little run." So, he and Jim ran up the beach, and they ran another six miles to the end of the island, Ocracoke Island, and ran back. And I said, I better get exercised. So, from then on, I did, with Jim and then we did the Charlotte marathon together.

AK: What's the Charlotte marathon?

BiP: It's a 26.5-mile run originating in the city of Charlotte, North Carolina. We ran that together . . . That was part of our friendship. (laughs)

AK: So, when you were walking, you were talking about your respective interests . . .

BiP: Yeah, we talked about what we learned at Harvard.

(19_Peck_Aug_26_2019)

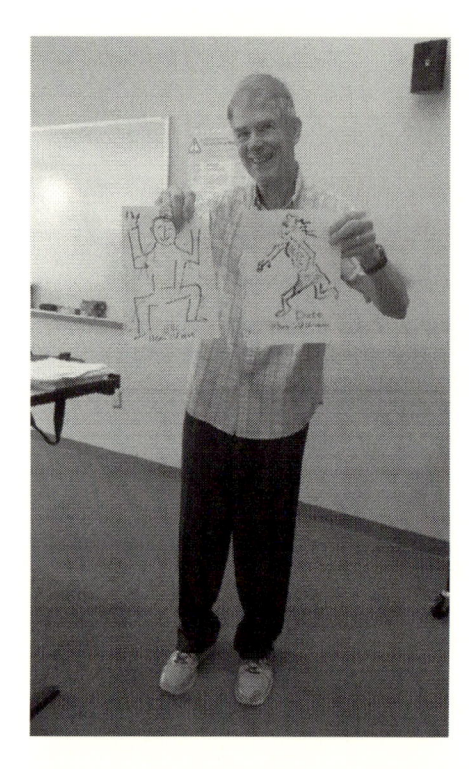

Professor Peacock's illustrations for the students of Consciousness and Symbols class, 2014. Photo: A. Kushkova.

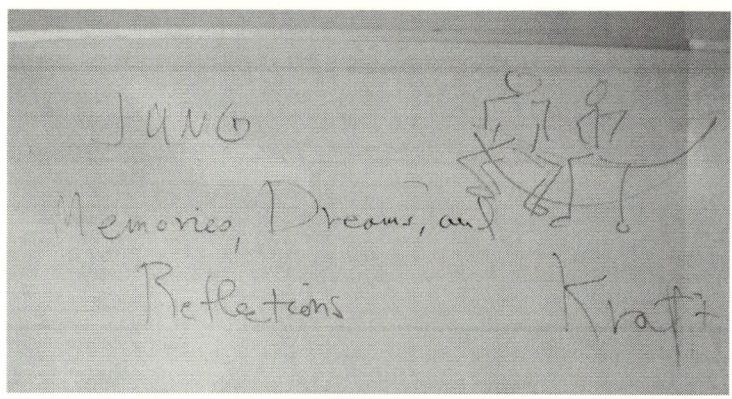

Professor Peacock with a student, Consciousness and Symbols class, 2014. Photo: A. Kushkova.

Student's optional presentation, Consciousness and Symbols class, 2011. Photo: A. Kushkova.

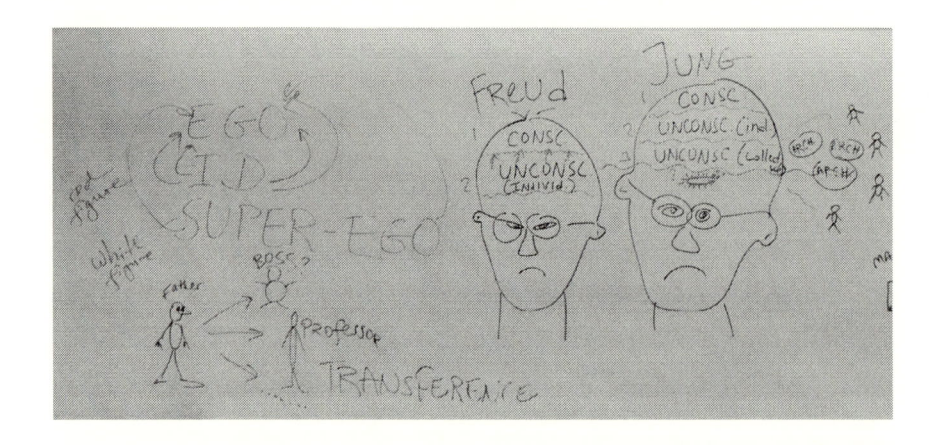

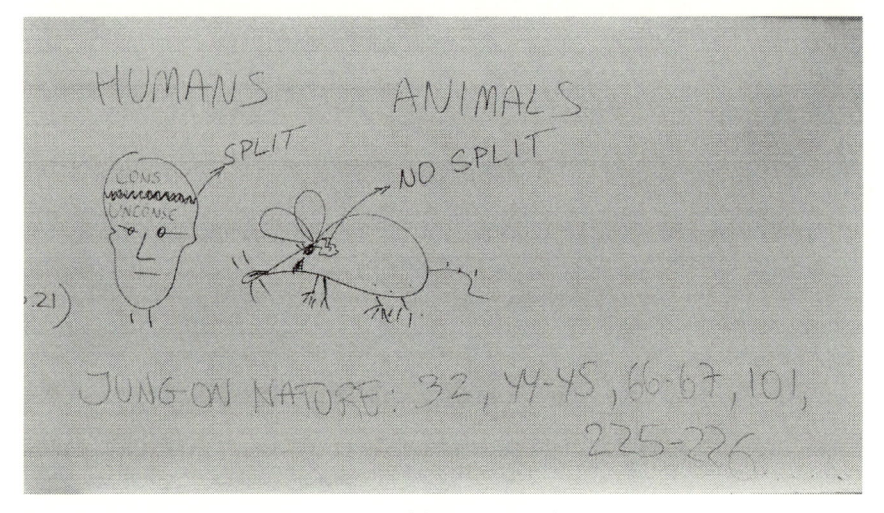

Recitation on Jung and Freud, 2014 (A. Kushkova).

Students' Thoughts on Consciousness and Symbols, from Final Exam, 2014

As far as the geographical US south is concerned, I believe the pride of the Southerner will allow us to incorporate the multiple facets of globalized life in a way that is still unique to the region.

Including the state of liminality as a phase of a rite of passage has helped me not to focus on a direct relationship between cause and effect, between start and finish, and between input and output. Rather, I am able to better see processes as a whole, with a definite phase of "in-between-ness," in which the poles of beginning and end simply become markers of a transition. The transition itself holds more information. Before the course, I can

Select students' drawings: Symbols of My Life: Anthro-435, Consciousness and Symbols, 2014.

honestly say that I was less focused on what happened in the middle, as long as there was a conclusive result. With the idea of liminality, we can zoom in on an event and better see why/how we end up with particular results. (Nick Bowden)

The course combines multiple perspectives that give it a rounded approach that encompasses a magnitude of human experience through just a few texts and themes. I think the main contribution is to think holistically about our own experience and the world. We must remember that each person is an individual and has his or her own feelings. We must also recognize that he/she is widely influenced by his/her immediate social relations and his/her socioeconomic conditions as a whole. Every situation has a context that extends to the global realm. When we treat others as subjects who feel joy and pain like us, along with the effects of social conditions, we come into a state of empathy and better understanding of various perspectives. To extend this beyond humanity, when we accept the environment as a multitude of subjects, instead of an object to be exploited, we come into a better harmony with this manifestation of energy.

Human experience is tiered. We have the level of the body, the individual, then the social, the society, the environment, the nation, and the global relations/context. Some are more obvious in our everyday experience, but they all exist in relation to us or within us.

Our reality is just perception, viewed through various prisms of context. I think it is essential to try to remember and be aware of the contexts of every situation. It is difficult to do this at times because we are often just rambling through the day trying to do what we think we should do or want to do. Many philosophers have said that contribution starts with the self. I and others necessarily must incorporate the global awareness that the course has helped teach.

I'm not sure exactly where the South will go, but I hope it becomes more accepting of people from all over the world. My critical prediction is that the South will further polarize in the next several generations, with many becoming totally accepting, while others become totally rejecting. I think it is my duty, and this generation's duty, to make sure the polarization is minimized and leads to acceptance of people from other places with various skin colors. In the long run, I truly believe that these superficial boundaries will not divide us. (Steven Crocker)

The main contribution of this course is that it makes you think outside of the box and view the world as a whole entity. (Oksana Goshovska)

The most important insight I have gained from the discussion sections is the in-depth analysis of individualization through discussing Jungian concepts and theories. The visualization and collaboration of the various levels of consciousness as well as sharing our own stories of individualization laid the groundwork to the various perspectives and identities discussed in the later portions of the course. (Andrew Nam)

What I gathered from the course as a whole was how very egocentric my view of the world had become, possibly because of my experience in the Marine Corps. Throughout this course I have witnessed the vast array in which symbols can be defined, and because of that I now challenge myself to think of all possible definitions of a symbol. This has aided me in viewing the world more critically and has greatly expanded my perception of a global connection that all humans share.

I may be from the South, but I feel that I don't fit in with the typical North Carolina Southerner. That is to say that I'm not a big fan of hunting or sports, nor do I salivate over the thought of BBQ and grits. However, after reading *Grounded Globalism*, my perception of what it means to be Southern changed. I realized that I was looking at one small description of what it means to some to be Southern, but I failed to realize the diversity of identities just in North and South Carolina, not to mention the other states that form the American South . . . The South is still in the midst of defining its identity, however, an attempt to offer a general description of any group of people is extremely risky because there exists too much diversity in our identities to be generalized.

There exist a lot of divide among "Southerners" and what it means to be Southern, however the South is an interpretive concept.

The most important thing I received from this class was the impact of small changes in perception. From having lunches with Prof. Peacock before class to the weekly recitations, I was almost constantly reevaluating various aspects of my own perception of the world . . . My lunches with Prof. Peacock gave me confidence to pursue my goals regardless of how radical they may seem, by allowing me to discuss something as taboo as the productive use of psychedelics during class. I gained the confidence needed to not assume that relaying these facts would be met with ridicule and disbelief. Rather, one student actually watched a documentary on psychedelics that she previously may have ignored. (Aaron Varner)

I think that the incredibly different views of all five authors above give this course the ability to compare and contrast diverse opinions. As someone who studies (nearly) exclusively chemistry and biology, it is has been valuable for me to learn to reconcile that multiple truths can exist within a philosophical framework. Self-scrutiny and self-improvement are more specific lessons that I believe all of these authors examine.

The most important insight I gained from recitation is that there is a constant connection between the works we were reading in this class. In

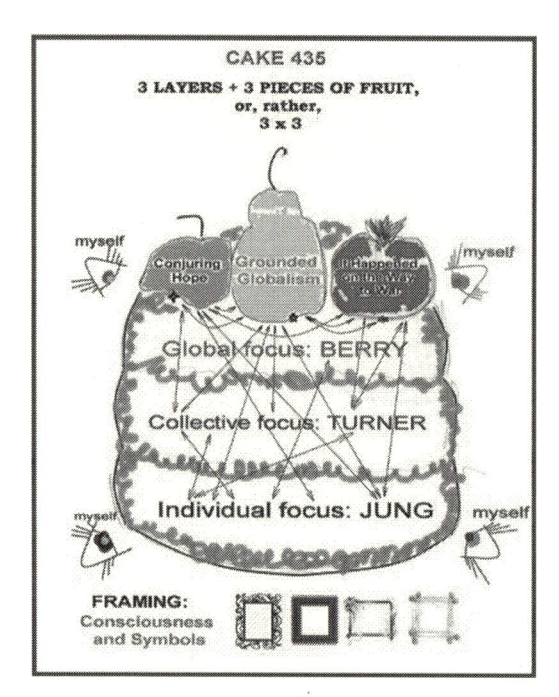

"Cake 435": Pictorial representation of the course structure used for recitations, 2014 (A. Kushkova).

recitation, Anna drew a diagram (she would later give us a handout with the same image) of a three-layer cake of Jung, Turner, and Berry with three fruits adorning the top (*Conjuring Hope*, G.G., and *It Happened on the Way to War*). I think that our constant incorporation of every single book and excerpt was a great way to move forward with a new discussion each week while covering old material simultaneously. (Wylder Fondaw)

The Nike Course

AK: So, what do you remember about this Nike course, or . . . Nike controversy, I guess . . . ?

JP: I have actually written some of it up, briefly, recognizing what Pete Andrews accomplished. Because Pete was the leader of the Nike course. So, in a nutshell, here is what happened. The athletic department made a deal with Nike, and I think it was thirty-seven million dollars that Nike offered to the Athletic Department for . . . apparel.

AK: So, they could not buy anything but Nike?

JP: Well, I don't know if it was that limited, but they gave them this huge amount of money where they could . . . clothe themselves with Nike shoes and uniforms. Some students protested, because they said Nike had sweatshops. So, then Pete had the idea—OK, if they want to protest about Nike, they need to know something about it. And so, he had an idea of organizing a course, which was later called a "Nike course," and he asked the two of us to join him . . . I was one, and Nick Didow was the other one, from the business school . . . we joined him. We created this course, and about twenty students signed up for it, and they ranged from freshmen to graduate and professional students. We met for a semester and discussed and had experts come in who dealt with labor issues. The last day of the course the students presented their proposals to Nike. And it so happened that day . . . I was standing outside where we met, which was the Coates Building, and this guy showed up, and he had dark glasses and a suit . . . And I said, "Hello, I'm Jim Peacock," and he said, "Hi, I'm Phil Knight!"—the head of Nike. And I said, "That's a surprise!" And he said, "I meant it to be." And he said, "Could I attend this class?" And I said, "Certainly." And so, the class met, they presented their proposals, and about two weeks later, Phil had a press conference in Washington, DC, and he invited all the students to come, and he thanked them, and then he presented their proposals. And he said, "These are the proposals, and we are going to accept them." And sure enough, he more or less did! And so, he became kind of a . . . champion of . . . labor rights.

JP: So, we set up a committee—at some point I chaired it, at some points, other people—and it consisted of students, and faculty, and administrators, and we examined the conditions of factories with whom Nike contracted . . . And if something was wrong, they would report it, and they would be warned . . . and we did this not just with Nike. It turned out that UNC had almost five hundred factories manufacturing their apparel. They perhaps had more factories than any other university in the world. And so we would look at the reports, and if a report said, you know, this or that is wrong, we would say: "Well, can you correct this?" And if they did not, we would take it to the administration, and they would cancel the contract. And Pete was a big leader in all this. And by the way—it was kind of funny: our committee would meet . . . oftentimes we would meet in my office, in Alumni Hall. (laughs) And then there was a group . . . some of them were students, and some of them were faculty, but they were a committee to protest labor abuses. And we would be meeting, and they would be protesting. So, we are all meeting, we've got ten people or something, and sometimes they included people from Nike, because by then we were in it together. They were trying to improve things, and we were trying to improve things, and the best weapon that we had was them! Because if they cancel the contract, the manufacturer was out of luck, so if something was wrong, the manufacturer would put it in shape. If it was just us, they wouldn't give a damn. So, Nike was our weapon. But this group (laughs) kept walking around with big signs saying "Nike get out!" "Nike go home!" Well, the last thing we wanted was for Nike to go home, because if Nike went home, the game would be over.

AK: But why do you say that they wouldn't care . . . if it were just the academic community that would protest? From what Pete said, and how I sort of see it in general, it was a great example of how civil society works in this country.

JP: Well, what I meant was that the factory was a lot more concerned about keeping their contract with Nike than about civil community or anything like that. We were concerned about the civil community, but our weapon to bring about labor rights was Nike.

AK: But you would have continued even if you didn't have this group of Nike, the internal group at the company who . . . .

JP: We would have, and did sometimes, but . . . anyway, this was only a little sideline. So, they would come with those big signs saying "Nike, get out," and meanwhile Nike would be sitting in my room, with us . . . by that time Nike had appointed a couple of representatives who would work with us. So, this led to another step—and Pete had a lot to do with this—and that was when Rut Tuft came in. Rutledge Tuft was an administrator at UNC, and eventually he organized a consortium, which had about a hundred universities and a hundred corporations, including Nike, to gather to improve labor conditions. What it was was a consortium of companies and universities to improve labor conditions. So, that was kind of a next step in development . . . So, at this point, the companies and the universities were working together to improve labor conditions. And then at the same time we had a committee at UNC that did that. But these were two different things: one was this labor . . . union, or whatever you want to call it, and it was based in Washington, DC, and so Rut Tuft left UNC because they invited him to be president of the union, and he moved to Washington.

AK: I am really amazed, because this story sort of undermines this stereotype of corporations whose only goal is profit-profit-profit, and they don't care about anything else . . . That's the opposite example.

JP: It is. And it's not to say that Nike was any different . . . By the way, who invented the name Nike? It was an anthropology graduate student. And it's in the book called *Swoosh*, which is the story of Nike.* Swoosh—that's the symbol of Nike. He was a student at the University of Oregon, I believe, who was a runner himself, a really good one. And so, the president of Nike had invented the shoes, which were much better than other shoes, and he didn't know what to name them, or he had some dumb name like Imperial or something. (laughs) And this student said, why don't you name it Nike? The goddess of speed!

AK: Nike is the goddess of speed?

JP: Uh-huh, that's what he said. That's how the name . . . and I asked Phil Knight, the head of Nike—what happened to him? And he said, "He's very, very rich, because as a result of him inventing this name, he got, you know, a million shares of Nike."

AK: Just for the name . . . ?

JP: Oh, maybe other help he gave . . . And so, he said, then he became a track coach at UCLA, I think, and so, he was a track coach, but he was very rich. (laughs) That was a side story that Phil Knight mentioned when I met him. That was the only time I ever met him, but then later, as we got to know various representatives of Nike, then there were other opportunities, and so we continued with this committee at Carolina, and I think they saved the chancellor a lot of trouble because what happened later, it was a kind of militant group of students, and at some universities, I think, one in Colorado, one in California, they induced students, persuaded students to do a hunger strike, you know, they would refuse to eat unless the administration changed the labor situation. And so, when they came to Carolina, these militant ones, it turned out . . . we already had students involved, and so, they couldn't persuade them to join the hunger strike because they were already more or less successful. And so, we did not have a hunger strike, whereas these other schools did, several of them.

AK: And those labor conditions that needed to be improved—we are speaking about the United States or other countries?

JP: Everywhere, everywhere.

AK: Everywhere where they had factories, right?

JP: Correct. So, for example, one of the things that factories had done

---

*J. B. Strasser, *Swoosh: The Unauthorized Story of Nike, and the Men Who Played There* (San Diego, CA: Harcourt Brace Jovanovich, 1991).

around the world was to hire Korean managers, and the Koreans were allegedly cruel, or rough—I mean, they would not allow the workers sufficient water breaks, that kind of thing. So . . .

AK: And probably not paying them enough . . .

JP: All that kind of thing . . . the usual worker rights situation . . . I was chair of this labor rights committee for about ten years. The chancellor, whose name is Bill McCoy, asked me to chair it, and I just kept chairing it for a long time. (laughs) For about ten years! And that's when hunger strikes and things like that came up. So, that's the story from my point of view, but Pete is much more informed. And one of the things he did, and I helped do, was—we had just a huge file of information and documents about all of this, and we put it in . . . he can tell you, where, but I think it's in the archives of the university.

AK: I know that he kept teaching this course under different names . . . it was never called "Nike course." It was something like Labor and Justice . . .

JP: Right. Something like that. And I never taught it again, I just did it one time, but I kept serving on the committee.

AK: I downloaded the syllabus from his website. And also, he said that both you and him have a video tape that was done during this last class . . .

JP: Oh! He thinks I have those?

AK: He does. I already inquired in the Media Resource Center . . . [about plans to digitize the old VCR]. Pete also said, Nike invited one person, him, to go to Vietnam, I think, to look at the actual labor conditions . . . But he said, he had known by that time a similar story when somebody made a similar trip and then he was immediately fired in his American university . . .

JP: Oh, really?

AK: . . . so, it was a dangerous thing to do in terms of keeping his position, so he decided not to go.

JP: Well, I did not go to anything like that. But Rut Tufts did—he did several of those visits.

AK: It's interesting because we were speaking about service, the aim of which is serving the community—not necessarily just students and faculty, but local community in general. And I think the Nike course is both, it's a great example of . . . it's teaching, so, it's about the academy . . .

Creators of the Nike course
Source: UCIS, *Global View*
15 (Spring 1998): 1.

We need to pay much more critical attention to the globalization of the economy and I see this as a pilot for a course on that subject. It is the defining force in our world, post Cold War...

Pete Andrews
Chair of the Faculty

Professors Pete Andrews, James Peacock, and Nick Didow.

JP: Yup! I agree.

AK: . . . and it's business, and it's community service . . . It's an amazing example of all of this.

JP: It is! And . . . Nick Didow and I—he just retired from the business school—so, Nick and I encouraged Pete to tell this story and publicize it because of what you just said.

AK: It's a great example of everything!

JP: I thought it was, too, and I still think it is. And I think Pete should be encouraged, because he is really the creator of all this.

Pete Andrews (PA): The big issue that I thought you were going to ask me about . . . that I will tell you about, was the Nike course. This was the closest thing that I worked with Jim on, and we really loved it and had a great time doing this together. In . . . just as I became chair of the faculty, the students were beginning to protest . . . The university had signed its first all-sports contract with Nike. Before that different sports . . . like, Nike had the football team, but Adidas has the soccer team, and Adidas made very good soccer equipment. So, all of a sudden UNC decided that it would be in the economic interest to do . . . Nike would pay them more for UNC to be branded as a "Nike-school" for all its athletic equipment. And a couple of our Morehead scholars, one a freshman and one a junior, a Canadian junior and an American freshman, started protesting—why UNC has this . . . We have a Public Ivy record as . . . having absolutely clean reputation—that was before the football scandal, of course. We had such a clean reputation in sports, so why would we want to sully our name by being associated with this company that was then being accused of running sweatshops in Asia and so forth? So, they had protested with literal sit-ins and then sleep-ins in the South building. So, this was a hot issue when I became chair of the faculty, and Chancellor Hooker and I had met to establish our working relationship as I came into that role. And we promised each other two things: one, that we would not reveal confidences, and second, that we would not surprise each other. However, in September 1997, my first Faculty Council meeting, the chancellor walked in and announced, without telling me ahead of time, he said, "I talked with Nike on the phone, and they want to pay the chair of the faculty and take a group of students to inspect one of their factories in Vietnam. And report back to the campus." (laughs) That was Friday, and thought about it over the weekend, and I thought—better people than I, more knowledgeable people than I were shredded for taking those kinds of trips, and that's what Andrew Young, a UN ambassador, an African American mayor of Atlanta . . . he had taken one of these trips to look at these factories, and come back, and got (?) no job (?). He did his best, but he . . . So, I decided, this was not something I wanted to do, I'm not qualified to do an inspection like that.

AK: And of course, with all those inspections they'll show you the best of the best, and . . . you won't see everything else.

PA: Of course! As a Russian, you know the phrase "Potemkin village"! (both laugh). So, I thought about it overnight, and said, this is not something I can do, but maybe I can identify some faculty members who could do that, but meanwhile, what I can do is I can teach a seminar, an ad-hoc seminar, on the economic ethics and impacts of the global economy. Using Nike as a case study. And I called Jim, literally on a Saturday, and I said, how would you like to do this together? Because I knew that his research was in Indonesia, with people some of whom work in these factories. And he said, "That's great, we'll do it together!" And then Nick Didow from the business school called and said, hey, can I join you, too? He was teaching sports marketing. So, on Monday I held a press conference and announced that it was very generous of Nike to pay for this, but if they were serious, they should send Professor Leon Fink from the History Department, who does economic history and Southeast Asia, actually, and knows that sort of thing, and Lory Todd from the Environmental Sciences Department, who was, number one, a woman, and number two, an ocean inspector from New York. They can do an inspection like that. But what I'll do, I'll teach a seminar. It was the greatest teachable moment that I've ever had, and I think Jim would say the same.

AK: So, you cotaught it basically?

PA: We team-taught it. We put it on a flyer, as an ad-hoc seminar in the spring semester of 1998, and we opened it up for students, and we got eighteen students, ranging from . . . I mean, it was an incredible group, all the way from a freshman Morehead scholar, a junior activist to several students whose families ran sports shoe stores, and the president of the Vietnamese student association to several business students who wanted to have a job with Nike and a journalism PhD student who had twenty-six years of experience as a reporter (laughs)—I mean, it was just an incredible group! And the chancellor gave us money to bring the speakers, so we brought in experts on different kinds of issues involved, we brought in a senior manager from Nike, we brought in their worst enemies, the national critics of Nike, and we ran this seminar and talked about all the issues, and then the students' big learning from this was . . . we put them in three teams; the first team was to say, what should Nike do better? Another was: what should the university do? And the third one was: what should students do, as a matter of conscience, themselves? And toward the end of the semester, they were going to give their reports, and Nike promised to send one of their senior managers to hear students report on what they should do. And it turned out that that team, the presenter of that team, was the freshman activist and the Morehead scholar. And he came half an hour early to set up his presentation, and he got it set up about ten minutes to the hour, ran down the hall for a drink of water and . . . (laughs) He came back, entered the room with his jaw dropping down his chest—he said: Phil Knight is sitting out there! Phil Knight, president or CEO, founder of Nike. And he bumped into one of the senior managers who came to listen to the students himself. And he spent two hours with them, just listening to his recommendations, explaining, how he had made the decision he'd made, and it was just a great experience for the students! And two weeks later, he gave a speech at the National Press Club, announcing some reforms in what Nike was doing, and credited our students for that. So, it was a really amazing experience!

AK: That's the juncture of education, business, public policy—everything!

PA: Exactly, exactly, yeah! And there were two other moments in that seminar . . . semester that were particularly interesting. One was about early April. ESPN, the sports television network, was planning a full-hour documentary on this whole issue of labor rights and labor safety, and these sport-shoe factories. And they came and videotaped the class. And they spent six minutes out of that hour, which on TV is huge, just playing that video—and Jim might have that copy as well. The students debating what to do about this kind of issue. [The video doesn't exist in digital form, only on a VHS. Later on, AK asked IT people in the undergrad library, and they said, if a person brings his own non-copyright tape, they will digitalize it for free.] So, that was another exciting thing that happened, and off the back end of it, ESPN asked us if we would host an online e-mail thread, and we did that for about a month, we monitored this—fascinating responses from ex-patriate Vietnamese, from people who had relatives, who had worked in the factories, and that was really, really interesting!

AK: And the students who were taking this class, they were actually getting their credits?

PA: Yeah, yeah! It was a regular class on the one hand . . . and I actually continued teaching it under a new number as a freshman seminar for quite a few years. It didn't stop at that, but it was the one Jim and I did together. Now, the other thing that happened was . . . when we were trying . . . setting up a seminar, we were trying to find a classroom where we could meet. So, Jim offered us a conference room in what was the International Studies Center . . . what is the name of the building? Coates. It's just across from the Rose Garden . . . Anyway. We met in that little conference room; it was a beautifully paneled conference room on the first floor of this building. And one of the people we had to come to talk with us was President Friday. Because even though his daughter works for Nike, he had very strong views about not doing this sort of thing. And we invited him to come and talk to the class one day, and he was telling us why he opposed this, and he said, you know, when I became president of the university, the first big issue I had to deal with was an athletic scandal. It was the Dixie classic basketball game—a huge economic event of the year, big basketball rivalry between UNC, Duke, and NC State. It was held in Raleigh. But, President Friday said, that year a gunman put a gun against the rib of an NC State player who had not made as many points as he promised. It was betting stuff . . . big scandal. So, I decided that the Dixie Classic had to be canceled. It's a huge decision. And then I called the chancellors of UNC and NC State, and he said, the UNC Chancellor sat right there, and the NC State Chancellor, right there. (laughs) We were sitting in the room that was President's Friday office, realizing that we are sitting in the middle of this history. So, that was quite a moment as well. Anyway, Jim and I really had a wonderful team-teaching together. I really loved this experience! . . . In the '70s there was this great turn that eventually led to deconstruction and so forth. But in the meantime, the debates were about theories. And what my sister-in-law thought was important, and what Jim thinks is important, were the fieldwork and the housework. It's actual deriving things from what is observed rather than just imposing theory on it. And to me it's a really important distinction. One of the reasons, I think, Jim is widely respected and so good at what he does.

AK: And that makes his writing so much more accessible to people.

PA: Yeah! I mean, it's writing about really . . . it's inductive rather than deductive type of thinking. So, we are actually working with . . . working from the data rather than trying to create great theories of everything and then imposing that lens on everything you see. And I think those are very different styles, and I think the best anthropologists are the ones who derive it from observation. This is true not just in anthropology but across most of the social sciences. And I think it's really quite problematic. I think history will not necessarily judge it well. But of course—the other side of that coin—you also have to be self-aware of the lens you are imposing from your own experience—these are all those battles about Margaret Mead and others . . . I'm trying to think of the names . . . I don't know much about anthropology, but I'm thinking about Clifford Geertz and some of the other segments of this . . .

AK: Writing culture, thick description . . .

PA: Yeah, yeah.

AK: Dr. Peacock was encouraging students to do small ethnographic projects in their homes—like, they would go home for Thanksgiving or something, he would encourage them to do some participant observation and write a small paper . . .

PA: Well, we did this with the Nike seminar as well. I can't remember whether we did it the first year, but after I started doing it as a freshman seminar, I said, as they went home for the fall break, I said to them: What effect does globalization have on your home town? I want you to go ahead and interview the mayor or town manager or some other respected adult . . .

AK: Or even your grandmother, exactly!

PA: Even your grandmother, exactly! I can't remember whether we incorporated that when we team-taught with Jim, or whether I added it later, but it was a really powerful experience, and it triggered these students from all over North Carolina, these freshmen . . . Some of them came from towns that were thriving on globalization and some that were devastated by it. So, it was really interesting to hear it from each other to realize the ways this manifested itself in such different ways in their own communities.

AK: Can you say something about Dr. Peacock's style of teaching, the way you remember it from the Nike course?

PA: It's again, it's this shy style that speaks from his own experience but also is always open to the students, always trying to empower and engage them in a conversation and draw out . . .

AK: It's never a lecture—in my experience, as far as I remember. Never, like, "Get your pencils and write after me . . . "

PA: No, this is a seminar, and we were serious about it. This is not . . . we had a number of guest speakers, and I think in his presentations, what he was doing, you know, the lectures, were just some good articles about the experience of workers in that area. And then the seminar was about how, OK, what did you read in that? What did you experience in that? Just really debating what they learned from the readings. And of course, that suits my style as well, I have a very . . . Socratic approach to teaching. Actually . . . actually, better than Socratic, because Socrates was always leading his students Somewhere. (laughs)

(16_Andrews_Aug_12_2019)

AK: And you were working together for how many years?

Ruel Tyson (RT): Well, we did a course together! Well, that may be even secret (?) . . . we did a course with Jim, the two of us, and not all of this had to do with fieldwork—it was a typical collaborative work. We were in an old-mode conversation about Primitive Baptists, some other theological issues, and we were going back and forth, and one of us . . . and truly neither of us can remember who, said, "We can't just side this issue, why don't we go to church?" So, we started going to church on Sunday nights, in the local area here. And we exact . . . we were on the way . . . the first . . . (laughs) . . . the first time we went into a church, we were all dressed up with our ties, and so were they. We sat in the back row, and then we were called out by the pastor: "We welcome . . . so-and-so." And at first time there was a witness for . . .

AK: Testimony?

RT: Testimony. That was a part of the service. And we heard three testimonies that evening. And of them . . . by my count . . . had . . . I'm not dead sure about my number here . . . had four sub-narratives within the initial beginning narrative. Boy, did that . . . that just . . . and interestingly enough, the revolution in my thinking . . . I was giving courses . . . and the books, and I said (?) So, that's when Jim and I started teaching together. Because he was accustomed to translating fieldwork into teaching. So, that was a big change in my professional profile.

AK: Anthropologists influenced you!

RT: That's right. After that, I think I (laughs) began calling myself . . . anthropology of religion. . . .

AK: So, in the 1970s, roughly, there was this major theoretical turn, in social sciences in general: one now had to frame and reframe everything, use all kinds of theories and concepts . . . Did this produce any impact upon your own and any common projects?

RT: Within the context of our joint work together we were already in a sense doing that. Because I hadn't read some of the stuff he was using and vice versa. That might not be a satisfactory answer, but I never thought it was a bump in a road, it was an expansion . . .

(6_Tyson_21_01_2019)

CHAPTER 7

Service

Center for the Study of the American South

Jim Peacock (JP): For several years in the '90s I was both chair of the UNC faculty and president of AAA. So, I would go to meetings with AAA on weekends, and then I'd be chair of the faculty at Carolina, home, during the week. And that was, actually, not very difficult, I mean, AAA meetings were usually in Washington, it's easy to go back and forth. So, that's what I did for several years. Then in '96 they needed somebody to be the head of the newly organized International Studies Center. It's called UCIS, University Center for International Studies, here at UNC. And so, I did that until 2003, roughly for six years. And during that time, we created a . . . FedEx Global Education Center and Rotary Peace Fellows, and some other . . .

Anna Kushkova (AK): Rotary Peace Fellows that exists only here at UNC?

JP: In the United States. There are five others around the world. And also, what's called the UNC World View Richardson Lecture, which is the organization . . . it's twenty-five thousand teachers at K–12 schools. I was not the creator of that, the creator of this is Robert Phay, but I facilitated. And some other things like that. All these were, essentially—all at the same time . . . but earlier in the '90s I had been one of those who helped create the Center for the Study of the American South and was involved in the creation of the Center for Black Culture. The Sonja Haynes Stone Center. And I could go into all that, but that was all organizational stuff. You could call it "service," "leadership.

So, an example would be this: When I was chair of the faculty several of us managed to get a piece of legislation passed. I believe it's still active—and that is, for out-of-state graduate students to get in-state tuition. Many international students have benefitted from this, because they are from out-of-state; it doesn't matter that they are out-of-country. Our Peace Fellows for Rotary get in-state tuition because of that provision. And that's a major savings. Well, to get that legislation done involved getting to know and working with local politicians and lobbyists, and connected people. It had similarities to being field work in that you have to mix with people and explain who you are and what you are doing. I had to do that in a thousand different ways and so its kind of and extension of fieldwork. Now, that's service. So, you think of the universities as having three features: teaching, research and service. That is service.

AK: Would any administrative responsibility be seen as "service"?

JP: Yes. It would be.

AK: Paid or unpaid?

JP: Largely unpaid. (laughs) Largely unpaid—I'll give you an example—to jump way ahead. So, in . . . let's see . . . so, I continued doing various kinds of service, including chairing a department. A stipend for chairing a department was very, very low, maybe $1,500 or something like that. Even though the amount of work for chairing a department was large! And then later, much later, when I basically built the international, or global, part of UNC, it was in 1996, that's when I became chair of the University Center for International Studies, and that was the beginning of creating all this global stuff. My stipend for doing that was $10,000 per year. And I never asked for a raise, and I did that until 2003, that was about seven years. So, for that stipend, $10,000 per year, I led an organization that brought in many millions of dollars in grants, ended up with building a building, the FedEx Global Education Center, which is a thirty-million-dollar building. And lots of other things, and lots of other programs, which you know about. And for all that work, I was earning $10,000 a year. But I was getting a normal salary, which was for being teacher, a professor, was my main income. The extra part, which was for service, was very small.

Working with Legislature

JP: Let me shift from national politics to state politics. So, my involvement there was when I chaired the faculty. There are two things, I will mention them and then maybe go into more detail. One of them was a . . . it was called "faculty legislative committee." And the other was the Black Cultural Center. I will say a little bit about both of those, because those were two of the main ways I was involved with state politics. So, I became chair of the UNC faculty, which meant the Faculty Council, or the Faculty Senate, but literally it meant all the faculty. All the fourteen schools—Medical School, Law School . . .

AK: But that's not the president of the university?

JP: No, it's different, it's the faculty, it's like the Senate. You know, the president of the university, or the chancellor, that would be like the executive branch, but the Senate, that would be like the Congress.

AK: So, what were your responsibilities there?

JP: A lot! . . . There are a lot of responsibilities, but one that I undertook was to relate to the legislature. Now, the legislature for the state of North Carolina is . . . it's a Senate and the House. There are senators, who are in the Senate, and there are representatives, who are in the House. And they come from one hundred counties of the state of North Carolina, which has about ten million citizens at the moment. It's in the top ten in terms of size. So, we created this faculty legislative committee, and we did many things, but there are two things I'll mention. One of them did impact you, I think, maybe.

AK: The Royster Society of Fellows?

JP: Not the Royster . . . I helped create the Royster, but what we did, we created, or strengthened, the provision where out-of-state students who are doing either research assistantships or teaching assistantships could get in-state tuition, which is a considerable bonus. If you think about it . . . the cost of doing that is millions of dollars, many millions of dollars.

AK: And historically everywhere in the States, if you're local, if you're from this state . . .

JP: . . . you can receive in-state tuition. And if you get in-state tuition, your tuition is a fraction of what it is if you are from out-of-state.

AK: What's the difference in percentage . . . roughly?

JP: I don't know—it has changed . . . it might be 6 or 7 times as much for out-of-state . . .

AK: And when was it introduced, this difference?

JP: Oh, it has long been there. And it's a simple reason: the legislature believed . . . that people from in state paid the taxes, and so if you are from out of the state, you don't pay the taxes, therefore, you should not receive that benefit of cheaper tuition. However, Thomas Meyer, a professor of chemistry, and I campaigned to get in-state tuition for out-of-state and out-of-country students who were doing a service for the university, like being a TA. So, we did that, and I'll tell you how, in a minute. Our other goal was to get raises for the faculty—not just Carolina, but on all seventeen campuses. And the reason for that was, at that time, this was in the 1990s, the salaries, especially for full professors, were in the lowest category among research universities. So, we were really low, and so faculty were leaving because they could get better salaries elsewhere. So, we had two goals: in-state tuition for out-of-state graduate students, and higher salaries for faculty. So, here is how we went about it. First, I went to the legislature—I had never even been there. And most faculty never did, actually. (laughs) But I went over there and I just kind of learned about it. And I went around and I just gave facts . . . I went into the offices of many of the legislators, and I just gave them the facts, you know, about . . . OK, our salaries are way low, and we're losing . . . the point was, the quality of the university, and the university is an economic engine for the state . . . You know, you have to give two or three simple reasons. And then, to help us in our lobbying . . . and by the way, we could not officially lobby. We were banned . . . faculty can't go all over and officially lobby. But informally we could make our point. So, we got somebody to help us. Two people to help us . . . three even. The first one is . . . was—he is dead, all three of them are dead—but his name was Walter Davis. Walter Davis . . . there is a whole long story about him, he was from Kitty Hawk, North Carolina, originally, he was a high-school dropout who became a billionaire. In oil. And then he became a champion of the University of North Carolina. To try to improve it in some way. (laughs) So, what he did with us was—he helped us set up meetings with some of the most influential members of the legislature, and also with the governor. Governor Hunt at that time. And at those meetings we got some of the faculty who had the most cogent arguments. For example, somebody who has a cure for cancer, and he can say, "We are one of the top cancer centers, but we're losing our best people because our salaries are so low"—that kind of thing.

It wasn't that simple, but it had to be something simple to show that the faculty were worth paying.

So, in the end . . . and then we got all the other campuses involved. At the time, I think, there were sixteen, not seventeen. So, we had people from Appalachian State and other places. People like Cece Conway joined us . . . and people from all over. And we went as a body, and we met with the budget committee.

AK: And you were the head of this . . .

JP: Yes, and Tom Meyer was helping . . . the chemist. And so, here is where anthropology kind of came in in an indirect way. This group of ours, from various faculty, went to the meeting of the budget committee for the legislature.

JP: And the chair of that was somebody named Gene Rogers, whom I had met, and accidentally, really, found out that he was a Primitive Baptist by background . . . And to make a long story short, he and I shared some things about Primitive Baptists. I did not know that he was a Primitive Baptist, but I learned it at this meeting.

AK: But by that time, you had already done your research on Primitive Baptists?

JP: Was doing . . . involved in. Anyway—so, we met, he was chair of the budget committee, and I was representing the faculty, and there were others, but they were trying to decide what salaries to pay. And I just gave them the facts—here is how we rank. And by the way, we never mentioned the actual amount of our salaries, and the reason we did not is because if you heard the actual amount, and then compare it to the actual amount that most citizens of North Carolina made, you would say: "Why do they need higher salaries?" Because they made . . . you know, the average citizen makes $30,000, so why does somebody need to make $50,000? So, we gave percentiles, not actual figures. So, we were at the bottom percentile nationally. And we really were. And we had charts . . . Anyway—he knew those things. So, the committee was debating . . . whether to give a raise to the faculty, and if so, what percent.

AK: So, this question was decided at the state legislature? They allocate money for universities . . .

JP: Correct. That's right. And they have these committees, and he was the head of the budget committee. Anyway, so they were discussing it, and

I had arranged for him to get a very rare book, which was the history of Primitive Baptists in this state. Anyway—as they were discussing, he came over, and he sort of tapped me on the shoulder, and he said, "By the way, I am a Primitive Baptist." And I thought—well, that's nice. Well, nothing more was said, but we got the highest raise in recent times, and that was not just for UNC-CH, it was the entire state . . . it's like fifty thousand faculty.

AK: Hail to the Primitive Baptists! (laughs)

JP: Exactly. And I think in some small way . . . and later we became friends and visited Mr. Rogers . . . So, two things about that—I think that . . . personal contacts, giving the facts . . . oh, and then we had these two allies. I already mentioned Walter Davis, but we had two other crucial allies: Al Adams and Zeb Alley. They were two top lobbyists for the North Carolina legislature. They normally would lobby for all kinds of things—they were paid lobbyists. People would pay them to lobby for whatever need they wanted. But they also were alumni of UNC. And so, we didn't pay them anything, they just volunteered and they helped us to figure out what to do. And actually, Al helped write the bill, the appropriation that gave the raises to all the state . . . it was actually all the state employees, and it passed. So, this is one thing we did. It was in the 1990s.

AK: Can you say a little bit about the Public Ivy? Because we are that. How did the concept of a public ivy evolve, and how did we become that?

JP: Well, it's just kind of an informal designation. It's not anything official. You know, the standard category of the Ivy League—you know, who they are: the Harvard, Princeton, several of those. The term "Public Ivy" is sometimes applied to the University of Virginia, University of North Carolina, Michigan . . . maybe Berkeley. In ranking of the public universities, these are often the top four. And so, some people call them Public Ivies.

AK: It's actually in the Wikipedia, so it's a pretty official name.

JP: Oh, is it? Well, what this basically means is: these are publicly funded universities, but in some way they . . . resemble the Ivy schools. Royster Fellowships, or honors programs like the Morehead—they provide special support, special programs somewhat like the Ivy Leagues provide—but they are state universities.

AK: Do you think the perception, or even the name of UNC as a Public Ivy university has to do with this huge project that you just described—raising of the salaries and keeping the best professors?

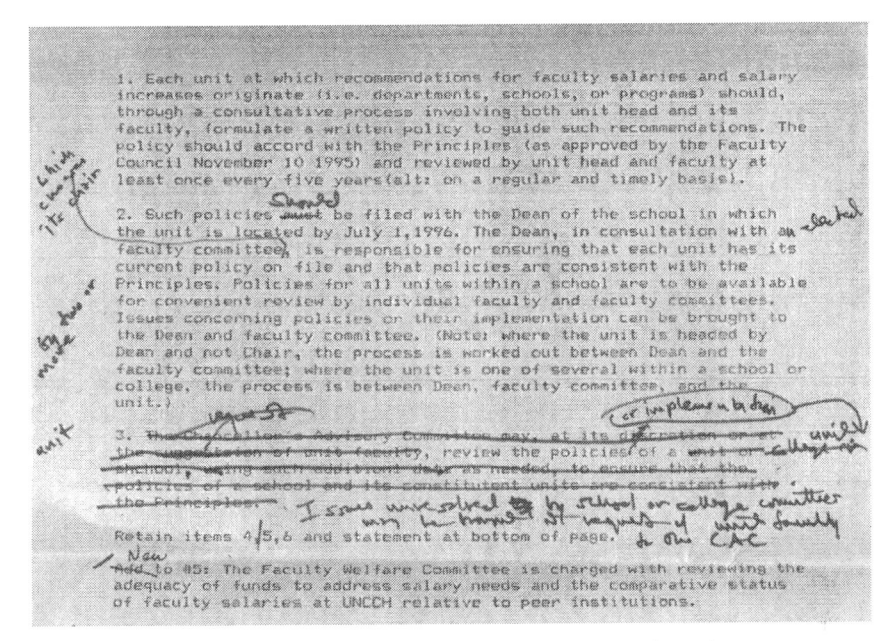

James Peacock's notes on a document draft related to faculty salaries.

JP: I'll tell you the truth: not as much as you might think. And the reason is, it probably means more to wealthy donors who probably got their degrees at Harvard or something, or have children who go to the . . . The majority of the legislators—remember they come from all one hundred counties—and so, when we were lobbying, trying to make the case for Carolina, we would never say anything like Public Ivy. But we would say things like, well, this is what people are paid . . . but we were not even emphasizing that. We would say: "They are important for the economics of the state." For example, businesses come here because they think they can employ educated workers, that sort of thing. We would emphasize the economic side, we would emphasize the more practical side, like, if you compare the top hospitals, the two of them, Duke and Carolina, one is public, one is private, but both are better than they would be if they did not have support.

And by the way, people almost never realized that I was an anthropologist. If they asked me, I would tell them, but Zeb Alley made a little introduction one time . . . Zeb was this guy from the mountains, smart as a whip. Florence and I used to go to his house and would have a barbeque in his backyard, and one time he and Al Adams actually went to a recital that Florence did, in Raleigh, and they were so nice, they put on their coats and ties, and they sat there . . . I mean, they were smart, very smart people. I think, Al went to an Ivy League prep school. But anyway—I'm getting off the subject. Zeb Alley—one time he introduced me as an anthropologist to some of his friends. He said: "This is Jim, he has come to measure your heads." (laughs) So, that was their picture . . . if any picture, of someone who measures your head . . . And then now and then somebody may say, "Well, in my county we have some really interesting grave-sites." If they heard anything about me, they thought, oh, he is an archaeologist.

AK: What did they think you were?

JP: Oh, they never asked . . . rarely asked. They knew I was from UNC. Some of them, of course, knew a lot . . . [but] people have all kinds of backgrounds . . . But we were trying to go to the basics first.

This is still when I was president of AAA . . . and in a minute I'll go into the global thing. When Annette Weiner was president, and I was president elect, and she died of cancer prematurely, but at a certain time we were working together. So, one of the things that she and I chose to do was to sell the building where AAA headquarters were. And it was an old house on Dupont Circle. We sold it for one million dollars, and we sold it to a Black sorority. And then we moved all of the offices out into the suburbs of Virginia and rented offices. And so, we had a million dollars to invest, and we invested it, and we had now about sixteen million.

AK: Endowment?

JP: Endowment. Now—that's perhaps the only endowment for AAA. Now—at a recent meeting a particular person who is a Marxist protested the fact that we have an endowment, and he said, "It's obscene that AAA has this endowment when so many of its members have a need." Of course, it's true . . . many have needs.

AK: But you're creating more money out of what you had . . .

JP: That's what we thought. So, an example of how we use this money is the following, and it's kind of related to the Marxist versus capitalist procedure. I can't remember the exact year, but maybe in the teens, 2010 or something like that, Hilton Hotel in California—maybe it was San Francisco, or maybe it was LA—there was a strike, workers' strike. And some of the anthropologists joined the strike and boycotted the meeting at the Hilton Hotel in California, because, they said, they were unfair to workers. So, the AAA president of that time canceled the AAA meeting. They rescheduled the meetings and put them in Atlanta a month later . . . the problem is, normally at AAA meetings about eight thousand people attend, and they all pay the registration fee. And that's the main income of AAA.

AK: Membership fee and registration fee.

JP: Precisely. OK, when they canceled it and then moved it to Atlanta, a very small number of people came there, about five hundred. And so, they lost . . . most of their income for that year. Fortunately, we had created this endowment, and we could cover the loss. That's my simple capitalistic view, and if you think about it, if you don't have any backup money, then sooner or later you don't have the organization anymore, which does many things, including, supposedly . . . help placement and . . . the rest.

AK: Any organization needs money to function!

JP: To function, yes.

Public Anthropology

AK: Leedom Lefferts mentioned that you as president of AAA were responsible for convening groups on Black studies, LGBT studies, and so on. And his—and my—question is: were you selected or even appointed to do this, or did you somehow volunteer to chair those meetings?

JP: Let me think about that. OK, first of all, I was certainly involved with all those groups—in fact, during the recent meeting in California I ran into Tony Whitehead, a Black man, who was president of the Society of Black Anthropologists. And who also used to be at Chapel Hill, a good friend.

AK: There is a separate society for Black anthropologists?

JP: Yes. AAA probably has fifty different . . . there is another one for Hispanic anthropologists, and there is women's issues, or studies . . . feminist . . . all that. So, I was not really responsible for organizing these groups, they just . . . they organize themselves usually. What we had were called "sections," and they had different specialties. And then we had interest groups. And the interest groups were created usually . . . by the groups. So, we had both, and I did not really create these. But I'll tell the main thing I created . . . I guess. It was called "public anthropology."

AK: When did this happen and what was it about?

JP: It was when I was president, and I think it was probably 1994. And I was chair of the faculty at UNC during the same time. So, each president was giving a presidential address, and mine was called "The Future of Anthropology." And that was published later in *American Anthropologist*. But in a nutshell, it was simply this: it was a call for anthropologists to become engaged with public issues . . . I had a little slogan, which is not in the essay, but it was in the speech, and it said: not only "publish or perish," but "public or perish." And that was the point. So, we have all this knowledge, so let's apply some of it, addressing public issues. And those public issues would of course include things like feminism, and immigration, you know, all of them—a lot of what we are talking about right now in the world. This was one of my . . .

AK: Basically, you initiated what's now called "applied anthropology"?

JP: No, it was not. Let me show you something . . .

AK: And what's the difference between "public" and "applied"?

JP: I'm going to explain it right now. [shows a book]

AK: *An Anthropology of Anthropology.*

JP: This is a new book . . . by Robert Borofsky.* And he asked me to write a comment on the back, which I have done. He basically copies my proposal, except he goes to extremes, in my opinion. He has me cited somewhere. So, if I were to mention my most distinctive contribution, it would be to underline the importance of addressing public issues through anthropology. Now—by the time it was published it was 1997, but the speech was in 1994—many societies have copied that idea. American Society of Sociology—they had a presidential address maybe two years ago for "public sociology," and historians have one for "public history" . . .

AK: They came with those ideas themselves, or they copied your idea?

JP: I don't know. But I used the term first . . . Here is the difference between "applied" and "public." Of course, they are quite similar. The idea is that we apply our knowledge, but applied anthropologist . . . and there is a society for applied anthropology—often do things that are very specific, for example, work with women to improve their birth process . . .

---

*Robert Borofsky, *An Anthropology of Anthropology: Is It Time to Shift Paradigms?* (Center for a Public Anthropology, 2019).

AK: Or applied anthropology of obesity . . .

JP: Obesity, or urban anthropology to improve cities—you know, it's a more specific type thing. OK, "Here is a problem, let's help solve it." Public anthropology included that, but it also put forward the idea of addressing public issues, you know, like immigration . . .

AK: Like, larger issues?

JP: Larger issues. Immigration is a national and an international issue . . . And there are others, like racism, then . . . you know, you could list fifty. So, the idea of public anthropology was simply: "Let's get into the arguments and try to consider actions." Not too long ago I wrote a piece called "Muslims: Friend or Foe?" And it tried to combat the idea that all Muslims are foes.

AK: So, public anthropology is a broader pursuit, and more theoretical in some sense?

JP: Correct. More theoretical and more . . . outreaching, further out, and including writings for larger audiences.

AK: But it sort of grew out of . . . I mean, public anthropology sort of launched or created the background within which applied anthropology as a focused, project-oriented pursuit emerged later?

JP: No, it was the other way. Applied anthropology has been around for a long time, but the public anthropology was a later addition . . . You know, the idea of a "public intellectual"?

AK: So, the succession is from applied to public, right?

JP: Yes, it is.

AK: And so, you have already been known for this "public anthropology."

JP: Probably, somewhat.

AK: And so, would you say this was the reason why you were asked to chair all those committees . . .

JP: Right. Who knows, why I was asked to chair those things, but I can tell you about some of them.

AK: It's 2007.

JP: Yes. So, this one was partly about the "human terrain," There was a controversy about the CIA . . . they posted an advertisement, or they proposed to post an advertisement, recruiting the anthropologists to join the CIA.

AK: So, it was not, like, "We need your knowledge on this particular military conflict, you have to join the CIA . . . "

JP: That was one proposal. And so, there was a controversy, shall we join the CIA, or allow the CIA to invite people to join it through the AAA, and many opposed that idea. And so, that got into a larger question of what should the anthropologist's relation to the military be? And to other security groups? And there was a lot of debate about that, and so they asked me to chair this committee.

AK: There is George Marcus here . . .

JP: All those were on it. I was the chair, and these are all the people who were members of the committee, or commission, I think, it was called.

AK: And this was like a round table, or . . .

JP: It was a lot more than that. So, anyway, I invited people to be on it, some of whom, like David Price, were adamantly against any involvement with the military at all. And then others were actually employed by the military.

AK: So, you collected a diverse group of people?

JP: Correct. Laura McNamara was employed at the atomic project in New Mexico, and . . . Kerry Fosher, she works in Quantico, Virginia, the Marine base . . .

AK: So, you intentionally put different people together?

JP: I did. That's the way Abraham Lincoln did it: he assembled a cabinet of people who disagreed with each other. Because his idea was: I'll get many points of view, and that way I can arrive at a more considered conclusion.

AK: So, you followed the path of . . .

JP: Abraham Lincoln, yeah. So, we had many meetings, mostly virtual at first. We mainly just communicated by telephone or by email. But then we also set up some conferences at Brown University—they have a University Center for International Studies there, it's called the Watson Center, after the founder of IBM. Thomas Watson.

AK: Why not here? We already had the FedEx building . . .

JP: I'll tell you why: because the Watson Center has lots of money, and we didn't have any money, that's why. So, we met there, and we debated various things, including the Human Terrain. That was something that people like anthropologist David Price opposed, because the Department of State at that time was apparently recruiting anthropologists and other scholars into working with the military.

AK: How popular was this idea among anthropologists?

JP: Well, it varied tremendously! We did a study—it turned out that there were a hundred anthropologists whose career was currently with the military. And here is one outcome of chairing that committee. I got a telephone call from the Pentagon. Department of Defense. They asked me if I would meet with them in Chapel Hill. So, they sent a whole delegation to Chapel Hill from the Pentagon, and they met with three people: the chancellor, the head of computer science, because they had contracts with computer people, and me. And the reason they met with me was this issue: "Why is it that anthropologists alone, among all the scholars, are so stubborn about . . . so resistant to involvement with defense?"

AK: So, sociologists would not be as adamantly . . .

JP: Apparently not. Anyway, that was their reason. And so, we met.

AK: Were they wearing their uniforms and stuff?

JP: Yeah, some were. And I'll tell you one thing: They were better informed about this issue than any of the anthropologists who kept raising the ruckus, because most of those didn't really know anything. But these guys had really done their homework. So, what I did was, I explained to them why the anthropologists were up in arms about it, and one of the reasons was that the anthropology code of ethics basically has one rule: "Do no harm." And many of the anthropologists were afraid that if military and fieldworkers got enmeshed with each other too much, it could endanger their informants. That was their reason. And the guys in the Pentagon were *very* understanding of that!

AK: Really?

JP: Absolutely! And they said: "Is there a way that we could deal with that problem?" And so, they tried to think of ways . . . I remember one guy . . . the head of that [group] was a particle physicist. And later he said, "You know, we just think the same way: particle physicist and anthropologist."

AK: One of the guys from the Pentagon was also a particle physicist?

JP: He was the head of the whole Pentagon research team. So, they tried to think of ways that . . . tried to think of ways to do it ethically.

AK: So, they were not trying to hard-press you, like, here are national interests, why don't you join . . .

JP: No, they didn't hard-press at all, they just . . . they wanted to have anthropologists involved, because they know more about places than anybody else.

AK: But apart from anthropologists, whom else were they trying to involve? Sociologists, maybe . . . who else?

JP: Well, in the Human Terrain . . . it turned out that at that time there were 405 scholars who were doing the Human Terrain. And later I met many of them.

AK: And they were coming from which disciplines?

JP: Many: religious studies, sociology . . . various things. And there were only four anthropologists. Out of 405. And all the controversy, you know, was about . . . and probably for that reason very few anthropologists joined that, but there were many from other fields. Many people who were specialists in Far Eastern Studies, for example.

Anthropologists' Involvement in War Actions

AK: Did you have any rivals in the proper sense of the word during your career?

JP: Did I have rivals? Oh, sure, I had lots of rivals (laughs) . . . in a way. Well, here is one rival. So, I came to Carolina, and there was a guy here named Stephen Polgar. He was Jewish, and his specialty was population planning and birth control. He was in the Population Center.

AK: So, he was not in Anthropology?

JP: He was. But he also was in the Population Center. And he was somewhat older than I, probably not much older. And I wouldn't say we were rivals, but we had different approaches to things . . . Let me tell you a little bit about him. He was a survivor of the Holocaust. Apparently, he was in a concentration camp—he was from Hungary—when he was maybe twelve years old or something like that he might have been in the camp with his mother. That's just background. And within anthropology he was part of a faction within the AAA that was opposed to the Vietnam War, and so he was an activist. And at that time, which was in the late 1960s, or maybe into the 1970s, you know, it was when the Vietnam War was at its peak, and the CIA was apparently recruiting anthropologists to be their so-called advisors . . . Berkeley tended to be kind of a hotbed of opposition to that, and there was a guy at Berkeley whose name was, I think, Gerald Berreman, and he and Polgar were comrades in this opposition. I really wasn't involved in it at all. But if I had been, I probably would have been more sympathetic to the military. After all, I had a father who had been in the military.

AK: But your experience and the experience of a person who as a child was in a concentration camp would have been very different.

JP: I know. Totally different. And I understand that, and I completely agree. So, I'm just saying . . . you said "rivals"—no, we weren't "rivals" exactly, but he had different views. And he was also a bit older than I was, probably eight or nine, or maybe ten years older.

AK: Speaking of this, there was another thing that I paid attention to in Leedom's interview. He said, "Anthropology in WWII was very different from anthropology in the Vietnam War." And he said this in response to my remark that as far as I know Cora Du Bois was a spy during the war.

JP: I don't think . . . not a spy . . .

AK: Not a spy, but she was working for the government.

JP: She did. Correct.

AK: Leedom said, everybody did that during the war . . .

JP: Precisely. No, he is absolutely right. During WWII . . . it was considered a "good war" by comparison to Vietnam. So, during WWII a lot of the major anthropologists worked for the US government and maybe other allied governments.

AK: So, when those debates opened about the Vietnam War, did you think of the past . . . did you refer to this involvement during WWII as an important precedent or an important chapter in the anthropological involvement with their governments?

JP: I guess I did, but it seemed like a contrast. So, I knew a lot about the involvement of the anthropologists in WWII, and they were people like Margaret Mead and Gregory Bateson, and I read a lot of about that . . . *Cul-*

ture at a Distance* . . . all those people . . . many of them were at Cornell and Columbia Universities. And many others . . . including Mead and Bateson . . . and Cora Du Bois. During that time, it was an admirable thing to do from the American point of view and the allies' point of view, and a lot of the interesting research was being done under that rubric. And a lot of the early schools of thought, including psychological anthropology, and then later "national character studies," which were the first studies of the Nazis, the Germans, and the Russians . . .

AA: The major enemies . . .

JP: Yeah—the Japanese . . . think of Ruth Benedict and the study of the Japanese.

AK: *The Chrysanthemum and the Sword.*

JP: Right . . . think of Margaret Mead's book *And Keep Your Powder Dry*.[†] She equated fighting for the allies with the Americans fighting for the revolution in the 1700s. So, it was a patriotic thing to do—to fight. And if you were an anthropologist and could help the cause—fine. So, it was a positive thing then, during WWII. I think that's what he is [saying].

AK: So, this "National Character studies," it was a special program that was initiated . . . ?

JP: It was an approach, but a lot of it was being done at Columbia.

AK: And when did they initiate this program?

JP: After WWII. It was when the Cold War had begun. But it really started during WWII . . . *The Chrysanthemum and the Sword* and other studies of the so-called "national character."

AK: And this approach would presuppose that each nation would have a certain typeset . . .

JP: Precisely. And in that early time, they also had a psychological basis, like, Russian are . . . what are they . . . ?

AK: Swaddling!

---

* Margaret Mead, *The Study of Culture at a Distance* (Chicago: University of Chicago Press, 1953).
† Margaret Mead, *And Keep Your Powder Dry: An Anthropologist Looks at America* (New York: Morrow, 1965).

JP: Swaddling! That's the word I'm looking for.

AK: Like, they lack initiative because the first months of their life they are tightly . . .

JP: Actually, it was a binary thing: they are swaddled, but then, when they can get loose . . . ! They go wild and they do . . . the balalaika plays and . . . So, that was kind of a stereotype . . . and there was a British guy who wrote about that.

AK: How many years did this approach exist?

JP: Ten.

AK: And then why did it . . . ?

JP: Because it was too imperfect. You know, there are too many stereotypes about different nations . . . it got a lot of criticism.

Robert Daniels (RD): I met Cora Du Bois [at Harvard].

AK: Yes, that was his supervisor.

RD: Right. Who was described to me as having a mind like a steel trap.

AK: During the war she was in the military, I think . . . a spy or something . . .

RD: You know, it turns out, they all were. My sort of inspiration, Gregory Bateson . . . well, I never actually knew him, it turns out it was through Margaret Mead . . . they all . . . everybody was in the war. Which they didn't see any ethical problems with that I can see. And maybe they need to have ethical problems, for god's sake. In the introduction to *The People of Alor*, which was republished in paperback, she writes about the agony of having worked in this community, where she was "America," and then having to flee in front of the Japanese, and then coming back after the liberation to find out that anybody who had spoken to her were killed by the Japanese. Because of the association with her. I mean, it's a bleak . . . she obviously doesn't spend pages on that . . . But she talks about this moral burden of . . . fieldwork in that kind of situation.

(1_Daniels_22_09_2018)

AK: What about Cora Du Bois?

Leedom Lefferts (LL): She was initially a Southeast Asianist. Southeast Asian anthropologist.

AK: And also a spy during the war . . . ?

LL: (laughs) Well . . . anthropology in WWII was very different than anthropology in the Vietnam War. And maybe he talked to you about it to some extent.

AK: He said, she was doing some governmental . . .

LL: Sure, sure . . . well, everybody was. It was a kind of national mobilization that . . . didn't occur in the 1960s.

(2_Lefferts_23_09_2018)

RD: You know, for the AAA he also did a big study about anthropology in the military. The Human Terrain project—are you familiar with that term?

AK: That's when they hired anthropologists . . .

RD: . . . to figure out who to shoot in Afghanistan.

AK: This was about seven or eight years ago, pretty recently, right? Anthro in the military . . . he did a presentation at AAA . . . ?

RD: No, he chaired, I guess, a report about this . . . OK, if you go to the website with my papers on it . . . there are a bunch of papers about Africa, and there is one called "Where Is Anthropology When You Need It?" Which I wrote ten years ago. It's all about the energy problem. But in there, in the midst of it all . . . it rambles all over the place, I happened to get into this whole question of anthropology in the military.

AK: There was AAA statement on ethics . . .

RD: And Jim Peacock chaired that. And . . . I think it pleased no one. You know, it harkened all back to Vietnam, and the great . . . uncovering of how anthropologists were used in Vietnam to decide who to shoot.

(1_Daniels_22_09_2018)

LL: If you look at the list of presidents of the American Anthropological Association, he is . . . up until 19 . . . until the 2000s, he was the only one from the South. Look at what he did! He worked on ethics things, he worked on the LGBT thing, he worked on the minority thing, the Black... he was central to those, at least organizing them and getting them moving. So, there is something there. People recognize that he is a person that can hopefully get things done.

LL: Well, there are not so many anthropologists in the South. Worthy of the name. And these are . . . by the way, most of the presidents are from an Ivy League or across the North there. Stretching . . . Wisconsin, Minnesota, all the way there! Down the West Coast to California, Berkeley and the UCLA—I mean, I'm giving a . . . There might be Chicago there, and . . . Saint Louis. And he is there—and so, there is something interesting there. There is something interesting. He was the only . . . at the time he was elected president of AAA, he was the furthest south president they ever had! (laughs)

(2_Lefferts_23_09_2018)

AAA: The Napoleon Chagnon Case

JP: Then not too long after that I was asked to chair another controversial committee, and that was about Napoleon Chagnon.

AK: Yes, I heard about it—it's about ethics of field research . . . could you remind me about this?

JP: Sure. Napoleon Chagnon, who is still alive . . . he is my age—had done fieldwork in Brazil, among the Yanomamö, and he wrote many renowned and widely used books. Well, somebody wrote a book called *Darkness in Paradise*, and it was about ways he and some others did fieldwork among the Yanomamö.[*] And there were a number of accusations, but basically it was that they violated the precept "Do no harm." Well, one thing about that was when he did that work, we did not have an ethics code. He was doing his research in the 1960s, at the same time I was doing mine. So, again, it seems when something was controversial, they would ask me (laughs) to chair a committee, and I chaired this one . . . And the way that they asked me to do it, was—they said, "Would you please, you and your committee, consider the issues and the accusations, and advise us, should we investigate them at length?"

---

[*] Patrick Tierney, *Darkness in El Dorado: How Scientists and Journalists Devastated the Amazon* (New York: Norton, 2000).

AK: Like, real, legal investigation? There was something with biology?

JP: Yes, there was a biological component, it was blood samples, and whether they should have taken them . . . So, we did that, and I wrote a report . . .

AK: And this was recently? The Chagnon case?

JP: Maybe 2000 and something. He responded later in a book, which is called *The Noble Savages and Not So Noble Anthropologists*.* And if you read that book, he does mention me and my part, and he says something like, "He has a reputation of being fair." So, what happened, was this: So, we looked into it, and then we came up with a report, a recommendation. And it was "Yes, investigate it." I presented that to the board of the AAA, and so they did instigate an investigation, and Jane Hill chaired it—she was a previous president.

AK: So, was Chagnon accused . . . ?

JP: It was not really a legal . . . not a court trial, it was more of an investigation by an academic society, the ethics of one of its members. But it was not a legal trial . . . he was not endangered with being sent to prison or anything like that, but it was more of a censure of him. And then there was a lot of controversy about that: Some people defended him, and then he wrote this book noted above . . .

AK: Did you regard participation in these projects, like, chairing of special committees as part of your service or part of your professional . . .

JP: Service. It didn't have any research . . . it might have some, but it was service, not research. And it wasn't teaching.

AK: And you did this without any compensation?

JP: Correct. No compensation . . . I was on thirty doctoral committees probably. And there were other faculty, like Julia Crane—she arrived the same time I did. She was probably on thirty committees also.

AK: Bob Daniels told me that because he is of the generation that got a four-field training, he was asked to be on archaeological committees . . .

JP: Oh, yeah, I was on those, too. I was on archaeology committees, probably committees on public health, various things.

---

*Napoleon A. Chagnon, *Noble Savages: My Life among Two Dangerous Tribes—the Yanomamö and the Anthropologists* (New York: Simon & Schuster, 2013).

AK: All four fields . . .

JP: Well, I don't know if I was ever on a biological one, but I was a lot on the archaeology ones.

AK: But approximately how many PhD students did you have over your career?

JP: I'm not sure. Maybe fifty, something like that. I could tell you the names of just about all of them.

AK: Give me some names—who was . . . ?

JP: Cece Conway. But I was not her chair—she was in English. Bill Lachicotte. Let me think . . . if I just go back . . . Page Guttierez . . . and I remember what most of them were doing, I mean the topic and the work they did, and I was involved in it sometimes. Like, mule trading. And the topics have changed. The trends were just the same as with anthropology in general: postmodernism started coming in, maybe more studies focused on identity of this kind or that kind, gender . . .

Dan Patterson (DP): FedEx . . . I guess he must have pushed for the wider perspective here at UNC. Because he and Florence were behind this Global South . . . his name is on it, isn't it?

AK: The atrium in FedEx.

DP: And that was because of their efforts to raise money for foreign support. I think that must have been one of his major contributions to the university—adding something that was not here before. Other people were doing . . . several other ones, at least one, Brockington was working in Mexico, they were all going places . . . Anthropology by nature was sending people out, but he wanted to incorporate it, I guess, into the larger campus perspective.

AK: UNC is unique in having an international building like FedEx as a separate building—usually international programs are scattered around various buildings on campus. That's one of his achievements—not an exclusively personal achievement, but he contributed a lot to it.

DP: And he wouldn't claim it to himself—he always worked with other people, and that was his other major strength . . . helping people.

(7_The_Pattersons_Feb_9_2019)

Herman Greene (HG): From my perspective, which is not from within the academic community, he is more known for being kind of an ambassador . . . he served on . . . I mean, as for the University Center for International Studies, he would go to different places in the world, to talk about the university. I think one time they were thinking about having a foreign campus . . . I'm pretty sure there was one going to be in the Middle East, but that never came to be . . . But yeah, he served on so many different boards, I don't know, if you have a record of those, but . . . but I think his work in establishing the International Center, and all his different roles as faculty, and different committees, and his role in the community as . . . civic role . . . I think, for me those are what stands out.

(8_The_Greenes_March_28_2019)

AK: He is unique in that he was the only president of the American Anthropological Association who was not only born in the South but worked all of his life in the South.

Sandra Rich (SaR): Others are from larger well-known communities . . .

AK: East Coast, West Coast, and the North, like, Chicago. But he is the only one . . . the Southerner.

Steven Rich (StR): Born in the South, worked in the South.

AK: Right.

SaR: And he is proud to be—but he represents the South beautifully. I wish more people could learn from him on being representative of Southern culture and background. Because he is just so accepting and . . . even, you know, when he speaks, it's slow and deliberate . . .

StR: No judgment . . . and Florence is the same way.

(9_The_Riches_July_24_2019)

AK: Do you know about their atrium in the FedEx building?

Nerys Levy (NL): Without Jim there wouldn't have been FedEx. I don't know exactly, how it's . . . he helped the International Center. And the person who can tell you more about this International Center would be Sharon Mujica. She was in charge of Latin American studies outreach. And she lives in Chapel Hill still. But she worked in this building they had on

Franklin Street before they moved. Sharon is a resource! They worked with Jim for years in the international center. And he kept saying: "We've got to get out of this building." Because she was on the top floor with her Latin American studies, and Jim was in there, and I think he was one of the people who started to build that relationship . . . whether the university can grow it into something bigger. And now . . . when we did our polar show, we had . . . in 2010, I worked both in the Arctic and Antarctic, and I also went to the Arctic with Jim and Florence and Brooks de Wetter-Smith. And we were going to have a show in the FedEx Global Education Center on climate change—the Ackland didn't want to. And Jim and I and Brooks went to the Norwegian Arctic, on a boat. So, I've traveled with Jim as well. But then Jim realized the importance when he could see . . . climate change at first glance—he got the money. Through the FedEx Global Education Center, through departments to fund this exhibit. And from the exhibit that was going to be just photographs and paintings . . . it lasted for six months! And we ended up bringing in the law department, geophysics, environmental studies, eighteen schools . . . I was already doing the big polar project in the middle school here with Brooks, we brought the animals that kids had made . . . And we had an opening, which was video with music. And Terry Mizesko from North Carolina Symphony composed a composition, and Florence sang, and we had harp, and flute, and . . . It was a big deal, you know.

AK: When was this exhibition?

NL: In 2010. February 2010. It was a huge thing! It was called Ice Counterpoint. And so, it's in the archives of the FedEx Global Education Center. And so . . . Jim got money for us for this, like, $20,000, you know. Because to pay the composer, and then Brooks had a lot of photographs . . . the painter doesn't get paid . . . my hand nearly . . . burst! But we ended up with a program . . . and I was telling Jim—he didn't know that: but they set up a polar department after our show. Because they never knew how to deal with Alaska. And I think there is still a polar studies section in FedEx—and that's because of us. Because of our show and because of Jim. But he doesn't know it's there—I hope it's still there; the last time I looked it was still there . . . I said, you need to have polar studies, I was involved, you know, with all these conversations. So, we had this go on for six months. I worked with Jim on it, so, you know, we worked together getting the show, and that was really important in the wider context of applied anthropology in a sense. And applying it not only to cultures but also to areas, regional areas, under threat. And that still applies, you know. But he is also in his peace studies, and he has brought in, as you well know, all these different students. And giving

Professor Peacock's retirement party in the FedEx Global Education Center, 2015.

those people a life-line in their own country as a result. But also giving them a break to think about . . . their whole status in the world.

(10_Levy_Nerys_July_27_2019)

AK: [About FedEx building and the history of its construction]

Cece Conway (CC): When Jim was running the global education before there was that building, he was trying to do fundraising, he may have been contemplating applying for the president of the university, provost or president at some point.

AK: You apply for this—or you get appointed?

CC: Or . . . maybe he was nominated, I don't know. But he might have been contemplating the possibility of being nominated or applying. And I know he had some major fundraisers before he made the move to the FedEx building. [CC asks AK to tell the whole story, AK tells about the bonds to raise money.] Maybe Niklaus Steiner helped broker the FedEx part . . .

And he works there . . . There is the Rotary and Peace scholarship that he has done—he helped make it happen, and it's still . . . and World View over there—a hundred teachers there, one from every county, come to these events that they put up every year.

AK: And he initiated this?

CC: He helped . . . make it happen. I don't know the details. And the Rotary Peace Fellows is huge! And they support the symphony, and even in places like Hendersonville, North Carolina, which has been able to at least have the symphony come once in ten years, thanks to them! That's getting more into Florence's interests, but also that's his . . .

AK: Service! That's his service!

CC: Service to the community! Exactly!

(11_Conway_July_29_2019)

AK: So, these are not end-of-the-year parties?

JP: No . . . often, they had a political speaker—maybe Congressman David Price or somebody like that. They are always to the left I would say. Students could also come . . .

CC: If they were invited.

JP: I mean . . . neighbors from down the street would be there and various people. I think they were not exclusive—anybody who knew about it could come.

CC: But then meanwhile Jim and Florence were having major political parties in their house, and they were having end-of-the-semester parties for students of the Global South and Dream Group people. And they had a lady who did fabulous fried chicken at some point . . .

JP: I think they were joking because these gatherings, they usually were mix-up things—neighbors sometimes, and students, and faculty, and . . . whoever. A lot of it is neighborhood.

AK: Probably, they walked in and heard words like "paradigm" and "discourse" . . .

CC: Didn't you have one for service dogs?

JP: Oh, yes, we had those. Florence got involved in all those things . . . She might have . . .

Service

AK: Service dogs?

JP: They are rescue dogs, and she had some of those gatherings, and there were dogs all over the house. (all laugh) Florence would have all those things for this or that cause or group, and who knows, maybe Mensa was one of them, and I wouldn't know who they were!

CC: But then one time not too long ago, and I forget which party this was, Charles Frazier, who wrote *Cold Mountain*, was there—that was exciting.

AK: Who is Charles Frazier?

CC: He wrote a very famous novel *Cold Mountain*, and another one called *Thirteen Moons*.

AK: And a movie was done . . .

JP: *Cold Mountain*, with Nicole Kidman starring in it. And then they made an opera from it, and that's where Florence came in, because the North Carolina Opera Company, which is really very good, they are based in Raleigh, they produced *Cold Mountain*. And so, that's when Charles Frazier came, because they produced an opera based on his novel. And so, he came to our house. He is a very empathetic type of person. You talk to him and he's just like your brother, and maybe that's why he is a good novelist. Florence was the instigator for most of these parties, I rarely . . . my job was to carry things. (laughs)

CC: The harpsicord!

JP: Yeah!

AK: So, these were themed parties, but you were . . .

JP: They weren't even themed, who knows, I mean, there were so many . . . a lot of times it might have been like . . . The *Cold Mountain* one was around the author, but other times it was more a political thing. Somebody like David Price . . .

(13_Peacock_Conway_McCanless_July_31_2019)

SaR: We moved here . . .

StR: . . . the very end of 2003.

SaR: December. We came from Atlanta, Georgia, we had been students at Carolina in 1964—Stephen and I were married in the fall of his senior year, in

1963—it would be my junior year here. Took us forty-two years to come back to Chapel Hill, but we are very happy we did because we got to meet people like Jim and Florence Peacock. But we'd moved in with our two dogs and my sister. And we'd gone out for the evening, and we came back, and there was a note that our dogs had escaped the little gates, and the note was from Florence Peacock. She had found them and put them back in the yard . . .

AK: I can't imagine Florence chasing the dogs . . . (laughs)

SaR: . . . other than she is a kind, gentle person, and the dogs realized that, and they probably came to her. Because that is her nature. They felt her caring. And I guess they probably wanted to get back to the house.

(9_The_Riches_July_24_2019)

Pete Andrews (PA): So, I don't remember when I first met Jim—I remember he was chair of the faculty in the early 1990s, and then Jane Brown followed him, and I thought of Jane starting in 1997. So, clearly by that time I knew him through . . . one of his greatest contributions was creating the Executive Committee of the Faculty Council, ECFC. He may not have done it alone, there might have been others—he could tell you whether there were other collaborators on that, but it was during his term, in the early 1990s, that . . . The chair of the faculty is elected from the entire university faculty for a three-year term. I've been chair of the public policy since then as well. This is part of university governance, faculty governance. In the early 1990s, when he was chair of the faculty, I became . . . or maybe right after that, I became a member of the Executive Committee of Faculty Council, which he was largely responsible for creating. I don't know the exact history of that . . .

AK: What's the council about?

PA: The chair of the faculty, he chairs the Faculty Council, and so represents the interests and the views of the faculty to the larger world. To the university administration, to the public, to the legislature . . . Until the early 1990s, it was kind of a solo-job, you know, and . . . how do I represent the views of the faculty, and also, what happens in the summer when faculty is not around? Do I just . . . you know . . . So, Jim created the Executive Committee of the Faculty Council, a small working group of about a dozen respected faculty members who could act in the absence of the faculty, to represent the views of the faculty to the administration, and also to give the chair of the faculty a stronger base from which to represent the faculty. So, if the chair of the faculty had to argue with the chancellor or something like that, it was not just one person, it was . . . it was very smart. So, he and his successor, Jane Brown, in the end . . . the executive committee, which I was a member of, would meet to talk about the role of the chair of the faculty, and what were the issues we needed to deal with.

. . .

PA: I came into that role when I was chair of the faculty, and one of the major issues that I dealt with as chair of the faculty was changing the tuition model. For decades, you know, there had been this conventional wisdom that . . . propagated by President Friday, President Spangler, and others . . . that low tuition was the best form of financial aid. And when I became chair of the faculty, one new and brilliant person on the staff, the director of financial aid, she brought data to me and said: "It's not true. Low tuition is the best form of financial aid for rich kids from Charlotte, who could go to an Ivy League, but their parents would promise them an SUV if they go to Carolina." She said: "We are actually thirty-seven in access for low-income kids." So, we went through a real . . . the faculty was very divided, but I, and several people, and Jim of course, were involved in this. The leaders for that were a couple of professors from chemistry and economics, who were closely associated with that, and we . . . First proposed that we need to increase tuition but provide more financial aid and one of the reasons for increasing tuition was to provide more money for the faculty salaries. That's why I said it—back to your question. But the legislature was gradually underfunding faculty salaries, and we were at risk of . . . we still are, even more so, at risk of competitive offers from other places and so forth. So, yes, Jim was involved in that at an earlier stage than I was, but they sort of came to our head during my term, from 1997 to 2000. So, that was one of the two big legislative things I worked on, but it was actually more within the university, to change the tuition policy. And the keys to that—something I'm very proud of actually—the key was, we would raise tuition, but we would never raise it beyond being in the lowest quartile of our peer institutions. So we would still be one of the most affordable places, just at face value. And we would also allocate, from any tuition raise, we would allocate up to 40 percent of that increase to kids who had financial needs. It was a tough issue, I mean, people including a former chair of the faculty, who were very much against it, and who attacked me in the letters to the editor as . . . we as former chairs of the faculty disagreed with this, and fortunately the secretary of the faculty said, "Let me respond to this." But it was deep mythology that low tuition was the best form of financial aid.

AK: So, you basically won?

PA: We won the issue, yeah! And later, the next step from that was the Carolina Covenant—that was one of the greatest innovations in financial aid that Carolina did. It was about creating . . . piecing together different forms of financial aid so that we could guarantee students whose family made 130 percent or less of the federal poverty level could come to college and graduate without debt.

AK: Without debt—it's a big issue right now.

PA: Yeah, it has been ever since! And it was an issue then, and it was piecing together federal, state, and university financial aid, using some aid from the change of the tuition model, and also, they would have, like, scholarship jobs . . . work-study jobs.

AK: I was a Royster Society Fellow, and one year we were working with "covenant students" . . .

PA: Yeah, this was hailed as a national model, and other universities copied UNC . . . and about in the late 1990s, I think, *Kiplinger* started rating universities on the basis of affordability of . . . value for money. *Kiplinger*—that's a magazine, financial magazine. It began rating universities as . . . how they value for the cost. UNC has been number one on this list ever since. Every year. Because of this model. I mean, it's just such a great innovation. But it started with this . . . this changing of the tuition model.

AK: How about international programs? Because I know that this was happening approximately at the same time: the FedEx building, and the whole idea of . . .

PA: And Jim, of course, was deeply involved in that. The atrium is named for him and Florence!

AK: Was it part and parcel of this . . . creating of the new intellectual . . . ?

PA: I don't think so. That was certainly going on at the same time, and it was a big deal, and Jim of course was director of the International Center at that point, which was then across from Morehead Planetarium. I'll come to that because that's another big area where I worked with Jim. But I was not much involved in the big international . . . in the internationalization of the campus. That was more his issue. I should go back and say, another legislative issue I worked on back then was convincing the legislature of the importance of tuition remission for TAs and RAs. Because they were

Service

threatening . . . they saw this money as a slush fund of the university, and there were serious proposals to take that money back. And I did a lot of just personal work of the legislature—meeting with them, and telling them, what . . . how important that was, and so on. And we won that battle, that was . . . I'm not sure, I can't remember, what role Jim had in this.

I can't remember the details . . . The big set of policy questions beyond the tuition model that I worked on as chair of the faculty was the tuition model, that came to me from Jane Brown, the person between us as chair of the faculty, and that was in the mid-1990s, when the university ran through an accreditation process, and the particular focus of that was the intellectual climate of the university. And Jane . . . maybe with Jim's help, I mean, they worked very closely together. If you haven't talked to Jane, you have to do that. She is here, in Chapel Hill. She is retired but very active in women's health issues. She appointed a committee of faculty members to come up with a report on how to improve the intellectual climate. And they came up with a long list of really good recommendations that included freshmen's seminars—that was the biggest one, but also themed dorms, I think . . . whole series of recommendations. And the initial summer reading that the undergraduates read, so that they have something common to talk about. A whole series of important recommendations, and Jane's committee bequeathed that to me as I became chair of the faculty, so that was a big portion . . . implementing that report, it was a big chunk of what I did as chair of the faculty.

(16_Andrews_Aug_12_2019).

Diane Robertson (DR): They [The Peacocks] have a heart for the international . . . the world! And then I did know them because after meeting them I went to work at the . . . as a development director, at the American Dance Festival, and we had a big program with Indonesia. And I contacted them to see if they would be willing to support two dancers to come study for the summer and present their work at the American Dance Festival. That would have been in 2014 probably—they supported some artists to come and work here. So, you know, leveraging our interest in arts and politics and global education . . . I just have all these different touch points with them.

They've changed the community through their engagement in the arts and in the academy—everything from the service dog training and the symphony and the opera!

AK: Service dog training?

DR: Yeah, yeah—she has donated to this service dog training in Carrboro, where they take these dogs, and train them, and give them to people who need service dogs. So, their impact is just so big! And yet, you know, even though if someone tells somebody . . . because they don't toot their horn at all! (laughs)

I also know that he has a strong commitment to global education and was instrumental in founding Rotary scholars, and the FedEx . . . making sure that this education was lifted up.

AK: It's a very unique situation: not many universities have a separate building for international studies, usually those are spread around campus . . .

DR: Right. And that he saw the need for that synergy and interconnectedness of students . . . And then they hosted so many good programs there, bringing people into the space . . . !

They [The Peacocks] feel blessed to have what they have, and they see it as something that benefits not just them—the community and the world. And if you go to them with something you are sincere about and they think is important—they'll help you. I don't know that they turn anybody down. Their sense of philanthropy and civic-mindedness is huge!

(17_Robertson_Aug_12_2019)

AK: And he was on so many committees, boards, and so on . . .

Bill Peck (BiP): Yes, yes—he does it all sotto voce, he is not . . . power hungry, but he makes great contributions just for that reason . . . And . . . delicacy and . . . non-pushy, but effective. He is great!

(19_Peck_Aug_26_2019)

HG: We were struck by his contact with foreign students like yourself . . . I mean, you came here as a foreign student.

AK: Right.

HG: And how he reached out to all those people, especially the peace scholars—that was one of his . . . I don't know: did he start peace scholars, or he was just a . . . ?

AK: I'm not sure he started it, but he certainly participated very actively—because of his connections with Indonesia.

Service 227

HG: Yeah . . . this became a center . . . there was more than one center, but I know that some of the major fundraising was done out of here, and he did that.

AK: I know that UNC is unique in having FedEx—a whole building dedicated to international affairs.

HG: Right.

AK: Because on other campuses it's more spread . . . little centers spread around campus.

HG: Yeah. And of course he started the University's . . . when he was the first . . . as far as I know he was the first director of the university's International Studies. So, he brought that international perspective, and I'm sure you've talked to him about his life in Indonesia, and while his circumstances here seemed grand—not that he lived in a grand way, but it was a grand house.

(8_The_Greenes_March_28_2019)

Sandy Greene (SG): That's a big gift of his! Being a connector! He knows how to find people, how to take ideas and nurture them, find someone to carry it on. Working within the seminars . . . just was so characteristic of him to be open and supportive. I think . . . you work in the university system, there's always someone who says why you can't do something in a certain way: "It has never been done that way before, it's not how we do it . . . " There are so many restrictions, cubbyholes that . . . things have to fit into. And Jim in his way would approach things . . . "Well, we've not done it before, let's see how we can get that to work. Let's find a way." And that was recognized and really appreciated, because he is a generous person, and creative, and excited about new things, and was ready, I guess, to take risks. "Let's get it to work, if it doesn't, well, we tried, but let's not just shut it down." Yeah, he is creative and open to ideas, and that worked really well with our program. If someone had a seminar, and it just didn't quite work . . . he was willing to take a risk and just to give it a try.

(8_The_Greenes_March_28_2019)

AK: What about the national political developments that impacted your career? Here in the United States. Different presidents . . .

JP: I'm thinking of national and local . . . I was probably involved with both by being the president of the American Anthropological Association, which was in the 1990s, in the mid 1990s. I have to check the dates, but it might be around 1995 . . . And at the same time being chair of the university faculty. So, the one got me involved in the state politics, and the other one, a little bit, not so much, in the national . . . Now, the part where anthropology might have come in was this: Carter had an idea, which was instead of giving foreign aid to our friends . . . to people who like us, like Saudi Arabia or something like that—his [Carter's] idea was no, we don't give it to people to be friends, we give it to people who need it. And so, he asked theAmerican Anthropological Association to do an analysis of need: who needs aid the most? There are probably people who are not our friends, and not our useful allies, people like Ethiopians, or Sudan, or . . .

AK: North Korea!

JP: North Korea—things like that. Well, what happened, though, was—as that project was under way, and I was slightly involved, because I was on the board of the AAA, but as it was underway, then Reagan defeated Carter. And Reagan of course had no interest in any of that. So, it did not continue.

AK: But Carter addressed directly the American Anthropological Association?

JP: He had an assistant whose name was Elliot something, he was British, and he was working for Carter, and he was actually a member of the AAA. He joined the AAA, and he brought it to the board. But Carter also . . . he did a retreat, or a conference at Camp David, and he invited top scholars to assess the reason for disillusionment in the nation. So, one of those top scholars was my former teacher, Robert Bellah, for example. So, Carter was reaching out in ways most presidents had not. Not so much for anthropologists, although they were a little bit involved, but more to other . . . .

AK: So, not only anthropologists were invited to Camp David?

JP: I don't know if any were, but Robert Bellah was, and Robert Bellah was a sociologist at Harvard . . . he was on my dissertation committee.

AK: So, Carter was exceptional in that sense?

JP: He was. Still is.

"Jim welcomes Bill to UNC-CH's Two Hundredth Birthday Party, October 12, 1993." Source: *AnArchaey Notes* 2, no. 1 (October 1994): 1 (newsletter for the Department of Anthropology, UNC-CH, edited by Dorothy Holland).

CC: They used that beautiful house to host many political events for worthy candidates. I've been there for lots of them . . . Going to the legislature was huge, to begin to have relationship with the legislature . . .

AK: Everybody who spoke about Dr. Peacock's role on campus stressed his ability to be an intermediary, to do networking . . . would you agree?

CC: Oh, of course! And, look, he worries about all sorts of important issues . . . I don't know his role in a lot of things, even though I know he was involved conscientiously with them. One of the ways he helps me with my grant proposals is, like, he knows Ellie Kinnaird well, who was a legislator, and she was the former mayor of Carrboro. And so, when I was writing my first town grants, I needed letters from the mayors, and you can start asking them, and it's, like, they are too busy with their meetings or something, but . . . When Jim and I asked Ellie, and Ellie asked them, they would go ahead . . .

AK: So, everybody would do things if Dr. Peacock asks, right?

CC: Yes, yes—or he knows a person to help him ask.

(11_Conway_July_29_2019)

The Only Southern President of the AAA

AK: You were the first, and maybe so far the only president of the AAA from the South, right?

JP: That's true.

AK: So, after you there was nobody from the South?

JP: Not that I know of. I think we need to be clear about it: "from the South" and "living and working in the South" would be the definition. So, as far as I know, I'm the only president who was both from the South and currently working in the South.

AK: That's a very important specification. And not only "currently" but your whole academic career basically . . . your couple of years at Princeton don't really count.

JP: Basically . . . so, the reason I made this clarification is that one other person was president and was working at a Southern university, and that's Ernestine Friedl, who recently died. And she was at Duke. But she was from New York, and I believe Jewish—I'm pretty sure, Friedl. And I think along the way there have been one or two presidents who may have roots in the South but who were teaching in other parts of the country.

AK: Do you think there is a certain bias here?

JP: Yeah, I think the bias . . . depends on history. Historical. So, in the history of anthropology, as we know, Columbia University was the beginning for American anthropology. And Boaz was one of the key people. And Boaz was German Jewish but based in New York. So, Columbia, and then there were other places like the Smithsonian in Washington, DC, and then the Ivy League schools, mainly Harvard and Yale, also in the Northeast. Later Berkeley in California. But in the South, when I was an undergraduate student, there were no . . . well, maybe I shouldn't just say "none" . . . there was no prominent department of anthropology that I can think of in the South at that time. Right after I started graduate school . . . so, when I applied to graduate school, I applied to four places: Chicago, Yale, Harvard, and Stanford. And I was admitted to all four, and I chose Harvard. Being admitted to all four was not a big deal then.

AK: So, there is a historical development behind the fact that you were the only anthropologist from the South and working in the South [who became AAA president]?

JP: That's right. One of the earliest departments of anthropology in the South is right here, Chapel Hill. And this department was created just a year or two before I came here, 1965 or something like that. And that was true for many anthropology departments around the country, including the South, because in the 1960s a lot of different departments were created, new departments. And new schools, like the UNC system. But there is also another aspect, which you already alluded to, and Leedom does, too. And that is—probably, the majority of anthropology students, people who chose to go to anthropology, were not from the South. Maybe the majority were not. There was kind of a tradition for Southerners to go into fields like history and law. Accounts of USA scientists I have seen indicate more in regions other than the southeast. Sort of similar to what it was in anthropology. And there were a few exceptions like Watson, the behaviorist psychologist, who was from South Carolina. Now—how did that happen? And there were some prominent physicists who came from the South, but on the whole the tendency in science, including anthropology, and maybe in academics generally, was to be from somewhere else, not the South. Except in literature or law or history.

AK: And in relation to this, Leedom says, according to his knowledge, there were "two contenders" for the position of AAA president. And so, "Who was he against? Who else was running? And . . . but that's something you can ask him . . . maybe he wouldn't mind talking about it."

JP: I think the contender that year was Richard Baumann. He was probably better known as a folklorist. And I think was at that time at Indiana University.

AK: And how does the election proceed? I mean, two people get nominated, right?

JP: I'm not sure it's restricted to two, but I think probably that's right. There is a committee, they come up with nominees, and then they have a ballot, and people vote.

AK: And so, you won over Richard Baumann?

JP: I believe that is correct. It's something that could easily be checked with the AAA office. But that's what I . . . my impression. And if that's true, then I would guess the reason was that he was better known in folklore than in anthropology. He was well known in folklore, and I was maybe better known in anthropology.

Southern Anthropological Society

JP: Many of us at UNC were active in the Southern Anthropological Society, which started pretty shortly before the year I came.

AK: Is it based in our university, or is it larger than that?

JP: It's all over the region and includes people from all over the country. It's a regional organization. And it still exists, but it's probably not as active as it was then. SAS, the Southern Anthropological Society. So, what I was coming to, it's the students. A lot of students would present papers at the Southern Anthropological Society meetings. Because they were closer. We would have those meetings in Atlanta or the beach . . .

AK: And you don't have to travel to San Francisco . . .

JP: Precisely. And so, many of the students whom I supervised, and Bob [Daniels] supervised, and others supervised, presented at those meetings. And we had colloquia, all kinds of things, and we published a lot of those. Initially a lot of it was published by the University of Georgia Press. It's still an active organization, but Chapel Hill is not as active in it as we used to be.

AK: Were you one of the initiators of . . . ?

JP: Not really. I was one of the early members, but I was not an initiator. The initiators included several people. John Gulick, John Honigmann . . . these were people who started the department. At that time, I was a new assistant professor.

By the way, I was the person who hired the first African American person at our department. And that was Norris Johnson. I'm pretty sure he was the first African American faculty member we hired in our department. I hired not the first, but among the first, woman. Carol Crumley, she was an archaeologist.

Global South Seminar

AK: And so, you found out about this "Global South"...

LL: Global South Seminar. But I found out... basically, it was through... because Peacock has worked in Southeast Asia, and he was the known person.

AK: So, he was the key... bridge type of person?

LL: Right.

AK: And so... describe your first encounter with him.

LL: Oh, goodness... I think I called him up on the phone, said, "Can I come to the Global South Seminar?" He said, "Sure!" That was at his house, and I just came and introduced myself, and he said, "Sit down, enjoy!" I think the idea of the Global South Seminar... what it has done, is giving me a hunger to compare what I see going on in Southeast Asia, or part of Southeast Asia, with issues of the "South." The South as a discriminated-against area and that kind of thing.

AK: Everywhere, more or less? Not just in the United...

LL: Right. For Thailand it's Northeast Thailand, which is the area I worked in. So, I began to see that. And then there was an article in *Southern Cultures*, this magazine that comes from the Center for the Study of the American South, or whatever it is...

AK: I think it's "South writ large" or something...

LL: No, no... There is an article in there about Northeastern Netherlands... I call it "the Siberia of the highlands," of the Netherlands... now, how many feet away is that? (both laugh) But evidently, there are these areas on the world where... the countries that define certain peoples in the world... in these countries... they are just... backwards, and discriminated against... I think it [the seminar] lost its focus, though. I believe that it started out on a definite focus about the Global South, and talking about issues of the Global South and all like that, but then it sort of moved in the direction of psycho... psychology... psychiatry... (laughs)... psychoanalytic things, and also authors. I think they probably invited authors who were Southern authors, but then it got to be more... critique of the author, not of the "why this person is a Southern author, or not." That kind of thing. So, I think that it drifted... the topic drifted....

Global South Seminar at The Cedars, March 11, 2019. Photos: A. Kushkova

AK: So, this Global South Seminar was instrumental in many ways, but then it started losing its . . .

LL: I had a feeling it did. The "golden days" of the seminar were before I got there.

AK: Did Dr. Peacock initiate this seminar?

LL: I don't know. I assume so. I assume he and some other people were sitting around and said, "Hey, let's do this." I don't know how it got going. I think it may have been an offshoot of some Global South initiative at the university itself.

(2_Lefferts_23_09_2018)

Sonja Haynes Stone Center for Black Culture and History

JP: The Black Cultural Center. Let's go into that, then. The whole time that I was doing all this here, I was president of the AAA. So, two things were happening at the same time, but—here, at Carolina. So, there was the faculty salary and other stuff, with the legislature. And more or less at the same time there was Black Cultural Center issue.

There was a Black woman who died abruptly. Sonja Haynes Stone was her name. And I was supposed to go to her wedding, no . . . to her daughter's wedding, whose name is Precious Stone. And she had been a student of mine as well. And that's why I was going to her wedding. And I had a relation with Sonja Haynes Stone because I hired the first Black faculty member in anthropology, Norris Johnson.

AK: Which year was this?

JP: It was probably in 1978 . . .

AK: So, affirmative action and all this . . . right?

JP: Well, I don't know about the affirmative action part, but it's just that he happened to be Black, and I was chair of the department, and I hired him. And the way that I hired him was in collaboration with Sonja Haynes Stone, who was the chair of the Department of African American Studies. And so, the way that I got money to hire him was by . . . it was related to affirmative action, and it was by collaborating with the Black Cultural Center I got money to hire a Black person.

AK: Was the money specifically for somebody who would be African American?

JP: Yes. They might not call it that, but it was affirmative action. So, that's how we got the money and I hired him, Norris Johnson. And then sometime later . . . much later, actually, Sonja Haynes Stone's daughter Precious was to get married, and then she abruptly died—not the daughter, but the mother. Well, her best friend at that time . . . Margo Crawford—Sonja was the chair of African American studies, and her best friend was the head of the Center for African American Studies, or Black cultural studies. She was very distraught that her friend, Sonja, had died, and she wanted to honor her, and so the way to honor her . . . they already had the Black Cultural Center, it was in the Students' Center, it was a part of the Students' Center. But she wanted . . . and then the whole group, the BSM, the Black Student Movement, joined in, and so what they wanted was an independent . . . no, wait a minute . . . a freestanding Black cultural center. This was about 1995 maybe.

AK: So, like, not part of the existing building, but . . .

JP: Correct. They wanted it "freestanding," that was their word, "freestanding," to say they didn't want to be . . . subordinated to somebody else, they wanted to be free . . . standing. The chancellor at the time, Paul Hardin, who died last year, his father was a friend of Martin Luther King Jr. And his father was a Methodist bishop. So, King and Hardin's father were friends, and they stood for civil rights. And that meant—integration. So, Paul Hardin wanted not a freestanding, separate Black Cultural Center but an integrated area. So, he said, and I heard him say it, I was there, on the steps of South building: "I want a forum, not a fortress." Forum, not a fortress. Forum meant collaboration; fortress meant independence.

AK: Two different ideologies.

JP: Yup.

AK: How did the Black students . . .

JP: That's what I'm going to tell you. The reaction was almost violent in several ways. One—they built structures all over the campus that said "Paul Hardin's plantation." . . . Second, they . . . a thousand people marched on Paul Hardin's House. Then the student groups began holding weekly speak outs in The Pit. Spike Lee, the black filmmaker and activist heard about the speak outs and decided to attend one. The event then grew to a large size with him becoming the key note speaker and was held and the Dean Smith Center. I went there, and there were thousands of people, and there was a little comical incident. (laughs) One of them was a former student of mine, a Black student, and she had been in the course, the 135. And she was shouting angry chants, and I was standing right behind her, and she turned and said, "Hello, Professor Peacock! It's so nice to see you!" So, there was a kind of friendly relation coupled with protest. And as part of the protest, they condemned various people, including several Black faculty. And two of those condemned were Trudia Harris, who later left because what happened was . . . the so-called activist arm of the Black Student Movement threatened the life of various people, including the chancellor and two Black faculty. One of them was Trudia Harris, and a second one was Chuck Stone. Chuck Stone was an eminent journalist who had been in Philadelphia but who was now at the Department of Journalism. Later, by the way, he and I arranged for Jesse Jackson to speak to the American Anthropological Association meeting in Washington, DC. And I can tell you about this later, but the point is, Chuck and I were friends. But they condemned and threatened the life of Chuck Stone, who had been a member of the Tuskegee Airmen, a famous group of Black airmen, Black pilots and bombardiers, who flew missions in WWII, and they were trained at Tuskegee, Alabama. It's a name of a town in Alabama, it's an American Indian name. It's a Black college there right now, a renowned Black college. So, anyway, Chuck Stone and I were friends, but the militants condemned him because he was a moderate, he was for cultural diversity, and he used to wear a hat that was from Guatemala, and I think he was a mix of various things. Trudia Harris was also condemned, I guess because she was somewhat moderate as well.

AK: And probably supporting the "forum" idea?

JP: I think so. So, all that was going on. I was the chair of the faculty. So, I did several things. One was I got the Faculty Council to issue a proclamation condemning the threats of murder. And it stopped, amazingly. I don't know whether it had to do with us condemning it, but it stopped. Second, I wrote an editorial in *Daily Tar Heel*, which said that I supported the idea of a separate center for Black culture, provided it was inclusive, not exclusive. In other words, that it would include white . . . and many cultures, and different perspectives.

AK: Inclusive internally, but it would be independently standing . . .

JP: It would be independently standing, but it would reach out and include . . . And so . . . amazingly enough, it actually did that and still does. So, what happened was . . . several things. A so-called blue ribbon panel was created that included about ten people, including me, but also Michael Jordan's mother, you know, Michael Jordan, the great basketball player. Harvey

Gantt, who was an architect, and who was a candidate for the Senate, opposing Jesse Helms and other people, was also included.

AK: Racially mixed?

JP: Racially mixed, yeah. Stick Williams, they called him "Stick" because he used to hit the ball with a stick. And he was . . . I still know him and see him frequently. People, Black and white, we adopted the idea of inclusive center . . . Well, there were two issues remaining. One was how to pay for it and, second, where to put it. So, remarkably, an alumnus from Alabama died and left the university I think it was twenty-six million dollars. With no designation—they could use it any way they wanted to. They used it to build the Black Cultural Center. So, paying for it was an issue, but an alumnus inadvertently solved this problem—he left the money. Second, where to place it. By the way, what had happened in the meantime was I had been designated the chair of the committee to decide what to do, make a plan. And on that committee were Black faculty and white faculty—and I was the chair. And we came up with a proposal to build a center, to make it inclusive, and to put it across the street from Wilson Library. And that was partly suggested by the architect Harvey Gantt. Because if you look at it, it's a grove of trees. In the summer, the board of trustees approved that plan, but there was one part that the Black activists disagreed with, and that was the location.

AK: Why would they oppose the location?

JP: Because they wanted it in the central campus, not across the street.

AK: Wilson Library is in the center anyway . . .

JP: Yes, it is, pretty much . . . But where they wanted it was right next to Wilson Library. Unfortunately, there was already a plan to build the science center, which is now there. And so the alternative was to put is across the street. But a local minister got students to sign a suicide pact that said they would commit suicide if they did not put it in the central campus.

AK: I never heard of practices like a "suicide pact" . . .

JP: Well, it was. Now—I don't think anybody actually committed suicide, but some students, including some of my own students, went to jail, in protest. But to put a long story short, eventually they put it next to the Bell Tower.

AK: These were Black students who signed . . . ?

JP: Some of them were white, some Black. Yeah, I remember some of them taking 135, actually. But eventually it was built, and they appointed a director. And the director followed the idea . . . and the current one, whose name is Jordan, he is very collegial, and outreaching, and inclusive—so, they had tried, all these years, tried to follow the inclusive idea. So, that was that—that was the Black . . . but as part of all that I participated in hundreds of hours of discussions with the Black Cultural Center. Anyway . . . that's where it came out.

In the 1990s . . . AAA invited Jesse Jackson to speak, and Chuck Stone was a friend of Jesse Jackson. And I asked him if he would introduce him, and he agreed. And he came to Washington, and he and I were standing out in the lobby of the hotel. And there were about two thousand people in the auditorium, waiting for Jesse Jackson to speak. And we waited, and waited, and his secretary kept saying, "He is on the way! He is on the way!" But he never came, and it turned out that he had chosen a photo op in the White House rather than speak to two thousand anthropologists. Meaning, he was at the White House and he had a chance to be with the president.

AK: But what was he supposed to speak about? What was the topic . . . ?

JP: Whatever he wanted to. So, that was a failed effort . . . But I also had some successful efforts at the AAA. One or two of those were when we met in Atlanta, I got Coretta Scott King, Martin Luther King Jr.'s widow, to speak to the AAA, and Johnetta Cole, an anthropologist who is about the greatest speaker you ever could hear. And she spoke, and then later, by the way, I got her to deliver the commencement speech at UNC, which many said was the best they'd ever heard. I thought it was terrific. Obama had appointed her head of the National Museum of African Art in Washington, DC.

AK: This is all very interesting, these two different philosophies, exclusion versus inclusion, fortress versus forum . . .

JP: Now remember, all of this is happening in the South, where segregation was the tradition but where living together was the reality. So, it's both. And by the way, a lot of anthropologists, in my experience, here, at least, and maybe in general, are big on diversity but not so big on creating diversity at home . . . or, let me put it another way: They are not always so good in relating to diverse people who are not minorities. I mean, diversity includes conservatives as well as liberals, and a lot of anthropologists have problems with that.

AK: Do you know the story of the Sonja Haynes Stone Center . . . ?

CC: I was thinking about that—he may have been chair of the faculty during that, and there may have been some issue of whether it should be an African American center or whether it should be a multicultural center.

[AK tells the story of "forum" versus "fortress" and Paul Hardin, and how JP mitigated the conflict.]

CC: It's an independent building, and in a way . . . as we think about it . . . and I didn't keep up with the whole thing . . . African Americans are the primary ethnicity of our settlement, and . . . I mean, what we did to the Native Americans was wretched, but it was theirs, but . . . well, anyway . . . I think it's appropriate that the Sonja Haynes Stone Center is for Black Americans, because it's our . . . primary effort, that's what we haven't . . . that's the personal relationship that was the most . . . prominent, that we created and haven't solved.

(11_Conway_July_29_2019)

The Royster Society

AK: One more question, about the Royster Society of Fellows.

JP: How did that happen? OK. That was around the same time. I think that was around the time that I was chair of the faculty. Maybe a little bit later. It might have been the early 2000s . . .

AK: I think we just celebrated twenty years, so it might have been 1997 . . .

JP: Probably. So, here is what happened: Tom Royster, who was a physician and graduate of UNC, and his wife, who is a daughter of the head of the Merck drug company. They met with the chancellor, Paul Hardin, and I was invited to that meeting. The Roysters asked this question: "Where is money most needed?" And I said, "Graduate students!" And the reason was, at that time, there were very few graduate fellowships at UNC compared to other universities. So, that was my suggestion. And I suggested the model of the Harvard Society of Fellows. And lo and behold, they accepted that suggestion. And they gave the money that started the Royster.

AK: And that's also an endowment?

JP: It's an endowment, absolutely, from the Roysters . . . Also, in addition to that, another person I knew well, whose name is Lovick Corn . . . he died, but he was an alumnus of Carolina, and he lived in Columbus, Georgia. I happened to go to a football game. This was when I was chair of the faculty. And the alumni were hobnobbing with each other, and I noticed this one man who was standing in the corner and not talking to anybody. So, I went over and introduced myself. And he said, "I live in Columbus, Georgia." And I said: "That's where my father is from!" And it turned out that he knew some of my relatives even better than I did. And then . . . my father was still alive, and I mentioned that I met this man, and my father said, "Do you know who he is?" I said, "No, I just know he lives in Columbus . . . " He said, "He is the husband of so-and-so, who is the daughter of the founder of the Coca-Cola company!" And so, he showed me, he went to the *Forbes* magazine, and it had the five hundred richest people in America, and there she is! So, Lovick Corn was not there, because he is the husband . . . So, then I went to the fundraising group, and I said, "Did you know that this alumnus is the husband of the daughter of the head of the Coca-Cola company???" Well, they had not known this, apparently. So, then they began looking for money. And so, Lovick Corn came here for lunch with us, and Florence (laughs) went to the grocery store and brought back this horrible lunch. (laughs) This was an awful lunch! She was in a big hurry, the way she always is. Anyway, here is Lovick, and we ate this horrible lunch, and later . . . by the way, Florence's brother-in-law, who was a cattle farmer, knew Lovick, and he asked him about that lunch, and Lovick said, "It was an awful lunch!!" And Sam, teasing me, said, "Did you have that awful lunch???" And he said, Lovick kind of smiled . . . But he then donated . . . oh, he asked me the same question, "Where is the biggest need?" And I said, "Graduate students." It was the first time that they had realized that he has all this money. He had spent millions of dollars in Columbus, Georgia, to restore the . . . civic opera house and many other things. But this was one of the first donations he made. And if you look at the Royster fellowship, there is another one, which is from Lovick Corn.

AK: Mine was called William Reynolds . . .

JP: That's another major family in North Carolina.

AK: So, it's called the Royster Society of Fellows, but there are many donors who contribute to this endowment?

JP: Exactly . . . One of the fundraisers went with me to Columbus and we met with Lovick and continued this discussion, and that's when he donated . . . Lovick Corn was a real gentleman, he was just as decent and "fine" as they come . . . And by the way, Florence is a big plus in all of this, because she is friendly, and she doesn't mind talking to . . . some whom our colleagues will have nothing to do with, say, businesspeople, or wealthy people. Florence doesn't care; it doesn't bother her to talk to anybody.

University Center for International Studies, UCIS

JP: Anyway—I'll move on to the global, because Florence was involved in it, too. So, the next thing that happened with me, was . . . this was still in the 1990s, 1996. Quite a lot of the money-raising was going on during the bicentennial of UNC. But one thing that happened in 1993 was Craig Calhoun.

AK: I know this name—I read his critical theory of . . .

JP: Correct, about Habermas. Precisely—he is a very well-known sociologist. Well . . . in 1993, in addition to other things, he started the University Center for International Studies, UCIS. It was small, and it was newly organized, and it was across the street from the Morehead Planetarium building, what is now the Coates Building. That was in 1993. In 1995 or 1996, Craig got an offer to go to New York University and also to become a president of the Social Science Research Council, SSRC. And he did, he left. And so they needed somebody to replace him as the head of the UCIS. And they asked me to do that. And at first I was supposed to do it for one year. And I said, fine, I started doing this . . . it was just . . . a part-time job, and I got a stipend of $10,000 a year to do it. In addition to other stuff I was doing, teaching and all that. So, we had . . . just a handful of people working there, including Bogdan Leja, who was Polish, and Niklaus Steiner—I hired Niklaus, by the way. Raymond Farrow, whom I also hired . . . And so, with Raymond and Niklaus, we created a board, first of all. UCIS was a newly created organization, so we had no alumni. So, we went back into the records of UNC, for the last twenty to thirty years, and we found people who had done international things. One of them, by the way, was just in our house a few minutes ago, and he is coming back in a little while. His name is Arthur Deberry—and if you're still here, I can maybe introduce you. He is about ninety years old. To make a long story short, you know the place in the Global Education Center that says, "Florence and James Peacock Atrium"?

AK: Certainly.

JP: He is the reason for that. He and another person, to honor Florence and me for creating a lot of this, they got some people to donate . . . Some people think we gave the money—we didn't give the money. Many people gave the money. And he and this other person, Margarete Hutchins, who is now deceased, led that. And if you go upstairs . . . you'll see a seminar room that's called "Deberry Room." It's named for him. So, we went back and we found people who were alumni of Carolina and who had something in the international arena.

JP: And so, we created a board of those people. And then, to create sort of a movement, I hired Raymond Farrow, who had returned to the university to continue this global work. Raymond helped to do two things: one was to raise money, and another was to plan a building, because we really had no adequate place to meet . . . we had a place at the Coates Building. So, we created a board and began to plan an organization, which is now Global Carolina. And we also planned a building, which is now FedEx. And I have to admit—at first I said to Raymond, "I don't think we need a building. We need to focus on building programs." So, we did, and we got lots of grants; we had many millions of dollars from just about every foundation you can think of: Ford, Rockefeller, and so on. This grant-getting was owing largely to Craig Calhoun. For various programs, for instance . . . we had a postdoc programs. The Rockefeller . . . and the first Rockefeller program, by the way, was for the Global South. And in fact we had all in all three Rockefeller grants, and those financed postdocs for people who were doing research for the so-called Global South. And they were people from all over the world. There was one Japanese person who was studying the Ku Klux Klan in Alabama, for example. And so, we had a seminar, which met for several years . . .

AK: In the Coates Building still?

JP: Sometimes . . . but we were also meeting in the Institute for Arts and Humanities. And that was kind of the ancestor to this group that meets here at our house sometimes, the Global South. So, that was going on for several years, and then later it became the Center for the Study of the American South. And it was related to the Black Cultural Center. So, we had a board, we had grants, we had activities, and some of them were really large-scale. For example, we would meet at Morehead Planetarium. A speaker was the major translator for Rumi, the great mystic from Persia. Also we would have dinners at our house. And Florence had a lot to do with that. We had one major event at the Singapore embassy in Washington, DC, and the ambassador of Singapore hosted us. Raymond Farrow was involved in that, and that was all related to fundraising. But not just that—some people would say "friend-raising." And then a great opportunity came up. So—a bond package. Reportedly the largest higher education bond-package in the history of the United States.

It was about three billion dollars, and the idea was to raise money to build buildings and repair buildings on all seventeen campuses of the UNC system and for community colleges. Amazingly enough, all one hundred counties of the state voted in favor of that bond package. This was back in the . . . either late 1990s or early 2000. It was before the recession of 2008.

AK: And who purchased the bonds?

JP: The citizens. Through their taxes. People were paying taxes, and a portion of these taxes, probably a very low percentage, went for this. Three billion dollars. The bond package passed the vote of all one hundred counties.

The question then was which buildings would be built? For our UNC campus.

AK: And you were competing for the building . . .

JP: Well, we were, in a way. Because they said they would choose two buildings to be built. So, the humanists were one group. The scientists were another. The scientists had their act together, they had their plan—the humanists failed to get their act together. So, Raymond Farrow and I got the global act together. What we did was we interviewed every global organization on campus, there were thirty or forty, to see "what are your space needs." And at that time various global activities were just anywhere—they were in basements, attics, anywhere. And so, we made a plan to show how each of them would fit into this new building. And we brought the plan to the College of Arts and Sciences. And our plan, and the science plan—the two of them were chosen. So, that's where most of the money came from for the FedEx building.

AK: Why is it called FedEx?

JP: That's another story. So, most of the money was raised by the bond package. But later another fundraiser, who is now the head fundraiser for the global ed, he wanted to raise some additional money for the fourth story. And he approached FedEx, and they agreed. So, FedEx chipped in some extra money. We had raised about thirty million dollars through the bond package. But they needed some more money for the fourth story. And FedEx agreed to pitch in, so they named it the FedEx building.

AK: When I first saw this building, I thought it was some services . . .

Service   245

JP: Yeah, it sounds like it. Anyway, that's how the FedEx building got to be created. Oh, and there is a lot more to it, though. So, then the question was who would be the architect. We had about thirty-nine proposals. And some of them were from very famous architects like Pei, who designed the Woodrow Wilson building at Princeton. Or Portman, who designs Hyatt hotels all over the world. The best plan, we thought, came from two unknown women from Cambridge, Massachusetts, who were partners—a small firm, just two women. So, we chose them, they oversaw the building . . . Andrea was the key architect. And since then their firm won an award as an outstanding architectural firm.

AK: Would you say that a building intended specifically for global studies is unique on US campuses?

JP: Good question—yes and no. So, before we built it, we flew all over the United States, looking at other buildings. One of the alumni had a private plane, and he let us fly to Yale, we went to Michigan, we went to other places, and we looked at their buildings. And to make a long story short, none of them was as good as this building. Because we wanted it comprehensive . . . we called it a "one-stop shop." It would be—people coming in and people going out. People coming in meant people from all over the world. People going out meant students and faculty who are going to do international research. And so, in it you find various centers for overseas research, like the Islamic center, or Latin American . . . And you would also see Study Abroad, and you would see the International Students Center, it assists international students, who have various needs. So, the idea was that it would be a one-stop shop, and it has an auditorium, and it has classrooms, all that. And then at the top it has offices, on the fourth floor, and those are designed for cutting-edge scholars. Then it includes a major in global studies for undergraduates and also a master's for graduate students, and the major is one of the largest in the university, I think they have about eight hundred majors.

AK: Global studies as a major is a little bit tricky, because whenever you study something abroad, it's already global, right?

JP: Right. It's broad . . . we went through various definitions and so forth, and it keeps changing, but . . . it's global.

JP: I can illustrate a few of the activities that have come out of that. One is the UNC World View Richardson Lecture. It's an organization of twenty-five thousand teachers in all one hundred counties of North Carolina. And what it does is help teachers K to 12 and community college teachers to

At professor Peacock's retirement as a director of UCIS, 2003. Niklaus Steiner displays the "Globgro" shirt.

think internationally. And so a lot of their work is at the Friday Center. They have conferences every month, just about, on various topics, and teachers take these workshops, so their workshops are on different parts of the world, their workshops are about issues, leadership, or economics, or whatever. That's outreach.

AK: Peace Fellows?

JP: Yes, Peace Fellows is another one, of course! The Peace Fellows—there are about a thousand Peace Fellows around the world, doing many, many different things. There are seven Peace Centers in the world; this is the only one in the United States now. And it's both Duke and UNC. And the peace program here, and also at the other five—which, by the way, are in Sweden, England, Australia, Japan, Africa, and Thailand—the money for them comes from the Rotary Foundation. And the Rotary Foundation raised about 150 million dollars to endow the peace program—not just this one, but all of them.

AK: That's where Paolo Bocci was?

JP: Correct! That's how he came here. And then he got a doctorate. The peace program provides support for two years to go through whatever graduate program you wish. He went to anthropology, others went to many things. And they get a master's degree at the end of the two years. And half are in Duke, half are in North Carolina, but they all study together, they do an internship during their first and second year. Often an internship leads to a job. Sometimes at the World Bank, sometimes at the UN, sometimes in various countries.

AK: Once I came upon a fellowship, or a program, under your name, to go . . .

JP: Oh, yeah, that's different. That's under the program that Niklaus Steiner has . . . yeah, I created that program. It's endowed by one of our persons who was on our board, and the idea is it will pay for a year of fieldwork for a graduate student, provided he or she teaches for a year, and they pay for that also. So, the idea is you do fieldwork for a year, and then you teach what you've learned for a year. And you get paid for both.

Bringing Gamelan to North Carolina

AK: What is the story of you bringing gamelan to North Carolina?

JP: I don't think it was quite true, but it's somewhat true. So, in the Music Department of Carolina there was a musicologist, at Yale now. She had done research in Java, in Indonesia, on gamelan, and was a world expert on it. So, she located a gamelan—it's a percussive orchestra, like a symphony orchestra for Java. And it's a whole bunch of percussive instruments, something like a xylophone, and then there is a big gong, and then there is a little drum and other percussive instruments.

CC: And lots of them, about twenty or . . .

JP: She located a gamelan in Java that you could buy, it was for sale . . . A Carolina grad plays a tuba, and he is interested in music, a music supporter. I wrote him a note, and I said: "Would you be interested in donating to buy a gamelan?" And he basically wrote back and said, "Fine." It was not that expensive, it was like ten thousand dollars.

AK: But the shipping charges!

JP: (laughs) Oh, that was the next thing . . . We got the dean to pay the shipping charge. So . . . the dean paid the shipping money, but we paid the rest of the cost. We had this donor who paid . . . it wasn't very much, it was like twenty thousand dollars total—shipping and the instruments. We bought it, and it's here now—you can hear it any Tuesday night.

CC: Where?

AK: Global building?

JP: There is a place for it in the Global building . . . The architect went over with Florence to the emerging building, and she designed the whole building around the site for gamelan.

AK: On which floor is the gamelan in FedEx?

JP: It's in the auditorium, and also the Kenan Music Building. Well, it can be in both places. The gamelan is large but portable like a symphony orchestra . . . Anyway, that's how the gamelan got here, and the interesting point is that the architect designed the building so as to surround the gamelan, which nobody realizes.

AK: But who can play it?

JP: Oh, there is a whole orchestra, ensemble, students who have learned . . . one of them is an archaeologist, and she has been playing that thing since the beginning, for twenty years. Tuesday nights at six o'clock. It's orchestral, but it's percussion. And it's a mystical sound. It's very beautiful, it's very dreamy . . . and Indonesian music is many, many types, but this one started as a supreme form, played in the palaces of the nobility of Java.

(13_Peacock_Conway_McCanless_July_31_2019)

Service: Florence and James Peacock Together

Diane Robertson (DR): I've no first memory except that I knew about them [the Peacocks] before I knew them: their reputation precedes them . . .

AK: You said, their reputation precedes them—what did you hear about them before you actually met?

DR: Well, I knew that she was an opera singer, and I knew he was an esteemed anthropologist . . . I didn't know as much about them as, you know, their political stance until I was invited to this fundraiser, and then I saw that also . . . And I just admired them as this couple who comes from a generation so far from my own, and yet . . . and from a part of the country that you would not associate with the magnanimous values that they represent. They seem to be an exception to that, although I think there are probably more people like that, whom we know about, but they . . . their backgrounds do not necessarily put them in the direction that they've gone professionally and personally. So, that just intrigued me to meet people like that.

(17_Robertson_Aug_12_2019)

AK: Interestingly enough, so, he is famous for his broad networks in the world of the academia, and Florence is as famous for her connections in the world of performance and theater, and so together it's like a juncture . . .

CC: It pretty well covers the community! (laughs) And there would be several times when Florence would see what we need to do to solve our problem, you know.

(11_Conway_July_29_2019)

AK: So, how did you first meet with Dr. Peacock?

HG: Well, I remember, I was on a board of Magnolia opera, and Florence was on the board. And we met at their house for a couple of times . . . that opera company is no longer operating, but . . . it was based in Chapel Hill and gave performances. So, my first memory of Jim was coming to their house, and it was raining, and he was carrying . . . he was with an umbrella, he was going out and bringing people into the house. And somehow I knew a little about him, and it just struck me how humble that was . . . Of course, I've seen him doing that many times, but that was my first meeting with him.

AK: And that was when?

HG: Maybe 1998.

(8_The_Greenes_March_28_2019)

AK: Tell me a little bit about their house on North Boundary—or even their previous house . . .

NL: Their previous house was very modest, you know, very small . . . but Florence made it look regal. Every girl had a beautiful bedhead . . . decorated. But they were modest academics, you know. And Jim didn't really want to move into the big house; he was worried about it because it looked ostentatious—because he never wanted to look ostentatious. That was his style, as you know. But he got into it.

(10_Levy_Nerys_July_27_2019)

Katherine Leith (KL): They are both . . . so accepting of people! And so encouraging! And positive. Because I've seen both through rough times,

Florence especially . . . she comes out and encouraging others, so many others. And I don't know all the people she is helping and supporting . . . And people don't realize—they see her singing, glamorous and so forth, but they don't realize, what goes on in giving oneself to people. It could be visiting professors, it could be students, it could be somebody who just needs it . . . very, very generous. And Florence particularly has a knack for looking at someone so tenderly, saying, "You are important to me." And people feel that. And one of the wonderful things about their house on Boundary Street . . . I'm sure, it's here, too, with the elevator—people in wheelchairs can come and participate! And be just accepted . . . and it's a real gift!

(18_Leith_Aug_18_2019)

AK: Everybody compares how they dress: he is walking around with his shirt not always tucked into his pants, and she is walking around in her Japanese kimono.

NL: I know—but that's how she is. She's always been meticulous at that level. But she also . . . she didn't want anybody like that, she wanted Jim, because he was her opposite in a sense.

AK: Opposite?

NL: Not really . . . you know, he was her inside, her honesty, he reflected her values. And also—Southern women dress, you know. They all have a lot of clothes. And people who've been in the South, they all have these wardrobes. I'm always surprised . . .

AK: And it's a Southern thing?

NL: I think so. And an American thing, too. But it's a Southern thing.

[On the New Year's parties she convenes at her house] I invite somebody who knows somebody . . . and Florence does the same thing. She doesn't have everybody together—she has people who will work together. That's exactly . . . and it's sort of like "reading" people—it's inviting people who have a relationship. It's basically having people who would have a nice time meeting other people. So, you are a facilitator. It has to be meaningful. If you put somebody next to somebody, there should be some kind of relationship, not a bunch of strangers who have nothing in common.

A Democratic Party meeting at Professor Peacock's house on North Boundary St., 2014. Left, seated: David Price, representative for North Carolina's fourth congressional district. Center, standing, in white dress: Valerie Foushee, Senate Democratic Caucus Chair. Right, standing, in long dress: Florence Peacock. Photo: A. Kushkova.

AK: Florence told me that she loved doing parties all her life, even before they got married . . .

NL: Yes.

AK: Would you say it's also "Southern"?

NL: Oh, yes—I mean, I come from Wales—they don't do parties like that . . . Florence is very astute. She and Jim are very astute. She is probably more astute than he is about the practical side of things. He is more a theoretician at that level, she is the practical side of things. So, they make a good team, because she would say: "Jim, you can't do that"—you've seen her do that, or . . . They are a team! And I think that's why they are successful. Because they "read" each other, and . . . Yet Florence is an independent woman, she has her own self . . . She has a life of her own, and religion is very important to

Florence and Jim Peacock at 2022 farewell reception of Terry Rhodes (left), singer and dean of arts and sciences at UNCCH.

her. And the Methodist church. Her main close friends are in the Methodist church, you know. Very basic women. I mean, I'm a close friend, I'm not in the Methodist church, but she doesn't have "fancy" friends if you know what I mean. She goes for people she can trust. And that's important.

(10_Levy_Nerys_July_27_2019)

KL: They are a fabulous, fabulous couple! This spirit of adventure, and doing things, and learning about the world . . . I don't think he could have found a better wife in the whole world! So supportive, and positive, and interested, and involved . . . and caring about him.

(18_Leith_Aug_18_2019)

Service

Professor Peacock speaking at FedEx Global Education Center dedication as Florence looks on with Rye Barcott.

JP: Maybe I'm getting off the subject . . . I don't know if you've seen our plaque in the Global building, they dedicated it one night, and they asked various people to say something. And so, I said something, which was very dull, I mainly just acknowledged all the people who had had something to do with it, like a list of names. And I carefully prepared that, and Florence, they asked her to say something, and she hadn't taken but a few minutes to put together her . . . And so, she delivered it, and I remember it had . . . and it was not a blessing, it was a kind of an invocation of the future, you know, how . . . the world is going to be glorious and united and all the various people who had been involved would remember this occasion . . . I mean . . . and after that, we have a neighbor whose name is Steven Rich, who was present at that thing, and he said, "Well, Florence's speech was about twenty times better than yours." (all laugh) And I have to agree.

(13_Peacock_Conway_McCanless_July_31_2019)

AK: I wanted to ask another question, because you mentioned coming to his house and convening there, and because Florence was traveling with him to many . . . most of his trips—so, how do you see them in tandem? What's her role in supporting him or . . . ?

SG: Well—they are a pair! I can't quite picture either one of them alone! And he is also so incredibly supportive of her work. I think when she traveled with him, she continued with her music, she studies the music of where they were at the time.

AK: And she even helped him transcribe some music for his proletarian drama book.

HG: Well, I think he delights in Florence. She really gives him a lift . . . I gather she is rather astute at business, which is not evident when you first meet her, you don't realize that. And she is the one who makes the home so inviting . . .

(8_The_Greenes_March_28_2019)

AK: Is there, like, a local community of people, who are doing things together, or somehow . . . ?

SaR: Well, it's loose, but there is an annual neighborhood picnic. And it used to be held on a lawn here at the Horace Williams House, and now the neighbor . . .

StR: . . . three doors house . . .

SaR: . . . the white house on the corner going toward the Peacocks' house has it on her lawn. And neighbors come and get together twice a year, and say "hello." You bring your own whatever, and if it's really hot, people just come and say "hello," and bring a glass of wine for themselves, or . . . to share with somebody . . .

StR: But it's not a real "organization"—it's very loose, people come and go, there is turnover . . .

SaR: But we do live in what is called a "historic district"—there are three of those in Chapel Hill.

StR: This is what they call the Franklin-Rosemary historic district; it was the first back in the 1970s. So, I guess it's a little more established, but again, people are transient, since we came here, on our side, half the people are different, in fifteen years. So, it's not like some of the new "planned communities," with young families, and they all go to school together, and . . .

AK: But were the Peacocks active in whatever was happening locally?

SaR: Yes, we have been . . . former presidents of the board at the Preservation . . . it's Preservation Chapel Hill, which is located inside of the Horace Williams House. The Horace Williams House is owned by the university, and they allow us, for a dollar a year, to have our offices there, but we are also responsible for all the upkeep, repairs . . . It's been there since 1978, that's when it was founded, and its goal is to preserve natural and historic communities, and natural landscapes as well. And . . . there are issues, because houses that have been built in the historic district, they are changing the whole . . .

AK: Landscape, yeah.

SaR: Yeah, and they want us . . . the whole Preservation to take a stand, which we can do, but it's really the town that has to make that final decision. But we can make recommendations. Florence has been past president; she has done, for years, concerts called "Baroque and Beyond." And they used to hold them at the Horace Williams House, but they got to be so large that they are mostly held in the Chapel of the Cross—in the sanctuary, in the smaller sanctuary there. But . . . she is always getting back to . . . you know. And there has been an endowed fund in honor of "Baroque and Beyond," has been established at Preservation, for Florence and all that she has done, which is a lovely tribute to her.

AK: And Dr. Peacock was also active there . . . ? He was also a member . . . ?

StR: Not as much as Florence—because he was still working, still teaching. That kept him busy. . . .

SaR: And she is also very bright. When she was president, and on the board, she was one of the people . . . not everybody goes through the treasury report to know . . . it's just, like, OK, we accept it!

StR: Growing up in a banking family . . .

SaR: . . . she knew how to read . . . she would ask wonderful financial questions and kept the treasurer on their toes . . . [to StR] At one point it was you!

StR: You had to be ready for Florence's good questions! (laughs)

(9_The_Riches_July_24_2019)

NL: I knew Florence because I'd done community things, and Florence does not have an "ego," a big ego, you know—she is very . . . how could I say? She does a lot of things anonymously, and she would not be someone who would complain. Last thing you need—somebody complaining. Somebody who is worried, complaining . . . you know. And she always puts the best side on her . . .

(10_Levy_Nerys_July_27_2019)

AK: Have you ever been to those parties, or meetings, that they were holding at their house?

NL: Yes, lots of them, yeah. And Florence always had those caterers, you know, provided, and then she would have everybody there. She would invite everybody, she was always inclusive. Always inclusive. And I think this was really important. Not . . . you know, I have a community dinner, she loves the dinner, it's very important to her . . . Our big thing is feeding seven hundred people every year. We've done twenty-three of them. At Mama Dip—I started it at Mama Dip. We are doing it at school here, with entertainment. And Jim and Florence were big on Preservation Chapel Hill, and Florence has run a music program for years, and I'm in charge of the other program, so I had a lot to do with her. She never wanted personal credit. Never.

AK: But she was president of the Preservation Society based at the Horace Williams House.

NL: Yes, yes. But she never wanted personal credit—it was always for the cause. Then the North Carolina Symphony, Carolina Performing Arts, the North Carolina Opera—they would not be here today if it wasn't for her. I'm not saying there aren't other donors, but she has been very important to arts in North Carolina. And Carolina Performing Arts—but you would not know. She does not "push her weight," as they say, everything is low-key, very, very low-key. She doesn't want . . . she gives to people—you wouldn't know it.

AK: It's interesting: he has a dense network of his professional, anthropological relations, and she has a dense network of community . . . and relations in the arts . . .

NL: Yes, yes . . .

AK: And you say the name "Peacock," and everybody reacts . . .

NL: Yes, yes—basically, you know, it's not just involvement, it's generosity, because they can. Because not everybody can, some people have to do it through their work—well, she does both, you know. She works, but also she gives. But she is not . . . she doesn't give away lightly. She is very careful, because her father was a banker. So, she has to know where everything goes.

(10_Levy_Nerys_July_27_2019)

DR: My experience is knowing them as philanthropists, as progressive political thinkers, as people who invest in something they believe in. And I'm just amazed at the breadth and their capacity . . . breadth of their interests, their ideas, and their generosity. And not because there aren't other people who do this—they do this with such humility and lack of interest in building themselves up. They just have the pure sense of doing it for the right reasons. Because it's the right thing to do. Because the community needs this. Because the country benefits from this. Because the university will be better for it. Nothing to do with themselves personally . . . to be elevated by it. At least that has been my experience.

(17_Robertson_Aug_12_2019)

Florence and Jim Peacock, 2003. Photo: Lance Richardson.

CHAPTER 8

Scholarly Impact

> **AK:** *How did your parents view your choice of major?*
>
> **JP:** *Oh, I think they didn't care. You are not going to amount to a hill of beans, and the reason was . . . I was supposed to have . . . I was supposed to mow the lawn, and I think I didn't finish mowing it.*

Anna Kushkova (AK): In your personal perception . . . you wrote a number of books . . . Here in the American Anthropological Association, how would you rate your books according to their degree of importance? From the point of view of the academy? What's your most important book?

Jim Peacock (JP): (laughs) Oh, my gosh! Frankly, I don't think any of them is a world shaker, but . . . let's see . . . depending on your point of view . . . ah . . . It's hard for me to rank them. In some ways, they each had something to contribute, but nothing of a world-shaking importance, I would say.

AK: But wouldn't you say ludruk played an important role when it came out? Was it widely read in certain . . .

JP: I would say, it played a small role. But it did one or two things: it helped . . . it sort of encouraged the study of folk drama, and it encouraged, a little bit, the field called "symbolic anthropology." And maybe that was about it. And that's true for the *Rites of Modernization*, and a lot of times that's the one people remember.

I don't say in that book [ludruk book] very much about my fieldwork. Unlike today . . . people talk today a lot more about how they did their fieldwork. In my time most of us did not. I will check in my book, but I think the only thing I did is just at the end, I have a note, saying "Note on fieldwork."

[Looking at the pictures in ludruk book:] I did the drawings, and then the editor at the University of Chicago basically modified them a little bit, for the design, and then put them in the book. And I don't think in that book, by the way . . . it does not mention that I did the drawings and all the photographs. Because I just didn't think to do that. I thought—it's a book, it's writing . . . I wrote this . . . and I submitted it, and they sent it to several commentators, several people. One of them was Dell Hymes, the second one was Clifford Geertz, the third one was Fabian Bowes, who was a drama critic, who had written a book about theater in the Far East, or something like that. Hymes wrote the most . . . discerning critique and comment on the book, and they asked me would someone like to write a preface, and so I asked him to do it. Even though I didn't really know him—I met him briefly when he was teaching at Harvard, temporarily, when I was studying there. But I didn't really know him. But he wrote what I thought was a really terrific introduction.

AK: How would you evaluate his impact on sociocultural anthropology, with him being a specialist in Indonesia primarily . . . ?

Robert Daniels (RD): I know, obviously, he is very widely read beyond . . . outside of the specialist level. I mean, his original work was greatly admired in sociocultural . . . the ludruk stuff. And the whole . . . you know, you couldn't talk about drama in anthropology without getting into James Peacock. If you'd read something about street theater in South Africa, you had to know your James Peacock, or you're lost. And of course, his book was published in how many languages? Look it up! And of course, he is also . . . his work with the Muslim fundamentalists.

You have to find somebody to talk about how many people he has touched. Because it's an enormous number. And how many graduate students, and how many undergraduate students, and how many people read his books . . . but the question is, how many people . . .

AK: It's impossible to count!

RD: Right. But he has helped an enormous number of people. And I'm sure he doesn't know.

(1_Daniels_22_09_2018)

AK: Would you say that Professor Peacock's name is more known to anthropologists who are doing general sociocultural stuff, like, ethnography of the field—or he is more known for his Indonesian stuff?

Leedom Lefferts (LL): I think he is more known for doing a book on Indonesia.

AK: This ludruk book?

LL: Yes, which he . . . which got translated, which he keeps talking about . . . Another aspect of his work, of course, is anthropology. I mean, Indonesia . . . anthropology in some sense informs the way he approaches the world. I think his own personality, though, is also the way he approaches the world—very . . . not-pushy, humble, or . . . I don't know how to talk about that . . . deferential, deferential is, I think, another word for it.

AK: Not "prescriptive," but "descriptive" . . . ?

LL: Right, right. I have run across his name when reading other people's comments about anthropology, recent anthropology, the last twenty to thirty years. About some role that he plays in it.

(2_Lefferts_23_09_2018)

AK: What do you think Dr. Peacock is most famous for in anthropology? What kinds of books, or ideas, or concepts, or fields . . . ?

Cece Conway (CC): I don't really know. He is the most preeminent anthropologist, and you know, it's one thing after another—even as little as I know about the field of anthropology, I mean, the ludruk drama, it's a fascinating application of what was going to become Consciousness and Symbols, the Primitive Baptists, *Pilgrims of Paradox, Diversities of Gifts,* and the Muhammadiyah study . . .

AK: *The Anthropological Lens* . . .

CC: *Grounded Globalism* . . . this book is more related to Consciousness and Symbols than the study of a particular [religion], and the ludruk drama had both the symbols and . . . consciousness.

AK: And the ritual.

CC: And the ritual, yeah . . . Jim Peacock was a reader on my dissertation, which was on white banjo players. And I found him to be . . . to understand what I was trying to do, and why it is important, more easily than almost anybody. There were others . . . Dan Patterson was an incredible dissertation director at every level, and I think . . . it was harder for him to understand why I was going down certain paths—than for Jim. Dan was a perfect director and knew the folklore resources and was ready to deal with sentence suggestions. He was willing and able to go into every level, and he also had some big ideas about what I was talking about—for us to think about. But Jim was the one, I think, who seemed most easily to appreciate what I was trying to do—in broader strokes, in the meaning of this stuff. And it had all to do with the Symbols and Consciousness. And so many people had written about how Black people were inadequately represented in white ballads. And so, I had to go all the way around that and try to understand their aesthetic, which is different . . . I mean, it's not conservative, and "learn it word for word" like the ballads sung by your daddy or granddaddy or neighbor. But improvisation is what's at the heart of Black aesthetics. And learning how to talk about that was very important.

(11_Conway_July_29_2019)

AK: So, Dr. Peacock worked in Indonesia, and then here in the United States, in the Appalachians, and then he considers his service as the third type of his major involvement. So, he speaks about his fieldwork, lawnwork, and housework—that's his tripartite structure. But speaking about Indonesia versus the United States: where do you think he is more famous, as a specialist in Indonesia or as a specialist in . . . what you were doing together with him? What's his major contribution in anthropology?

Dan Patterson (DP): I won't be in a position to answer this because I don't know that many anthropologists very well. But I think . . . from my perspective, he is taking in folklore students and training them, and supporting, and learning from them, probably. Going with them places that he might not otherwise have gone. That was for the folklore program an enormous benefit. And he was always one of the people they most often talked about, and I thought it was a great benefit to folklore.

Beverly Patterson (BP): He did so many things!!! With students, with other faculty . . .

DP: It's his curiosity—he is just curious about everything! And he was open to what everybody was interested in. And he was interested in doing and seeing whether he can learn from it. And how he could help. And I felt one of his contributions was his curiosity and supportiveness. And no competitiveness at all!

BP: He is supportive of everything!

DP: Everybody! (7_The_Pattersons_Feb_9_2019)

AK: And yet, what is your general impression: what is he most famous for in his writing . . . ?

Sandy Greene (SG): My general impression would be—his Indonesian work. Thinking of both music and puppetry . . . I mean, he brought, as far as I know, he and Florence brought the gamelan to UNC, and . . . I just . . . when I think of Jim, I think primarily of his work in Indonesia . . . But thinking about his involvement with Muhammadiyah: that's incredibly significant. Those are things that really stand out for me . . .

(8_The_Greenes_March_28_2019)

AK: What do you think is his most significant contribution to anthropology?

Nerys Levy (NL): Well, I'm a historian, but I think for anthropology he made the subject accessible. Because of his personal touch. I think a lot of anthropology is very remote for a lot of people, because it requires such dedication to these traditional field studies which he did, and my husband did, Skip did. People don't do that in the same way anymore, only a few people do. Because the world has changed. It's very difficult to go and park yourself in a country for three to four years. But also he was able to go inside, you know, this Islamic country, which has radicalized, and even maybe provide a longitudinal study, because he early on built trust. And I think what's very important for all anthropologists is to keep the trust of the people you study. And not to have an imperialistic relationship.

(10_Levy_Nerys_July_27_2019)

Bill Peck (BiP): I would describe him as a human being with a great sense of humility about what he knows and so on. He is reliable because he really thinks for himself, and has contributed to the field of anthropology greatly.

AK: Everybody stresses that he is accepting of everybody.

BiP: Yeah, that's really true. That makes him a true anthropologist—in my opinion. And he is very generous.

(19_Peck_Aug_26_2019)

AK: Did you come to any of those parties [at their house]?

Sandra Rich (SaR): Always! Whether it was for academic or . . . political, and we are proud to say, we are on the same side politically, so . . . They would just give so much back to the community all the time. But the interesting story: when Jim was recovering with the broken leg after an incident in New York . . .

Steven Rich (StR): It was right after we got here.

SaR: They went to New York, and he was helping Florence into a cab, and he opened up his side, and he was struck by another car. And they ended up having to fly him home, and he had surgery, and was off his leg for months. And so, people . . . all of these meetings were taking place in the house, so, I called and said: "I have my matzo ball soup and challah, and, you know, I'll bring you something." He said: "Sure, any time!" So, we walked to his house, which is around the corner, and we knock on the door, and he says: "Come in!" So, we go in, and he is having his Mensa group meeting. Mensa—it's for elite intelligence, you know, for people with very high IQs . . .

StR: . . . and they are in a very deep conversation . . .

SaR: . . . deep conversation. And he says: "Come in, sit down, join the conversation!" And we said: "We probably have said all we could contribute by saying 'Hello' to this group." (general laughter) I mean, they were just . . .

StR: But Jim is always inviting.

StR: He wasn't going to exclude us.

SaR: You know, he would just not distinguish someone with an IQ . . . high or low—he is just a good person welcoming everybody and just cracks me up! So funny! "Come, join the conversation!"—I don't think we can . . . I don't think we're capable of doing it. (laughs)

(9_The_Riches_July_24_2019)

Susan Reintjes (SR): I see him [Professor Peacock] as very balanced, his anima is well developed. He has a very strong balance . . . my work is about masculine and feminine, so what I see in him is a very strong balance between masculine and feminine . . . I just respect him so much, for his insight and his . . . I'm a perennial student, so it's this continuing to . . . just, like, know how little you know. He knows how little he knows, and then he wants to know more, and then he knows now he knows even less, now he needs to know even more, I mean, the more you know, the more you . . . So, he knows that, and I espouse that, so I feel this kinship.

(14_Reintjes_Aug_9_2019)

Professor Peacock awarded George H. Johnson Prize, 2014. Photo: A. Kushkova.

Pete Andrews (PA): He is such a modest man. It's so ironic that his name is Peacock, because a peacock is anything but modest. (laughs)

(16_Andrews_Aug_12_2019)

Florence's Influence

AK: Do you think Florence helped you promote your career in general, or in any particular . . .

JP: Of course! Except on the whole we divided our labor—you know, I did mine, and she did . . . music basically. But you're right . . . people would

Scholarly Impact   267

never have met me, or heard of me, but they would always know Florence. Because she sang, she did a lot of concerts. And so, they would just know her, remember her. Even to this day, you know.

AK: Do you think she had to forego certain possibilities in her career . . .

JP: Oh, absolutely!

AK: . . . because she got married to you and traveled . . .

JP: . . . yes, she did give things up.

RD: There was always a very interesting contrast between Jim and Florence.

AK: Was she part of what was happening at the department?

RD: No, no. But . . . Jim very generously invited me to a lot of things. And other people. And Florence is both extremely effusive and extremely formal at the same time. And I remember her one time serving tea in her parlor—it was a parlor, not a living room.

AK: At North Boundary?

RD: No, no, over when they lived at Willow Drive. And watching her serve tea was like . . . a wonder bird . . . and it was fully as complicated as a Japanese tea ceremony. I mean, she was so elegant, and *studied*—it was just amazing, absolutely amazing. And she wasn't in any sense artificial. She wasn't putting any of that on—that was Florence.

(1_Daniels_22_09_2018)

PART II Reflections
by Jim Peacock

Gratitude

Much gratitude is owed to many. Here is one debt I could not have anticipated before embarking on this journey. In 1969 and 1970, I carried out research in Indonesia, as described. My focus was on Islamic groups. In late 1969, while we were in Singapore, our middle daughter had a kidney infection that required an operation, so she and her sister and Florence returned to the United States. Since I had a grant for research, I went on to Indonesia.

I had not arranged for the work I would do there, but I decided to focus on Muhammadiyah, one of the two largest organizations. After some weeks, Muhammadiyah accepted my plan to study them. I then began to travel to Muhammadiyah branches throughout the islands. I traveled deck-class, sleeping on the deck of a boat along with hundreds of Indonesians and stopping at ports, then contacting local branches of Muhammadiyah and some other organizations. Eventually I also traveled by bus. I traveled widely—and cheaply; I stayed at one place in Garut for ten cents a night, including a cup of coffee and a tiny crib in which to sleep. After completing the boat trip, which extended to the outer islands including Sulawesi and beyond, I traveled by various means to West Sumatra, then Sumbawa to the east.

In Sumbawa, at a guest house, I met a fellow guest from Bima, the other side of the island. He lived in Surabaya, where he ran a pornographic movie theater, though he came from a deeply Islamic family in Bima. We both embarked on a boat to Bima, a strongly Islamic place who claimed a citizen that had once attempted to assassinate Sukarno, the president of Indonesia, for being too syncretic. After waiting for a week to board a delayed small boat and then sleeping on the boat deck all night in the rain, we arrived at Bima at dawn. My new friend was greeted by his father and brothers and we went to their house, whose walls were covered in pinups. Some of my photographs of Bima appear in *Gerakan Muhammadiyah*, a translation by Muhamadiyah of a short book I wrote on that movement published by UNC Press as well as by Muhammadiyah.

After a few days, mosquito and malaria season set in as I caught a ride with some Indonesians on the back of a truck crossing the island west to Sumbawa Besar. We traveled all night, following wild horses running along the riverbed, which was then dry and thus could serve as our road. This

This photo of a tomb in the town of Pare (Modjokuto) was provided by Sudibyo Markus and holds Sudibyo's parents, whom Jim met in 1970.

travel was heavy going, as the riverbed was rough and I had caught a flu en route. Nevertheless, we arrived at dawn and I found a way to get back to Jakarta, the capital of Indonesia, from which I continued my travels throughout Indonesia.

My travels duplicated somewhat a trip undertaken a hundred years before by Snouck Hurgronje, the eminent Dutch Islamist. He had the advantage of traveling in a country then under the governance of his own nation, the Netherlands, whereas I was a mere visitor in the relatively new nation, thanks to Chapel Hill's Frank Porter Graham, who had represented Franklin Roosevelt in negotiating Indonesia's independence from the Netherlands after being a Dutch colony since 1596.

Eventually I reached Yogyakarta, a city in central Java and one of the two Javanese kingdoms and the headquarters of Muhammadiyah. I introduced myself to the chief administrator, Pak Jindar, and he helped me find lodging with a local family. That connection led to contact with a youth group, Pemuda Muhammadiyah, where I met two of the leaders, Amien Rais and Sudibyo Markus. This in turn led to my participation in training camps at levels ranging from youths to branch heads. By this time, I spoke fluent Indonesian, which was the language the Muhammadiyahans used in all of their camps, even though many also spoke Javanese in several dialects. During this time, I also collaborated with Niels Mulder, a sociologist from the University of Amsterdam who was studying another group, Sumarah, which was somewhat opposed in belief to Muhammadiyah. I was later chair of his research committee in Amsterdam.

These months of moving about were often lonely and sometimes risky, and the friendships with Amien, Sudibyo, and in a different way, Niels, were extremely meaningful to me. Amien's brother lived in our house for a time in Chapel Hill and Amien himself was and is an important leader in Indonesia. Among other things, he persuaded General Suharto to step down as president and facilitated the appointment of Megawati, daughter of Sukarno, as president of Indonesia, the fourth-largest nation in terms of population. All of this activity fell under the rubric of fieldwork (as compared to lawnwork or tourist travel), and I cannot imagine doing it without these friendships. I am deeply grateful to Sudibyo for our long friendship, and I deeply admire his own work.

A Historical Footnote: From Clifford Geertz to Sudibyo Markus via Christiaan Snouck Hurgronje

Christiaan Snouck Hurgronje was an eminent Dutch scholar of Islam who also was a leader in Indonesian culture and government in the nineteenth century, during colonial times. Not only did he lead in policy and perform such feats as residing in Mecca without converting to Islam, but he also wrote a description of Islam in Indonesia that foreshadowed syntheses such as Clifford Geertz's *The Religion of Java* and carried out fieldwork that foreshadowed that of Harvard anthropologists Clifford Geertz, Alice Dewey, and others who lived in Mojokuto (actually Pare) in the 1950s. Mojokuto is the hometown of Sudibyo Markus, who was a young boy when the Harvard team lived in that community—Clifford and Hildred Geertz actually in Sudibyo's family home. In 1970, I joined this parade by studying Muhammadiyah, the Muslim organization based in Yogyakarta, and met Sudibyo and his friend Amien Rais, who were leaders of Muhammadiyah's youth movement. Recently, Sudibyo has published his excellent book *Islam and the West: A Light on the Horizon*. Sudibyo traces the history and culture of Islam and Christianity and proposes ways they can unite. His work is an excellent expression of this century's interchange between Islam and the West, as represented by Muhammadiyah and Aisjijah, the women's branch, which nourished its own superb scholars, such as Ibu Barororh Baried. Offshoots of this history include President Obama, whose mother studied under Alice Dewey, a member of the Harvard team. Doubtless more "lights on the horizon" will appear as anthropology joins in this promising history.

Prof. Azyumardi Azra (far right) at Sudibyo's book launch of the Indonesian edition of *Dunia Barat dan Islam*, organized by the Muhammadiyah Central Board, October 29, 2019. The English translation *Islam and the West: A Light on the Horizon* launched in English translation on November 12, 2022, with a Zoom presentation in Indonesia. It is a real breakthrough in the analysis of relations between Muslims and Christians and includes accounts of fieldwork completed by anthropologists.

Anthropology

The field of anthropology is a mystery to most even today, when it is found all over the world and there are ten thousand or so members of the American Anthropological Association and many similar groups globally. Perhaps one reason for the mystery is that anthropology focuses on the long ago and far away—ancient pasts and exotic customs—although much effort is given to cultures today as well. One of the seeming oddities is the importance among humans, as well as other animals, of kinship: the relationships based on birth, hence bonds between cousins and ancestors ranging from royalty to the rest of us. Some of us travel far to see our relatives or expect our relatives to come see us, but others couldn't care less.

Claude Lévi-Strauss wrote brilliantly about kinship around the globe, including cross-cousin marriage, a custom wherein a marital union between a mother's brother's daughter and a father's sister's son is preferred in many societies, especially in parts of Asia where this practice serves to unite clans spread across thousands of miles throughout the mountains that otherwise are not integrated. Such phenomena and the analysis of them expanded into complicated mathematical formulas and studies that Lévi-Strauss, Sir Edmund Leach, Floyd Lounsbury, and others developed into a science in order to demonstrate how and why kinship is so crucial for humans, not to mention other primates.

Well, then, how and why do kinship relations matter for some of us sometimes? Obviously inheritance is one reason, but beyond that, pride in ancestry, or shame for the lack thereof, and also, more complicatedly, shame for having kinfolk, as with our daughter who asked us not to visit her school together when most of her classmates came with a single parent.

In old age, such matters matter, and anthropology is a relevant approach for understanding all of it, but a lawyer is needed first, to formulate wills and other mechanisms.

Face Cards and Connections

Florence's uncle Bob Arnold told a story about riding in a car in Washington, DC, to a meeting pertaining to his position as chair of the board of regents at the University of Georgia. He told the driver where they were going and for what purpose, to which the driver replied, "I knew you were face cards."

Years later, I was in a bar at a hotel in Cambridge, Massachusetts, where I was staying to attend a meeting to chair a committee of the board of trustees of Harvard University. A woman and I at the bar conversed about her work at MIT and our shared links to Alabama, especially Tuscaloosa, and she mentioned my uncle Clayton Rogers, who was an executive of the Alabama Power Company and worked closely with her father. "My father's best friend," she called him.

Much more far-flung is the relationship revealed between Florence and me and Haryo Marsosudiro. He and I met while we were waiting in line at a picnic for a performance of a dance troupe from Indonesia held at Duke. I asked him where he was from, and he said, "Surabaya, Indonesia," to which I replied, "We lived there on Jalan Gundih, number 16," to which he exclaimed, "That is where my mother lives!" And we then realized our connection.

Face cards, addresses, license plates—all have been small but sturdy islands in vast seas of society. Some, however, reject such relationships. A college fraternity to which I belonged was holding a "rush" to which were invited new students. One, a chemistry major from Georgia, had a photographic memory. He instantly memorized a group photograph with names on the wall, then introduced himself to the brothers, referring to each by name. The brothers, largely from the Northeast, deemed this behavior "not cool" and rejected consideration of this person. No networking for this bunch!

Friendship

One downside of networks and friendships is corruption, the breaking of laws and violation of ethics, which supposedly is rife in developing countries. An example might be the black market for money exchange in Indonesia in the 1960s, when a dollar brought forty-five rupiah at the bank and twelve hundred on the street. On the whole, however, during that period and ever since it ended, when Suharto became president, I have found most friendships and relationships in Indonesia to be ethical. Rarely did anyone seek money unethically, despite living often very frugally if not desperately. In fact, I feel guilty that I got much more than I gave. Like most anthropologists who are fortunate to live in a wealthy nation, we try to reciprocate but often fall short.

Commitment and Unity

When I began my fieldwork among the Muhammadiyahans, one of them asked, "What is your religion?" I replied, perhaps jauntily, "Saya perjaja Ilmu Kebudaan" (I believe in the science of culture, that is, anthropology, that is, the study of belief, but I do not necessarily profess a belief). Later, in the middle of the training camp, after the trainees and I had been through a lot together, one of them said jokingly that I had been *hit* with evangelism, the pressure to convert. Later, in a mosque service, some of that pressure was expressed. Later still, in a discussion following dawn prayer, someone asked if I believed in the trinity and I mumbled something like "maybe." This led to an article in *Suara Muhammadiyah*, the Muhammadiyah newspaper, under the headline "Peacock May Convert to Islam."

This sounds like heavy-duty evangelism, but in the hours and days and nights of the training camp Darul Arqom, there was little of this. Mainly I just joined the other trainees in the daily routines, exercises, and lectures and listened to accounts of their lives and beliefs, sometimes accompanying them to their daily prayers. I did not join in those prayers, whereas I did join in all of their physical exercises, as was noted appreciatively by one of them in a public comment at the end of the camp. On the last day, we went on a tour of mosques and other parts of local Islamic practice. Sudibyo told some very good jokes and I chimed in with one of my own. That night, an army general spoke inspirationally, and Sudibyo and I parted early the next morning as he went off to speak at various gatherings and I myself did some of that, invited by fellow participants in the camp to offer "critique" at their branches.

I did not see Sudibyo again until the hundred-year anniversary of Muhammadiyah many years later, in 2010. I was deeply touched by our reunion. Ever since, we have corresponded and collaborated, including on his new book. I got back to work teaching, undertaking administrative roles, and engaging in a long stint of fieldwork not among Muslims but among Christians, Pentecostal and Primitive Baptists, in North Carolina.

Here too the conflict between observing and believing in a faith was evident. The late Ruel Tyson and I were interviewing a tall Black Pentecostal preacher, a woman, in Durham, when she put one arm around each of us and forcefully exhorted us to go beyond just observing. Around that time, a layman told us flatly that we would never understand if we did not convert and believe. Later I returned to Java to join my student, David Howe, who was studying with and later professed the Kebatinan, a mysticism sect known as Sumarah. To me and my colleague from Amsterdam, Niels Mulder, on our return late at night from the mountains of Java, a Javanese mystic said gently "Kita Bersatu" (We are one), the word "Bersuta" signifying a deeply inclusive oneness.

The Long View

In 1959, I graduated from Duke University and matriculated at Harvard, one of a half dozen students in a graduate program in social anthropology. This program was associated with both the long-established anthropology program at Peabody Museum, which included archaeology and physical or biological anthropology, as well as a program ("Social Relations" or "SocRel") that included social psychology, clinical psychology, sociology, and a course in statistical analysis. I had chosen this program for its interdisciplinary curriculum, which included psychology, my undergraduate major. My teachers included Cora Du Bois, Talcott Parsons, Robert Bellah, Kwangchih Chang, John Pelzel, and Evon Zogt. Fellow students were Tom Kirsch, Terry Turner, Chris Boehm, Fran Waxman, and Nahum Waxman, as well as others at the Peabody, notably Joan Bamberger, Karl Heider, and Gene Ogan. We took courses, underwent a qualifying exam, and wrote dissertations. Fieldwork was expected, and most succeeded in achieving a doctorate. I did so in 1965, then taught at Princeton until 1967 when I moved to Chapel Hill and then returned to Indonesia for fieldwork in 1969.

I returned from my fieldwork in Indonesia at the end of the summer of 1970 and began my service as associate chair in August, working with John Honigmann, who was then chair. This was an abrupt transition, from "fieldwork to lawnwork," so to speak. In the early 1970s, Honigmann retired owing to illness, and I replaced him as chair, a position I held for five years. Later, I was again chair for one year and then was elected chair of the entire faculty of UNC-CH, serving a term of three years in the 1990s. While carrying out these administrative tasks, I continued to teach a normal load of four courses per year.

As a departmental chair, I oversaw and "managed" a faculty of approximately eighteen and the teaching of hundreds of undergraduate students and perhaps forty graduate students while also teaching and advising students. One activity I found demanding was hiring and evaluating new faculty. If a position became available, through an application to the administration, which was itself challenging, we would undertake a process that included advertising the position, interviewing top candidates, initially at professional meetings, bringing them to our campus, arranging for them to give a presentation about their research, reading their work, setting up committees to evaluate it, discussing and comparing the various candidates, ranking them, approaching the top ranked ones with an offer, working through to hiring them, and, some years later, usually between five and seven years of "trial" employment, undertaking an evaluation of their publications and the like, hopefully offering tenure, and sadly sometimes recommending termination. Overseeing this process was demanding for the overseer and for the candidate. Usually the outcome was positive but stressful if assessment resulted in termination.

More positive were opportunities to build and produce. Over the years and continuing today, I write recommendations and otherwise support numerous students and colleagues who seek jobs, research funds, and other opportunities.

Beyond the department and campus, I participated in national and international organizations and conferences. The organization I know best is the American Anthropological Association (AAA). When I served as its president, it had about eleven thousand members and hosted an annual national conference that drew as many as eight thousand participants. Several thousand presentations would be made, several thousand books exhibited, and several dozen officers elected to serve. During my time as president, we made one significant step toward improving our finances. We sold the building that housed our office in downtown Washington, DC, and invested the proceeds, which to date have grown to an endowment fund sufficient to cover our needs in the event of a mishap.

The AAA is more than a century old, not quite as old as the Royal Anthropological Institute or some others, but perhaps the largest. In the United States, the earliest centers were in New York and Washington, DC, at Columbia University and at the Smithsonian, respectively. In the 1960s, many new departments of anthropology were created, but officers of the AAA have tended to come from elite universities in the East and the West, namely California and New York and Washington. I think I am the only AAA president from the South and a Southern university; Ernestine Friedl from Duke was a New Yorker, so she was a partial exception.

Since the time of Anna's interviewing, I have also served as president of the retired faculty association for UNC-CH; facilitated the completion of the FedEx Global Education Center, and carried out various activities in and around it; and worked on the Nike project with Pete Andrews, formerly chair of the faculty of UNC-CH, then president of the retired faculty association of UNC-CH.

A number of new programs were created, including the Sonja Haynes Stone Center for Black Culture and History, Center for Southern Studies, Center for Humanities at Hyde Hall, and FedEx Global Education Center. I was involved in each of these, as noted below. They were all created around the time of the bicentennial in 1993 or soon after. Instrumental was one of the largest educational funds of this time, $3.1 billion for the construction and repair of campus buildings in the UNC university and community college systems. Leaders at the time were UNC presidents C. D. Spangler and Molly Broad. The fund was supported by citizens in all one hundred counties of North Carolina. This was altruistic support, since only a small number of citizens who voted would make use of the programs that would be supported.

The Rotary Peace Center

The Rotary Peace Centers are international. The Duke–UNC Center, jointly hosted by both schools, was among the first and remains one of the most prominent. How did the Rotary Peace Fellows come to UNC? The process began when my phone rang at UCIS a decade or so ago. It was E. T. York, president of the University of Florida and member/chair of a search committee for Rotary International, asking if we might be interested in applying to be a peace center, a new program Rotary was planning. I said yes, and he asked for a proposal, which we submitted. That led to several site visits with York and another board member of Rotary International.

I think the winning touch for us was Florence. She and E. T. hit it off, and we all had a few things in common. He had a doctorate from Cornell and had been the head of the US Department of Agriculture. His alma mater was Auburn, and he was a native of Alabama. Florence's brother-in-law, Sam Hay, was a cattle farmer who played on Auburn's football team. Cornell University was a candidate for hosting a peace center, as were a hundred other schools, but Rotary chose Carolina plus Duke as a pair and UC Berkeley, the only other school in the United States, as well as schools in Australia, France, Great Britain, Japan, and Latin America. Today, Paris and Berkeley no longer have Rotary peace programs, and UNC is the only US program.

A considerable endowment, more than one hundred million dollars, has been raised for the centers. The funds go primarily to fellowships for the Peace Fellows, who earn a master's degree and are then employed by the World Bank and similar institutions globally; they are professionals in the endeavor of building peace. Several hundred peace fellows now work at this task internationally. We are in close touch with our fellows and alumni of both Duke and UNC. Approximately six fellows are admitted at each institution annually, producing graduates now employed across the globe.

Frances Lethem at Duke and myself at UNC-CH worked together as coheads of the paired centers at our institutions. Frances and I, as well as many other faculty and students, have taken part in a range of projects and events. A memorable one was a peace conference in Puna, India, held at the large MIT University campus there. Several dozen speakers, including Frances and I, presented ideas about paths toward peace. As the program began, the event leader, Darshan Mundada, a Peace Fellow from Puna, asked me to offer brief opening remarks. I told of the Bhagavad Gita, the famous legend of the war between the Kauravas and the Pandavas in ancient India. The warrior Arjuna was distressed that he would have to kill his cousins, the Kauravas, but as he rode in the chariot piloted by the god Siva, he received advice: "Sustain peace in your inner being even while coping with the outer world." It turned out that this legend had special meaning for Puna. Several hundred years ago, a young man in the village had completed a massive analysis of the text of this legend and had then told the villagers, "Bury me alive for I have completed my life's work." They did as he asked, and his grave is in a temple at Puna, where he is a patron saint.

We were in Puna as the life and death of Mahatma Gandhi was being celebrated. Francis and I were lifted up several stories in a pea picker to hang wreaths around the bust of Gandhi. In another ritual, we deposited

Peace Fellows and US leaders, April 2005.

Graduating Duke–UNC Peace Fellows with managing director Susan Carroll (fourth from left), April 2023.

UNC-Chapel Hill's website featured the Duke-UNC Rotary Peace Center on March 27, 2023. https://www.unc.edu/posts/2023/03/27/duke-unc-rotary-peace-center-celebrates-20th-anniversary/

our sins or shortcomings in a pool. Music, dance, and eloquence enriched this remarkable conference. These were among the special events pertaining to our peace center. These experiences and connections benefit UNC and Duke by sharing our campuses and institutions with thousands of leaders and citizens of many countries affiliated with Rotary and working in leadership roles. At present, the head of the peace program at UNC and Duke is Susan Carroll, a distinguished international leader.

Balancing the exotic were of course the basics. For example, I was called on a Friday with a request to speak at a meeting in Scottsboro, Arizona, where I met one of the first donors. I said something mundane and he donated a million dollars to kick off the endowment; among those present were some from Hollywood who vacationed in Scottsboro. The mundane was essential, as when an administrator at UNC agreed to set up a fund which provided peace fellows with tuition equal to that of in-state students' reduced charges. Those of us administering the peace program participated in many meetings in Evanston, Illinois, where the central offices were located, as well as our state senate and house programs. These contacts were both essential and instructive, though not so exotic as the rituals of Puna.

A Launching Pad for Angels: FedEx Global Education Center

Travis Venters, a poet and former student, coined the phrase "a launching pad for angels" in reference to my backyard as we sat together on our porch, and I quoted him in our launching ceremony for the FedEx Global Education Center. His phrase brilliantly suggests the center's potential: to integrate and inspire efforts to create a better world. Another student, Rye Barcott, created one such effort, Carolina for Kibera, which is based in Kenya. The Center houses the Nelson Mandela Auditorium, named for the first Black president of South Africa.

The Coates Building

The Coates Building served as the office for the University Center for International Studies from its founding in 1973 until its relocation to the new FedEx building. Gladys Coates, at nearly one hundred years of age, met with the UCIS staff and others at the Coates Building and described how she and her husband, who had also created the Institute of Government at UNC and at the NC legislature, led construction of the Coates Building. This building was once the office for the entire UNC system, as former president Bill Friday noted when he met with us in the building's assembly room.

Atrium in the FedEx Global Education Center. Photo by architecture firm Leers Weinzapfel Associates.

The Coates Building.

Sonja Haynes Stone Center for Black Culture and History

The Sonja Haynes Stone Center for Black Culture and History was inspired by the tragic death of Sonja Haynes Stone, former head of the program in African American studies. Following her death, many wished to construct a building as a memorial. The chancellor at the time, Paul Hardin, welcomed this proposal but favored a multicultural focus that would be open to various programs; he suggested "a forum not a fortress." Students and others reacted negatively to this language. They erected structures and signs lambasting the chancellor's view as "Hardin's plantation," they picketed his house, and Spike Lee attended and spoke at a large protest in the Dean Dome that targeted several faculty members as nefarious, allegedly threatening death.

At this time, I was chair of the faculty. I called for a more moderate proposal, affirming and studying African American culture while also welcoming other approaches. Some faculty members disagreed with me, while others agreed. I and some others, especially Robert Eubanks, an alumnus, met repeatedly with students and others so we could all share our opinions. The provost formed a committee consisting of prominent persons such as the mother of Michael Jordan and senatorial candidate Harvey Gant, an architect. This group produced a proposal for a center. I was appointed to chair the committee, and we prepared a proposal to submit to the board of trustees.

A sticking point, though, was the location of the center. Harvey Gant suggested a wooded lot near the Bell Tower. Some preferred a location across the street near Wilson Library, on the main campus, but that location was already committed to the new science building. A local minister called for suicide if the Wilson location was not chosen. Some students who protested were jailed.

During the summer, it was decided to locate the building near the Bell Tower, and plans proceeded. However, the question remained: how to fund the building? Fortunately, an alumnus who happened to be from Alabama had donated sufficient funds to build the center. It serves many activities, including meetings of the Faculty Council. Professor Joseph Jordan, a distinguished scholar of African American studies and other topics, has been director of the center until recently.

Mission Accomplished

The faculty requested an administrator capable in leading research. The chancellor, Paul Hardin, appointed an outstanding scientist. Three deans blocked funding for this work. As chair of the faculty I threatened to call for a faculty strike if the funds were not provided. Chancellor and provost did provide the funds. The scientist did outstanding work and went on to become a national educational leader.

Center for the Study of the American South

A third major center created around this time is the Center for the Study of the American South, which leads many activities. It is located on Franklin Street and publishes *Southern Cultures*. My involvement with the center coincided with the leadership of David Moltke Hansen. David was head of the Southern Historical Collection at Wilson Library and later the library of the Pennsylvania Historical Society in Philadelphia. He is a leader also of the St. George Tucker society in Southern studies and writes and edits with Cambridge University Press. During his time at UNC, David led many projects, including the civil rights project wherein scholars and others met with civil rights leaders in key cities throughout the US South.

Hyde Hall

Finally, a most important center, Hyde Hall, which houses Ruel Tyson's Institute for the Arts and Humanities. It began in West House, since destroyed, a small brick building near the current center. The former building was shared with Fred Brooks, creator of the personal computer when employed by IBM and a contemporary with Ruel, hailing from the same community in eastern North Carolina. The two men were very different in outlook, Fred being a computer wizard and Ruel a brilliant humanist, but perhaps a similarity is suggested by an anecdote. Fred met with the then provost and said, "Provost, I have invented a machine to increase the intelligence of the faculty. Are there faculty whose intelligence requires increase?" The provost reportedly grabbed a piece of paper and proceeded to make a long list.

Increasing the intelligence of the faculty was certainly a mission of both Ruel and Fred. Fred's building is named for him; Brooks and Ruel's is Hyde Hall. Noteworthy among the activities Hyde Hall sponsors is the family that supports it, the Massey family. Their support extends beyond faculty research and writing to work by staff of the university, such as mowing the football field, keeping up the campus grounds, and supporting students suffering from mental or physcial illness. The Massey awards each year reward such work and bring to attention the remarkable importance of community at the University of North Carolina at Chapel Hill.

Boundaries

A decade ago, I was invited to deposit my field notes in the Smithsonian National Anthropological Archives. Florence and I drove to Washington, DC, then to the gate of the Smithsonian Institution to deliver the notes in boxes in my trunk. But the guard at the gate said we could not enter—until he noticed my license plate and declared, "Hey, you are Tar Heels! Come on in!"

Also a decade or so ago, I drove together with two students to Washington, DC, to attend an anthropological meeting. As we were about to leave, a colleague from Duke hailed us and asked for help. She had attended the same meeting but could not get her car out of the garage, which was across the street from our garage. The guard for our garage, like the guard at the Smithsonian, noted our NC license plate and we talked a bit about his coming from NC. I asked what advice he could give for our colleague. He telephoned the guard for her garage but he was not on duty, so he proposed a scheme. Her deck adjoined a fast food place whose door opened onto the deck. He suggested that we access her deck through that door and then manually lift the outer door so that she could drive out. He warned us that when we opened the door, an alarm would sound that would bring the police, but he assured us that his friend would be in the police car and would let us leave with our colleague. We did as planned and the Duke colleague drove away—without ever thanking us, as I recall.

The power of the Tar Heel is suggested by a contrasting experience I had when driving with a Georgia plate. When studying in Cambridge, Massachusettes, I found a note on my parked car, saying, "Take this heap of junk back to Georgia." A similar comment was shouted when I drove our daughter's car with a Maine plate through downtown New York City.

Boundaries between anthropologists and their subjects, that is, those with whom we live during our fieldwork, are of course a major issue for anthropology and other kinds of research involving people. Here is a bit of experience. My first study abroad was in Ulm, Germany, where I lived with a family, Herr and Frau Beck and their sons, Gerd and his younger brother, at

Haryo Marsosudiro posed with two garage door opener remotes that he and his son, Philindo, had just reprogrammed.

11 Rechsberg Weg for four weeks and traveled with Gerd and others for two weeks. We became quite close, and Florence and I also visited them on our "honeymoon" passing through Ulm en route to Indonesia in 1962. In Indonesia, we met Joko Sanyoto in Jakarta, then traveled to Surabaya and lived with the Marsosudiro family at Jalan Gundih 16, then with the Soeyoenoes family at Panglima Sudirman in 1963. Remarkably, a son of Marsosudiro, Haryo, and his son now live ten miles away from us. Florence and Haryo have the same birthdays and celebrated together this June 13. Haryo's son Philindo is good friends with our daughter.

Since the late nineteenth century and early twentieth, anthropology has evolved from expeditions to participant-observation fieldwork. Much of the credit goes to Bronisław Malinowski, the Polish anthropologist who did intensive work among the Trobriands in the Pacific islands and also happened to be an acquaintance of the sociologist Howard Odum, who arranged for Malinowski to visit Chapel Hill in the 1920s, stimulating the teaching of social anthropology here. I learned about the huge Polish contribution when I was the only American to participate in the hundredth anniversary of the Polish anthropology society in Poland several years ago.

Carolina, then, was a pioneer in anthropology in the US South, stimulated by Georgian Howard Odum (who happened to grow up a mile away from where Florence was born) thus carrying the germ to Charles Hudson, via Chapel Hill, thence to Athens, Georgia, where Odum's brother, Gene, was a pioneer leader in ecology. I, of course, was ignorant of all of this despite living in the same state, but in the wilds of south Georgia. My community had not sent its students into anthropology at Athens but instead into other fields, usually business or agriculture, though there were some exceptions, such as my close friend Bobby Burton, who became a philosophy professor at the University of Georgia.

Little if any of this is noted in histories of anthropology or related fields, which tend to focus on the major centers in the North or West, such as Columbia University, where Franz Boas led cultural anthropology, and the Smithsonian, which built a major museum. Balancing attention to region, notably the Southeast United States, was our increased globalism at Chapel Hill. In addition to the FedEx Global Education Center, there were numerous new international projects, such as our collaboration with Eritrea via grants from USAID, and with the Madame Curie Institute at Poznań, Poland; fellowships funded by Rockefeller to link scholarship in the US South with scholars and institutions abroad; and Fulbright fellowships. We began to win as many fellowships and grants as the institutions in the Northeast and on the West Coast. Niklaus Steiner headed our center, which developed these projects, while Bogdan Leya was a leader in others, such as the Curie Institute relationship. As the title of my book *Grounded Globalism* suggests, we strove to integrate research and work abroad and in our region.

When I left Princeton, my first job, for UNC in 1967, my former advisor, Cora Du Bois, remarked, "James, you are crossing the Rubicon," alluding to the boundary separating civilization from outer darkness. Today, we cross many Rubicons globally. This is no problem for our multicultural grandchildren and their friends, whom they treasure even as they do have to cross boundaries and encounter change.

Three Fields or Four?

This modest controversy represents a division within anthropology and, indeed, within the sciences more broadly. In brief, Charles Darwin's theory of evolution is one guiding perspective, and British social anthropology is another. The theory of evolution covers all of life, including the rise of humans from primates and previous organisms. Thus, the "four fields" that are traditional in American anthropology—biological, cultural, archaeological, and linguistic—can be included in that theory.

An alternative, stemming from British and French anthropology inspired by Emile Durkheim, focuses on the social basis of life and derives everything from that. At Oxford, the two approaches are divided between two institutes. I participated in both and was the only person who did so then. At UNC-CH, the two were also divided, between downstairs and upstairs: the archaeologists and physical anthropologists downstairs in their labs, and the sociocultural anthropologists upstairs, along with the linguists, who were located in another building with the language departments. Nationally, we were also divided. Vincas Steponaitis was president of the Society for American Archaeology and I was president of the American Anthropological Association, which included all four fields but did not so completely focus on archaeology and physical anthropology. Thus, finally, at UNC we underwent a transition that Bob Daniels describes as being from four fields to three, as illustrated in the approach of Carol Crumley, who is an archaeologist of France, and including somewhat contemporary culture.

Vincas is a superb thinker and analyst, which is why he became the secretary of the faculty for UNC as a whole and joined me on the committee appointed by Harvard to assess its Department of Anthropology, which was divided between Harvard's Peabody Museum, which focuses on archaeology and physical anthropology, and William James Hall, which focuses on the social sciences, including social anthropology. These "lenses" are articulated in my book *The Anthropological Lens*. Different lenses come to life in debates and plans like ours at UNC, not to mention in life itself and in our human efforts to apply these viewpoints in our governance and work.

Grandparents and Parents

I turn now to more personal reflections. I describe Florence's ancestors in *A Truly Lucky Jim*, beginning with their arrival in America in the 1600s, where they settled in Connecticut, notably Milford near New Haven. A museum there tells of their mill, and they also built mills elsewhere, including in Torrington, where a house bears a sign "Ye olde fowler home." This is Florence's father's forebear; her mother's family came from South Carolina. Her grandfather and grandmother met in Milledgeville, Georgia.

My mother and father both had ancestors in North Carolina but grew up in Alabama and Georgia, respectively, and met in summer school at Auburn University. Here is a bit about them. Mother's father, Clayton Rogers, was a businessperson in Elmore County, near Montgomery, who served in the legislature. My father's mother, Minerva, was first cousin to Miss Lillian, mother of Jimmy Carter, who became the governor of Georgia. They did not have close contact because she moved to Columbus as a child, whereas Carter remained in the county near Plains. Minerva and her siblings moved to Columbus, possibly because of the pandemic that killed their parents.

Minerva and her siblings went on to work in various fields: Mary and Minerva to normal schools and then to become teachers; Schley to become a successful contractor and builder; and the oldest daughter to marry a lawyer who later served on the board of regents of the University of Georgia.

Minerva and Mary pursued higher education. Minerva was a teacher and administrator in the Columbus school system and Mary was a faculty member in Florida and Tennessee. Minerva, at sixty, matriculated at Auburn focusing on mathematics and education and graduated when she was sixty-four. All of us, my mother, father, sister, and I, went to Auburn's commencement ceremony and saw Minerva onstage with the other graduates, many of them GIs. Mary entered a graduate program at the University of Chicago.

Both ladies were blunt and no-nonsense. Aunt Mary arranged for the adoption of my cousin Emily. She was teaching at a college in Tennessee, which had a nursery for orphans. She was impressed by one young child, Emily, and told the head of the college she wanted to adopt her. He said, "If you do, I'll fire you, for you are single." She replied, "Fire me, I am adopting her." So he did fire her and she did adopt Emily, and then later she arranged for her niece, Mary, Minerva's daughter, to adopt her. Emily is our first cousin.

A classmate to my father and aunt in Columbus school, Carson McCullers, was the author of *The Heart Is a Lonely Hunter*. Minerva told me, a mere

The cabin depicted is part of approximately three hundred acres in Stewart County that were recently sold, while fourteen or so acres are retained by James Peacock III. This cabin is the birthplace of Minerva.

teenager then, about McCullers, who was the daughter of a jeweler known to Minerva and from whom Minerva bought a silver dish that she gave to Florence as a wedding present. McCullers had won a scholarship as a pianist at Julliard but lost her purse on a subway. To survive, she played piano in a bar and during the day wrote her famous book (*The Member of the Wedding* is another). McCullers married a man whom both my mother and her sister, a concert pianist, Louise, had dated. I heard these accounts when I was a teenager in south Georgia and sometimes visited grandparents in Columbus, Georgia, and Speigner, Alabama, as well as cousins in Tuscaloosa.

My connections to North Carolina were via both my mother and my father, though I did not visit North Carolina until I was a teenager. Yates Mill, near Raleigh, was built by a relative on my mother's side and then later was sold or otherwise passed over to Yates.

Back to Georgia. At the office of the clerk of court in Stewart County was a box with a Confederate uniform worn by an ancestor of the Gordy family from that area who was shot at Petersburg, Virginia. That family was related to Minerva as well as to Miss Lillian, mother of Jimmy Carter. The cabin depicted is where Minerva was reportedly born, and the land on which it stood was inherited by my father and his sisters.

My father, James Lowe Peacock Jr., grew up in Columbus, Georgia, graduated from Auburn with a degree in electrical engineering, was employed by Georgia Power Company, was inducted into the army as a lieutenant, as World War II began, was shot during the invasion on D-Day, and while recovering was head of a prison camp for German prisoners. After the war, he joined a friend in Tifton, Georgia, to open a business for electrical contracting. He did this until his retirement at the age of seventy-five and he died at ninety-four. My mother, Claire, lived to be 101.

A family that was prominent in Columbus and related to my father was the Schleys. They were reportedly from Bavaria and had helped found a town in Maryland, and then one of their relatives was governor of Georgia when it was a colony. Minerva's brother was named Schley Gordie; we called him Uncle Schley.

Minerva and James Peacock, my father's parents, lived on 1520 Fourth Avenue in Columbus, Georgia. Their house had several bedrooms, a large front porch, and a walled-in backyard with a garage. It was an easy walk from downtown Columbus and fairly close to the Bradley Library. It was a bit more than a hundred miles from Tifton, where we lived, which was a small town lacking the amenities found in the city of Columbus, which had the iron industry and wealth. Columbus boasted a bookstore, a library, a department store (Kirvins), a football stadium, and even an opera house once visited by international performers and now renovated with the help of a wealthy alumnus of UNC-CH. Carson McCullers suggests Columbus's cosmopolitan in *The Heart Is a Lonely Hunter*. The story goes that Fort Bening was built on farmland of one of my relatives, which the government had confiscated; the relative sued and vowed not to shave until he won the suit; he never did win, so he had a very long beard. In short, Columbus and our grandparents and other relatives were a welcoming contrast to the small town where we lived. Importantly, Minerva, Mary, and others gave us a glimpse of the education to be gained in schools such as Auburn and the University of Chicago.

My mother's parents and siblings lived in the country but also in cities such as Birmingham, Montgomery, and Tuscaloosa. When my uncle's wife Emily went to school at Radcliffe, her father is quoted as quipping that Boston is fine but won't amount to much because it is too far from Tuscaloosa.

In short, I am very grateful for my relatives. We have faithfully and regularly driven the miles to visit them, especially on holidays, and we regret the intrusion of the pandemic into this custom.

Selendang

Selendang refers to a sling by which a parent carries his or her child; the verb for that action is gendang. Either father or mother uses that technique. Aside from a technique to carry or hold a child, releasing the hands for work or other action, the selendang expresses protection, affection, and warmth.

Our first child, Louly, was born slightly premature and had difficulty breathing; hence she looked bluish when newly born. Her life was saved by Dr. Brazelton at Boston Lying-In Hospital. He massaged and worked with her all night while I watched, and she emerged ruddy and healthy.

When Louly was small I would often walk while carrying her wrapped up against the chilly Massachusetts winter. I unthinkingly emulated the selendang way of parenting.

In the painting on the cover of this book the elderly man does not show a sling but simply holds the child, accomplishing a similar action. A mother and child are perhaps more typical in western painting, following the story of Mary and Jesus.

I close this account with a treasured memory of our first child. I should add that Louly moved out of a selendang to full mobility. When she was in college, she would leap from the top of a stair and turn over in midair, landing on her feet at the bottom.

Louly's dramatic flips down the stairs at a fraternity house (SAE) at Davidson provides an introduction to her generation. She finished at Davidson then went to France, passed an exam at the Louvre normally for French citizens, published and presented her dissertation about Bashkirtseff, an early leader in post modernist art, then taught for some years and currently is a singer. Her sister Claire earned a degree in philosophy at Yale followed by a doctorate in literature; she has written several books including *16 Ways of Looking at a Photograph* published by Oxford University Press. Next came Natalie, her sister, a social worker whose work and writings are now gaining note.

Currently, Louly's son, Nicholas, earned a bachelor's degree in physics at UNC-Chapel Hill and is a graduate student at Duke University. Her daughter, Flora, is at Davidson College and is majoring in English. Claire's and Mark's son, Yanni, is at Harvard University and is majoring in mathematics and history. Natalie's and Emiliano's daughter, Bella, is in high school at Cary Academy, the SAS school in Raleigh, NC, and their daughter, Lucia, is in middle school at Duke School in Durham, NC.

Yanni and Bella at Harvard University

Jimmy Carter

In the spring of 2023, as Jimmy Carter is preparing to die, commentators including the *New York Times* are reassessing his presidency and life. He and I are relatives, though not closely acquainted. My grandmother on my father's side, Minerva Gordy, was first cousin to Miss Lillian, his mother, but they did not grow up together because Minerva moved from Plains to Columbus, Georgia, when she was a child, allegedly because her parents died.

When our children were young, Florence and I visited Plains and met Miss Lillian at the Plains train station. She was sitting in a chair on the station platform and was very friendly. Jimmy was not present.

When my mother was in her nineties, I drove her and my sister Laurie to Plains, Georgia, and we heard Jimmy give a Sunday school lesson, which he did expertly. Many visitors were present from many places. A female leader in the church announced that visitors could have a photograph with him but should not speak to him. This command annoyed my mother, so we left after the lesson.

On several other occasions, including his inauguration in Washington, DC, I heard him speak. But I never met him, other than for a brief three minutes in Durham, North Carolina, when he was greeting people in a line as he campaigned for the presidency.

Based on all that I have read or heard, especially recently, I agree with the positive assessment.

Ironic Juxtapositions

Having described Tift County, Georgia, where I lived for a while starting at age eight, I cannot escape without a word about Covington, Georgia, where Florence grew up and formidable characters resided. Some evoked mirth, such as the local politician who presided at a funeral and cremation and then announced, "The ashes of the deceased are deposited in the urinal." More formidable was Florence's ninety-year-old Uncle Bob, who was chair of the University of Georgia's board of regents and was asked what the speaker said at a local Kiwanis meeting; he replied, "He didn't say." These Covington figures contrasted with Howard Odum, whom the UNC-CH chancellor told me was the most important North Carolinian, owing to his social and educational contributions. I met Odum's son-in-law through a sad circumstance. A colleague in anthropology, Stephen Polgar, died while jogging, and I, as department chair, was asked to identify him in the morgue. While there, I also met the husband of Odum's daughter, who was employed in the morgue and was the son of a professor of music at UNC, a native of Vienna.

Connecting all of us, in various ways, was Sam Hay, Florence's brother-in-law who was married to her sister Louly. Sam was a cattle farmer and former football player at Auburn who came from a distinguished line of Presbyterian leaders reaching back to Scotland. When he died, the lengthy driveway surrounding his and his in-laws' house was filled with hundreds of mourners. He was a great person and storyteller. A family joke was the time Sam and I, adults and in-laws, were seated at the children's table at Thanksgiving. He was also a committed Democrat, sometimes a counterpoint to the more conservative locals, including the sheriff who happened to be the uncle of the film stars Dakota and Elle Fanning, the latter recently cast as Catherine the Great of Russia.

Outshining all by wit was Louly Fowler, Florence's mother, whom Sam described as "having more sense before breakfast than anybody else." Here is a brief interview with her conducted in her later years:

> After I finished Covington High School, I went to Shorter College, where I was really cut down to size. After being a glorious high school senior, there is no worse contrast than a college freshman. I've never recovered.
>
> Received a B.A. from Shorter in 1931 with a major in music. Lived a completely worthless life for two years until I married my Robert Fowler.
>
> We have two daughters: Louly (Mrs. Sam B. Hay Jr.), and she has five children; Florence (Mrs. James L. Peacock III), she has three children, and Robert R. III has one child. Out of these eight grandchildren, only one boy, Sambo Hay III.
>
> All our children have college degrees; the girls have masters and they are fine citizens, I think. All eight grandchildren are geniuses!
>
> Sara Clyde told me to say that I was president of my class for four years at Shorter, and since then every fool thing I belonged to has foisted the dubious honor of the presidency on me, since nobody else would do it. Now I don't join anymore, and there are no more cake sales or rummage sales and best of all, no more PTA.
>
> So! The best thing I ever did is get old. I love it.

Tift County, Georgia: A Breeding Ground for Anthropologists

Charles Hudson, my late colleague in anthropology from the University of Georgia, joked that something in the water of this small town and county bred anthropologists, including his wife and several others of our vintage. Charles was a leader in much, including the Southern Anthropological

Society, founded in the 1960s and based in Athens, Georgia, home of the University of Georgia, which, by the way, competed with UNC for status of oldest public university in America; it turns out that UGA submitted the first legislative claim and UNC was the first to open its doors. William and Mary was much older, founded in the 1600s, but it was a private university until it became public relatively recently as part of the UVA system. Anyway, the anthropologists in Tift County to whom Charles referred were Holbrook Peterson, Charles's wife, Joyce, me, and one other, a linguist. Just a few, but representing a small place, which deserves a comment. Why anthropologists here? Was it because we were culturally deprived? That is, primitive? Perhaps so; this place once received an award recognizing its cultural deprivation. Do anthropologists require a primitive setting?

Charles's joke is an excuse to say a word about Tift County and the Southern Anthropological Society. Tift County and the town of Tifton are located more or less as follows: two hundred miles or so south of Atlanta, the capital of Georgia, ninety miles north of Tallahassee, the capital of Florida, and a considerable distance from Savannah and the Atlantic Ocean, as well as from the mountains near North Carolina, Virginia, and Tennessee to the west. Georgia is about as long from north to south as North Carolina is wide from east to west. South Georgia was seen as a backwoods area, illustrated by an image in *Gone With the Wind* by an Atlantan, Margaret Mitchell, of a skinny and pallid hick on the road from south Georgia—a far cry from Scarlett and Rhett. Nearby, however, is the last hiding place of the president of the Confederacy, who was captured by federal troops near Irwinville, a few miles from Tift County. The Tifts were from New England, came to south Georgia to cut timber, and founded Tifton and Tift County in the early 1900s; some Tifts still resided there when I lived there and, in fact, owned the local newspaper.

What, then, might such an area offer to budding anthropologists? I moved to Tifton at the age of eight when my father joined Hull Atwater in opening an electrical contracting company after he'd completed his stint in the US Army at the end of World War II. A small gang in the neighborhood greeted me by pelting me with pine cones and sticks. This was a rite of passage, as delineated by anthropologist Arnold van Gennep, but to me it simply signaled rejection. I caught some of the missiles and threw them back. Eventually, we were friends.

As I've noted, Tift County was a bit isolated. However, several local institutions added some diversity. Abraham Baldwin Agricultural College and the Coastal Plain Experiment Station, more recently the Agrirama, a museum of agriculture, are state and federal institutions that attracted agronomists and others from other states and occasionally other countries. Some of these brought families and children who were friends to my parents, siblings, and me and mixed in with locals who themselves often had other associations.

Let's recall a few people who imbibed the drink Charles Hudson attributed to Tift County. Holbrook Peterson, my age, was son of the dentist Dr. John Peterson. Dr. Peterson taught Sunday school at the Methodist church, as noted, the tree class. His passion was historical research into religious traditions, Judaic, Christian, and others, which inspired him to learn Greek and Hebrew, to read works by Carl Jung or Lévi-Strauss, and to analyze cultural trends and issues. Holbrook, his son, earned a doctorate from the University of Georgia under the tutelage of Charles Hudson. He joined the faculty at the University of Mississippi. Joyce Hudson took the path of writing novels about Native American culture, which was the specialty of her husband, Charles. I preceded them both by a bit.

Southern Anthropological Society (SAS)

The Southern Anthropological Society was established in the 1960s with leadership from several anthropologists located at Southern universities, notably Charles Hudson, University of Georgia, and Miles Richardson, Louisiana State University. SAS chose not to become a member of the AAA. I was once president of SAS, as was Charles Hudson. The University of Georgia Press was a major publisher of SAS materials, while the University of North Carolina also published materials about the US South but has not focused on anthropological materials to the extent that Duke University Press has, for example, publishing the dissertation of Obama's mother, who earned a degree in anthropology at the University of Hawaii.

I first attended SAS at a meeting in Dallas, Texas, shortly after I moved to Chapel Hill. On stage were several speakers, memorably Miles Richardson. He sat respectfully erect until his turn to speak, then did so in his Texas accent although he was teaching at LSU in Baton Rouge and had done a doctorate at Tulane along with doing fieldwork in South America. Miles followed another speaker who was so academic that she read aloud each footnoted reference. Then, as always, he was original, insightful, and witty. A hint of his work is in his excellent book on the anthropology of religion, which begins, as I recall, with an account of his mother falling into a well.

SAS meetings often had remarkable presentations. For example, a former missionary told about being captured during the Mau Mau rebellion in Africa. He was tied to a stake, beaten, but then administered a powerful aphrodisiac that induced an instant erection.

SAS did not join AAA, the national organization, but kept its localized identity, which saved money as well as preserved its culture. Charles, Miles, and others were very effective leaders. Charles sat on the front porch of my parents' house in Tifton, and Miles went fishing on Stuart Marks' pond near Chapel Hill. We had a good time.

Globalization

This theme continues to resonate, in the sense of "grounded globalism," to take a phrase from a book I published with the University of Georgia Press. The theme is depicted by the cover, which I borrowed from a Confederate flag I bought at the state fair of North Carolina with a tag that reads "Made in China." The book depicts ways the US South was and is global as well as regional.

Tifton is a good illustration. Next door to my parents' house, built of thirty thousand bricks I collected and transported from a school that burned down in nearby Ashburn, lives two of their best friends. They are Peter and Faith from South Africa. They moved to Tifton from Mexico so that Peter could take a job with a large agricultural enterprise. Faith is an artist, and she and my mother, in her nineties, enjoyed coffee at the shop off Highway 85.

Heck Dodson, a friend from high school, had a large agricultural enterprise and was, I noted recently, listed in the local Episcopal church as a sponsor of the Jungian "journey into wholeness" and had a member of his family studying literature at UNC. George Wright, son of a drugstore owner, joined the Peace Corps and adopted a child from Latin America. My mother's close friend has a grandson who joined several Chinese students as valedictorians at Chapel Hill High School. My father retired from electrical contracting at seventy-five or so and began making furniture as a hobby. He then traveled with Mr. Bargeron, a master furniture craftsman and also librarian at Abraham Baldwin Agricultural College, around England purchasing antiques that they would then emulate in their shops. Examples are now in our apartment.

From England to Indonesia, our families have usually experienced friendship and kindness as well as occasional conflict, illustrated by my father in D-Day and other veterans from Tift County, such as Mr. Cohen, who was with General Patton's tanks, or my uncle Scott Madding, who was in Burma with Merrill's Marauders and later led in establishing the Green Berets.

A kind of globalism continues with our grandchildren. Bella and Lucia's father and paternal grandfather are from Mexico, Yanni's mother is Greek, and Louly's son attended a scientific meeting in Singapore. Their classmates and friends in school, college, and beyond are from many places, as is true for their generation.

Kin and Travel

Bat Masterson's "Have Gun Will Travel" and Johnny Cash's "I've Been Everywhere" evoke the itinerant aspect of Florence's and my life. Her sister called us "academic gypsies." Actually, much of our travel has been to stay in touch with that sister and other relatives but also for other reasons. Here is a brief account.

Between the ages of three and six, I moved frequently, as my mother, sister, and I followed my father as he trained for D-Day. We moved from Fort Gordon in Augusta, Georgia, and Fort Benning in Columbus, Georgia, as far north as Massachusetts, as far west as Oklahoma, and as far south as Tallahassee, Florida. I attended four schools in first grade—in Tallahassee, Columbia, South Carolina, and Deatsville, Alabama—finally settling down in Tifton, Georgia, after World War II until I went to college. Florence, by contrast, remained in Covington, Georgia, until she went to Hollins College, then Yale.

After we married in 1962, we lived in Indonesia and traveled in Europe and Asia until we settled in Cambridge, Massachusetts, until 1965, then on to Princeton, New Jersey, and finally to Chapel Hill, North Carolina. Since then, we have driven back and forth repeatedly between here and our families in Georgia, as well as some relatives in Alabama and various children who live in Maine, Virginia, and elsewhere, including France, where we have visited them. Either singly or together, we have traveled and lived in Indonesia, England, Singapore, and briefly various other places. Florence went to the extreme by traveling with her friend Nerys Levy on a Norwegian icebreaker to the South Pole. We both went to the North Pole on a more conventional ship.

Brook de Wetter-Smith is at once a renowned flautist and superb photographer of the south and north poles. His forebear was an official with the Czar of Russia when Bolsheviks were taking over. Accompanied by Cossack guards, he and his family traveled on the Siberian railway with the guards freezing on the train roofs. Brook's ancestors thus managed to escape Russia and migrate to the United States. Brook's photographs, Nerys's paintings, and Florence's singing combined in a concert and exhibit at the FedEx Global Education Center and Morehead Planetarium to address climate change.

For many years, Florence has attended the Baroque Performance Institute at Oberlin, Ohio, where she performs. My travel is often to conferences in the United States or overseas, plus a longer stay at Oxford, England, in All Souls College and in Yogyakarta, Indonesia, and elsewhere for fieldwork.

Regarding travel, cosmopolitan and provincial outlooks of course mix even in a place with a global center. A few examples are notable from local sports. A local author wrote a book about how great it is to hate Duke. The Presbyterian minister was invited to comment, and he replied, "God does not distinguish between Duke and Carolina, but he does distinguish between good and evil."

My favorite comment, though, came from Florence's mother about the rivalry of Georgia Tech and the University of Georgia. The Tech coach at the time was Bobby Dodd and at Georgia it was Wally Butts. At their game, the Tech students displayed a banner that read "In Dodd we trust to beat Georgia's butts." Far less clever is a T-shirt at a Duke football game that shows a baby saying, "I dream of a world where there are no Tar Heels." Even while war wages between Russia and Ukraine, sports rivalry dominates local media, and this caption may reflect Duke's propensity to look down on the locals. That attitude is common, perhaps, among private schools toward locals; I recall a Yale football game with the University of Connecticut when the Yalies snubbed UConn's effort to start a cheer uniting the two schools.

When I was chair of the faculty at UNC, I invited the president of Duke, Nan Keohane, to speak at our Faculty Council meeting at UNC. She did so powerfully, and Ron Hyatt, our faculty marshall and a leader of athletics, responded with an eloquent greeting taken from classical rhetoric. Later, Nan joined Chancellor Moeser in welcoming the new Rotary International Peace program UNC shared with Duke. Apparently, such a union of Duke and Carolina was unprecedented and went on to reinforce other collaborations. I also invited the president of Durham's predominately Black university, North Carolina Central, which also led to collaboration when he asked me to join the board he chaired at the UNC-CH law school. Sports aside, such collaborations were numerous and successful.

Ian, Singapore, and Parallel Histories

As I write, Hurricane Ian is threatening North Carolina, having flooded Florida. Yesterday evening was a celebration of the fifteenth anniversary of the FedEx Global Education Center at the university of North Carolina. Two histories resonate with these concurrent events.

The first unfolded in Singapore in 1969, a flood in December. Florence, myself, and our two children, Louly and Claire, were residing there in the Katong area near the coast. In the morning, I drove William Schneider, his wife, and their son to the Singapore airport, where they boarded a plane to fly to Borneo for William to do fieldwork for a doctoral thesis in anthropology at UNC-CH. After they embarked, I drove our car, an old Ford, returning to our apartment in Katong. However, the road flooded owing to a storm and the water rose above the hood of the car, forcing me to stop. I waded back to Katong, where the first floor of our apartment building was partially underwater.

It so happened that Florence's parents, who were traveling in Asia, had arrived in Singapore, and were staying in a downtown hotel. To meet them there, Florence, Louly, Claire, and I waded into town. The water then reached Louly's neck and I carried Claire on my shoulder. We arrived safely and returned to Katong that afternoon.

After several days, the water receded, and I retrieved our car. It started promptly.

The second event was the celebration of the fifteenth anniversary of the FedEx Global Education Center. The speaker was Mr. Smith, the retired head of FedEx. He was invited to speak because the building was named FedEx to acknowledge his gift when the building was built.

So far as I recall, based on my own participation and later observation, this was the process. More than fifteen years ago, in 1970, I returned from Singapore and Indonesia, where I had been doing fieldwork supported primarily by a grant from the National Science Foundation. In 1993, UNC celebrated its bicentennial, having been founded in 1793. That year, Craig Calhoun created UCIS, the University Center for International Studies. After several years, Craig moved to New York University and I replaced him as head of UCIS. The offices of UCIS were in the Coates Building. Raymond Farrow, who had joined me and others at UCIS, proposed that we seek to build an adequate building to house our expanding projects. Fortunately, Presidents Spangler and Broad, head of UNC's campuses for both universities and community colleges, led a bond package that raised more than three billion dollars to repair and construct buildings on the various campuses. The bond was voted on and accepted by the counties of North Carolina. Various teams were invited to submit proposals for the buildings. Led by Raymond Farrow, UCIS submitted a proposal. Two proposals were accepted, one for a science building next to Wilson Library and one by UCIS. A site was determined and an architect selected to utilize the funds committed. FedEx then offered additional funds, for the construction of a fourth floor.

During the fifteen years of service, the FedEx building has become a leading site for UNC-CH, housing many programs and projects, including study abroad, area studies, and cutting-edge initiatives that support Carolina's leadership internationally.

Tragedy in Malang, Indonesia

In Malang, a city in East Java, on the weekend of October 1, 2022, the local soccer team was playing the team from Surabaya, the second-largest city in Indonesia. Rowdy crowds led to police overdoing it with teargas and beatings, resulting in more than one hundred deaths, one of the worst incidents at a soccer match in world history.

This tragedy evokes many memories of Indonesia for me, some involving crowds and violence. The largest loss was probably Gestapu, the murder of as many as a million alleged communists by the military in 1965. A relevant concept and term is *dikroyak*, which refers to a crowd attacking an individual, as happens, for example, when an automobile driver runs over a pedestrian in a village and the villagers attack the driver. An opposite kind of attack is by an individual on a crowd, as occurred in 1963 when Pak Sakera, a worker in a sugar factory, used his parang, a kind of knife, to attack his Dutch bosses. Then there is the general reputation of Surabaya, Indonesia's second-largest city after Jakarta, where Florence and I lived from 1962 to 1963. An anthropologist, Dr. Kennedy, was reportedly killed by a crowd there during the revolution of 1945 when he was mistaken for a Dutchman.

In 1962–63, when Florence and I lived in a kampung in Surabaya, the US Peace Corps sent a team of athletes to that city only to withdraw them for fear of violence. We were fortunate to experience nothing untoward, unless I count the drunk man who attacked me shouting *Merdeka!* (Freedom!), alluding to Dutch colonialism, which cast Americans as neocolonialists, according to President Sukarno. I gently pushed the attacker aside, and no one joined him. We lived in that kampung, Gundih, with a family, the Marsosudiros, whose son and grandson, amazingly, now live ten miles away, in Hillsborough. The headman of the kampung, a communist, and everyone else was always friendly to us, which is the more typical habit of Javanese people, in my experience, except when poverty prompted dangers, especially in crowds.

Java is crowded; it is an island the size of North Carolina with ten times the population. Hence, crowd pressure is common, for example, on the train we rode when we left, with people packed in, in seats, on the floor, and on laps. Indonesia is the fourth-largest nation in terms of population.

Chinese Connections

On a Sunday afternoon in May of 2023, a gathering at the Horace Williams House celebrated the life of a kind and wonderful leader in Chapel Hill who died of cancer. The redeeming aspect was visiting with the remarkable people who came from many places to attend. One of them was Jun Wang. Jun came from Beijing to earn a doctorate in anthropology at UNC. With her she brought notable skills—one was Thai Chi, in which she was a collegiate champion in China. She began a demonstration at the local junior high school by standing in front of the approximately 3.5-foot-high stage. Suddenly she was standing on the stage, somehow having leapt to a height almost equal to her own. Amazed at her magic, many of us awkwardly joined her Thai Chi sessions. Jun was also trained in Chinese medicine. Once she observed that my hand and wrist were warm; she said I had a symptom called "warm" and gave me an herb which I boiled and consumed. Later I visited my own doctor who checked me for a sinus infection and said it was gone. I told him about the herb that she termed "waxy"—he said he wished he had such a "waxy remedy."

Once Jun was walking down the path near Franklin Street in Chapel Hill when she met a remarkable person, "The Man Who Stayed Behind"—that is the title of his memoir. A Jewish man from Charleston, SC, Sidney Rittenberg graduated from UNC soon after World War II. As a student activist and labor organizer, he was involved in the Communist party. Drafted and sent to China, he became proficient in Chinese and participated in the Long March led by Chairman Mao. He became involved in Mao's outreach to the West and was reportedly the only American member of the Chinese Communist party. Unfortunately he angered Mao's wife and was imprisoned for more than a decade. After he was released, he returned to Chapel Hill. Many of us, included Jun, met him when he spoke at meetings of an organization for international studies led by then-student Rye Barcott. Jun remarked that his Chinese was perfect and included some vocabulary used by the Communists in China.

Danger

The "year of living dangerously"—to use Sukarno's phrase—coincided somewhat with the time Florence and I lived in Indonesia; our locale had a reputation of danger. That brings to mind danger more generally, so I'll add a brief reflection on that aspect of fieldwork and also lawnwork.

Actually, dangerous episodes for me were more in the USA than Indonesia. The first day of high school my books were stolen. I went over to the thief's house and beat him up. That person later spent years in a federal penitentiary. A few years later I was selling pots and pans in rural Georgia. I went to a house out in the country and was showing my wares to a young woman when her father came out from a back room. He was large, barefoot, in overalls, had a shotgun, and told me to leave. I packed up and tried to arrange a later appointment with the young woman. As we spoke in the driveway, he threatened me again, so I drove across the road to another prospect. I was stupid and lucky.

Qatar

The recent football excitement in Qatar evokes memory of our international program's ventures there. Several of us from UCIS were invited to visit in order to learn about prospects for setting up a branch program there. Several schools had already done so. Ours would be for women and focused on arts and sciences and we had discussed the possibilities with several officials from Qatar whom we met with in Chapel Hill. So, one evening a queen of Qatar, who was also a sociologist, sent her personal airplane to pick up and fly over night to Qatar about fifty of us faculty and administrators of UNC-Chapel Hill. We attended a feast in our honor at the palace and spent a day learning about Qatar and its prospects for the program by UNC-CH there. After that visit, the faculty council of UNC-CH voted to proceed toward setting up a program, but the board of trustees voted against doing so, hence this venture was terminated. A year or so later a smaller group of us visited Jakarta at the invitation of a major Chinese bank to consider a UNC-CH branch there, but this one also did not gain trustee support. Despite one of the best international programs nationally, UNC-CH did not choose to create an extension of itself internationally.

Hail to the Queen and Certain Other Brits

The very moving remembrances of Queen Elizabeth evoke appreciations of certain other British persons. These are teachers and friends noted by my father and now by me.

When my father was preparing for D-Day, he took part in exercises on the ship called the *Black Prince*, which held a mock invasion on the River Clyde. After D-Day, he was in a hospital in Britain, where he recovered from his leg injury and pneumonia. My first thanks go then to those who treated him and secured his recovery. During that time, he sent me two small books about the Iron Age in Britain, which led six-year-old me to fashion stone axes. Decades later, he and my mother visited us when Florence, our children, and I spent the year in England on a Guggenheim fellowship at All Souls College, Oxford, and the fellows of All Souls treated my father with respect and courtesy. We drove over to the coast where he had embarked for the invasion, and he recalled every twist and turn, lane and road, in the area.

My own first major involvement with a British person was in graduate school at Harvard. In my second year of study, a new anthropology faculty member arrived, David Maybury-Lewis. David and his wife had come from Oxford, where he had studied with E. E. Evans-Pritchard, a leading social anthropologist. They invited our small group of students over for a weekly reading group, which David's Scandinavian and energetic wife enhanced with sweets as we gathered in their apartment. We read and discussed social anthropology for hours. Once we had a distinguished visitor, Edmund Leach from Cambridge University. Sir Edmund, a strongly built veteran of guerilla fighting among the Kachin of Burma, sat down in a chair, which immediately broke. He laughed, brandishing the broken leg.

Maybury-Lewis's arrival had a strong impact on us students at Harvard in 1960 and in the years following. He had done fieldwork on the tribes of Brazil, a time he describes in a vivid book as well as in complicated analyses of kinship systems. Several of us, Terry Turner, Chris Crocker, Jean Lave, Roberto Damatta, and others, joined Maybury-Lewis's field project in Brazil. I did not because I had decided to go to Indonesia. However, in 1962, when my advisor, Cora Du Bois, was in India, David was kind enough to chair my doctoral exam. I was the first in our class, I believe, to take and pass the exam, and David invited me to lunch afterward. He told me a funny story about his time as a student at Oxford. He was an outstanding runner when Roger Bannister, on the same team, broke the world record for the four-minute mile. David said he warmed up for a race in his warm-up suit, then sprinted onto the track and ripped it off only to realize that he had forgotten his shorts.

Maybury-Lewis was also a brilliant linguist who spoke many languages, including those of the Brazilian tribes. The author of the film *Jurassic Park*, formerly a student at Harvard and then a doctor from Harvard Medical School, once served with several of us on a committee and expressed his admiration for David, including his linguistic and speaking prowess. More than anything, David was an immensely kind person. At an AAA meeting in New Orleans, his former student, Roberto DaMatta, gave a magnificent remembrance of him.

A few years later, Leach became tutor to Prince Charles, now King Charles, who was a patron of the Royal Anthropological Society. Leach followed Isaac Newton by becoming provost of King's College and then was knighted, which led to a witty talk I heard him deliver in London at a meeting of the Royal Anthropology Society. It was titled "Once a Knight Is Quite Enough."

Still later, Leach and several other British anthropologists visited and spoke at Chapel Hill, as Bob Daniels recalls in his interview with Anna. Bob muses about how these British visitors came to UNC, which leads to an account of our family's year in England.

In 1965, I received my doctorate from Harvard and we moved to Princeton, New Jersey, where I joined the faculty and, as noted, helped start an anthropology department with the help of David Crabb and Cyrus Black. I published my first book and, with David, started a series with the University of Chicago Press just after we moved to Chapel Hill in 1967. I delivered my first paper to the AAA around that time. It was early on a Sunday and only a couple of persons attended to hear this neophyte. One of the two, however, was the editor of a major journal, and he invited me to publish my paper with that journal, which I did.

Also in 1965, we left Harvard and moved to Princeton, New Jersey, where I began my first job, as an assistant professor at Princeton. Louly, our first child, born in 1964, was followed by Claire, in 1967, and later Natalie, in 1970. I taught a large class at Princeton, of approximately one hundred students, and led a dozen discussion sessions. I also revised my dissertation, creating *Rites of Modernization*, a book published by the University of Chicago Press as the first title in a new series, coedited with David Crabb, titled Symbolic Anthropology, which we created for the study of symbols.

In 1967, we moved to Chapel Hill, and I carried on, as already described above. I joined the American Anthropological Association and began attending their meetings. A major boost came from the Wenner-Gren Foundation. Wenner-Gren is based in New York City and once had a castle in Austria where conferences were held. As I began to publish, I was invited to present papers at several of these conferences, where I met both new peers and older leaders from around the world. These included, for example, Gregory Bateson and his daughter with Margaret Mead; Max Gluckman; Victor Turner; as well as peers such as Roberto DaMatta, whom I knew in graduate school.

In 1973, I taught as a visitor for two quarters at the University of California in San Diego, actually La Jolla. This was a wonderful time for our children and led to our sojourn in England later on. At La Jolla was the superb

Reflections 307

British anthropologist Freddie Bailey, who, among other things, edited a series of books published with Blackwell's. He invited me to write a book on symbolic anthropology, which I did, titled *Consciousness and Change: Symbolic Anthropology in Evolutionary Perspective*. It received a very kind review by the *Times Literary Supplement*. Then, as summer arrived, so did Rodney Needham from All Souls College at Oxford University. Rodney was teacher to Tom Beidelman, who had arrived at Harvard when Maybury-Lewis did and who became a friend and teacher to many of us even as he moved later to Duke and then NYU. Owing to Tom, Florence and our three girls got acquainted with Rodney when he arrived in California; he had come there partly because one of his sons was living there, working as a tennis pro, while the other was studying physics at Cambridge. Since we had learned the ropes and sites around San Diego, we helped Rodney get oriented while he also got to know our daughters, who were ages two through nine. We treasure four-year-old Claire's question to him, based on her seeing an exhibit on birth: "Professor Needham, if a man's seed enters a woman's egg, she borns a baby; if a woman's seed could enter a man's egg, would he born a baby?" He was impressed with her and later encouraged her and her sister to study at Oxford High School for Girls when he invited me to spend a year as a fellow of All Souls College at Oxford University.

That year led to many excellent experiences for our family and hopefully contributed to our hosts. I gave talks at Oxford, King's College of Cambridge University, Canterbury, and Edinburgh, and at Oxford I joined colleagues Bob Barnes and Peter Carey in their course on Southeast Asia. I also spent a month in Sweden, thanks to Ulf Hannerz and others, where I lectured at Stockholm and elsewhere.

For me, these opportunities offered time to write a book, *The Anthropological Lens: Harsh Light and Soft Focus*, which was published by Cambridge University Press and has been translated into half a dozen languages. Funds for the year came from the Guggenheim Foundation, to which I am grateful. Wenner-Gren, Guggenheim, and other foundations have been most helpful.

So those projects and opportunities led also to contacts, including in England, where I was invited to give presentations at various universities and other venues. That led to further contacts, which then led to the visits from British colleagues to which Bob Daniels alludes in his interview with Anna Kushkova. They also had enduring effects on Florence and our children. Two Italian organ makers engaged Florence to sing while they demonstrated their organs in churches in England. The churches were ancient and unheated so that Florence's vocalizations were emitted with large clouds of mist wafting into the air. Later, in the summer, Louly and Florence replaced the boy choir at Christ Church Cathedral in Oxford during the summer when the boys were on vacation. This happened partly because Louly responded to a notice at her school, which called for "sopranos to audition" and Louly as a soprano showed up, only to realize boy sopranos were sought. The director very kindly appreciated her interest, which may have led to the two Tar Heel sopranos replacing the choir at Christ Church during the summer. Claire joined drama performances as well as dance, including the Royal Academy of Dance in London during that summer, which led us to be present as Lady Di and Prince Charles rode by on Fleet Street a few feet from us on the way to St. Paul's Cathedral for their wedding ceremony. That afternoon, Claire and I returned to our neighborhood at Kennington in time to spot Florence leading neighbors at the train station in singing "God Save the Queen."

Mishaps happened. The first was during our vacation to Tunisia in January. It was planned as a break from the winter season in England, and for a day we swam in the ocean. The next day brought the first blizzard Tunisia had experienced in a century. Finally, in the summer, we sadly bid our friends goodbye. We had collected nineteen bags of stuff the children had acquired, and our friends helped us take them to the station to get a train to Gatwick Airport. Fortunately, I found an empty wagon and was able to load the bags on the train during the five minutes it stopped. Next morning, we went to the airport only to discover that Ronald Reagan had fired the controllers, which meant most flights to the United States were canceled. Thousands of passengers were stranded at Gatwick, including us. Luckily we were able to get a flight to St. Louis and then to Atlanta. Thus, the year ended with both a bang and a whimper.

Our time in London has had enduring effects. Claire, for example, has published numerous books of both poetry and literary criticism with British publishers, including Oxford University Press and Blackwell's, usually under her husband's last name, Raymond, rather than Peacock. Of the three, Natalie, the youngest, brought back perhaps the strongest British accent, which induced her experiment with an interview survey. When she and her junior high classmates back in Chapel Hill were asked to do a telephone survey about nuclear disarmament, she conducted some of the interviews with her British accent and others with her American one, leading to her discovery that the British accent elicited more people to agree to be interviewed.

To conclude, I join in a salute to the Queen and the new King that is nurtured by gratitude to British friends who have enriched the experiences of my family and myself with their kindness.

Lawnwork and Fieldwork

Fieldwork is a staple of anthropology. One example is my note taking during discussions by Muhammadiyah at the training camp. The Muhammadiyah commentator described my practice: "His pencil was moving rapidly across the blank sheet as he listened and watched" (see Gerakan Muhammadiyah in *Purifying the Faith*, 1978). Bronisław Malinowski's classic depiction is a colonial era anthropologist who interviewed and took notes while sipping a gin and tonic on a porch. Since Muhammadiyahans did not drink, I did not, but I certainly took notes. Circumstances varied, of course. For example, during the two week workshop of Muhammadiyah, my activities included the following: exercise at dawn with participants, taking notes during lectures, prayers, lectures, arguments, walking . . . I did not have or need a translator. The recorder I brought failed to work, so I took detailed notes by hand. I took some photographs and sometimes joined discussions and arguments (including the sessions of jokes). Eventually my text was translated by the Muhammadiyahans into Indonesian and published in Indonesian or English by the Muhammadiyah press.

To conclude, I will reflect on ways anthropology and related efforts exemplify the scope of lawnwork and fieldwork. One could begin with the standard definition of anthropology covering the living and dead, the huge variety of cultures and creatures all studied and dealt with through fieldwork and lawnwork, then move on to issues and problems treated ranging from war to administration and economics. Examples encountered by the author and colleagues include the following:

Roy Rapaport led a project funded by the Wenner-Gren Foundation and involving many of us based at a ranch in Arizona. This effort endeavored to apply anthropology to issues facing the world ranging from war to climate change, inequities to mental illness. Our group of several dozen met several days per year for several years. The result was one book edited by a member of the Ford Foundation with chapters by each member of the group (mine dealt with the USA). An additional result was inspiration for each of us to apply our discipline. I had an opportunity to do so as chair of the faculty for my university and as director of a new center for international studies. Colleagues worked in other areas; one example is preserving grave sites of African Americans in New York. Yolanda Moses, I, and others published a book with the American Anthropological Association that explored the work of applying anthropology to issues ranging from inequity to climate change. Beyond publications, I and others moved into administration as well as scholarship.

Examples from other fields suggest further developments. For instance, Oberlin Conservatory of Music holds summer workshops which Florence, my wife, has attended for many years. The musicians study then perform at a high level.

At age 85 I recognize much that can be done, hence I treasure this drawing—completed in 5 minutes by our granddaughter Bella—which depicts a variety of cultures and entities delicious enough to evoke the world's comment "yum."

Drawing by granddaughter Bella Corral depicting a global world containing various cultures then saying "Yum," affirming that all are good.

AFTERWORD

The One Hundredth Anniversary of Muhammadiyah, Work and Fieldwork

In 2010, Muhammadiyah celebrated its one hundredth anniversary in the mother city of Yogyakarta Java, Indonesia. Florence and I had not planned to attend, but then I met a young Korean political scientist who was a panelist on a symposium at the Association for Asian Studies. The symposium was led by Bill Liddle, a distinguished political scientist, as well as an old friend of mine from Yale and a groomsman in Florence and my wedding in Georgia in 1962. I introduced myself to the young panelist, who flatteringly exclaimed "Rock star!" and then invited me to the anniversary celebration. She subsequently contacted Din Shamsudin, then president of Muhammadiyah, who confirmed the invitation. So Florence and I attended. To my surprise and delight, also present was Sudibyo Markus, whom I had not seen or been in contact with since I attended Darol Arqom, the Muhammadiyah camp, in 1970.

Sudibyo was a prominent speaker at the Muhammadiyah celebration, and I was invited to speak also. Recently, he has launched his monumental book *Islam and the West: A Light on the Horizon*. I have been honored to assist slightly in this work, which sets forth an important vision for peace, especially between Christians and Muslims.

In addition to Sudibyo's book and other achievements, his peers in Indonesia have made powerful changes in recent times. For example, Amien, Sudibyo's close friend, was a leader in bringing about the retirement of General Suharto as president of Indonesia, an office he had held since Sukarno died in 1970. Suharto had replaced Sukarno, the creator of the nation of Indonesia, and initiated the murder of as many as a million alleged Com-

Sudibyo Markus received the Honoris Causa Degree at this February 2023 event. This was in honor of his life's work in the field of Peace and Humanity and his book *Islam and the West*.

munists, after which he led a corrupt government. His retirement, prompted by Amien, arguably saved Indonesia from an uprising along the lines of those constituting the Arab Spring. Amien, as president of Muhammadiyah, helped increase its membership from six million in 1970 to thirty million and built educational and health programs such that Muhammadiyah is now an important civic as well as religious organization. Other activities by Amien's peers include Doctor Ariawan Soejoenoes's campaign "dua tjukup" (two is enough), which calls for lowering birth rates to two children per family.

Compared to such impactful efforts as these, undertaken in a nation with approximately the same population as the United States, my fieldwork and lawnwork, or that of my colleagues, would seem modest in impact. I do not argue otherwise. Compare, for example, the populations involved. Muhammadiyah claims some thirty million members, far more than the organizations in which I am involved claim; Rotary, for instance, has about one million members and one thousand Peace Fellows across two hundred nations but not thousands of schools and hundreds of hospitals like Muhammadiyah. The American Anthropological Association draws as many as eight thousand people to its annual meetings, but these are neither nations nor churches. They are scholars who do research, teach, and apply their knowledge; they do fieldwork and lawnwork, neither of which are slam dunks. They offer passes or blocks, and perhaps wisdom and insight, that builds offense and defense, or at least the possibility of systematic understanding. In the case of my Indonesian friends, I am deeply and forever grateful for their example and their kindness and friendship.

APPENDIX I

Belief Beheld: Inside and Outside, Insider and Outsider in the Anthropology of Religion
James Peacock

The issue I address can be stated simply: the relation between inside and outside in religious experience. "Inside" refers to what we often term "private," "personal," "the psyche," or perhaps "the soul." "Outside" refers to what we often term "public," "collective," or "the world."

A counterpoint to this inside/outside dialectic within the experience of the believer, the religious actor, is the relation of this actor to the observer: the believer as insider, the observer as outsider. This introduces the issue of reflexivity. These two insider/outsider pairs are not precisely parallel: in fact, their asymmetry leads to my conclusion.

This format may seem abstract. My materials will be concrete. They are ethnographic, drawn from fieldwork done over the past quarter century in Southeast Asia among Muslims and in the Southeast United States among Christians.

Both inside/outside aspects pose an issue in theory and method for the anthropology of religion. This is so at two levels. The first is at the level of the believer/participant. The second is the relation between the outsider/observer, the beholder, and the believer/participant. Let us examine the first level first. In the contemporary anthropology of religion, it is still fair to say that the two greatest inspirations are Emile Durkheim and Max Weber.

Out of this Durkheimian/Weberian framework has come the pervasive anthropological perspective of an anthropology of religion: emphasizing its collective, public symbols and beliefs, an outer aspect. (For those who wish names, I am thinking of the British/European social-anthropological tradition extending from Durkheim through Leach, Douglas, Needham, Turner, and Lévi-Strauss and the American cultural anthropological stream extending through Clifford Geertz and Roy Rappaport.)

What are the reasons for this emphasis on the public, the outer symbols? Most salient are two. First, public symbols make meanings public, hence observable, recordable, and analyzable, while private meanings are unobservable. Second, public and collective phenomena crystallize patterns that are somewhat structured and predictable, while private experiences—insofar as we can know anything about them at all—seem ephemeral, irregular, and unpredictable.

A related and basic reason is this existential condition of our practice: the anthropologist is by definition an outsider (this would be true even of a believer who, for the moment, is acting as an anthropologist—a beholder of beliefs). He or she, in the role of anthropologist, is the beholder of belief but not a believer. Paul Rabinow puts it simplistically and accusingly but cogently: "The anthropologist thus ends up studying what is serious and truthful to others without it being serious and truthful to him" (quoted in Lawrence 1989). Aside from such a cognitive gap, there is an experiential one between the methodologies and technologies of observation and the spiritual experience observed. Montana Locklear, a North Carolina Lumbee Indian Pentecostal preacher, described this situation with admirable pith. As my fellow fieldworker and colleague Ruel Tyson staggered into Locklear's church, laden with audio and video recorders, Montana introduced him: "Here's the brother professor. He's come to record the Holy Ghost."

This dilemma of being outside to the insider, beholder of the believer, is not lost on the anthropologist of religion. Essentially two solutions have been proposed: to get inside or stay outside. The first option is advised by Evans-Pritchard, who, after pessimistically surveying anthropological theories of religion, quotes with approval Wilhelm Schmidt, who says, "If religion is essentially of the inner life, it follows that it can be truly grasped only from within" (1965:121). So Evans-Pritchard suggests becoming an insider, which he himself did, in a sense, by converting to Catholicism. But he does not consider this option within the scope of anthropology itself, which, for reasons already mentioned, remains essentially focused on the externals of religion. The second option is advised by Clifford Geertz: stay outside. We cannot know other minds, much less, one would assume, other souls. Therefore, concentrate on that which we can know: the external symbolism, the performances. Geertz advises: "Understanding the form and pressure of, to use the dangerous word one more time, natives' inner lives is more like grasping a proverb, catching an allusion, seeing a joke—or, as I have suggested, reading a poem—than it is like achieving a communion" (1983:70).

Here, then, are wise precedents that advise us, as anthropologists, (1) to be outsiders and (2) to focus on the outside. Outsiders, beholders rather than believers, we treat religion only in its externals, such as its rites and publicly affirmed beliefs. And yet, so much of what our informants' experience tells us, what our own experiences tell us, points not only to the significance of the inner, as Schmidt stated, but also to the interplay of outside and inside and of outsider and insider. A more porous boundary is implied than by the dominant classic emphasis of our discipline.

Of course, there are sub-emphases, subtexts, we say, to the dominant formula: be an outsider, focus on the outside. Like psychoanalysis, anthropology also claims that as an outsider you can probe the inside better than the insider can. Objectivity is claimed to penetrate subjectivity in a way the subject himself or herself cannot, at least not without the help of the observer—the analyst, the ethnographer—who may in fact take a psychoanalytical perpective.[1] Even more convoluted dialectics are offered by some of our subjects, the fundamentalist Primitive Baptists. They argue that the apparent outsider may actually be more of an insider than the apparent insider, but neither should make what Calvin termed the "dread presumption" and claim to know the significance of evidence from inner experience.

Permit me to introduce a spokesman whom we'll encounter again: Elder Walter Evans, a recently deceased stonemason from the Blue Ridge Mountains, who was a Primitive Baptist elder. Elder Evans is preaching on pilgrimage. He says:

> If you feel today, or ever feel, that you're a stranger or pilgrim in the earth, listen to what's said in the following verse: "They confessed that they were strangers and pilgrims in the earth." I'm not saying this to make you sad. What I'm dealing with this morning, endeavoring to, has given me perhaps more consolation than any one verse or verses in all the Bible. . . Because so much of the time . . . I'll not go into that, but I've felt so much of my time in my life like a stranger.

We could devote a lecture to these lines, but three quick points are in order here. First, although words like "felt" are used, Evans's main referent is not psychological but theological. As he explained to me, his feeling like a stranger hints that he may be a child of God, a member of the Elect, predestined for salvation. Second, feeling like a stranger may also mean feeling estranged from your own faith, as Evans himself testifies to having felt on occasion: "Observing the baptism, it meant nothing to me." Finally, anybody, including non-church members, unbelievers, even the anthropologist, may be a child of God.

Paradoxically, the more you feel outside, the more you may, in fact, be inside, because to feel outside in this world is a sign, ambiguous to be sure, of possible elect status in the next.

So the Primitive Baptists provide a theology and imagery to refute and enrich too stark a distinction between inside and outside and to suggest a dialectical relation between the two. The believer/participant himself oscillates between estrangement and commitment, inside and outside. And between believer and observer the line is porous. Your stance of outsider is no unambiguous sign that you really are outside: in fact, it may be "evidence," as they say, that you are not. The more we would tell the Primitive Baptists that we were just observers, the more they would remind us that they, too, were observers of us and would discern small evidence that we were more than observers. Hear Mamie Osborne, another Blue Ridge Primitive Baptist, a beauty parlor operator, speaking to Beverly Patterson, a musicologist who was working with us:

> **Mamie:** This is really fascinating, that you do want to learn about us. I detected the enthusiasm that you had, and even seeing the two men, Mr. Peacock, and what was the other one's name?
>
> **Beverly:** Patterson and Tyson.
>
> **Mamie:** Tyson, Tyson . . . I wasn't thinking that the service was all that good, and here they had their ears just peeled, close you know, and I thought, well, it either had to be that they were wanting to learn for a job, or they were interested in what was being said for themselves . . . I thought they were interested somewhat for themselves.

"Somewhat for themselves": She is astutely cautious, but hopeful, in integrating our statuses as observers and participants.

My quick survey of the anthropology of religion needs a brief supplement. Anthropology, like other humanistic fields, still grapples with a perspective often termed "postmodernist." Postmodernism shifts the emphasis from what is known to the process of knowing and the stance of the knower. Postmodernism appears to assume that nothing can be known by the knower except his or her processes of knowing; hence the experience of knowing—observing, listening, interacting—becomes our frame and our data. In philosophy, Hans-Georg Gadamer exemplifies this emphasis when he stresses that the truth of the message of a text is relative to the perspective of the interpreter of that text: we cannot know what the text says except by exploring our own perspective or horizon as we encounter the text (1982). In anthropology, Vincent Crapanzano exemplifies this viewpoint, emphasizing how his informants' narrations depend upon, virtually derive from, himself, the interlocutor, the ethnographer (1980). So, as postmodernists, we get preoccupied with ourselves as observers and our impact on others, those whom we observe, encounter.

Yet such "others" can exert, I find, a power and constancy independent of any influence I as observer may exert: furthermore, I discover that, far from me influencing them, it is they who are working on me. Especially is this true when those we are studying are of a conversionist, evangelical group. These "Others" feel empowered as a voice and vehicle of the all-powerful Other, the numinous supernatural Other, to whom the believer has converted and to whom he invites or exhorts the observer to convert. Just what impact such an invitation may have on the beholder is a further question: the point here is to affirm the empowerment of those beheld, of believer through belief, of narrator through narration. As Erik Erikson wrote concerning his work on Martin Luther, the clinical biographer attempting to deal with a client finds that the client has been dealing with him (1958).

We turn now from this methodological issue of the relation between outsider and converted-converting insider to our substantive focus: the movement from outside to inside, the conversion experience. What follows is a comparison, which I introduce with two epigrams.

E. E. Evans-Pritchard: Social anthropology has but one method: it is the comparative method: it is impossible. (quoted in Needham 1983:62)

Jonathan Z. Smith: In comparison a magic dwells. (1982)

The conversion experience is, as we know, central to the history and phenomenology of Christianity. From Saul on the road to Damascus and Martin Luther on the road to Erfurt to John Wesley at Aldersgate and contemporary fundamentalism, testimonies and other accounts tell of dramatic experiences of conversion. The conversion is from some previous state of sinfulness or unbelief to a categorical and absolute commitment and belief in Christ and Christianity. Such conversion is often dramatic and emotional, entailing some vision or altered state of consciousness. The convert experiences a loss of his or her old self and the rebirth of a new self. Theologically, the experience is interpreted as evidence of being saved or at least renewed or given some hope of eventual salvation. Among the "fundamentalists" I studied, this familiar general pattern was typically narrated by the men, to me at least, and it is men on whom I shall focus. One typical male narrative tells of a misspent wild youth and early manhood, drinking, dancing, chasing women, maybe staying out in the woods to hunt and make liquor. Then the wild man becomes convicted of his sins (i.e., found guilty by God), asks Jesus for forgiveness, accepts Christianity, joins a church, gives up his wild ways, and is now found with his family in the pew, or even, after further struggle to escape the call, in the pulpit or at the stand. More dignified variants resemble Puritan conversion narratives. Here are excerpts from Elder Walter Evans, the Calvinistic stonemason mentioned earlier:

> In the latter part of my twentieth year... when I cared nothing for God nor his people, satisfied with my big times attending places of worldly pleasure—my father insisted strongly that I attend a meeting being held by people of the Regular Baptist denomination, of which he and Mother were members. I finally agreed to go: however, my purpose was to walk home with some of the girls from the meeting.
>
> It was on Tuesday night while standing in the back of the house, a strong power arrested my heart and soul to the extent my body trembled under the weight like a leaf on a tree shaken by a mighty wind. A voice from somewhere, a still voice taut with power, said, "You are lost without God or hope in the world."

Walter Evans felt himself a sinner "by nature... doomed without God's mercy." He knelt at the altar, or "mourner's bench," and "begged God for mercy and pardon of [his] sins." "I was in desperate need of something to give me relief from this awful feeling of condemnation," he said. He left the meetinghouse and went home, but nothing could bring relief: "Neither prayers of Dad and Mother, preachers, nor no one else could reach my case." Evans prayed and suffered for two days and three nights, until a voice said, "Your sins are all forgiven." He was raised to his feet "one happy man" and joined the congregation singing "Christ will bear the Christian higher. When the last trumpet shall sound," his mountain tenor no doubt ringing out all over the voices, as it could still do in his eighties. "Before the song ended, a call or strong impression came to me... O, how I desired to tell what the Lord had done for me, I was in a new world." He was baptized on Sunday, November 16, 1930.

As I was working in 1970 among Muslims in Southeast Asia—in Indonesia primarily, but also in Singapore—I was struck by the absence of such conversion narratives. Certainly there were conversions. Objectively considered, some of the conversions to Islam entailed quite a radical change of commitment, for example, from Christianity or communism or syncretism (by "syncretism" I mean a distinctly Southeast Asian mix of Hinduism, Buddhism, and animism) to Islam, which is considered in many cultural, political, and phenomenological respects to be the polar opposite of these other faiths. But, however radical the conversion would seem, the Muslims did not, with one or two interesting exceptions, report a conversion *experience* with the emotional and altered states of consciousness noted in the Christian testimonies.

I turn now to a particular Muslim group, the Muhammadijah of Indonesia. Muhammadijah is a reformist Muslim movement in the basic sense that it strives to return to fundamentals: to return to the Qur'an as the literal word of God and to follow that word in stripping religion of irrelevant syncretic practice in order to re-create the pure Islam of the Prophet. In certain respects, Muhammadijans are militant zealots, in others moderate rationalists, but certainly to join Muhammadijah is a radical step for most Indonesians, especially Javanese, who are reared in the looser Hinduized syncretic setting of the larger Javanese culture.

In this context, consider the following account. Ahmad says that like many of village origins he remembers the day but not the year of his birth (this is owing to the Hinduist-syncretist calendar system), and he confirms that he was from a family of this syncretic persuasion, which did not recite the prayers of Islam. But he learned to pray, and praise be to God, he is now a Muhammadijahn. (The group echoes, "Praise be to God.") Ahmad goes on to tell how he helped crush a syncretic mystical movement, which, he says, "threatened the safety of society."

This is one of many similar statements that I noted, rendered as verbatim as possible. They were made in the Indonesian language by trainees in a Muhammadijah training camp called Darul Arqom. This was a two-week, eighteen hours per day, intensive camp for branch leaders of Muhammadijah. (I went through the training myself as a participant-observer. Among the participants, incidentally, was the current head of Muhammadijah, Amien Rais, now a leader in Indonesian politics.) The trainees were all Javanese, ranging in age from their early twenties to mid-thirties. The statements were made as part of an exercise called "personal introduction," which most trainees (twenty-three of the thirty-eight present) were called out to perform at various points during the training. These statements were the closest approximation I heard to what Christians term "testimonies." The testifiers described how they came to be committed to a faith manifested in a sect, Muhammadijah: they did this publicly and elicited a supportive response.

But, although these accounts reported conversion and took a kind of testimonial form, none of them described a Christian-style conversion experience. In none of the twenty-three Darul Arqom accounts is there any mention of an emotional experience or altered state of consciousness. Yet the accounts described a shift in belief, membership, and sociocultural identity.

The absence of emotional language was especially striking given recent history. This was in 1970, five years after Gestapu, the massacre of some half a million Indonesians in a conflict that was, in part, between the purist

Muslims and the syncretic Communists. Muhammadijah, including some of the Darul Arqom testifiers, had been involved in the murder of their own neighbors. Yet remembered violence did not translate into emotion and drama even as Muhammadijans narrated their conversion from the cultures of those some had killed.

Struck by the absence of the conversion experience accounts, I discussed the matter with one of the instructors as we strolled beside a rice paddy on one of our habitual walks. He seemed to recognize the sort of experience I described but assured me that he had never heard of any Muhammadijahn reporting or having one. However, he mentioned suggestively, he had heard of such among the Chinese. This is suggestive because many of the Indonesian Christians, including fundamentalists, are Chinese.

Away from the camp, I did a number of interviews eliciting life histories from Muhammadijans and also other Muslims, including Malays, Pakistanis, Indians, and Arabs from Singapore. None mentioned a conversion experience, with one interesting exception, to be noted shortly. In similar interviews with fundamentalist Christians in the southern United States, the conversion experience was almost always mentioned quickly, without prompting, and served as the cornerstone of the life history narration.

We come, finally, to the one partial exception to my failure to discover a conversion experience among Southeast Asian Muslims. This man, from Singapore, is half Chinese—his father Chinese, his mother Burmese—and he had taken his father's name, Tan, until his conversion to Islam, when he became Abdul Talib. He was educated in a Christian, Anglican school. His father, who owned a perfume factory, was wealthy. His brothers and sisters were all non-Muslim: they represent Buddhist, Christian, and hedonistic-materialistic orientations—a cultural diversity equal to the family of Sanyoto and indeed to Singapore itself but lacking any affiliation with the Malay-Muslim element. Talib's first wife, a Chinese woman, left him with six children. He then married an Indian-Malayo-Muslim woman who also had six children. With these twelve children, as well as a baby of their own, they lived, when I knew him in 1969, in a two-bedroom apartment provided by the army, in which Talib was a warrant officer on the island then known as Belakang Mati, or "Behind Death" (now, under another name, the site of an amusement park).

Talib is a dedicated Muslim, strictly following the fasting and other rules; when I knew him, he was praying five times a day, reciting extra prayers every evening during the fasting month, and fasting extra days. But he is a deviant Muslim, for he has joined the radical sect, Ahmadiyya,[2] which some Muslims consider outside the fold of Islam. Ahmadiyya proclaims Ahmad, a Pakistani teacher, to be the successor to Muhammad. When I first met Talib, at an Ahmadiyya meeting in 1969, he told me, with no prompting, the story of how he converted to Islam. He was at Sarawak, engaged in a shirt-selling business, when he had a vision in which a figure in white entered the room and told him to go to the mosque. He did so and joined Islam.

That's all he said about that, although later he made it a point to tell and show me many aspects of his life, rather consciously making plain how his conversion entailed a radical break from the lifestyle of his generally rather materialistic and Westernized family and Chinese milieu. Note his Chinese (rather than Malay-Indonesian) ethnicity and his Chinese background.

The final bit of data is to note that if one moves outside the Islamic arena, one can hear standard Christian testimonial accounts of the conversion experience among ethnic Malayo-Indonesians. I heard one such account from an ethnic Javanese man at a Jakarta meeting of the Full Gospel Businessman's Association. So ethnicity alone does not preclude the conversion experience, or at least the narration of it.

What is the significance and meaning of the seeming lack of conversion experience and testimonial in the phenomenology of Southeast Asian Islam, at least so far as I have discovered?

I raised the question on two occasions at study groups of Muhammadijah, one organized by the Young Muslim Intellectuals and the other held at the home of Professor Mukti Ali, a well-known Muhammadijahn and Muslim scholar of comparative religion and later the minister of religion for the Republic of Indonesia. These discussions suggested the following comparison between the fundamentalist Christian and fundamentalist Southeast Asian Muslims, especially the Muhammadijans.

Believing that he is born sinful or has sinned, the fundamentalist Christian feels guilt, which is absolved through the conversion experience when he accepts Jesus. The Muhammaijan does not, in the first place, believe in original sin, and Muhammadijans emphasize that they do not see as an important motivation for their actions the desire to be saved from a state of sin. They emphasize instead that they would always sustain peace of mind, ichlas, through consistent conformity to the law set forth in the holy Qur'an.

To generalize this contrast a bit, Muhammadijans and fundamentalist Christians could be characterized as guided by contrasting paradigms of action: the dramatistic and the legalistic. The legalistic Muhammadijan sustains his struggle in order to continuously—some would say relentlessly—conform to the laws of the scripture. His action is dictated and explained as belief codified in law. The dramatistic fundamentalist Christian derives from his belief a torment that is resolved only through the conversion: his action stems from tension and guilt generated by inner belief rather than from conformity to belief instituted as outer law.

This contrast is an instance of the general contrast often made between Islam and Christianity: the one a religion of law, the other of a life. The drama of Christ's birth, life, and death assumes mystical meaning in the life and experience of Christians: this narrative archetype transcends any legal code. So the contrast reflects fundamental differences between two world religions. But many other questions and implications are suggested as well.

What is the role of ethnicity and culture? Not only Islam but also the Javanese culture of the Muhammadijans with whom I dealt would seem to dispose them toward reticence, constraint, calmness, and other values that oppose the dramatic emotional abreaction of the conversion experience. And non Javanese (i.e., the Chinese) reputedly have such experiences. Yet at least one Javanese did, in a Christian context, testify to such an experience. Visions, transformed states of consciousness, as in trance, occur in other Javanese situations. An interaction of religious and ethnic background is suggested in the contrast between Talib and Sanyoto.

Social-psychological differences doubtless contribute. For example, the Muhammadijan congregation is essentially male, while that of the Christian fundamentalist is of mixed gender. The wild one, a reprobate, a man's man, becomes, through Christian conversion, domesticated. Ceasing to run around with the boys, he began to stay home with his wife and children and becomes part of a partially female congregation. Joining the all-male congregation of the mosque and the Muslim community, the Muhammadijan male is not domesticated or effeminized: in fact, his joining affirms his identity as a man, at least in terms of the machismo model of Islam. Because the Muhammadijan can join the congregation without sacrificing his masculinity, he can do so without undergoing the drastic (and in some ways emasculating) conversion experience of the male Christian fundamentalist. This explanation, however, does not consider why women convert, either in Christianity or in Islam.

Rhetorical genres differ. The conversion account is grounded in a language and literature that is biblical but also Western, including a general emphasis on introspection, psychological development, and climax in contrast to a literary tradition in Java and Malayo-Indonesia, which is generally more cyclical than climactic, more conventional than introspective, and more classificatory than developmental.

Transformation of identity does occur but often by means of magic or simply a change in status rather than through psychological development.

These observations lead toward an assessment of the phenomenology and psychology of change of identity, especially from outside to inside, in these two cultures, in their lives, in our lives. To remind ourselves of a few points about our own culture, though some may claim that in the postmodernist West identities are changed as easily as underwear, much cultural apparatus still defines the self as continuous. For example, we do not normally change names after an illness or promotion, as Javanese do, nor do we normally say some of the things some Javanese do (e.g., Haryo was a murderer yesterday, but today the spirit has gone out of him, so he is not a murderer today). We still tend to assume continuity of self such that transformation of it entails struggle, introspection about one's past self in relation to the present self, inner growth, and, finally, choice. If for liberal intellectuals the conversion experience is not the normal vehicle, processes like psychoanalysis resemble the conversion experience in that the old self is broken down while transferring attachment to an authority figure in relation to which the new self is built.

What of the cultural background of the Muhammadijan? A clue is given by a comment made to me by a prostitute of pious Islamic rearing. She said: "When I am practicing my profession I don't pray: when I'm not practicing, I pray." In other words, ritual purity is an issue for her: she doesn't imagine that a conversion has to transform the sinful self into a new self before she can resume her pious ritual, but she does imagine that a polluting action has to cease before she can be ritually pure. This is akin to various Muslim concerns with menstruation, copulation, and the like that pollute the pure body, if not the self, that should be present in a prayer ritual.

This ritual emphasis in Muslim identity is reflected in the various kinds of rites of passage that lead to being Muslim. At the daily prayers, one has to wash before entering the mosque, for example. But most important, though as custom not creed, is circumcision. This is the great ritual act for male Muslims, which moves them, through trauma and pain and comradeship, from being essentially female—a child in a female-oriented household—to a member of the male Muslim community. In Southeast Asia, the greater the Muslim identity the sooner circumcision is performed, as though it becomes more urgent to complete this rite of passage the more one values the Muslim self.

Yet, paradoxically, Muhammadijans never mention their circumcision in their autobiographical recollections, unless, as in one instance among the narrations in the training camp, there was a problem with it. For the Muslims, this rite is a given, setting a framework that need not be mentioned. For Christians, the conversion experience is not a given but a gift. However culturally stereotyped narrations of the experience may be, it is perceived as unique to the individual—a gift of God (grace) that the recipient has chosen to accept in his or her own way. It is this fact of choice, or personal decision, that gives impetus to narration.

Becoming Muslim, then, occurs through a collectively dictated ritual: so, to a great degree, is becoming Muhammadijan, for example, through the training camps and schools that indoctrinate. The process is not necessarily mechanical and unreflective: there may be pain, as in circumcision, and reflection and even psychologizing (a tendency that prompted participants in the Darul Arqom to propose to substitute certain psychological terms for theological ones). But these processes are group-controlled rituals that indoctrinate and solidify rather than calling for either the experiences or the narratives of conversion: inner struggles and agonizing lonely, individual decisions.

In the broad cultural background of Javanese Muhammadijans is another kind of transformation that transcends both the conversion experience and the ritual mode of joining. This is identified by the term *kebatinan*, which means "inside" and refers to mysticism. In *kebatinan*, through meditation and other exercises, one unites with a cosmic ground of being. Through such unions, the self can be transformed without the emotional upheavals of conversion. Self is within totality so that self-transformations are absorbed into this unity and hence rendered relatively insignificant and benign. One can be cured of hallucinations or fever, and one grows and deepens while remaining part of this constant unity. Outside and inside, outsider and insider cease to oppose each other since the unity encompasses both. The deeper one goes within, the wider one's resonance with the cosmos without becomes. Inner order automatically yields outer order. And *kebatinan* membership and belief are not exclusivist, so one can theoretically become an insider without giving up outsider statuses, all of which are encompassed by the greater unity anyway.

This transcendental, mystical alternative to both conversionist and ritual modes of moving from outside to inside is on the edge and underneath the culture of the Muhammadijans just as the more passionate Catholic mysticism of Eckhart, Suso, Tauler, Teresa, and others lies obliquely behind the Christian fundamentalist conversion experience. Occasionally, the mystical mode seeps into the ritualist, as when an orientation session for a Muhammadijah recruitment camp titled "Giving Love" makes an analogy between stages of mystical attraction and affection and the process of being drawn into the Muhammadijah. Yet cosmic mysticism is resisted by both kinds of Muslim and Christian fundamentalists, the one reducing recruitment to ritualization, the other to an individualistic decision to accept a gift and make a commitment.

Our inquiry has been couched as an effort to explain an absence of the conversion experience in the Muslim case, as though the Christian one is the norm. We could just as well have taken the other viewpoint—that the Muslim way of experiencing and narrating movement from outside to inside is more normal and the Christian one the aberration that needs explaining. In fact, this is the way it seems from the position of reason and common sense (this is how psychiatry tends to view it), or maybe we see it as miraculous. Believers speak of it this way, and so it is, in that it is not explicable in terms of worldly processes such as the social, psychological, and cultural factors that I or anyone else has adduced. Such explanations never fully account for the transformation from being one creature to being another, from inhabiting one phenomenological world to inhabiting another. Such a movement in this sense really is miraculous. But so is any radical transformation, whether in the human or the natural worlds, and no analytical explanation, necessarily reductive, will suffice. The best we can do is what Max Weber termed *verstehen*, which means to try to grasp the viewpoint of the other, not by becoming the other or even by total empathy with the other but by some kind of intellectual construction of guiding cultural values and social context of the experience of the other. For Weber as for us, comparison can be useful, though not of course perfect, as Evans-Pritchard reminds us.

This allusion to *verstehen* forces a brief return to the nagging issue, which becomes for some more a shout than a nag, and a shout that deafens them to all else. This is the issue of reflexivity: the relationship of insider to outsider, the beholder to the believer. This dialogue is tense when it is conversion that is beheld, for conversion is itself an experience of engagement; hence the study of it is engaging. Further, the convert often wishes to convert someone. Pentecostal informants recount their own conversion experiences, which they tell me I can understand only if I myself convert: they not only tell but embrace and exhort. And Muslims apply pressures, too (they would joke that I "am hit by their da' wa" [evangelism] and one of their newspaper headlines forecast that I was about to convert to Islam). Beholders' feelings of being drawn to believers and their beliefs would seem unavoidable and perhaps necessary for *verstehen*, as was probably true for Weber himself. Studying conversion, then, has, as my computer disk tells me, a "double-sided density." The subject itself, like Frankenstein, comes to life and invades the life of the investigator, challenging any barrier between beholder and believer. The scholarly stance one takes, even if it is resistance, detachment, or categorical assertion of one's stance as an outsider, is a kind of engagement. So there is some slight resonance between the research experience and the experience researched. This is the lesson of the postmodernist who detects reflexivity. Against this emphasis, however, I assert the point of the believer and, I suspect, of the anthropology of religion. The experience researched (i.e., "natural religion") is incomparably more interesting and significant from the standpoint of constructing a theory of religious experience than is the research experience, which can be, from this standpoint, a weak, secondary vision of the religious experience.

To conclude, we have explored two relationships: that between the inside and the outside of the experience of the religious actor, as he or she moves from outside to inside through conversion; and that between outsider and insider, as observer encounters actor and beholder encounters believer. The two relationships are themselves related inasmuch as the outer to inner movement of the believer is replayed by the outer to inner movement of the observer as he engages the engagement of the believer. Engagement with engagement, which is the fate of the student of religious experience as of other human experiences, is one of the fascinations of postmodernism. This fascination has the advantage of focusing on what the researcher knows best, namely, the researcher's own research experience, but it has the disadvantage of diverting us from what is least known but perhaps more profound, namely, the religious experience.

Notes

1. Examples range from extravagantly clinical views like those of Weston La Barre in *They Shall Take Up Serpents* (1962) to the nuanced analysis, also treating snakes, of Gananath Obeyesekere's *Medusa's Hair* (1981). The focus on symbols as the strategic convergence of the unconscious (thus, outsider to one's inside) and the objectification of the subjective (thus, again, outsider to one's inside) to which the analysis has a special access (again, outsider to one's inside) expresses a dialectic that deserves an elaboration that is not possible here, where I followed my informants in emphasizing a nonpsychological view.

2. Ahmadiyya (not Muhammadiyah) is a Muslim organization founded in Pakistan with branches worldwide. It was founded in the nineteenth century by Ahmad, designated successor to Muhammed. At one time Indonesia banned the organization, although an active branch recently existed there, as in Singapore—the branch I researched in 1969. Tan was a member of this branch. The head was from China and was probably an ethnic Uiggur. Members explored unorthodox (by Muslim doctrine) practices and doctrine and were varied in ethnicity.

References

Basch, Linda, Jagna Scharff, Lucie Saunders, James L. Peacock, and Jill Craven. 1999. *Transforming Academia: Challenges and Opportunities for an Engaged Anthropology*. American Ethnological Society Monograph Series, no. 8. Arlington, VA: American Anthropological Association.

Crapanzano, Vincent. 1980. *Tuhami: Portrait of a Moroccan*. Chicago: University of Chicago Press.

Erikson, Erik H. 1958. *Young Man Luther: A Study in Psychoanalysis and History*. New York: Norton.

Evans-Pritchard, E. E. 1965. *Theories of Primitive Religion*. Oxford: Clarendon.

Forman, Shepard, ed. 1994. *Diagnosing America: Anthropology and Public Engagement*. Ann Arbor: University of Michigan Press.

Gadamer, Hans-Georg. 1982. *Truth and Method*. New York: Crossroad.

Geertz, Clifford. 1983. *Local Knowledge: Further Essays in Interpretive Anthropology*. New York: Basic Books.

La Barre, Weston. 1962. *They Shall Take Up Serpents: Psychology of the Southern Snake Handling Cult*. Minneapolis: University of Minnesota Press.

Lawrence, Bruce. 1989. *Defenders of God: The Fundamentalist Revolt against the Modern Age*. San Francisco: Harper and Row.

Needham, Rodney. 1983. *Against the Tranquility of Axioms*. Berkeley: University of California Press.

Obeyesekere, Gananath. 1981. *Medusa's Hair: An Essay of Personal Symbols and Religious Experience*. Chicago: University of Chicago Press.

Smith, Jonathan A. 1982. *Imaging Religion: From Babylon to Jonestown*. Chicago: University of Chicago Press.

APPENDIX 2

The Narrated Self: Explorations in the Psychology of Religion
Lecture by James Peacock, March 14, 1990

Freud, in his analysis of Dora, characterized neurosis as the inability to narrate one's life story coherently; therapy was complete when the patient could tell her story straight.

Freud says, "The patients' inability to give an ordered history of their life in so far as it coincides with the history of their illness is not merely characteristic of the neurosis. It also possesses great theoretical significance." Later he continues, "It is only towards the end of the treatment that we have before us an intelligible, consistent, and unbroken case history. Whereas the practical aim of the treatment is to remove all possible symptoms and to replace them by conscious thoughts, we may regard as a second and theoretical aim to repair all the damages to the patient's memory. These two aims are coincident. When one is reached, so is the other; and the same path leads to them both" (32).

Here, Freud connects self and story, construction of the individual personality and the narrative process.

But as we know from reading Dora, and from reading commentaries, such as that of Steven Marcus, Freud's notion of a straight story was couched very much in his own terms, rather than the patient's. He tells Dora that when she says no she means yes; he controls the treatment and the narration. And his characterization of the self deploys narration rather than respecting it in its own terms as constitutive of self; ultimately, the individual is reduced to a system of forces, with narration only symptomatic or symbolic of these deeper forces. But both tendencies—a hermeneutical attention to meanings, which included narration, and a scientific impulse to explain meanings as symptoms of underlying causes and forces—are, as has often been pointed out, present in Freud, with the hermeneutical coming to the fore, as here is rediscovered in recent humanistic reflections.

Anthropology and the social and psychological sciences have developed two major views of the life story. One emphasizes the "life," the other the "story." The first approach is concerned less with the story as such than with some reality external to the story but that the story is presumed to mirror; analysis of the story is a means toward grasping that reality—the "life" narrated.

This first approach then divides into two sub-types. One treats the life narrated as an objective account of events, the other as the subjective experience of the narrator. In the objectivist approach, the life story is regarded as a datum for history or ethnography or biography—a source for reconstructing a record of events. In this approach, one is concerned to check the validity of the narrated account against other data about the events narrated; the narration is only one datum among others for reconstructing events. Often, there is concern that the narration be recorded as impartially as possible—the ethnographer serving as scribe to record this historical record, which is presumed to have truth independent of the scribe. This approach is found in older ethnographic studies (a classic account is Kluckhohn's 1945 monograph on the use of personal documents).

In the subjectivist approach, the life history is viewed as an expression or projection of the subject's psychological disposition and dynamics. As in the first approach, the concern is not so much with the text as with some presumed reality—that of an individual personality—that the text mirrors, but unlike in the first approach, this reality is not so much the external events of someone's life but the inner forces of the narrator's personality. The narration is a datum—usually one of several—to diagnose these psychological forces. This approach is illustrated by many life history analyses in psychoanalysis, psychology, and psychological anthropology, especially that of the so-called culture and personality school.

Whether conceived as objective events or subjective experience, a presumed reality external to the narration is the focus of these first two approaches. The narration is only one datum for learning about that reality, and whatever reality the narration itself may have is secondary to this external reality; hence relatively little attention is given to the narration itself.

My approach does emphasize the narrative itself. Whatever the source of it—whether actual events, personality dynamics of the narrator, or the interaction between narrator and listener—it is the story that is the focus.

In life stories, one might distinguish between surface and deep structures. The surface structures include conventions of language and literary style as well as contexts of performance. These are entailed in the telling of a story. The mode of telling will vary with form and context—whether the story is oral or written, for example, or whether it is told in a ritual or as an interview. Telling the story contrasts with the story told. The story told, which includes importantly the basic plot and the existential world entailed by it, remains more or less constant in these varying contexts. It is this story told—the basic plot of an individual's life and the existential world entailed by it—that is the deep structure of the life story. Especially deep structure, but also surface structure, is entailed in what I call "the narrated self."

What kinds of life stories are told by my subjects? Here I am dealing with religious people, believers, and with the stories of their lives as religiously constituted. For them, like certain philosophers, life seems a preparation for death. These religious lives are depicted as a process of moving from one phase to another of life, toward death, and into the next life. This is their plot, their narrated self.

Before taking up some examples, let me briefly remind you of the format of this series of lectures, of which today's is one piece. The series follows a plot or movement in religious experience: from outside to inside, then back to outside. The first lecture treated the movement from outside to inside, epitomized by the conversion experience. Today's lecture picks up the believer as he (my cases are, for better or worse, all male) is now converted—a believer who is struggling to deal with his belief: to deepen it, ground it, then apply it and proclaim it. This latter movement is back toward the outside: the world.

As explained in the first lecture, my materials come primarily from fieldwork I have carried out among so-called fundamentalists: Muslim fundamentalists in Southeast Asia, Christian fundamentalists in the Southeast United States. A sub-theme of my talks is to explore the experience of fundamentalism. So doing, I contend, we learn not only about fundamentalists but also about our fundamentals: our elementary forms of religious experience, so to speak. A sub-sub theme concerns methodology, such as issues in the study of life story narration.

The First Account

Rutledge is a tall, blond, athletic man, well-mannered and well-spoken. Employed as a front-end mechanic in a garage, he is a Sunday School teacher in Mount Pisgah Pentecostal Church, in a small Southern city.

At Rutledge's house, we began by asking him, "Will you tell us the history of how you came to be a member of the church?" He asked, in turn, "Do you want me to begin with my childhood?" "Sure, any way you want," we invited. He replied, "I was not raised in a Christian home at all, my parents are not Christian, neither were my brother and sister . . . I wasn't spiritual at all when I was a young man. I was vain in the world of the devil." This was all Rutledge said about childhood and family. Now he moved straight to his spiritual quest. One Sunday, when he was twenty-five years old, his wife tried to get him to go to church. He replied, "I don't want no part of it," so she left him at home. Rutledge recalls: "That Sunday she went I was sitting on the porch, and became real miserable all of a sudden for some reason, as if something was drawing me—spiritual. I'll never forget the experience of that, the leaves on the trees were weeping, and it's amazing how nature spoke to me. I began to think of the lines of the Creator . . . I remember praying, I never prayed any, so I asked God in a simple way to have someone invite me to church and I'll go."

He did go, for six nights straight. "I would stand there and shake in the pew, I would not give into it . . . it was a force pulling at me. The sixth night was when I accepted it . . . the burden was lifted, I felt new, I felt clean." Thus, Rutledge experienced being saved. He tells us, "The Church I was saved at is just right up the road here." This is a Freewill Baptist church.

The experience of being saved was not sufficient for Rutledge: "I was hungry for deeper things . . . I said, 'Lord, if you will manifest yourself to me it will help me to believe and be strong in the things of the spirit.' This is what I began to seek after, a manifestation of the spirit of God. I wanted to see him in a vision."

At a place called Timberlake, about a year after being saved, Rutledge had such an experience: "A force, it just drew me to him, it anointed me all over, it was joy that I had never experienced." Rutledge called the pastor of his church, then called a deacon to tell them about his ecstasy. The pastor had not had the experience and discounted it; the deacon had, but thought such experiences came from a demon.

These interpretations disturbed Rutledge "for seven long years. This was such an experience, there was so much glory, and so much joy . . . But I had never heard of the Baptism of the Spirit, or nothing. All I had ever heard was get saved, sit in the church, and go through the rituals of every day and every Sunday service."

He left the church. Leaving the church, Rutledge also left his job. Three new opportunities were "sent by God," and he emphasizes that he chose the job which on rational grounds was least desirable. But this proved to reflect the mysterious workings of God, for this job led to his second experience with the Holy Ghost. This occurred at the body shop.

He met a Pentecostal, Billy, at work. Rutledge now explains that he had always thought of Pentecostals as "Holy Rollers, jump pews and swing from the lights." Rutledge went with Billy to a Pentecostal service, which he found "really funny. A woman threw a leg up on a table and talked about how God had healed it . . . I went home and me and my wife laughed about it for several hours."

One day, everything was going wrong: "It seemed as if a force was fighting me." Finally, at about four in the afternoon, Rutledge went to the body shop to see Billy: "Billy, I'm about to give up, and be like I used to before I got into Religion at all." But at 4:15 p.m., Rutledge had another experience: "I just looked up and, for some reason, said, 'Father,' and the Holy Spirit moved me, praise God, I can feel it now. It moved on me and it seemed like everything changed . . . and I spoke in tongues."

Rutledge then described the force that was in him, how he touched a policeman, Frank, who had come to pick up his car. Frank "threw both hands up in the air, and began to confess to the Lord . . . The power that was on me at the time was unbelievable."

Thus Rutledge experienced the Holy Ghost again. Still, he had no church. He continued to look for one, and as he looked he saw many strange things. He describes what he saw with a certain detached disdain—not unlike that of an Enlightenment philosopher or old-fashioned traveler who witnessed savage rites: like moralist Hume, or Lord Monboddo who wrote on "Men living in a Brutish State, without Arts or Civility." Rutledge went among snake handlers but stood aloof: "I got by the door, and said if they bring out snakes, I'm gonna be gone." He went to a service where they carried his friend Ruth to the altar, "screamed in her ears and spit in her face . . . trying to beat the Holy Ghost into you." Finally, he came to Mount Pisgah Church, where Ruth, his wife, and he himself received the Holy Ghost again. (There he remains.)

The Second Account

Walter Evans is an elder in the Mountain District Primitive Baptist Association, a group that spans two Virginia and two North Carolina counties in the Blue Ridge Mountains. Evans, now eighty, is a stone mason, farmer, and gifted preacher. He has written his life history, titled "The Life and Experience of Walter Evans," and elaborated it to us orally and visually, not only telling about but also showing us the sites.

Evans hews to the sternly Calvinistic belief in predestination, that before the foundation of the world God had decided who would be of the elect and who damned. A brilliant theologian, whose seventh grade education has proved sufficient for the most discerning analysis of Calvin's Institutes and subsequent theological writings, he is careful to remain consistent to this doctrine in his ingenious interpretations of scripture; he appears to interpret his own life similarly. He presents his life as seemingly guided by some divine plan, but he would never make what Calvin termed the "dread presumption" that he knows definitely that this is so, knows certainly that he is of the Elect, or indeed knows anything for certain about God's will.

Elder Evans begins: "I have a deep conviction that the Lord has motivated some of my activities" IF (he continues) "if I have not been deceived."

Evans's intimation of some foreordination is reflected in his use of foreshadowing. Early in his narration, he states that his grandmother said to his mother, when he was still a small baby: "Annice, that boy will make a preacher." "This," Evans writes, "I didn't know until I was exercising [he uses the old word meaning preaching] in public." Here he retrodicts, reflecting backward about a prediction of things to come, implying that even at this early time God had set His hand upon his life. By locating a sense of destiny within the mind of a third person—the grandmother—and emphasizing the absence of this sense from his own mind, Evans emphasizes the objective of his calling: that it was out of his control and his knowledge.

His next scene is of his youth; he recounts that in his early teens, as he "followed a yoke of oxen to a plow or harrow, I would sing some of the old songs of Zion. Guide me, O' Thou great Jehovah / Pilgrim through this barren land / I am weak, but Thou are mighty Hold me with Thy powerful hand." He introduces here an image that he continues to explicate a half-century later; he is the pilgrim, the lonely sojourner, traveling through this life guided only by Jehovah. He continues, "As I would sing these old hymns, a sad lonely feeling would come over me that someday I would have to preach, but when or how I didn't know." Again, he alludes to a destiny that was out of his control or knowledge, and he foreshadows his calling to preach.

He continues his account through his teenage years, telling of attending a singing school in the mountains that taught shape-notes. He was singled out by the teacher, he tells us, as he shows us the site of the school, Union church. "And he spotted me singing, he called me out, said, you back there (he didn't know my name), says, you back there singing with that strong voice, says, come up here a minute . . . you lead."

His text continues. "I thought I would make a singing teacher, but gave up, and went to rambling and sowing wild oats, which in time I had to reap." Note again his referring forward, reflectively, retrodictively/predictively: which in time I had to reap.

His story continues, rather predictably for those who have heard Christian accounts of salvation experience at a church, and he was given, he says, "liberty," and for four years led public prayers, while "my burden to preach grew heavier." A dream ended his public exercises for a while.

In this dream, the full imagery of which we do not have time to tell, he is on a stool preaching and is lifted so high he loses sight of the people. A casket and corpse present earlier in the dream disappear, and his earlier sadness is gone, and he is "rejoicing in hope of the glory of God." But he awoke "disturbed and troubled." He interpreted the dream as telling him he was trying to climb too high, that the exaltation was illusion, and God was warning him not to preach. He accepted this warning and stopped praying publicly.

Now follow months of roaming the mountains and rock cliffs "begging the good Lord to show me what to do. I could not understand my dream and I was in deep trouble."

He recounts, "One lonely evening I wanted to pray once more, so I told my companion [his wife] I was going out to see the corn, and did walk through the field. I shall never forget this experience. As I walked through the field of corn, it appeared to be mourning with its blades bending toward the earth."

He climbed the mountain, passing grazing cattle who also appeared to be mourning. He reached the top of the mountain, Sheep Pen Ridge: "As I stood there alone, Oh! So dark and gloomy, late in the evening. I turned down the other side. This side of the mountain was a wooded area, so I roamed among the trees, trying to find some place to pray . . . such a burden I was carrying."

He prayed, determined to find relief, but he failed, and finally he said, "Amen." But "this time I thought it was to my condemnation—that I had been deceived in it all." He climbed back to the top of the mountain: "Suddenly there shined a light around me, a complete circle fifteen feet in diameter, or more, the resemblance of a rainbow's many colors but brighter. Such as this I had never seen nor felt. Every doubt and fear left me as quick as a flash. I felt so light in my feelings. I actually thought I was going to be taken from the earth."

He walked down from the mountain; the cattle now appeared ready to shout. He tried to get in the house without showing his wife the difference in himself, but she saw it (she, incidentally, was always a bit skeptical of his enthusiasms; she died a year ago, and a couple of weeks after he remarried, to a woman more of like mind). Anyway, he was so ecstatic he took his little boy on his knee and sang, "Children of the Heav'nly King."

After "constant research and review," he reinterpreted the dream he had previously attributed to Satan. The stool was now the three persons of the

The Narrated Self 339

Trinity, the foundation of doctrine. He saw his being carried above and the banishment of the casket as signifying the power to preach, given him by God; the loss of his sadness was from taking up this task. In short, he reinterpreted the dream as a calling to preach rather than as a warning against it.

The story continues through many trials, but we must leave it.

It is now fifty years later. Elder Evans, now in his seventies, has been moderator of the Mountain District Association for twenty-one years. A certain incident that I cannot go into here (see Peacock and Tyson, *Pilgrims of Paradox*, 1989, for an elaboration of this) has brought the Association and Elder Evans's leadership to a point of crisis. He is being challenged by the assistant moderator. Some think he will fall at the election to be held in the annual meeting of the association, in September.

In several sermons he preaches during these months preceding the meeting, Elder Evans develops the idea of "translation." By "translation," he means something is changed into something else through powers of a third party rather than its own. Language can't translate itself, he notes. He recounts the experience of Elijah. He was lifted up and taken to heaven by God. Elijah was translated. He parallels his own experience on Sheep Pen Ridge to Elijah's translation. Having exhausted his own capabilities, he, Evans, as an utterly passive agent, was lifted up and translated by God into a higher realm.

Consider this sermon, preached at Antioch Church on July 24, 1983. Evans follows the classical Primitive Baptist format, known as "types and shadows." He arranges a sequence of types, great figures of the Bible, who have been "translated." He modestly and obliquely alludes to his own experience of translation on Sheep Pen Ridge as in this line of experiences. He terms Elijah's translation "the greatest such event, other than the day the Lord of glory died." He moves from Enoch to Elijah, each a foreshadowing of Jesus's resurrection:

> In the second King, second chapter, you'll find one of the greatest, most mysterious days other than the day the Lord of glory died, when there was a great earthquake and shook this old earth, and it quaked and trembled, and one said reeled him like a drunken man, and the sun went out, as the old colored preacher said, the middle of the day, refused to shine, everything got dark and black as sackcloth . . . the day of translation of the great servant of God that the ravens fed, one time and drank water from the brook and the ravens.

He alludes to his experience at Sheep Pen Ridge: "I can't hardly talk about this, cause it gets so close to some things that's, I've been so close to some things in my little time in this world, right on this mountain up here as you've heard me tell, but I'm embarrassed to speak of it this morning lest I'm just completely overcome with emotion, cause I've been so close to this thing."

He concludes with an explanation: "I'm dealing, Brothers and Sisters, with the power that's active, and subjects that's acted upon, or shortly to be acted upon."

In the weeks following, as we go with him to see sites of his life, he is gloomy about things to come. We ask him if he would like to visit Sheep Pen Ridge with us. He demurs, saying it's now fenced in. We can see it in the distance; in fact, you could see it from the church where he preached the sermon. Maybe, though he wouldn't admit this, he wants to retain its sacrality, prefers not to profane it by a visit.

Some commentary on these two accounts. First, a similarity. Both Rutledge and Evans narrate a spiritual quest, a religious life story. The language, the frame of reference, the plots—the deep structures—are essentially spiritual, rather than psychological, sociological, or economic. For example, both accounts see as the pivotal transformation not a sociological change (for example, of job or spouse, as in our so-called midlife crisis) but a spiritual change (which, of course, has sociological underpinnings and implications).

Some differences in the narrations can be seen as reflecting theological differences. Rutledge is Pentecostal, of the Arminian or Wesleyan tradition, which emphasizes the freedom of the individual to choose whether to accept the gift of salvation. Evans is Primitive Baptist, of the Calvinist tradition, which denies this freedom and decrees that whether one is saved or not is predestined before the foundation of the world and can never be known but can be evidenced ambiguously by signs. Further, the Pentecostal theology sees salvation as followed by sanctification: receiving the experience of the holy ghost. Whereas the Primitive Baptist theology decrees only that the conversion experience is a first sign, ambiguous like all subsequent ones, of one's status as being saved, and life is therefore a search for subsequent signs to affirm but never confirm that hope.

Rutledge seeks EXPERIENCE: the experience of the holy ghost, a quest that leads him adventurously from place to place. Evans stays in one place studying the scripture, seeking not experience but doctrinal resolution. His experiences are depicted as by-products of his struggle to discover such resolution. Rutledge first encounters spiritual forces, then finds resonance in scripture and doctrine; Evans depicts himself as first studying scripture, then experiencing spiritual forces as allegorical images in visions or dreams that are defined scripturally and theologically. As my colleague Ruel Tyson argues, the Primitive Baptist discourse is allegorical, harkening back to authors like John Bunyan (who, incidentally, Evans names as his favorite author) and to Classic schemas, such as their favorite: types and shadows. The Pentecostal is perhaps more akin to a Romantic tradition (one, incidentally, that informs symbolic or interpretive anthropology) where the symbol is encountered participationally and is then interpreted "thickly"—attributing multiple hidden meanings in a way that would seem undisciplined to the Primitive Baptist, who constrains interpretation by doctrine and scripture. The experiential (Evans would say, in the seventeenth-century language, experimental) emphasis of Rutledge set the value in terms of which he evaluates forms; repetitive songs are, he says, boring. Evans never uses such experiential criteria; forms are never for him boring; but they may be judged meaningless if they are not linked deductively to doctrine (this is his judgment of the shout, speaking in tongues). Finally, the plot of the narratives. Evans' predestinarianism is expressed narratively as foreshadowing; this device is present in Rutledge's story, but only once and later in the narration, rather than as a framing device at the beginning, as with Evans.

So here is a beginning for a reading of the two narratives, attempting to tease out some theological cultural patterns in the shapes of these two storied lives.

Our third account is drawn from a biography of the founder of the movement we discussed last time, the Muhammadijah of Indonesia.

K.H.A. Dahlan, Amal dan Perdjoanganja, Riawat Hidup, or *K.H.A. Dahlan, His Actions and Struggle; Life History* is the official biography of Muhammadijah's founder, written by Solichin Salam, and published in 1962 by Muhammadijah.

Riwajat Hidup, or "Life History," is actually only one section of the book, the others being devoted to such matters as the history of Islam and Muhammadijah. The life history is divided into five seemingly straightforward sections: Childhood and Youth; Education; Father and Husband; Struggle; and, The End of His Life.

After setting the scene in Yogyakarta, Central Java, Indonesia, birthplace of both Dahlan and Muhammadijah, the author describes the ancestry of Dahlan: "In the nineteenth century, there lived a religious teacher named Kijahi Hadji Abubakar bin Kijahi Hadji Salaiman."

"Bin" means "son of," reflecting a patrilineal emphasis among pious Muslims, which contrasts with the bilateral balance of most Javanese. The patrilineal stress is shown too in Salam tracing Dahlan's ancestry for eleven generations on his father's side and only four on his mother's.

The biographer gives the year of Dahlan's birth (1868 Christian calendar, 1825 Muslim) but apologizes because he knows only the year and not the day. This again contrasts with the wider Javanese pattern, where often one knows the day of one's birth but not the year. Pious Muslims are seemingly more concerned with the passing of unrepeatable years—in a word, linear time-history—while the syncretist Javanese stress the repeatable day, which bears a relation to cosmic cycles.

Essentially nothing is said of Dahlan's childhood, but a list is given of his siblings; he was number four.

The section of education provides two more lists: his books and his teachers. And it relates that he was "ordered" by his father to go to Mecca, for pilgrimage and study. When he returned, his name was changed from Darwisj to Dahlan.

The category Husband and Father picks up the story after Dahlan returned to Yogykarta. He is described as "replacing his father," by becoming an official of the Great Mosque of the Sultan of Yogyakarta, a position he occupied for the rest of his life. At the same time, he was a traveling merchant.

He married his mother's brother's daughter, Siti Walidah, then four additional wives, divorcing each after a short time but retaining his first wife, Siti. These wives and his children by each are listed.

Struggle (Perdjuangan) is a standard category in Indonesian narration of history and life history. This section tells how Dahlan came to found Muhammadijah, on November 18, 1912, when he was approximately forty-four years old. As is often the case in Indonesian movements, the early nucleus was the leader's pupils, the setting, a school. Note that as Dahlan was "ordered" to go to Mecca, so he is "urged" to found Muhammadijah. Perhaps the other-directedness reflects both a prophetic notion of being called and a Javanese de-emphasis of individual initiative and decision.

The End of His Life category contains one of the two efforts at dialogue in the life history. Dahlan became ill from overwork, his wife begged him to rest, and he replied: "I must work hard, in order to lay the first stone in this great movement. If I am late or cease, due to my illness, there is no one who will build the groundwork. I already feel that my time is almost gone, thus if I work as fast as possible, what remains can be brought to perfection by another."

He summoned friends and his brother-in-law to delegate tasks and died on February 23, 1923, at his home, Kauman 59, Yogyakarta.

Toward the end of the book are two sections: PEARLS OF WISDOM and SEVERAL ANECDOTES. PEARLS cites twenty-five aphorisms from Dahlan, ANECDOTES records twenty-six events. The PEARLS emphasize the need for salvation. For example, the first is: We humans are given as a wager only one life in the world. After you die, will you be saved or damned? ANECDOTES include tales of Dahlan's generosity and humility.

This is the material. What are the patterns?

Consider first the structure of the text. At first glance, this seems to be a developmental account like those customary in Western biography. Childhood leads to education, which leads to adulthood and finally death. On closer look, the pattern is as much classificatory as developmental.

No developmental psychology leads from one phase to the next. Most prominent in each section is a list. Under Childhood is a list of siblings, under Education a list of books and teachers, under Father and Husband a list of wives and children. The prominence of lists and absence of dialogue is an indication of the lack of a processual narration from "formative years" to "private life," to take familiar phrases from the bourgeois Western biographical genre. The last sections, Struggle and End of Life, are more narrative and include the only two instances of dialogue but are schematic.

The 25 Pearls and 26 Anecdotes relegated to the end of the book contain raw material that could flesh out this narrative. Why was it not so used? Partly, I think, because the author's conception of life history is somewhere between the developmental and the classificatory. Life is imagined as sequential, as history, but the concern is not so much with showing how individual experience unfolds psychologically as with exemplifying by each phase a category of culture. Hence the numbered lists, ordered not dynamically but thematically.

Now this third account differs from the first two in that it is a third-person official story of a founder of a movement; the first two were first-person accounts by lesser leaders. But other data show that the differences adduced hold if we compare first-person accounts of ordinary people or third-person accounts of leaders across the two religions and cultures; the difference is not due only to surface features.

The story of Dahlan differs from those of Evans and Rutledge in that his narrative does not turn around an intense inner struggle, a conversion experience, or a spiritual quest as with Rutledge or Evans; they in turn resemble in this respect the inner struggle entailed in Martin Luther's quest to discover justification or salvation. The surface result of Dahlan's reformism was not unlike that of a Luther, a Calvin, or a Zwingli: the stripping of ritual to its essentials, delivery of sermons in the vernacular, reliance on the books instead of the priest. But the formulation of a Luther, meaningful only in a culture imbued with the notion of original sin, was an inner solution to an inner torment. The reformation of Dahlan was an outer one: a legalistic attempt to impose a Middle Eastern ethic on a Malaya-Indonesian society.

After completing his education and pilgrimage, a phase we might term "initiation," Dahlan changed his name, signaling the end of the phase. His next phase, termed "struggle," describes not further education or questioning or inner searching but the application of doctrine, learned during his schooling, in a highly methodical and bureaucratic manner. The third and last phase, the end of his life, is depicted in a similarly bureaucratic way: no dramatic last words, as favored in Christian and Western biographies. (Max Weber, according to his wife's biography, died singing a Wagnerian aria.) He simply arranged for the organization to carry on.

Using these three phases of the life story narration—initiation, vocation, termination—we can compare the Muslim and Christian accounts. The Christian accounts dramatically separate the pre-initiation and initiation phases: the initiate, the convert, is a new person. (Clyde, a Pentecostal, formerly known as cowboy Clyde, answers the phone after his conversion: Is this cowboy Clyde? No ma'am, he's dead. A new Clyde is alive, born again.) But initiation is continuous with vocation in that the convert dramatizes his conversion in order to convert others, and the metaphor of rebirth energizes his life work: every day is giving birth and being born, again and again.

The Muhammadijah accounts, as with Dahlan, do not so sharply separate pre-initiation and initiation phases; Dahlan is not made a new creature through dramatic conversion. But there is a sharper separation between pre-vocation and vocation phases; Dahlan is a student, then he is a teacher, and the teacher is no longer a student. Experiences during his initiation period, his student years, do not feed his vocation through dramatizing metaphors; rather, creeds learned as a student are applied bureaucratically and legalistically now that the student is the teacher.

The device by which the Christian moves from conversion to vocation is the call: the call to preach. This typically is narrated as occurring when one's life reaches a crisis, and a terrible inner struggle ensues. To be in a crisis when much hinges on your decision, and then to DECIDE—This is the pattern prominent in Christian fundamentalist life history, not in the Muhammadijan accounts. After decision comes ecstasy. "I had the time of my life," says the Pentecostal preacher, Clyde, after accepting the call when his child teetered on the edge of death: "God heal my baby, I'll preach." God did, and Clyde did. Here, by revealing cliché, Clyde singles out a particular time, a single ecstatic moment: "THE time of my LIFE." No parallel moments exist in Dahlan's account or other accounts: time is flat, though progressive; each moment like the last, except an advance, and there is no inner struggle leading to a decision, then relief.

In sum, let us compare the Muhammadijan and Christian narratives in terms of the way the main actor moves through the phases of life: for Dahlan, this process is more bureaucratic and legalistic; Dahlan studies creed, then he applies that creed, then he dies. For Evans and Rutledge, the process is more dramatistic and metaphorical; Evans or Rutledge have a conversion or other experience that becomes a metaphor energizing their quest and calling. The hierarchical, rationalistic, legalistic structure of Islamic belief gets translated into one kind of self-narrative, the dramatistic belief structure of Christianity (which, fundamentalistic or not, is grounded in the drama of Christ's life, death, and rebirth and the mystical relation between that and the salvation of the believer) gets translated into another kind.

At this point, then, the first argument of this lecture has been completed. Some structures of these stories are apparent. Further, we have traced how these narrative structures embody cultural structures, specifically, theological ones: differences between Calvinistic and Arminian Christianity, differences between Islam and Christianity, differences between the particular Western and Asian cultures entailed.

To lay bare so laboriously the way life story narration embodies cultural patterns may seem unnecessary. Is that not obvious? Apparently not. Of the thousands of psychological, psychiatric, and psychoanalytical studies of life stories, few show much sensitivity to cultural and especially religious dimensions; and while cultural sensitivity may be increasingly fashionable, virtually none systematically analyze the cultural patterning as it is embodied directly in the mode of narrating. This lack in psychological studies has practical implications, for example, in the way psychotherapy is carried out. Therapy is essentially a way of helping a self to narrate. Is it not reasonable that the mode of therapy should be guided by a model of narration the client takes from their culture? Therapy aside, pop psychologies influence all of us to imagine our lives in certain ways—in terms of mid-life crises or certain kinds of aging, for example—and these psychologies are drawn from particular cultural models of self-narration while claiming to be universal. In fact, they corrode and destroy some of our models of self-narration, such as ones explored here, which, however, fight back.

This leads to the second and final task of this talk: to argue, as asserted at the beginning, that self-narratives are more than simply vessels of culture: they are themselves worlds, and they have integrity and power.

To see more clearly how each narration is constitutive of the self, let us focus more closely on the language of narration. You heard Elder Evans recounting his religious life history; now listen to him in a different context. Here he is showing, as well as telling and displaying to us, sites of his life; he's showing us the first stone structure he ever built:

That don't look too awful bad does it? To be the first. I mean that's been there. That stone'll be there. Now where's Jim Peacock [he wants me to take a picture]. You want to see something fancy! OK! (claps his hands). Claude Holloway and me laid every stone in that. If you want a pretty picture my friend Jim, you just take that chimney there. You see that's me, and Claude and Carl Andrews, we worked together so long, and we had the same pattern and you couldn't tell where one of us started and the other one quit, to save your life.

Compare this language, nimble and quick, to the ponderous retrodictive/predictive written narration: "I knew I was to preach, but how or when I could not say . . ." The shift in language is not just between writing and speaking but between the ordinary world of stones and friends and the spiritual world, his religious self as constituted through his narrative.

In the language of Rutledge, you can hear the shifts within the single narrative. Rutledge begins with a quiet question of fact, "Would you like me to tell about my childhood?" His manner of speech, at least in the beginning, is in a style of remembered facticity. The beginnings with reference to the world of ordinary experience are however soon transformed through the language of the spirit. Note Rutledge's words: "I was vain in the world of the Devil . . . I began to consider the things of creation. . . The spirit moved on me . . . It's amazing how nature spoke to me. Christ said . . . if you love me, you'll keep my commandments, and we will come and make our abode in you, and manifest ourselves to you."

Such words are spoken in the calm, matter-of-fact way that Rutledge describes the rest of his life, uttered fluently though (I sense) with a faint hint of embarrassment, signaled sometimes with a downward look or stumbling rhythm.

What is displayed in these passages, and throughout the narration, is the problem of connecting the spiritual and the worldly. The languages are different, the culturally accepted presentations of self and others different. The male, especially in this regional sub-culture, has a special problem in that acceptable male narration and presentation of self must stress action rather than feelings, depicting others unsentimentally and attaining drama by exaggeration of actions; it must also temper any dramatization by toned-down facticity, which must not be overly technical. This language of the everyday world must be connected to spiritual language that treats inner experience, dependency on others, and spiritual powers that by doctrine and belief cannot be treated demeaningly and so must somehow be honored, albeit awkwardly.

What is the point of these comparisons? They show there is a narrated self, which is distinct from selves constituted by other languages. This is a Lacanian point; the French psychoanalyst Lacan argues that it is language that constitutes the psyche; yes, and here is a particular kind of language that constitutes a particular kind of psyche, the narrated religious self.

Permit me to introduce two terms that help locate our perspective. These terms are "liminality" and "moratorium."

Liminality, associated with the anthropologist Victor Turner, refers to an in-between phase in rites of passage: a stage when the initiate is no more a child but not yet an adult, is isolated from the statuses and structures of the ordinary society. "Moratorium," associated with the psychoanalyst Erik Erikson, refers to a similarly in-between phase in the life course: a time when one is between one's childhood and one's calling, left free to explore one's gifts and neuroses.

During the liminal phase, normal conventions are reversed or negated; genders or classes exchange roles, and categories normally segregated are united (as in masks Turner describes that depict human faces as grassy plains, merging culture and nature). In later writings, by the way, Turner attributed such images to the reptilian mid-brain. During moratorium, too, normal conventions are suspended, permitting special kinds of inner search and development. One thinks of Jung's own account of his encounter with his unconscious when, having given up his university position, he builds toy villages on the beach and struggles with his anima through the night. For Turner, liminality is socially defined, a stage in a mechanically unfolding group process. Erikson gives moratorium more of a psychological emphasis; it is a stage in psychic development.

We've encountered our subjects today in a kind of liminal or moratorium phase of their lives. Rutledge is undergoing his spiritual quest; Evans is seeking an identity as a preacher answering the call; Dahlan, back from the pilgrimage, his moratorium, joins the struggle as a reformer. They hint of journeys into the deep, struggles with Satanic forces, sorcerizing spirits or possessing devils. So we acknowledge that Rutledge, Evans, and Dahlan pass through their versions of liminality and moratorium. But by focusing on their narrations, we stress something else: they are not just acting out a socially defined ritual phase (liminality) or carrying out a genetically programmed phase of psychological maturation (moratorium); beyond that, they are taking control. They are creating a world. They are constituting themselves through narration. All three display SELVES CONSTITUTED THROUGH NARRATION.

What kinds of selves are constituted? They are not primarily psychiatric or psychological selves, as Freud saw Dora, and as Erikson saw Luther and, for that matter, Freud. They are not primarily ritual selves, as Turner sees his characters: Kamahasany and others. Rather these are cosmological selves. They are stories of self as part of a great cosmic narrative: the combat between God and the Devil, Satan and the Holy Ghost, Allah and spirits, or more abstract negotiations between one's formulation of God's Will and one's own life, despair, and hope. These narrations place the self not in a ritual process or a psychological process but, to use a term reminiscent of Lukács, at an intersection of colliding cosmic forces.

We are accustomed to scorning the fundamentalists. They seem trapped in anachronism: an out-of-date cosmology. We, on the other hand, are in Walker Percy's phrase, lost in the cosmos, alienated from any cosmic narrative. They are trapped in it but also empowered by it—struggling, but, so far as their narration takes them, victorious.

The methodological premise enunciated at the beginning of this essay is that we should honor the narrated world. As we do that, we recognize its power. In a clinical or experimental or literary or linguistic or sociological approach to the study of the life story, narration may be regarded as a form of analysis. We do that too, by a kind of structuralism. Beyond that, though, we can recognize the narrative's empowerment: the narrative constitutes and empowers selves. It creates a Rutledge, an Evans, even a Dahlan.

In recognizing empowerment by narration and its way of joining worlds and selves of narrator and interlocutor, we accord with emphases already made in research (e.g., in the hermeneutical model of Gadamer) and in therapy (e.g., in Kohut's call for a more interactive therapy than that of Freud and Dora). Empowerment is a distinctive quality of the life story as a way of revealing the self. The self can be revealed indirectly, through dreams and gestures or remains left in garbage cans, but to narrate a life story is an assertive and energizing way to reveal the self. This feature is at once important to recognize in the study of life stories and a reason why life stories are important in study of the religious self.

APPENDIX 3

Public or Perish?
by James L. Peacock

A *News and Observer* article (November 24, 2000) tells of a new interdisciplinary institute at Duke University that provides faculty released time and a sheltered place to exchange ideas. The creator, Kathy Davidson, cites Princeton's Institute of Advanced Studies as the model. She might also have mentioned others closer to home, such as the National Humanities Center or our own Institute for the Arts and Humanities. She also might have recalled her own president's inaugural address, which began by describing a similar experience at the Rockefeller Foundation Bellagio Center at Lake Como.

Then again, the vision Nan Keohane, former president of Duke University, articulated during her speech moved beyond that idyllic retreat in Italy. Citing Duke's motto *eruditio et religio* (faith and learning), Keohane asserted that with the privilege of joining a community of thoughts comes the obligation to reach out to the public. Keohane was too eloquent to stoop to a pun like "public or perish," but that was her point. Many other leaders in higher education today agree.

There is a widespread call for academia to fulfill a social contract—if society supports higher education, then colleges and universities should give back to society in return. The question remaining, however, is how and with what pitfalls?

In a new book rather presumptuously titled *Transforming Academia*, I and several others explore this question. Our focus is the discipline of anthropology, but many points are applicable to other disciplines. One simple but useful distinction is between critical and constructive action. Critical action entails critique, perhaps public protest, concerning society and its leading forces—typically corporate structures, which are perceived as increasingly dominant and influential. Recent examples at Carolina include faculty and student protests against Wachovia Bank monopolizing public space at UNC-CH (the Pit), tuition increases, and the perceived threat of the World Trade Organization. Constructive action, on the other hand, includes critique but extends also into formulating policies, proposing plans, and leading and organizing people and groups to implement them.

Faculty and students, especially those in the liberal arts and sciences as contrasted to those in the professional fields, are inclined toward critical action for obvious reasons. Their intellectual training hones their critical capacities, and they are deeply, and often rightly, skeptical of ruling forces and are not in a position to make things happen easily.

Traditionally, they lack the power and resources that those in positions of leadership and those with wealth possess.

Perhaps quixotically, some people endeavor to strike a balance—to have a constructive impact while maintaining their critical edge. Here at Carolina, such efforts are illustrated by interdisciplinary centers and projects spearheaded by faculty but joined by "real people," citizens from outside the university. The logic of such efforts is, in part, that critical perspectives and critical thinkers (often academics) can join with constructive perspectives and "doers" from the wider society to move not toward agreement and compromise but toward dialogue and multilogues, synergies, and broadened perspectives that pave the way for positive action.

In this spirit, the Institute for Arts and Humanities has created "public fellows." These are alumni who have contributed much in society and who tap into academia by working with faculty. Each learns from the other. Many similar efforts occur at Carolina. UCIS is building academic/public linkages at several levels. Most obviously, we do outreach. We work with some one hundred K–12 public schools around the state; our outreach director, Bogdan Leja, with the help of volunteers, goes out to the schools and injects international information and insights. The UNC World View Richardson Lecture, directed by Robert Phay, complements this work by bringing school administrators and teachers to Carolina for intensive seminars to build critical awareness of world issues.

These efforts point toward a central theme for UCIS (and for Carolina): how do we sustain humanity in our globalizing world? Globalization, as we well know, is being driven by international business. As Dorrie Massie quips, dollars go round the world and dollars make the world go round. The information revolution is key, too. Immigration and increased diversity are other pieces. The question is how to sustain identities, anchored in place and community, as we globalize? The question is particularly pertinent in our own locale, the Triangle, and more generally in the South.

After a hundred years of relative stasis, the region is exploding into the global epoch. How can we sustain our humanity (keeping the good while losing the bad) as we do so?

To address this question, myriad disciplines and experiences must be consulted. In this vein, UCIS is organizing a seminar this year, jointly funded by the Mellon and Rockefeller Foundations, titled "Reading Regions Globally and Creating the Transnational South." Held on Fridays at 12:30 p.m., these sessions are open to citizens as well as faculty and students (a schedule is included in this newsletter). The objective is deepened and broadened critical and constructive thought, and who knows, maybe even action, linked to our own present lives and communities.

Action of this sort, for example, resulted from another, related project, the so-called Nike course. Stimulated by student protests about Carolina's contract with Nike, which allegedly created sweatshops in Asia, this course explored the various business, environmental, and cultural issues involved and then recommended reforms. A surprise audience for these recommendations included Nike CEO Phil Knight, who later implemented a series of reforms in his overseas factories, crediting Carolina students among others for acting as catalysts.

These and many other recent activities at UCIS highlight the increased dynamics and interaction between Carolina and the wider—and might we even say *world*—community. Even the new format of Global View itself represents an increased outward direction, as does an expansion with this issue of our mailing list to include persons outside the confines of traditional academic discourse. While UCIS remains committed to sustaining and furthering interdisciplinary and international scholarship among Carolina faculty and students, we are also striving to draw into this learning community a more diverse and larger group of participants.

As we experiment with various partnerships between academics and the public in addressing questions about globalization, many questions concerning such efforts will linger. Why are partnerships necessary at all? Does academia have a binding contract with society to contribute in some specific manner, in return for which society provides support? If so, how is this partnership best sustained? Should corporate America support academic institutions just in order to be the focus of constant critical analysis? Should constructive as well as critical efforts be launched? What strings are attached to outside support? How do we in academia sustain our critical edge? Might the critical edge include innovative proposals as well as the usual chorus of critique? What about communication blocks, for example, the "executive summary" that, for academics, omits nuance and the persistent stereotype that academics are rambling and administrators or businesspeople crisp? These and many other questions deserve our (and your) continuing and thoughtful attention.

For myself, I contend that just as the dictum "publish or perish" is justified in order to sustain the thoughtful exchange of ideas among scholars, "public or perish" is equally important to institutions of higher education. Only by reaching out to the public may our learning community build a strong and secure foundation for ideas, experience, and action. In the months and years ahead, we welcome your involvement and insights on this vital endeavor.

(File: UCIS_booklet_Winter_2000; Document: UCIS, Global View, Winter 2000. Wilson Library. James Peacock papers, 1969–1970. Peacock, James L. Southern Historical Collection. Call Number: 05570. BOX 7)

References

List of Interviews

1_Daniels_22_09_2018 (Inf.: Robert Daniels, b. 1940.; Int.: A. Kushkova. Chapel Hill, Sept. 22, 2018).

2_Lefferts_23_09_2018 (Inf.: Leedom Lefferts, b. 1939. Int.: A. Kushkova. Carrboro, September 23, 2018).

3_Rosefieldes_28_09_2018 (Inf.: Rosefieldes, Steven and Susan, b. 1942 and 1943. Int.: A. Kushkova. Chapel Hill, Sept. 28, 2018).

4_Peacock_Florence_05_11_2018 (Inf.: Peacock, Florence, b. 1937. Int.: A. Kushkova. Chapel Hill, Nov. 5, 2018).

5_Peacock_Florence_04_12_2018 (Inf.: Peacock, Florence, b. 1937. Int.: A. Kushkova. Chapel Hill, Dec. 4, 2018).

6_Tyson_21_01_2019 (Inf.: Ruel Tyson, b. 1930. Int.: A. Kushkova. Chapel Hill, Jan. 21, 2019).

7_The_Pattersons_Feb_9_2019 (Inf.: Dan Patterson, b. 1929, and Beverly Patterson, b. 1938. Int.: A. Kushkova. Chapel Hill, Feb. 9, 2019).

8_The_Greenes_March_28_2019 (Inf.: Herman and Sandy Greene, b.? Int.: A. Kushkova. Chapel Hill, March 28, 2019).

9_The_Riches_July_24_2019 (Inf.1: Stephen Rich, b. 1941. Inf.2: Sandra Rich, b. 1943. Int.: A. Kushkova. Chapel Hill, July 24, 2019).

10_Levy_Nerys_July_27_2019 (Inf.: Nerys Levy, b. ca. 1945. Int.: A. Kushkova. Chapel Hill, July 27, 2019).

11_Conway_July_29_2019 (Inf.: Cecilia Conway, b. ca. 1947. Int.: A. Kushkova. Chapel Hill, July 29, 2019).

12_Peacock_Conway_July_30_2019 (Inf.1: James Peacock, b. 1937. Inf.2: Cecilia Conway, b. ca. 1941. Int.: A. Kushkova. Chapel Hill, July 30, 2019).

13_Peacock_Conway_McCanless_July_31_2019 (Inf.1: James Peacock, b. 1937. Inf.2: Cecilia Conway, b. ca. 1941. Inf.3: Allen A. McCanless, b. ca. 1950 (?). Int.: A. Kushkova. Chapel Hill, July 30, 2019).

14_Reintjes_Aug_9_2019 (Inf.: Susan Reintjes, b. ca. 1948. Int.: A. Kushkova. Carrboro, August 9, 2019).

15_Nimes_Aug_11_2019 (Inf.: Cameron Nimes, b. ca. 1952. Int.: A. Kushkova. Chapel Hill, Aug. 11, 2019).

16_Andrews_Aug_12_2019 (Inf.: Pete (Richard) Andrews, b. 1944. Int.: A. Kushkova. Chapel Hill, Aug. 12, 2019).

17_Robertson_Aug_12_2019 (Inf.: Diane Robertson, b. ca. 1960. Int.: A. Kushkova. Chapel Hill, Aug. 12, 2019).

18_Leith_Aug_18_2019 (Inf.: Katherine Leith, b. ca. 1938. Inf.: A. Kushkova. Chapel Hill, Aug. 18, 2019).

19_Peck_Aug_26_2019 (Inf.: William (Bill) Peck, b. 1928. Int.: A. Kushkova. Chapel Hill, Aug. 26, 2019).

Additionally, 12 interviews with Professor Peacock, recorded in 2018-2019, are also used.

Archival Materials

Andrews, Richard, Letter, April 21, 1998.

Brown, Frank, and John Turner. Institute for Research on the Life and History of Blacks in America, UNC at Chapel Hill.

General Education Curriculum: additional recommendations. Probably 2002. 8 pages.

The Faculty Code of University Government. The University of North Carolina at Chapel Hill. January 1991.

Hadikusuma, Djarnawi, secretary-general of the Central Leadership of Muhammadijah, book preface, with the consent of Mr. A. R. Fakhruddin, the president. September, 1975.

Holland, Dorothy, and James Peacock. Life Histories: Cognitive and Symbolic Approaches. Anthropology Seminar. Fall 1985, Course syllabus.

Nike Seminar Explores Ethics, Impacts of University/Corporate Partnership in Global Economy. S/a. 3 pages. UCIS, *Global View* 15, Volume XV, (Spring 1998).

Peacock, James L. Anthropology 328. Diversity in the South. No date. Course syllabus.

Peacock, James L. Anthropology 105: Anthropology in the South. No date. Course syllabus.

Peacock, James L. Anthropology 129: Peoples and Cultures of Southeast Asia. Spring 1986. Course syllabus.

Peacock, James L. Anthropology 201-1: Socio-Cultural Theory and Ethnography. Fall 1985. Course syllabus.

Peacock, James L. Anthropology 431a/531a: Text and Person: Studies of Life Histories. No date. Course syllabus.

Peacock, James L. Letter to the contributors to the volume *Social Anthropology of Culture: In Commemorating a Half-Century of Social Anthropology at Chapel Hill* and a paper "Social Anthropology of Culture: Commemorating a Half-Century of Social Anthropology at Chapel Hill." December 1980.

Peacock, James L. Open Lecture at American Center, June 15, 1993.

Peacock, James L. *The Southern Protestant Ethic Disease*. Reprinted from *The Not So Solid South* (Southern Anthropological Society Proceedings, No. 4, 1971), edited by J. Kenneth Morland.

Peacock, James L., and Ruel Tyson. Anthropology/Folklore 188/Religion 288. Observation and Interpretation of Religious Action. Spring 1987. Course syllabus.

Peacock, James L. and Ruel W. Tyson. Anthropology 142 / Religion 142-13 / Folklore 142. Spring 1983. Course syllabus.

Peacock, James L., and S. Polgar. Family Religious Ideology and Adolescent Drinking.

Proposal for Committee G (Global Citizenship). February 2002.

Report of the Task Force on Academic Community, May 3, 1999.

Report. Recommendations for Development of the Center for the Study of the American South at the University of North Carolina at Chapel Hill. 1994.

Tyson, Ruel. Memorandum of September 6, 1979, Principles and Rationale for Course Planning.

The UNC Center for the Study of the American South: An Overview. Spring 2002.

UCIS, *Global View* (Spring 2002).

UCIS, *Global View* (Winter 2000).

University Council on International Programs, Meeting Minutes. March 19, 2002. Chapel Hill, North Carolina.

Wilson Library. James Peacock papers, 1969–1970. Peacock, James L. Southern Historical Collection. Call Number: 05570. Box 7.

Wilson Library. James Peacock papers, 1969–1970. Peacock, James L. Southern Historical Collection. Call Number: 05570. Box 9.

Wilson Library. James Peacock papers, 1969–1970. Peacock, James L. Southern Historical Collection. Call Number: 05570. Box 10.

Selected Work by James L. Peacock

BOOKS

The Anthropological Lens: Harsh Light, Soft Focus. New York: Cambridge University Press, 1986. This book has been translated into Japanese, Spanish, Italian, and Chinese.

Consciousness and Change: Symbolic Anthropology in Evolutionary Perspective. Oxford: Blackwell's, 1975.

Grounded Globalism: How the U.S. South Embraces the World. Athens: University of Georgia Press, 2007.

With A. Thomas Kirsch. *The Human Direction: An Evolutionary Approach to Cultural and Social Anthropology.* New York: Appleton-Century-Crofts, 1973.

Indonesia: An Anthropological Perspective. Pacific Palisades, CA: Goodyear, 1973.

Muslim Puritans: The Reformist Psychology in Southeast Asian Islam. Berkeley: University of California Press, 1978.

With Ruel W. Tyson. *Pilgrims of Paradox: Calvinism and Experience Among Primitive Baptists of the Blue Ridge.* Washington, DC: Smithsonian Institution Press, 1989.

Purifying the Faith: The Muhammadijah Movement in Indonesian Islam. Palo Alto, CA: Cummings Press, 1978.

Rites of Modernization: Symbolic and Social Aspects of Indonesian Proletarian Drama. Chicago: University of Chicago Press, 1987.

A True Lucky Jim. Chapel Hill, NC: Lucky Press, 2020.

EDITED BOOKS

With Ruel Tyson and Daniel Patterson. *Diversities of Gifts: Field Studies of Independent Protestants.* Urbana: University of Illinois Press, 1988.

With James Sabella. *Sea and Land: Cultural and Biological Adaptations on the Southern Coastal Plain.* Athens: University of Georgia Press, 1988.

With Terence Evans. *Transcendence in Society: Case Studies* Greenwich, CT: JAI Press, 1990.

Transforming Academia: Challenges and Opportunities for an Engaged Anthropology. Arlington, VA: American Anthropological Association, 1999.

With Patricia Thornton and Patrick Inman. *Identity Matters: Ethnic and Sectarian Conflict.* Oxford: Berghahn Books, 2007.

FIELDWORK

1962–1963	Study of ludruk and Surabaya in Java with funding from National Institutes of Health (NIH)
1969–1970	Study of Muhammadiyah and Ahmadiyya in Singapore and Indonesia with funding from National Science Foundation (NSF)
1979	Study of Kebatinan in Indonesia
1975–1985	Study of Pentecostals and Primitive Baptists in USA

ACADEMIC POSITIONS

1959–1965	Harvard University work for doctorate in social anthropology
1965–1967	Assistant Professor at Princeton University
1967–1970	Assistant Professor at University of North Carolina at Chapel Hill (UNC-CH)
1970–1972	Associate Chair of Anthropology at UNC-CH

	Associate Professor and Kenan Professor of Anthropology
1972–1975	Chair of Anthropology at UNC-CH
1975–1978	Chair of Faculty at UNC-CH
1977–1980	President of American Anthropological Association
1980–1993	Director of Center for International Studies
1985–1986	Fellow at All Souls College, University of Oxford, England
2018-2020	President of Retired Faculty, UNC-CH

NEXT IN LINE

Children of Jim and Florence Peacock: Louly, Claire, and Natalie. Louly and Claire are teachers and writers; Natalie is a social worker. All three daughters are singers.

Grandchildren:

Louly: Nicholas and Flora. Nicholas majored in physics at UNC-CH and is a graduate student and researcher at Duke University. Flora is at Davidson College (NC) preparing for study in France.

Claire: Yanni. He is majoring in math and history at Harvard University.

Natalie: Bella and Lucia. Bella is at Cary Academy and Lucia is at the Duke School. Both are talented artists, athletes, and students.

Acknowledgments

Special gratitude and appreciation to Anna Kushkova and Sudibyo Markus. Anna both conceived and implemented this work, including carrying out the interviews that are its key essence. Sudibyo contributed many aspects especially concerning Islam and Indonesia. Deep insight into that aspect can be found in Sudibyo's own writings especially in Indonesian *Jejak Diplomat Partikelir Muhammadiyah* and in presentations by him in varied contexts. Thank you to Chris Belcher for his help with this project. Deep appreciation to Julie Allred of BW&A Books for help in publishing this book.

About the Authors

Anna Kushkova has written two dissertations, the first, *Peasant Quarrel: A Study of Rural Everyday Life* (European University of St. Petersburg Press, 2016), on everyday conflicts and their resolution in rural Russia in the second half of the nineteenth century, and the second, "Navigating the Planned Economy: Accommodation and Survival in Moscow's Post-War 'Soviet Jewish Pale,'" defended in 2017 at the Department of Anthropology, UNC-Chapel Hill, on the persistence of Jewish ethnic entrepreneurship under the post–World War II Soviet "planned economy." Anna is currently a postdoctoral fellow at the Leonid Nevzlin Research Center for Russian and East European Jewry, Hebrew University at Jerusalem.

James L. Peacock is Kenan Professor Emeritus of Anthropology at the University of North Carolina at Chapel Hill. Peacock received a BA in psychology from Duke University and a PhD in Social Anthropology from Harvard. His publications include research in Indonesia and Appalachia. In addition to academic work, at UNC he was chair of the Department of Anthropology from 1975 to 1980 and 1990 to 1991, chair of the university faculty from 1991 to 1994, director of the University Center for International Studies from 1996 to 2003, and president of the Retired Faculty Association. He served as president of the American Anthropological Association from 1993 to 1995 and was elected to the American Academy of Arts and Sciences in 1995. Awards include Phi Beta Kappa (1959); Order of the Golden Fleece (1995); Thomas Jefferson Award (1995); Franz Boas Award, American Anthropological Association (2002); Citizen of the World (2006); Massey Award for Service (2008); Johnson Award for Excellence in Teaching (2008); President, Rotary Club of Chapel Hill (2013–2014); Davie Award (2018); and Order of the Long Leaf Pine (2019).

Made in United States
Orlando, FL
29 September 2023